CATHOLIC LITERARY GIANTS

JOSEPH PEARCE

CATHOLIC LITERARY GIANTS

A Field Guide to the Catholic Literary Landscape

IGNATIUS PRESS   SAN FRANCISCO

First Edition: *Literary Giants, Literary Catholics*
© 2005 by Ignatius Press

Cover design by John Herreid

Reprinted under new title in 2014 by Ignatius Press, San Francisco
All rights reserved
ISBN 978-1-58617-944-1
Library of Congress Control Number 2014908648
Printed in the United States of America ∞

To Giovanna Paolina

CONTENTS

ACKNOWLEDGEMENTS   11

INTRODUCTION

Converting the Culture: The Evangelizing Power of Beauty   13

PART ONE: TRADITION AND CONVERSION

1. Tradition and Conversion in Modern English Literature   21
2. Twentieth-Century England's Christian Literary Landscape   58

PART TWO: THE CHESTERBELLOC

3. The Chesterbelloc: Examining the Beauty of the Beast   65
4. Chesterton and Saint Francis   76
5. Shades of Gray in the Shadow of Wilde   80
6. Fighting the Euro from Beyond the Grave: The Ghost of Chesterton Haunts Lord Howe   85
7. Catholicism and "Democracy"   89
8. Fascism and Chesterton   93
9. G. K. Chesterton: Champion of Orthodoxy   105
10. Hilaire Belloc in a Nutshell   109
11. Belloc's *The Path to Rome*   112
12. A Chip off the Old Belloc: Bob Copper In Memoriam   125
13. Maurice Baring: In the Shadow of the Chesterbelloc   128
14. R. H. Benson: Unsung Genius   138
15. Maisie Ward: Concealed with a Kiss   146
16. John Seymour: Some Novel Common Sense   153

PART THREE: THE WASTELAND

17. Entrenched Passion: The Poetry of War   157
18. War Poets: Cutting through the Cant   160

19. Siegfried Sassoon: Poetic Pilgrimage   162
20. Emerging from the Wasteland: The Cultural Reaction
    to the Desert of Modernity   167
21. Edith Sitwell: Modernity and Tradition   179
22. Roy Campbell: Bombast and Fire   184
23. Roy Campbell: Religion and Politics   189
24. Campbell in Spain   200
25. Evelyn Waugh: Ultramodern to Ultramontane   210
26. Beyond the Facts of Life: Douglas Lane Patey's
    Biography of Evelyn Waugh   214
27. In Pursuit of the Greene-Eyed Monster: The Quest
    for Graham Greene   218
28. Cross Purposes: Greene, Undset and Bernanos   223
29. Muggeridge Resurrected   225

PART FOUR: J. R. R. TOLKIEN AND THE INKLINGS

30. Inklings of Grace   231
31. From the Prancing Pony to the Bird and Baby: Roy
    "Strider" Campbell and the Inklings   235
32. J. R. R. Tolkien: Truth and Myth   240
33. The Individual and Community in Tolkien's Middle Earth   247
34. Religion and Politics in *The Lord of the Rings*   257
35. Quest and Passion Play: *J. R. R. Tolkien's Sanctifying Myth*   261
36. True North   266
37. The Once and Future King   269
38. Tolkien and the Catholic Literary Revival   272
39. True Myth: The Catholicism of *The Lord of the Rings*   288
40. Letting the Catholic Out of the Baggins   296
41. A Hidden Presence: The Catholic Imagination of J. R. R.
    Tolkien   301
42. From War to Mordor: J. R. R. Tolkien and World War I   306
43. Divine Mercy in *The Lord of the Rings*   311
44. Resurrecting Myth: A Response to Dr. Murphy's
    "Response"   314
45. The Good, the Bad and the Ugly: The Successes and
    Failures of Tolkien on Film   323

46.   Would Tolkien Have Given Peter Jackson's Movie the Thumbs-Up?   326

47.   The Forgotten Inkling: A Personal Memoir of Owen Barfield   329

PART FIVE: MORE THINGS CONSIDERED

48.   The Decadent Path to Christ   335

49.   The Quest for the Real Oscar: A Century after His Death, Is the Real Oscar Wilde Finally Emerging from the Shadows?   338

50.   Making Oscar Wild: Unmasking Oscar Wilde's Opposition to "Pathological" Gay Marriage   342

51.   Truth Is Stranger Than Science Fiction   345

52.   Hollywood and the "Holy War"   348

53.   Three Cheers for Hollywood   351

54.   Purity and Passion: Examining the Sacred Heart of Mel Gibson's *The Passion of the Christ*   356

55.   Paul McCartney: A Grief Observed   359

56.   Above All Shadows Rides the Sun: The Poetry of Praise   361

57.   The Magic of Technology   364

58.   Russian Revelations   367

59.   Dante: Assent's Ascent   370

60.   Shakespeare: Good Will for All Men   376

61.   Modern Art: Friend or Foe?   380

62.   Salvador Dali: From Freud to Faith   384

63.   Mr. Davey versus the Devil: A True Story   394

64.   Totus Tuus: A Tribute to a Truly Holy Father   399

65.   Faith and the Feminine   402

66.   Our Life, Our Sweetness and Our Hope   404

67.   The Presence That Christmas Presents   407

INDEX   409

ACKNOWLEDGEMENTS

Most of the chapters in this volume have been published before in a variety of journals on both sides of the Atlantic. My memory is no longer equal to the task of remembering which articles appeared in which journals, but I can, I think, list the names of the journals in which they appeared. These include, in no particular order and with apologies for any sins of omission, the *Catholic Herald*, the *Tablet*, *Crisis*, *Gilbert Magazine*, the *Chesterton Review*, *Lay Witness*, *This Rock*, *Christian History*, *Catholic Social Science Review*, the *Review of Politics*, *Faith and Reason*, the *National Catholic Register*, *Catholic World Report*, the *C. S. Lewis Journal*, *Chronicles*, the *Nicaraguan Academic Journal*, the *American Conservative*, the *Naples Daily News* and *National Review On-Line*. My thanks are proffered to those many individuals who were responsible for commissioning and accepting these articles for the journals listed. I suspect, however, that the list is not complete and apologize, once again, for any lapses in memory.

Many of the chapters in Part V were originally published as articles in the *Saint Austin Review* (*StAR*), the Catholic cultural journal of which I am coeditor. The article on Belloc's *Path to Rome* was originally written for, and published in, the *Encyclopedia of Catholic Literature*, edited by Mary R. Reichardt and published by Greenwood Press in 2004.

Grateful acknowledgements are due, and are wholeheartedly rendered, to Father Joseph Fessio, S.J., for his continuing faith in my work and for his valued advice during the preparation of this volume. Similar gratitude is due to Father Fessio's colleagues at Ignatius Press, each of whom has worked tirelessly to bring this and my other volumes to fruition.

Final acknowledgement, as ever and always, goes to my ever-patient wife, Susannah, for all the support she gives and is, and to our two children: to Leo, our firstborn, and to little Giovanna Paolina, who rests in the arms of God.

INTRODUCTION
CONVERTING THE CULTURE:
The Evangelizing Power of Beauty

There is a story about an American tourist somewhere in the wilds of
rural Ireland. He is hopelessly lost. Desperate for reorientation, he is
relieved to see a rustic Irishman, sitting on a fence and sucking a straw.
This man has probably lived here all his life, the American thinks to
himself; he will surely be able to help. "Excuse me", he says. "How
do I get to Limerick?" The Irishman looks at him for a while and
sucks pensively on his straw. "If I were you," he replies, "I wouldn't
start from here."

Although one can obviously sympathize with the irate frustration
that our lost American must have felt at the unhelpfulness of such a
response, there is more than a modicum of wisdom in the Irishman's
reply. Indeed, if the characters are changed, the whole story takes on
something of the nature of a parable. Instead of an American tourist,
imagine that the hopelessly lost individual is the present writer and
that the rustic Irishman is Saint Patrick in disguise. The year is 1978
and I am in the Northern Irish city of Londonderry. I am there
because, as an angry seventeen-year-old, I have become involved with
the Protestant paramilitaries in Northern Ireland and with a white
supremacist organization in England. I am angry. I am bitter. I am
bigoted. I hate Catholicism and all that it stands for (although, of
course, I have no idea what it really stands for, only what my prejudiced presumption believes that it stands for). Shortly afterward I
will join the Orange Order, an anti-Catholic secret society, as a further statement of my Ulster "loyalism" and anti-Catholicism. During
this visit to Londonderry, I take part in a day and a night of rioting
during which petrol bombs are thrown and shops are looted—all in
the name of anti-Catholicism. It is then, at least in the mystical

fancy of my imagination, that I meet the rustic Irishman who is really Saint Patrick in disguise. "I am lost", I say to him (though I am so lost that I don't even know that I am lost). "How do I find my way Home?" "If I were you," the saintly Irishman replies, "I wouldn't start from here."

Wise words indeed, though at the time they would have fallen on deaf ears. Deaf, dumb and blind, I had a long way to go. The long and winding road that would lead, eventually, eleven years later, to the loving arms of Christ and His Church would be paved with the works of great Catholic apologists such as Newman, Chesterton and Belloc. Newman's masterful *Apologia* and his equally masterful autobiographical novel, *Loss and Gain*; Chesterton's *Orthodoxy*, *The Everlasting Man* and *The Well and the Shallows*; and Belloc's stridently militant exposition of the "Europe of the Faith"—each of these was a signpost on my path from homelessness to Home. There were, of course, others: Karl Adam's *The Spirit of Catholicism*, Archbishop Sheehan's *Apologetics and Catholic Doctrine* and Father Copleston's *Saint Thomas Aquinas*. I am, therefore, deeply indebted to the great apologists and, in consequence, retain the strongest admiration for those who continue the work of apologetics in our day. I hope and pray that the great work being done by *This Rock* and *Catholic Answers* will bring about a bumper harvest akin to that which was reaped by these great apologists of the past.

Although my own approach to evangelization is somewhat different, I share the same desire to win souls for Christ as do Karl Keating, Tim Ryland and Jerry Usher. I would, in fact, call myself an apologist, albeit an apologist of a different ilk. I would say that I am a *cultural* apologist, one who desires to win converts through the communicating power of culture.

Perhaps a short theological aside will serve as a useful explanation of how cultural apologetics is both different from, and yet akin to, the more conventional field of apologetics. Truth is trinitarian. It consists of the interconnected and mystically unified power of Reason, Love and Beauty. As with the Trinity itself, the three, though truly distinct, are one. Reason, properly understood, is Beauty; Beauty, properly apprehended, is Reason; both are transcended by, and are expressions of, Love. And, of course, Reason, Love and Beauty are enshrined in, and are encapsulated by, the Godhead. Indeed, they have their *raison d'être* and their consummation in the Godhead. Remove Love and Reason from the sphere of aesthetics and you remove Beauty also. You get ugliness instead. Even a cursory glance at most modern "art" will illustrate the negation of Beauty in most of today's "culture". Once this theological understanding of the trinitarian nature of Truth is perceived, it follows that the whole science of apologetics can be seen in this light. Most mainstream apologetics can be seen as the apologetics of Reason: the defense of the Faith and the winning of converts through the means of a dialogue with the "rational" and its sundry manifestations. On the other hand, the lives of the saints, such as the witness of Mother Teresa, can be seen as the apologetics of Love: the defense of the Faith and the winning of converts through the living example of a life lived in Love. Finally, the defense of the Faith and the winning of converts through the power of the beautiful can be called cultural apologetics or the apologetics of Beauty.

Throughout history, the Faith has been sustained by, and has built upon, each of these pillars. Saint Augustine, Saint Thomas Aquinas and other giants of the Church have laid the philosophical and theological foundations upon which Christendom has towered above superstition and heresy, creating an edifice of Reason in a world of error. Numerous other saints have lived lives of heroic virtue and self-sacrificial love, showing that there is a living, loving alternative to all the vice and hatred with which humanity has inflicted itself. Similarly, numerous writers, artists, architects and composers have created works of beauty as a reflection of their love for God—and, through the gift they have been given, of God's love for them.

It is in the last of these three spheres of apologetics, the apologetics of Beauty, that I have found my own vocation, and it has become my aim, indeed my passion, to evangelize the culture through the power of culture itself.

In recent years, with the possible exception of Mel Gibson's film *The Passion of the Christ*, the greatest opportunity to evangelize the culture through the power of culture itself has been the release of Peter Jackson's film adaptation of J. R. R. Tolkien's *The Lord of the Rings*. As the author of *Tolkien: Man and Myth* and as the editor of *Tolkien: A Celebration*, both of which were published before the release

of Jackson's movie, I found myself in the privileged position of being
able to surf the wave of Tolkien enthusiasm that followed in the
wake of the release of each of the films in the trilogy. In spite of
the efforts of Jackson and others to play down the importance of the
Catholic dimension of Tolkien's masterpiece, I found myself giving
talks on the Catholicism of *The Lord of the Rings* to audiences from
all four corners of the United States, not to mention Canada, England,
Germany, Portugal and South Africa. I have spoken to very large
student audiences at Harvard, Princeton, Columbia and several state
universities. How else in this agnostic-infested age could an avowed
Catholic give a lecture at a secular institution on Catholic theology
to a captive, and for the most part captivated, audience? Although
very few of those in attendance would have dreamed of attending a
lecture on "The Theology of the Catholic Church", they were happy
to attend a lecture entitled "Tolkien: Truth and Myth" at which
they received unadulterated Catholic theology. Such is the power of
art to evangelize.

In the knowledge that art has an enormous power to win souls for
Christ, it has been my desire to play a part in the nurturing of a
Catholic cultural revival in the twenty-first century to parallel the revival
that characterized the first half of the last century. With this in mind,
I am honored to be coeditor of a Catholic cultural journal, the *Saint
Austin Review*, or *StAR*, which aims to act as a catalyst for such a
revival in Christian culture. Launched in England in September 2001,
StAR represents a unique voice in the world of Catholic publications,
and my work on the journal is truly a labor of love.

Currently I find myself embroiled on the front line of the culture
war as a result of the publication of my new book, *The Unmasking of
Oscar Wilde*. My research revealed, among other things, that Wilde
had a lifelong love affair with the Catholic Church and that he considered his descent into homosexuality as his "pathology". Having recovered from his homosexual "sickness", Wilde finally succumbed to the
true love of his life when he was received into the Catholic Church
on his deathbed. This hard evidence, combined with the orthodox
Christian morality of the vast majority of his work, destroys the popular image of Wilde as a gay icon or as a pioneer of sexual (that is,
homosexual) liberation. Needless to say, this unmasking of their idol

has led many homosexuals to question their attitude toward Wilde; it may also, one may hope, lead some of them to question their attitude toward homosexuality itself. Either way, the book is receiving considerable attention in the homosexual media and has given me the opportunity to discuss the whole issue of Wilde's moral position at public debates on Wilde in both London and San Francisco. Once again, as with Tolkien, the successful application of cultural apologetics reaches audiences who would never dream of attending an overtly Catholic meeting. May such encounters prove catalytic and fruitful!

In these sad but exciting times, apologists of every shade should unite in the battle to win a doubting world to the timeless truth. Many years ago, in even sadder and even more exciting times, the Jesuit martyr Saint Edmund Campion stated defiantly that he would never recoil from his efforts to convert the English nation back to the faith of their fathers, "come rack, come rope". Campion's example speaks to us across the abyss of the centuries. He was a great and indomitable apologist who should perhaps be adopted as a model and patron of apologists everywhere. These days, in our hedonistic anti-culture of "sex, drugs and rock 'n' roll", the barbarism is more likely to find expression in rock and rape than in rack and rope. The enemy is, however, the same. His name is Legion. We might not face the martyrdom suffered by Saint Edmund Campion (though who knows what awaits future generations of Catholics if the totalitarian tide of intolerant "toleration" continues to rise), but we can be as dauntless as was he in our efforts to win our faithless or erring brothers and sisters back to the faith of their fathers. Another English Jesuit, Saint Robert Southwell, wrote some of the finest poetry of the Elizabethan age in an effort to woo his fellow countrymen back to the Faith. He too was martyred, but not before his verse had captivated the nation and not before it had influenced the work of a certain William Shakespeare. As such, Southwell should stand alongside Campion as the model and patron of apologists, particularly for those who choose cultural apologetics as their means to win souls for Christ. As with other Christian writers, before and since, Southwell employed the beauty of language as a means of conveying the beauty of the Faith. Today, four centuries after his heroic death, his poetry shines forth as a lucid testament to the truth for which he died.

Let folly praise that fancy loves, I praise and love that Child
Whose heart no thought, whose tongue no word,
   whose hand no deed defiled.
I praise him most, I love him best, all praise and love is his,
While him I love, in him I live, and cannot live amiss.
Love's sweetest mark, laud's highest theme,
   man's most desired light,
To love him life, to leave him death, to live in him delight.
He mine by gift, I his by debt, thus each to other due,
First friend he was, best friend he is, all times will try him true.

In Campion's and Southwell's day, the Catholic faith was illegal. Today, in our own darkened age, it is no longer illegal but is considered illegitimate. It is, however, in the very midst of this darkness that beauty enlightens the gloom. Great art. Great music. Great literature. They are all great weapons. Giotto, Raphael, Michelangelo, Fra Angelico. Weapons! William Byrd, Thomas Tallis, Anton Bruckner, Arvo Pärt. Weapons! Dante, Shakespeare, Hopkins, Tolkien, Waugh. Weapons! We might live in a land of exile and a valley of tears, but we are not lost. The whole unfolding of human history might be, as Tolkien called it, a "Long Defeat with only occasional glimpses of final victory", but we remain undefeated. Even in the Long Defeat there is the promise of victory. We *are* not lost and we *have* not lost. Nor are we left undefended. Christ brings us a Sword—the Sword of Truth. It is a magic sword. It has three razor-sharp edges: the cutting edge of Reason; the cutting edge of Love; and the cutting edge of Beauty. (Saint John will, I trust, grant me the literary license!) No, we are not defenseless. We have been given the weapons we need. All we need is to use them well. And to return to our rustic Irishman, he is right to muse that he wouldn't start from here. We have wandered a long way from Eden in the years since our first parents' first sin. No, indeed, we wouldn't have wanted to start from here. But here is where we are, and Home is closer than we realize.

PART ONE

TRADITION AND CONVERSION

I

TRADITION AND CONVERSION IN MODERN ENGLISH LITERATURE

A NYONE WISHING TO UNDERSTAND the relationship between tradition and conversion is confronted at the very outset with an inescapable paradox. Tradition, of its very nature, requires the tacit acceptance by those in the present of the ideas, beliefs and customs of the past. Tradition seems to require conformity. Conversion, on the other hand, requires the conscious rejection of the ideas, beliefs and customs that have been tacitly accepted in the past in order to embrace the creed to which one is converting in the present. Conversion seems to require nonconformity. Yet, in spite of this apparent contradiction, tradition and conversion are far from mutually exclusive. On the contrary, and as we shall see, they are ultimately in harmony.

A paradox, as G. K. Chesterton never tired of reminding us, is not simply a contradiction, but only an *apparent* contradiction signifying a deeper unity. At its deepest level, every conversion is not merely a rejection of a tradition to which one had previously subscribed but is, at the same time, the acceptance of another tradition that seems to make more sense than the one rejected. Conversion is, therefore, the acceptance of a tradition perceived as authentic in contradistinction to one perceived as false.

This is not simply a question of semantics. Since the Reformation, the received tradition of the majority of people in non-Catholic countries has been at loggerheads with the authentic tradition of the Church. In consequence, every conversion to Catholicism is a conscious rejection of the traditions of the non-Catholic majority in favor of the traditions of a minority. It is the rejection of prevailing fashion in the name of providential faith. As such, and contrary to the assumptions of many "progressive" thinkers, authentic tradition's relationship with the modern world is both radical and revolutionary. It is radical in the sense that it counters the accretions of post-Reformation tradition in order to remain in communion with the roots of Christendom, that is, the apostolic tradition of the Church. It is revolutionary in the sense that it seeks the repentance of post-Reformation society and its return to the faith of its fathers. All revolution, properly and radically understood, requires a *return* by definition. It is this understanding of the word that Chesterton must have had in mind when he wrote that evolution is what happens when everyone is asleep, whereas revolution is what happens when everyone is awake. Many so-called revolutions in the past have been, in reality, either iconoclastic revolts against the status quo or else violent reformations of it. Neither are revolutionary in the true sense of the word. True revolution requires a return to basic truths, a return to authentic tradition. This revolution, in individuals and societies alike, is normally called conversion. Thus, authentic tradition and conversion are seen to be in sublime harmony.

Writing of the Victorians, Chesterton spoke of "the abrupt abyss of the things they do not know". This "abrupt abyss" was the result of chronological snobbery, the assumption, at least implicitly, that the age in which the Victorians lived was more advanced and enlightened than any preceding era in history. With unquestioning faith in the concept of inexorable progress, the Victorians equated the wisdom of the ages with the superstition of the past. Thus, medievalism was mere barbarism, scholastic philosophy was dismissed as being little more than an obsession with counting angels on the point of a needle, and the holy sacrifice of the Mass was mere hocus-pocus.

The poetic counterstance to this cold rationalism and its supercilious religious scepticism emerged several decades before the dawn of the Victorian era with the publication in 1798 of *Lyrical Ballads*, coedited by William Wordsworth and Samuel Taylor Coleridge. In this ground-breaking volume, which served as the *de facto* manifesto of the romantic movement in England, the poets asserted their faith in the integrity of the human soul and derided the spiritual sterility of the sceptical philosophers. Coleridge and Wordsworth both embraced

Christianity, and Coleridge, in particular, became an outspoken champion of religious orthodoxy.

In "The Rime of the Ancient Mariner" there were early glimpses of Coleridge's later orthodoxy in the Marian invocation at the beginning of Part V:

> Oh sleep! it is a gentle thing,
> Beloved from pole to pole!
> To Mary Queen the praise be given!
> She sent the gentle sleep from Heaven,
> That slid into my soul.

In this, as in his beautiful translation of "The Virgin's Cradle Hymn", a short Latin verse he had discovered in a Catholic village in Germany, Coleridge was seeking a purer vision of Christianity untainted and untarnished by the embryonic scepticism of the more puritanical of the metaphysical poets of the seventeenth century. His defense of orthodoxy in both poetry and prose was an earnest endeavor to bridge the "abrupt abyss" of the age in which he was living. In the course of his life's pilgrimage, his journey in faith, he had scaled the schism of sects and the chasm of secularism to rediscover the wonders of Christendom.

> I walk with awe, and sing my stately songs,
> Loving the God that made me!

Coleridge was one of the first "moderns" to cast aside the "progressive" traditions of the post-Enlightenment in order to rediscover the authentic traditions of the Church. He would by no means be the last. In many respects he blazed a trail that many others would follow.

The year before Coleridge died, the Oxford movement was born. Those at the forefront of this traditionalist revolution in the Anglican church—Keble, Pusey, Newman and others—were inheritors of Coleridge's orthodox mantle and shared his desire for a purer Catholic vision of Christianity beyond the fogs of puritanism. Nowhere was the plaintive cry of the Oxford movement heard so starkly as in the opening lines of a hymn by John Mason Neale:

Oh, give us back the days of old! oh! give me back an hour!
To make us feel that Holy Church o'er death hath might
    and power.

A similar vision was the inspiration for a young architect, Augustus
Pugin, who converted to Roman Catholicism, probably in 1833, and
set about promoting the hugely influential Gothic revival. The combined effect of the Oxford movement and the Gothic revival changed
the metaphysical atmosphere considerably. As Victoria ascended the
throne in 1837, the medievalist winds of change were sweeping across
England.

The prophet of neomedievalism in the mid-nineteenth century was
John Ruskin, whose influence on his contemporaries was gargantuan
in its scope and impact. His art criticism developed into a spiritual
history of Europe, epitomized by his famous essay "On the Nature of
the Gothic", and his love for the Italian Renaissance was infectious,
introducing whole new generations to the art of the Church. For
Ruskin, aestheticism and morality were inseparable. Thus, he argued,
the beauty of early Renaissance art flowed freely from its creative source
in the moral foundations of medieval Christendom. Consequently, aestheticism inevitably suffered when the humanism of the late Renaissance weakened the link with this Christian source. The more the
Renaissance bloomed, he believed, the more it decayed.

Ruskin was an early champion of the Pre-Raphaelites, a brotherhood of artists who shared his aesthetic vision. Seeking a purer
perspective untainted by the decay of the late Renaissance, the Pre-
Raphaelites chose Catholic religious themes and scenes of mythic medieval chivalry as their subjects, painted in vivid color and detail. Their
opposition to the fashionable conventions of Victorian modernism,
both in art and morals, was itself a dissatisfaction with the drabness of
the Victorian spirit and a quest for the purity and adventure of a healthier age. Dante Gabriel Rossetti, perhaps the greatest of the Pre-
Raphaelites, chose Marian themes such as *The Girlhood of Mary Virgin*
and *The Annunciation*, or Dantean allegories such as *Beata Beatrix*, to
convey a Catholic vision to a sceptical world. He also wrote fine religious verse, overflowing with medieval spirituality, akin to Coleridge's
earlier poetic quest for pre-Reformation purity. Yet Rossetti, unlike

his sister, was not an orthodox believer. Neither was Ruskin, who spent several months in a monastic cell in Assisi, basking in the Franciscan spirit, before declaring that he had no need to convert since he was already more Catholic than the Church.

Ruskin's vision, and that of the Pre-Raphaelites, was, at best, a baptism of desire into the Catholic spirit; at worst, their vision lacked any ultimate reality. It would take a remarkable man to unite the vision with the reality.

John Henry Newman's conversion to Catholicism in 1845 sent shock waves through the Anglican establishment. Already well known as a leading protagonist of the Oxford movement, Newman's reception into the Church was a courageously decisive act by a catalytically incisive mind. His act of conversion united the Catholic vision with the Catholic reality, the artistic word with the flesh of the Divine Artist, and the creative mind with the Body of the Church. In Newman, the convert and the authentic tradition became one.

Newman endeavored to explain the process of conversion in his first novel, *Loss and Gain*, a fictionalized semiautobiographical account of a young man's quest for faith amid the scepticism and uncertainties of early-Victorian Oxford. It remains one of the classic Victorian novels. The novelist Mrs. Humphry Ward believed that it was one of the works to which "the future student of the nineteenth century will have to look for what is deepest, most intimate, and most real in its personal experience". Newman also addressed the issue of conversion in his historical novel *Callista: A Sketch of the Third Century*. Although the setting had changed drastically, the same perennial questions confronted the characters of the third century as had beset Charles Reding, the youthful hero of *Loss and Gain*, sixteen hundred years later. A similar novel, *Fabiola: A Tale of the Catacombs*, had been published the previous year by Cardinal Wiseman, who was somewhat less subtle than Newman in his use of the fictional medium for propaganda purposes:

> We need not remind our readers, that the office then performed was essentially, and in many details, the same as the daily witness at the catholic altar. Not only was it considered, as now, to be the Sacrifice of Our Lord's Body and Blood, not only were the oblation, the consecration,

the communion alike, but many of the prayers were identical; so that the Catholic hearing them recited, and still more the priest reciting them, in the same language as the Roman Church of the catacombs spoke, may feel himself in active and living communion with the martyrs who celebrated, and the martyrs who assisted at, those sublime mysteries.

Whereas *Fabiola* remains Cardinal Wiseman's best-known work, much of Newman's finest work was still to come. His *Apologia*, first published in 1865, remains probably the finest exposition of a religious conversion ever written in the English language. Its candor and clarity of vision won over many who had previously been hostile to Catholicism, and perhaps no book published since has been quite so instrumental in the popularizing of the Catholic faith in England.

In his *Sermons Addressed to Mixed Congregations*, published in 1849, Newman conveys with pyrotechnic profundity the fact that the modern world faces a stark choice between authentic tradition and the abyss of nihilism:

> Turn away from the Catholic Church, and to whom will you go? it is your only chance of peace and assurance in this turbulent, changing world. There is nothing between it and scepticism, when men exert their reason freely. Private creeds, fancy religions, may be showy and imposing to the many in their day; national religions may lie huge and lifeless, and cumber the ground for centuries, and distract the intention or confuse the judgment of the learned; but on the long run it will be found that either the Catholic Religion is verily and indeed the coming in of the unseen world into this, or that there is nothing positive, nothing dogmatic, nothing real in any one of our notions as to whence we come and whither we are going. Unlearn Catholicism, and you become Protestant, Unitarian, Deist, Pantheist, Sceptic, in a dreadful, but infallible succession.

Newman's message to his contemporaries, and to future generations, is clear: relearn Catholicism; that is, convert, or perish. Perhaps the inextricable link between tradition and conversion has never been put so forcefully, either before or since.

Reading these lines, it is easy to concur with the critic George Levine's judgment that Newman is "perhaps the most artful and brilliant prose writer of the nineteenth century". Such a judgment should not, however, detract from Newman's achievement as a poet. His most ambitious poem, and arguably his finest, is *The Dream of Gerontius*, which presents the vision of a soul at the moment of death, and its conveyance by its guardian angel to the cleansing grace of Purgatory. Although it is steeped in Catholic doctrine, itself something of a novelty in Victorian verse, Newman's poem has been compared with *Paradise Lost*. "It reminds us at times of Milton," suggests the critic A. S. P. Woodhouse, "and it strikingly anticipates T. S. Eliot in its presentation of Christ as the surgeon who probes the wound in order to heal." There is, however, none of Milton's deformed, darker spirit in Newman's poem. Instead, it resonates with the hopeful spirit of Dante's *Purgatorio* and the glory of Dante's *Paradiso*, which it resembles in faith, if not in form. *The Dream of Gerontius* is not a lament over a paradise lost but the promise of a paradise to be gained.

Newman returns to the purgatorial theme in "The Golden Prison", in which Purgatory is described as "the holy house of toil, / The frontier penance-place". As in all else that he wrote, it seems that Newman is more intent on instructing his readers than with entertaining them. Poems such as "The Sign of the Cross" and his hymn "For the Dead" are deliberately designed to elucidate those aspects of Catholicism that aroused the ire and suspicion of his non-Catholic or anti-Catholic contemporaries.

Paradoxically perhaps, Newman is at his most charming when he is at his least Victorian. In "The Pilgrim Queen", subtitled "A Song", he throws off the formalities of Victorian verse to unleash his muse on the simplicity of medieval rhythm and rhyme.

> I looked on that Lady,
>   and out from her eyes
> Came the deep glowing blue
>   of Italy's skies;
> And she raised up her head
>   and she smiled, as a Queen
> On the day of her crowning,
>   so bland and serene.

"A moment," she said,
   "and the dead shall revive;
The Giants are failing,
   the Saints are alive;
I am coming to rescue
   my home and my reign,
And Peter and Philip
   are close in my train."

Newman's choice of this particular and uncharacteristic verse-form to convey the story of England's rejection of the Mother of God is intriguing. The jauntiness and joyful rhythm is reminiscent of pre-Reformation religious verse. It evokes England's Catholic past, the mythic Merrie England that still had the power to move Newman's contemporaries to feelings of nostalgia for a lost pastoral paradise in which people were united by a sure and simple faith. The jollity of the pre-Chaucerian meter serves as a counterpoint to the Pilgrim Queen's sorrowful lament that England had betrayed and deserted her to erect "a palace of ice":

"And me they bid wander
   in weeds and alone,
In this green merry land
   which once was my own."

The betrayal, the desolation, the melancholy are all reminiscent of the anonymous verse "The Ballad of Walsingham", which laments the destruction of England's Marian shrine, once the most prestigious in Christendom, under Henry VIII. Yet unlike the sorrowful and plaintive passion of the "Ballad", Newman's "Pilgrim Queen" transcends and transforms the sorrow with the promise of future glory. Beyond the Passion is the Resurrection. The Queen will rescue her people, and, aided by the company of heaven, she will be restored to her rightful throne.

The balance and symmetry of "The Pilgrim Queen" is the balance and symmetry of the Rosary. England's destiny, past, present and future, is reflected in the Rosary's mysteries. From joy, through sorrow, to glory. As such, England emerges as a subplot in a far greater mystery play. The lost paradise of Merrie England is the lost Eden of humanity's primeval past. The paradise has been lost through betrayal, and all that remains is the deep sense of exile at the broken heart of humanity. The brokenhearted can only look with hope for the promised glory—the conversion of humanity, and of England, through the restoration of the King and Queen to their rightful place. In tapping into authentic tradition, and calling for conversion, Newman had tapped into a wellspring of faith and hope.

Similarly, Newman had tapped into the hopes and aspirations of his fellow English Catholics when, with characteristic eloquence, he described the reestablishment of the Catholic hierarchy in England in 1850.

> A great change, an awful contrast, between the time honoured Church of St. Augustine and St. Thomas, and the poor remnant of their children in the beginning of the nineteenth century! It was a miracle, I might say, to have pulled down that lordly power; but there was a greater and a truer one in store. No one could have prophesied its fall, but still less would anyone have ventured to prophesy its rise again ... The inspired word seems to imply the almost impossibility of such a grace as the renovation of those who have crucified to themselves again, and trodden underfoot, the Son of God. Who then could have dared to hope that, out of so sacrilegious a nation as this, a people would have been formed again unto their Saviour?

Having been received scarcely five years earlier, Newman was already emerging as a leading figure in English Catholicism and was the effective instigator of the Catholic literary revival, the beginnings of which coincided almost exactly with the hierarchy's reestablishment. Ironically, *Anglican Difficulties*, the title given to a series of Newman's lectures published in the same year, pinpoints the central difficulty at the heart of any discussion of Catholic literature over the following century and a half. There are "Anglican difficulties" in any such discussion because of the essentially Catholic nature of the work of some writers who belong to the Anglo-Catholic tradition in the Church of England. This tradition was responsible for the largely orthodox writing of, among others, Christina Rossetti, Dorothy L. Sayers and, most notably of all, T. S. Eliot.

Newman's example, his genius, his energy and the impact of his life and work provided the creative spark that ignited and inspired a new generation of Catholic literary converts. One in particular was to become arguably the greatest of all the Victorian poets.

Gerard Manley Hopkins was received into the Catholic Church by Newman himself in 1866 and became, in literary terms, a sleeping giant. His friend Coventry Patmore probably summed up the Victorian attitude to Hopkins' experimental approach when he confessed his critical reservations to Robert Bridges: "To me his poetry has the effect of veins of pure gold imbedded in masses of unpracticable quartz." Although he remained utterly unknown as a poet during his own lifetime, he would emerge, thirty years after his death, as one of the most popular and influential poets of the twentieth century.

It is often said that Hopkins was ahead of his time, and perhaps there are few people to whom such a judgment could be applied more truly. Yet Hopkins was more than merely ahead of his time. He was outside his time, beyond his time. His verse is ultratemporal. It is essentially free, philosophically and culturally, of the fads and fashions of the Victorian age in which he lived. It is, however, equally free of the fads and fashions of the literary avant-garde that "discovered" and championed it during the period between the two world wars. Certainly there is no logic in the oft-repeated claim of many modern and "postmodern" critics that Hopkins should be considered a twentieth-century poet. Regardless of his undoubted influence on the poetry of the twentieth century, the publication of his poems so long after his death was essentially no more than an accident of birth.

Since T. S. Eliot was the poet most responsible for popularizing the poetic avant-garde, one might have expected him to be one of Hopkins' most vocal champions. It is surprising, therefore, that he is less than enthusiastic:

> Hopkins is not a religious poet in the more important sense in which I have elsewhere maintained Baudelaire to be a religious poet; or in the sense in which I find Villon to be a religious poet; or in the sense in which I consider Mr. Joyce's work to be penetrated with Christian feeling. I do not wish to depreciate him, but to affirm limitations and distinctions. He should be compared, not with our contemporaries whose

situation is different from his, but with the minor poet nearest contemporary to him, and most like him: George Meredith. The comparison is altogether to Hopkins's advantage ... where Meredith ... has
only a rather cheap and shallow "philosophy of life" to offer, Hopkins
has the dignity of the Church behind him, and is consequently in closer
contact with reality. But from the struggle of our time to concentrate,
not to dissipate; to renew our association with traditional wisdom; to
re-establish a vital connexion between the individual and the race; the
struggle, in a word, against Liberalism: from all this Hopkins is a little
apart, and in this Hopkins has very little aid to offer us.

There is something almost patronizing in Eliot's criticism, and one is
tempted to see an element of professional jealousy in his words. They
were written in 1933, when Hopkins was at the very height of his
fashionable popularity and when he was being lauded by many as
the greatest of "modern" poets, a position that popular critical opinion had bestowed on Eliot during the previous decade. Yet, whatever the motives behind his criticism, Eliot's appraisal fell far short of
the perceptive qualities that permeated most of his critical essays.
Most notable was his failure to appreciate the depths of orthodox Christian philosophy that underpinned Hopkins' work. Eliot was
fully conversant with the neo-Thomism that was in the ascendant
during the early decades of the twentieth century, so it is curious
that he failed to recognize the omnipresence of scholastic philosophy
in Hopkins' verse. The latter's Jesuit training had grounded him in
the teaching of Saint Thomas Aquinas and Duns Scotus, and this
had inspired his notion of *inscape*, the central concept at the heart of
his poetry, which was itself a reflection of the teaching of Duns
Scotus that everything in Creation has a unique spiritual identity, its
haecceitas, or "thisness". Distilling, through medieval philosophy, the
purer spirit of faith and reason that had existed before the adulteration of the Enlightenment, Hopkins had served up Catholic theology to an unsuspecting modernity, which, accustomed to lighter fare,
became intoxicated by its heady effects. In effect, therefore, and with
more than a modicum of irony, Hopkins' much-vaunted status as an
honorary "modern" springs from his adherence to the authentic tradition of the Church, a powerful reminder that orthodoxy is always
dynamic.

Although Hopkins remained unknown as a poet until the 1920s, he was not wholly without influence during his own lifetime. He was a close friend of Robert Bridges, and his critical judgment was greatly valued by Coventry Patmore. On one occasion Patmore actually burned one of his own manuscripts after it had been criticized by Hopkins. Following Hopkins' death in 1889, Patmore wrote the following words of tribute in a letter to Bridges:

> I can well understand how terrible a loss you have suffered in the death of Gerard Hopkins—you who saw so much more of him than I did . . . Gerard Hopkins was the only orthodox, and as far as I could see, saintly man in whom religion had absolutely no narrowing effect upon his general opinions and sympathies. A Catholic of the most scrupulous strictness, he could nevertheless see the Holy Spirit in all goodness, truth and beauty; and there was something in all his words and manners which were at once a rebuke and an attraction to all who could only aspire to be like him.

Although Patmore enjoyed the critical acclaim that eluded Hopkins during his lifetime, it would be fair to say that his verse does not reach the sublime heights that Hopkins achieves in his greatest poems. Yet Patmore's finest poetry, which followed the death of his first wife in 1862 and his conversion to Roman Catholicism two years later, almost justifies Sir Herbert Read's judgment that much of his verse represents "true poetry of the rarest and perhaps the highest kind".

Perhaps Patmore's greatest champion in the final decades of the nineteenth century was Alice Meynell, herself a poet of some merit, who published popular anthologies of his verse. Together with her husband, Wilfrid Meynell, she edited several periodicals that were highly influential and that were instrumental in popularizing other Catholic writers, of whom the most notable was Francis Thompson. The energy and enthusiasm that the Meynells displayed in their tireless promotion of the Catholic literati in late Victorian and Edwardian England helped to oil the wheels of, and give momentum to, the Catholic literary revival as it entered the twentieth century. This was a role taken up with equal vigor by Frank Sheed and Maisie Ward in the years between the two world wars. Nonetheless, the Meynells' greatest gift to posterity was their responsibility for the rescue and rehabilitation of Francis Thompson from a life of poverty and opium addiction on the streets of post-Dickensian London. Without their timely intervention, it is likely that Thompson would have died in wretched obscurity, without ever writing much of the poetry that has secured his place alongside Hopkins as the greatest Christian poet of the Victorian era. Three volumes of his poetry were published by the Meynells between 1893 and 1897 to immediate critical acclaim.

Through the Meynells, Thompson got to know the aging Patmore shortly before the latter's death in 1896, and there are hints of Patmore's influence in some of Thompson's work. The most obvious example of this can be seen in a comparison between Patmore's greatest poem, "The Toys", and Thompson's "Love and the Child", both of which employ observations of a parent-child relationship as a metaphor for the relationship of man with God. There is also a remarkable affinity between Thompson's mystical vision of nature and Hopkins' notion of the intrinsic beauty, through *inscape*, of all created things. Thompson could not have been aware of Hopkins' work, of course, but the coincidental depth of affinity is clearly discernible, most notably in Thompson's "To a Snowflake".

One also senses an affinity in such poems with the philosophy of gratitude that characterized so much of the writing of G. K. Chesterton a few years later. It is not too fanciful to imagine that Chesterton had read Thompson's poetry when it was first published in the 1890s, and if he had done so, he would most certainly have recognized in Thompson a kindred spirit. During the years that Thompson's verse was gaining widespread recognition, the young Chesterton was passing out of the period of adolescent doubt and despondency that had overshadowed his time as a student at the Slade School of Art. Writing of this period in his *Autobiography*, Chesterton referred to a time "full of doubts and morbidities and temptations; and which, though in my case mainly subjective, has left in my mind for ever a certitude upon the objective solidity of Sin." Chesterton conceded that his morbidity "may have been due to the atmosphere of the Decadents, and their perpetual hints of the luxurious horrors of paganism" that prevailed at the Slade School of Art in the "naughty nineties":

Anyhow, it is true that there was a time when I had reached the condition of moral anarchy within, in which a man says, in the words of Wilde, that "Atys with the blood-stained knife were better than the thing I am." I have never indeed felt the faintest temptation to the particular madness of Wilde; but I could at this time imagine the worst and wildest disproportions and distortions of more normal passion.

Regardless of how they may be perceived by posterity, Hopkins and Newman saw themselves, first and foremost, as ordained ministers of the Church. They were priests first, and poets second. As obedient souls who sought to do God's will in their daily lives, they could be called converts of the light. There was, however, a parallel movement of rebellious souls who were intent on experiencing all aspects of life, both the licit and the illicit, and who, often shunning the light, walked in the shadows or stumbled in the darkness. These were the Decadents, adherents of a movement originating in France but that would spread infectiously across the Channel under the beguiling influence of Oscar Wilde.

In considering the relationship between the Decadents and the Church, one is confronted with another paradox. At first glance the precociously risqué image of Wilde would appear to sit uncomfortably beside the primness and propriety of Newman. Appearances, however, can be deceiving. At the deepest level, saintly souls like Newman and Hopkins have more in common with "sinners" such as Wilde and Beardsley than with the archetypal, stoically self-righteous and sceptic-souled Victorians. "I have dreams of a visit to Newman," Wilde confessed to a friend in 1877, "of the holy sacrament in a new Church, and of a quiet and peace afterwards in my soul." Two years earlier he had scribbled in his Commonplace Book the words of the father of French Decadence, Baudelaire: "O Lord! Give me the strength and the courage to contemplate my heart without disgust!"

In later years Wilde fell under the influence of Baudelaire's disciple, J. K. Huysmans, whose luridly licentious novel, *A Rebours*, had scandalized French society following its publication in 1884. Huysmans, like Baudelaire, had chosen to look sin straight in the eye, probing its allure and its ugliness, whereas respectable, "rational" society preferred to sweep it under the carpet or glance at it furtively or voyeuristically through a keyhole. Sin, for the prudishly prurient Victorians, was to be obscene but not heard. For the Decadents, however, the honesty of a sin confessed, even in the absence of contrition, was preferable to the hypocrisy of a sin concealed. For one as tormented by self-loathing as Wilde, this candid vision of decadence was alluring. Temperamentally tempted to despair, he saw Baudelaire and Huysmans as kindred spirits. They were seeking enlightenment from their own inner darkness. He was trying to do the same.

Far from vanquishing the religious question from their lives, the Decadents discovered that plunging themselves into the depths of sin brought them into closer contact with religion, even if the contact took the form only of conflict. Sin and despair were, after all, religious concepts. They were not physical, but metaphysical, realities. Furthermore, and crucially, despair was distinct from desolation. The former is the absence or the denial of hope, the latter the longing or the hunger for it. A desolate soul does not seek suicide; it seeks consolation. Ultimately, the hunger for hope engenders a hunger for faith. Thus, in the final chapter of *A Rebours*, the novel's principal character, des Esseintes, discovers that his lustful appetites have not satisfied his inner hunger. In his hour of anguish, he realizes that "the arguments of pessimism were powerless to console him, and the only possible cure for his misery was the impossible belief in a future life". At the very last, utterly desolate, des Esseintes breaks into a faltering prayer to the "impossible" God.

> Ah! but my courage fails me, and my heart is sick within me!—Lord, take pity on the Christian who doubts, on the sceptic who would fain believe, on the galley-slave of life who puts out to sea alone, in the darkness of night, beneath a firmament no longer illumined by the beacon-fires of the ancient hope!

In this agonizing *cri de coeur* we hear the embryonic convert pining for the authentic tradition, the "ancient hope", that is only dimly discerned. Leon Bloy, in a poignant review of *A Rebours* written within weeks of the novel's publication, wrote that Huysmans' supreme achievement was to demonstrate that man's pleasures were finite, his needs infinite. The choice that Huysmans had placed before his readers was "whether to guzzle like the beasts of the field or to look upon the

face of God". A similar conclusion was drawn in another review by
the aging romantic writer Jules Barbey d'Aurevilly, who highlighted
the suggestive parallel between *A Rebours* and Baudelaire's *Les Fleurs
du mal*.

> Baudelaire, the satanic Baudelaire, who died a Christian, must surely
> be one of M. Huysmans' favourite authors, for one can feel his pres-
> ence, like a glowing fire, behind the finest pages M. Huysmans has
> written. Well, one day, I defied Baudelaire to begin *Les Fleurs du mal*
> again, or to go any further in his blasphemies. I might well offer the
> same challenge to the author of *A Rebours*. "After *Les Fleurs du mal*," I
> told Baudelaire, "it only remains for you to choose between the muz-
> zle of a pistol and the foot of the Cross." Baudelaire chose the foot of
> the Cross. But will the author of *A Rebours* make the same choice?

Twelve years after these words were published, Huysmans recalled
Barbey's review: "Strange! But that man was the only one who saw
things clearly in my case ... He wrote an article which contained
these last prophetic words: 'There only remains for you to commit
suicide or become a Catholic.'" By this time Huysmans had indeed
become a Catholic, and he would spend the last years of his life in a
monastery. Wilde, whose novel *The Picture of Dorian Gray* was greatly
influenced by *A Rebours* and contains the same desolate *cri de coeur*,
responded approvingly when he learned that Huysmans had entered a
monastery, declaring his own desire to do the same. Like Huysmans,
Wilde came to Christ and the Church via desolation, and even today,
a hundred years after his death, he remains a controversial figure. Indeed,
such are the moral somersaults that society has performed in the century since his death that he is now vindicated for the very things for
which he was vilified. Sadly, Wilde is as misunderstood today as he
was in his own day, especially as the central theme of his late works
has precious little to do with the role of "sexual liberator" that posterity has thrust upon him and everything to do with the Christian
penitent seeking forgiveness. Wilde's "heart of stone" was broken by
the experience of the two-year prison sentence imposed in the wake
of the libel trial, and his two late works, *The Ballad of Reading Gaol*
and the posthumously published *De Profundis*, bear witness to his
eleventh-hour conversion to Catholicism. Three weeks before his death,

he told a *Daily Chronicle* correspondent that "much of my moral obliquity is due to the fact that my father would not allow me to become a Catholic. The artistic side of the Church and the fragrance of its teaching would have cured my degeneracies. I intend to be received before long." He was received on his deathbed.

It is indeed ironic that Wilde is remembered only for the tragedy of his life and not for its happy ending. His last will and testament remains, however, in the brilliance of *The Ballad of Reading Gaol*, a poem that bears a remarkable similarity to Thompson's masterpiece "The Hound of Heaven" in its description of the triumph of Christ through the suffering and desolation of a misspent life:

> And thus we rust Life's iron chain
> Degraded and alone:
> And some men curse, and some men weep,
> And some men make no moan:
> But God's eternal Laws are kind
> And break the heart of stone.
>
> And every human heart that breaks,
> In prison-cell or yard,
> Is as that broken box that gave
> Its treasure to the Lord,
> And filled the unclean leper's house
> With the scent of costliest nard.
>
> Ah! happy they whose hearts can break
> And peace of pardon win!
> How else may man make straight his plan
> And cleanse his soul from Sin?
> How else but through a broken heart
> May Lord Christ enter in?

Ultimately, the Decadents were far more in revolt against the humanistic "rationalism" of the post-Enlightenment than they were ever in revolt against the traditions of the Church. They sprang from the same romantic tradition as Coleridge and Wordsworth, seeking the soul and its secrets in a world that had seemingly lost its soul through a lack of belief in its very existence. Whereas Coleridge and Wordsworth had become sceptical about scepticism, the Decadents had become cynical toward cynicism. Furthermore, when their cynicism led them to sin, it brought them into contact with authentic tradition, specifically the Church's teaching on the seven deadly sins, reflected most sublimely in art by the divinely inspired infernal and purgatorial visions of Dante. The Decadents were groping uncertainly and sometimes blindly in search of the same Dantean vision. Their own visions may have been pale reflections of Dante's masterpiece, but they were visions of sublime reality nonetheless. The Decadents discovered the reality of sin and, having kissed it, recoiled from its embrace. Having experienced the dire consequences of the real absence of God, they hungered for His Real Presence.

Apart from the striking similarity between the Decadent and the Dantean, there is also an obvious affinity of inspiration and intent between Decadent works such as *A Rebours* and *The Picture of Dorian Gray* and the Faustian parables of Marlowe and Goethe. Perhaps the most striking example of a Decadent reworking of the legend of Dr. Faustus was "Finis Coronat Opus", a short story by Francis Thompson. The hero, or more correctly the antihero, of Thompson's tale is Florentian, a character cast in the same mold as Dr. Faustus or Dorian Gray, who also makes a pact with the devil in order to achieve his heart's desire. Whereas Dorian Gray had desired physical beauty and eternal youth, Florentian desires poetic genius and supremacy in the arts. In return for this, the devil demands the blood sacrifice of Florentian's wife. Florentian removes the crucifix from the altar, treads the prostrate cross underfoot and places a bust of Virgil in its place. He then murders his wife on the altar of Art. His wish is granted, but, as with Dorian Gray, it brings nothing but misery and despair. At the very last, as the unbarred gate of hell looms menacingly, he is granted a glimpse of lost innocence:

> I met a child today; a child with great candour of eyes. They who talk of children's instincts are at fault: she knew not that hell was in my soul, she knew only that softness was in my gaze. She had been gathering wild flowers, and offered them to me. To me, to *me*!

In many respects, the figure of Francis Thompson stands symbolically as a unifying force between the Decadent converts of the 1890s and the decidedly non-Decadent converts of the Edwardian and Georgian era, such as Chesterton, Benson, Baring, Noyes and Knox. Throughout the 1880s Thompson had led a life of penury, squalor and opium addiction. Homeless, hungry and befriended by prostitutes, his experiences inspired his most famous poem, "The Hound of Heaven", written in 1889. Although Thompson was a cradle Catholic, the poem, with its potent and poignant depiction of a reluctant soul's final acceptance of God's relentless and fathomless love, remains a classic of conversion literature.

Maurice Baring was another writer whose conversion to Catholicism was influenced, at least in part, by Huysmans. In the early years of the twentieth century, when Baring was grappling with the tenets of Christianity, the line of reasoning in Huysmans' *En Route* struck him very forcefully. It was, however, another Frenchman who would have the greatest influence on Baring's conversion. In 1898 he had met Hilaire Belloc for the first time, and the two men formed a friendship that would last the rest of their lives. Two years later Belloc and Chesterton met for the first time in a restaurant in Soho, and through Belloc, Chesterton became friends with Baring several years later. The friendship of these three men would later be immortalized in Sir James Gunn's group portrait, which can still be seen in the National Portrait Gallery. Belloc, Baring and Chesterton, both singularly and collectively, represented the dominant force in Catholic literary circles throughout the first third of the twentieth century. Baring is the least known of the three, and his own literary achievement is sadly neglected today. His *Collected Poems*, published in 1925, included many of considerable merit, most notably the sonnet sequence "Vita Nuova", written to commemorate his reception into the Church in 1909. Yet he was known principally as a novelist. His first novel, *Passing By*, was published in 1921 when he was already almost fifty years old, and his last was published fifteen years later, when his literary vocation was tragically cut short by the debilitating effects of Parkinson's disease. In between he commanded a small but passionate readership and enjoyed much critical acclaim. His novel *C*, published in 1924, was highly praised by the French novelist André Maurois, who wrote that no book had given him such pleasure since his reading of Tolstoy, Proust and certain novels by E. M. Forster. If anything, Baring was to enjoy greater success in France than in England. Ten of his books were translated into French, with one—*Daphne Adeane*—going through twenty-three printings in the edition of the Librairie Stock. Others were translated into Italian, Dutch, Swedish, Hungarian, Czech, Spanish and German.

Although Chesterton and Belloc were great admirers of Baring's work, others failed to share their enthusiasm. Virginia Woolf, taking the opposite view, attacked what she perceived as Baring's "superficiality". Largely neglected and misunderstood in England, Baring gained solace once again from the empathy exhibited by a more discerning readership across the Channel. In particular, he was "too moved to speak" when, six months before his death in 1945, he learned of the deep admiration that François Mauriac had for his novels. Mauriac had told the Catholic actor Robert Speaight: "What I admire most about Baring's work is the sense he gives you of the penetration of grace."

Perhaps the profundity at the heart of Baring's fiction was encapsulated in the words of one of the characters from *Darby and Joan*, his last novel:

> "One has to *accept* sorrow for it to be of any healing power, and that is the most difficult thing in the world ... A Priest once said to me, 'When you understand what *accepted* sorrow means, you will understand everything. It is the secret of life'."

These words, which for Virginia Woolf and others represented Baring's "superficiality", were at once both mystical and practical, so practical that Baring put them into practice, accepting his own debilitating illness with a contrite and heroic heart. In 1941, the year in which Virginia Woolf took her own life in an act of despair, Baring answered his earlier complaint that his body was "a broken toy which nobody can mend" with the reply that his soul was "an immortal toy which nobody can mar".

Baring's obituary in the *Times* on 17 December 1945 regretted that "many English readers" saw his novels as "a form of Roman Catholic propaganda" but maintained that he was "above all concerned to express a passionate conviction that belief in God can alone bring storm-tossed humanity into harbour". After referring to Baring's "friendship with the late G. K. Chesterton, and with Mr. Hilaire Belloc", the obituary concluded with an assessment of Baring's literary legacy: "Concerning his final position in literature, time may perhaps confirm the judgment of those who see in him one of the subtlest, profoundest, and most original of recent English writers."

The emergence of G. K. Chesterton, who entered the literary fray at the dawning of the new century, heralded the second dynamic phase of the Catholic literary revival. Indeed, it would be no exaggeration to say that Chesterton's role in popularizing Catholicism in the twentieth century was as crucial as Newman's had been in the previous century. It would also be fair to say that Chesterton's mind was akin to Newman's in its ability to communicate timeless truth with seemingly effortless clarity. He hammered the "heretics" in his book of that title and pitted their heresies against infallible "orthodoxy". Then, in 1909, he became embroiled in the controversy raging in the Church between the traditionalists and the modernists. In prose as profound as Newman's he argued the case for tradition, labeling it the philosophy of the tree.

> I mean that a tree goes on growing, and therefore goes on changing; but always in the fringes surrounding something unchangeable. The innermost rings of the tree are still the same as when it was a sapling; they have ceased to be seen, but they have not ceased to be central. When the tree grows a branch at the top, it does not break away from the roots at the bottom; on the contrary, it needs to hold more strongly to its roots the higher it rises with its branches. That is the true image of the vigorous and healthy progress of a man, a city, or a whole species.

The modernists, by contrast, did not subscribe to such a concept of tradition, believing instead in "something that changes completely and entirely in every part, at every minute, like a cloud ... Now, if this merely cloudy and boneless development be adopted as a philosophy, then there can be no place for the past and no possibility of a complete culture. Anything may be here today and gone tomorrow; even tomorrow."

Elsewhere Chesterton would describe tradition as the proxy of the dead and the enfranchisement of the unborn, and he also seems to have seen it as a weapon wielded by the Church Militant in her centuries-long war against heresy. The latter vision was never brought more vibrantly to life, quite literally, than in a memorable essay on Gothic architecture.

> The truth about Gothic is, first, that it is alive, and second, that it is on the march. It is the Church Militant; it is the only fighting architecture. All its spires are spears at rest; and all its stones are stones asleep in a catapult ... I could hear the arches clash like swords as they crossed each other. The mighty and numberless columns seemed to go swinging by like the huge feet of imperial elephants. The graven foliage wreathed and blew like banners going into battle; the silence was deafening with all the mingling noises of a military march; the great bell shook down, as the organ shook up its thunder. The thirsty-throated gargoyles shouted like trumpets from all the roofs and pinnacles as they passed; and from the lectern in the core of the cathedral the eagle of the awful evangelist clashed his wings of brass.

Chesterton's militant approach to the authentic tradition of the Church found expression in many aspects of his work. It surfaced in some of his finest verse, particularly in "Lepanto" and "The Secret People", in which the influence of his friend Hilaire Belloc is obvious. *The Ballad of the White Horse* captured the imagination of a whole generation and influenced some of the century's greatest writers. John Galsworthy, C. S. Lewis and J. R. R. Tolkien were among its admirers, although Tolkien later became more critical of its undoubted flaws. It was also one of Graham Greene's favorite poems. In an interview published in the *Observer* on 12 March 1978, Greene called Chesterton "another underestimated poet". To illustrate the point, he cited the *Ballad*: "Put *The Ballad of the White Horse* against *The Waste Land*. If I had to lose one of them, I'm not sure that ... well, anyhow, let's just say I re-read *The Ballad* more often!"

Neither does Chesterton's literary reputation rest solely on his poetry. On the contrary, his genius resides primarily in his prolific versatility. His many works of literary criticism were much admired, by T. S. Eliot among others, as were his biographies of Saint Francis of Assisi and Saint Thomas Aquinas, but perhaps he deserves to be remembered above all for his handful of novels. As with his verse, these sometimes suffer from a slapdash approach, a carefree and careless disregard for structural discipline, but what they lack in technical tuning they gain in sparkling spontaneity. His first novel, *The Napoleon of Notting Hill*, addressed one of the central political and cultural issues of the century, the belief that "small is beautiful". This was summed up by Adam Wayne, a character in the novel, with the proclamation that a place, however small, "which is large enough for the rich to covet ... is large enough for the poor to defend".

Chesterton's second novel, *The Man Who Was Thursday*, was published in 1908. It is arguably the best, and is certainly the most perplexing, of his works of fiction. On a superficial level the plot is literally a plot, in the sense of the Gunpowder Plot, revolving around a group of anarchists apparently intent on destruction. On this level, the book's subtitle, "A Nightmare", seems singularly appropriate. As a dreamer has difficulty unraveling the meaning of his dreams—if, indeed, his dreams have any meaning at all—Chesterton seems to have difficulty unraveling the meaning of his nightmare. On the deepest level, however, the novel explodes with the brilliance of paradoxical pyrotechnics, a fantasy of fireworks that illuminate the darkness with the deepest truths about God and his Creation. Years later C. S. Lewis drew a surprising parallel between *The Man Who Was Thursday* and the works of Franz Kafka:

> Is the difference simply that one is "dated" and the other contemporary? Or is it rather that while both give a powerful picture of the loneliness and bewilderment which each one of us encounters in his (apparently) single-handed struggle with the universe, Chesterton, attributing to the universe a more complicated disguise, and admitting the exhilaration as well as the terror of the struggle, has got in rather more; is more balanced: in that sense, more classical, more permanent?

In the light of Lewis' comments it is interesting to note that Kafka was familiar with *The Man Who Was Thursday*.

Discussing both *Orthodoxy* and *The Man Who Was Thursday*, Kafka remarked that Chesterton "is so gay, that one might almost believe he had found God ... In such a godless time one must be gay. It is a duty."

Another admirer of Chesterton's first two novels is Terry Pratchett, the modern author of popular comic fantasy:

It's worth pointing out that in *The Man Who Was Thursday* and *The Napoleon of Notting Hill* he gave us two of the most emotionally charged plots in the twentieth century: one being that both sides are actually the same side; it doesn't matter which side we're talking about, both sides are the same. This has been the motor of half the spy novels of this century. The other plot can't be summarised so succinctly, but the basic plot of *The Napoleon of Notting Hill* is that someone takes seriously an idea that wasn't intended to be taken seriously and gives it some kind of nobility by so doing.

Chesterton's religious faith, which was present only implicitly in his first two novels, was much more to the fore in *The Ball and the Cross*. The two heroes, a devout Catholic and a militant atheist, are ennobled by their arguments and by their adherence to the ideals they espouse. Their nobility stands in stark contrast to the cynical indifference of the world they inhabit. On one level *The Ball and the Cross* can be seen as a parable of Chesterton's arguments and relationship with George Bernard Shaw. Chesterton and Shaw disagreed passionately on most of the issues of the day but remained good friends. Their relationship was a living embodiment of the stricture to "love thine enemy".

Manalive is often overlooked when Chesterton's novels are discussed and is arguably his most underrated work. It contains the charm, mystery and adventure of *The Man Who Was Thursday* and *The Ball and the Cross* but also has a depth beyond either of these, especially in its characterization of women. In Chesterton's earlier novels, female characters play a peripheral role, whereas in *Manalive* they are not only central to the plot but possess a mystique that is absent, or at least only hinted at, in the earlier books. As *The Ball and the Cross* can be read as a parable of Chesterton's relationship with Shaw, *Manalive* can be read as a parable of Chesterton's relationship with Frances, his wife. The parallels between fact and fiction are obvious. The novel's hero, Innocent Smith, was Chesterton, trying always to stir the world from its cynical slumber, while the heroine, Mary Gray, was Frances, the silence on which he depended utterly, the power behind the throne. On another level *Manalive* was a further affirmation of Chesterton's philosophy of gratitude that had found its fulfillment in Christian orthodoxy. Ultimately, the novel's whole *raison d'être* was to illustrate that the intrinsic wisdom of innocence was unobtainable to the naïvely cynical. This, of course, was the motive behind Chesterton's creation of Father Brown, and it is no coincidence that the first volume of Father Brown stories, appropriately entitled *The Innocence of Father Brown*, appeared within months of the publication of *Manalive*.

Another noteworthy novel of Chesterton's was *The Flying Inn*, published in 1914, a romp across an idealized Merrie England in praise of good ale, good companionship and traditional freedoms. In some respects it bore a remarkable similarity to Belloc's *The Four Men*, which appeared two years earlier. The prose in both these works was punctuated with hearty verse, or drinking songs.

By the time that *The Flying Inn* and *The Four Men* were published, Chesterton and Belloc were seen so synonymously that Shaw had dubbed them the "Chesterbelloc". For all their similarities, however, there remained many significant differences between the two halves of the Chesterbelloc, both in terms of their respective personalities and in terms of their literary achievement. With the notable exception of *Belinda*, Belloc's novels were not as accomplished as Chesterton's, but his verse is more consistent in its quality and more considered in its construction. At its best, Belloc's poetry is better than anything Chesterton achieved, with the arguable exception of the latter's "Lepanto". Belloc's poems "Tarantella", "Ha'nacker Mill" and "The End of the Road" place him among the first rank of twentieth-century poets. His "Lines to a Don", written in defense of Chesterton, is a timeless classic of comic vitriol, while "Twelfth Night", "Ballade of Illegal Ornaments" and "Rose" are among the century's finest religious verse.

Besides Chesterton and Belloc, the writer most responsible for carrying the mantle of the Catholic literary revival in the early years of the twentieth century was Robert Hugh Benson. In some respects, Benson's life paralleled that of Newman. His conversion to Catholicism in 1903 and his subsequent ordination caused a sensation on a scale similar to that which greeted Newman's reception into the Church almost sixty years earlier. In Benson's case the sensation was linked to the fact that he was the son of E. W. Benson, Archbishop of Canterbury from 1882 until 1896. Like Newman, Benson followed a literary as well as a priestly vocation, and before his untimely death in 1914 at the age of forty-three, he had published fifteen highly successful novels.

The other obvious parallel with Newman was Benson's writing of a lucid and candid autobiographical apologia describing the circumstances leading up to his conversion. Benson's *Confessions of a Convert* warrants a position alongside Newman's *Apologia pro Vita Sua* as one of the great expositions of the spiritual and psychological background to religious conversion.

An early admirer of Benson was Hilaire Belloc, who wrote in 1907 that he had met him once or twice "and liked him enormously". Belloc was particularly impressed with Benson's historical novels: "It is quite on the cards that he will be the man to write some day a book to give us some sort of idea what happened in England between 1520 and 1560. No book I ever read has given me the slightest conception, and I have never had time to go into the original stuff myself. This is the most interesting of historical problems."

Benson's early death ensured that he was never able to fulfill Belloc's wish. In consequence, Belloc, increasingly frustrated at the Protestant bias of the Whig historians, would reluctantly take up the cudgels himself. In later life Belloc would publish studies of key sixteenth- and seventeenth-century figures such as Wolsey, Cromwell, James II, Charles I and Cranmer. His *How the Reformation Happened*, published in 1928, would endeavor to put the whole period into context. Yet to a large extent Benson achieved the same aim in his fiction. *Come Rack! Come Rope!* remains an outstanding work of literature in its prose, its plot, its characterization and its masterful control of the historical landscape in which it is set.

Nor did Benson restrict himself to historical fiction. He wrote novels that dealt with the contemporary religious and moral dilemmas of Edwardian society and, as in the case of *Lord of the World*, novels that conjured up apocalyptic visions of the future. The latter were a reaction to the optimistic science fantasies of Wells and a foreshadowing of the nightmare visions of Huxley's *Brave New World* and Orwell's *Nineteen Eighty-Four*. R. H. Benson, as a writer of fiction, was a master of the past, the present and the future. His *Poems*, published posthumously, mark him out as one of the most accomplished poets of his generation, and his *Spiritual Letters*, also published posthumously, display a deep religious faith rooted in a marriage of the mystical and intellectual. The neglect of Benson's literary achievement says more about the decline and sickness of an increasingly secularized society than it does about any alleged shortcomings in his writing.

Benson's biographer, C. C. Martindale, saw a "disconcerting affinity" between Benson's *Papers of a Pariah* and Wilde's *De Profundis*: "Benson had, and Wilde was resolving, so he thought, to get, that direct eye for colour, line, and texture that the Greeks possessed ... Benson, ... in his direct extraction of natural emotion from simple and beautiful elements, like fire and wax, as in his description of the Easter ceremonies ... reaches, sometimes, an almost word-for-word identity with Wilde." Martindale also wrote of the "Chestertonian quality" in Benson's work and quoted a letter Benson had written in 1905 in which he expresses admiration for Chesterton's *Heretics*:

> Have you read a book by G. K. Chesterton called *Heretics*? ... It seems to me that the spirit underneath is splendid. He is not a Catholic, but he has the spirit. He is so joyful and confident and sensible! One gets rather annoyed by his extreme love of paradox; but there is a sort of alertness in his religion and in his whole point of view that is simply exhilarating. I have not been so much moved for a long time ... He is a real mystic of an odd kind.

The writing of both Benson and Chesterton was a principal constituent in the conversion of Ronald Knox to the Catholic Church in 1917. Knox was only sixteen, "a schoolboy just beginning to think", when he had first read Chesterton's *The Napoleon of Notting Hill*. It affected him profoundly, as he confessed to Frances Chesterton shortly after her husband's death:

> He has been my idol since I read *The Napoleon of Notting Hill* as a schoolboy; I'll only hope that you, who know as no one else does what we have lost, will find it easy to imagine as well as believe that he is alive and unchanged. Thank God for that faith; that I have it when so many of my friends lost it was due, I think, under God to him.

Elsewhere Knox had written that "Chesterton's philosophy, in the broadest sense of the word, has been part of the air I breathed, ever since the age when a man's ideas begin to disentangle themselves from his education. His paradoxes have become, as it were, the platitudes of my thought."

The fact that Benson shared the distinction with Chesterton of being Knox' idol during the formative years of his life is well documented in Knox' *A Spiritual Aeneid*:

> It was at Manchester, on Christmas Day, 1903, that I read a book writ-ten (I was told) by an Anglican who had just become a Roman Cath-olic (actually, in that September). It was, of course, *The Light Invisible*, a collection of stories written by Mgr. Benson while he was still in the Church of England ... Most people find it an interesting book, but free from controversial tendency ... Yet, to me, that Christmas Day was a turning point. It was the setting of the book—the little chapel in which the priest celebrated, the terms in which he alluded to the Mother of God, the description of confessions heard in an old parish church— that riveted me even more than the psychological interest. All that Cath-olic system which I had hitherto known only distantly ... now for the first time entered my horizon.

Thereafter Knox always looked upon Benson "as the guide who had led me to Catholic truth", and in the last few days before his conversion, almost fourteen years after he had first read *The Light Invis-ible*, he read Benson's *Come Rack! Come Rope!* "Hugh Benson, who had set my feet on the way towards the Church, watched over my footsteps to the last."

It was no great surprise that Knox considered Benson his mentor. They had so much in common. Both were sons of Anglican bishops and were educated at Eton. They both belonged to remarkable liter-ary families and had brothers whose literary reputations were perhaps the equal of their own. Both passed through Anglo-Catholicism into full communion with the Catholic Church. There was, however, one major difference. Whereas Benson's literary achievement was truly pro-digious considering his early and untimely death, Knox failed to live up to his early promise. Evelyn Waugh, in his introduction to the 1958 edition of Knox' *A Spiritual Aeneid*, described the precocious and meteoric rise of the young Knox:

> He went up to Balliol in 1906 preceded by a reputation of unique lustre. While still at Eton he had written a book of light verse in English, Latin and Greek and he is still remembered there as the cleverest boy who ever passed through that school ... At Oxford all the coveted

distinctions—the Hertford and Ireland scholarships, the presidency of the Union, a first in Greats—came to him as by-products of an exuberant intellectual and social life ... In 1910 there seemed no limit to the prizes, political, academic or literary, which a smiling world held out to him.

Seen in this context it was scarcely surprising that Knox' conversion proved almost as controversial as that of Newman or Benson, shaking the establishments of both Canterbury and Oxford. Expectations were high, and many believed that Knox was destined to be a latter-day Newman. It was not to be. The reasons for the literary anticlimax were explained by Waugh:

> After *Caliban in Grub Street* (1930) and *Broadcast Minds* (1932), in which he dealt with opponents who were mostly unworthy of his attention, he decided that his vocation was not to discomfort the infidel but to work among the clergy and laity of his own Church to fortify and refine their devotion and remind them of their high calling. He drew apart from secular life with the result that the name of one of the very few prose stylists of his age was seldom mentioned in literary journals.
>
> Three books, certainly, *Enthusiasm*, *Let Dons Delight* and *God and the Atom*, claim a place in the library, however small, of anyone, however indifferent to religion, who recognizes distinction in literature, but it is by his Bible that he wished to be remembered. It took ten years of his life at the height of his powers.

Sadly, even Knox' translation of the Bible, painstakingly crafted into what he hoped was a "timeless English", was very soon eclipsed by later translations that were more accomplished academically. Knox, it seemed, was never destined to reach the literary heights of which Waugh and others believed he was capable. Instead, his importance to the Catholic literary revival has more to do with his place in what Barbara Reynolds, the Dante scholar, has called the "network of minds energising each other". He represented a significant influence on the conversions of both Chesterton and Waugh and, in Waugh's case particularly, provided spiritual succor and sustenance. Many years later, shortly before his death in 1957, Knox formed a late friendship with Siegfried Sassoon that proved instrumental in the poet's reception into the Church.

If Chesterton and Belloc represented the voice of dynamic orthodoxy in the early years of the century, a new and radically different
voice would be its principal exponent in the years between the two
world wars. T. S. Eliot was hailed by the avant-garde as the authentic
voice of postwar pessimism and scepticism, particularly after the publication of *The Waste Land* in 1922. By contrast, many of the poetic
old guard viewed him suspiciously as a dangerous threat to tradition,
an iconoclastic aberration who was thumbing his nose at convention.
In the confusion of the fray that followed the poem's publication, many
on both sides of the critical divide had obviously missed the poet's
point. Lack of understanding led inevitably to misunderstanding, so
that battle lines were drawn according to erroneous preconceptions.
The "moderns" hailed it as a masterpiece of modern thought that had
laid waste traditional values and traditional form. The "ancients" attacked
it as an affront to civilized standards. Both sides had made the grave
and fundamental error of mistaking Eliot's pessimism toward the wasteland of modern life for a cynicism toward tradition. In fact, Eliot's
philosophical foundation and aesthetic sympathies were rooted in classical and medieval tradition, whereas he despised modern secular liberalism. It was, therefore, a perverse irony that he was being vilified
by the upholders of tradition and championed by the doyens of secularism. Indeed, it would be fair to say that possibly no poem in the
English language has been as admired, as abhorred and as misunderstood as Eliot's *The Waste Land*.

It would be many years before a true perspective would begin to
appear of the poem, the issues it raised and the reaction it caused.
Although Chesterton had initially mistrusted Eliot's work, mistaking
the latter's antimodern pessimism for postmodern cynicism, he eventually came to see Eliot as a major Christian literary figure, expressing
admiration for Eliot's *Murder in the Cathedral*, which was published a
year before Chesterton's death in 1936. Nor would it be entirely correct to make such a simplistic comparison between Eliot's dark vision
and Chesterton's high spirits. Chesterton and Belloc had always combined their *joie de vivre* with strident criticism of a centralist industrial
system that they both despised. With the growth of the distributist
movement, under Belloc's ideological guidance and Chesterton's charismatic presidency, in the years between the wars, this criticism became

more robust than ever. Also, on a purely literary level, Chesterton's response to the horror of the war was not that dissimilar to the bitterness being expressed by the war poets. His "Elegy in a Country Churchyard" was as full of potent indignation against those responsible for the slaughter as had been Siegfried Sassoon's "Fight to a Finish" or Wilfred Owen's "Dulce et Decorum Est". After all, Chesterton had lost his brother and several close friends in the war. Belloc, who had lost a son as well as friends, never recovered the prewar jollity that was the endearing feature of much of his early work. Stricken with grief, he wrote in 1920 of his own "desire to be rid of life", words of desolation, not despair. For Belloc, life after the death of his son and the earlier death of his wife would still be enjoyed on the babbling surface, most especially in the company of friends, but was endured in the still depths.

Perhaps the hidden key to understanding *The Waste Land*, overlooked by almost everyone at the time and still ignored by many of the poem's postmodernist admirers today, is to be found in Eliot's devotion to Dante. Eliot perceived that Dante had been grossly misunderstood by the undue emphasis placed upon the "negative" *Inferno* at the expense of the other two "positive" books of the *Divine Comedy*, and there was something almost divinely comic in the fact that Eliot himself was to suffer the same fate after the publication of *The Waste Land*. As post-Reformation puritanism had stressed the punishment of hell in Dante and had ignored the "papist" parts about the cleansing grace of Purgatory and the Church Triumphant in paradise, so postwar cynicism had stressed the negative aspects of Eliot's *Waste Land* and had ignored the cathartic conclusion that pointed to a "resurrection". Typical of this myopic modernist miasma was the judgment of the literary critic I. A. Richards that Eliot in *The Waste Land* had effected "a complete severance between poetry and *all* beliefs". This generally accepted assumption was blown asunder in June 1927 by Eliot's conversion to Anglo-Catholicism, news of which was greeted with incredulity. How could the arch-iconoclast have become an iconographer?

Similar horror and incredulity greeted the news, three years later, that Evelyn Waugh had been received into the Catholic Church. By the end of the 1920s, he was seen as the ultramodern novelist in much the same way that Eliot had been perceived as the ultramodern poet.

As such, Waugh's conversion was treated with astonishment by the literary world. On the morning after his reception, there was bemused bewilderment in the *Daily Express* that an author known for his "almost passionate adherence to the ultra-modern" could have joined the Catholic Church. Two leaders in the *Express* had already discussed the significance of Waugh's conversion before his own article, "Converted to Rome: Why It Has Happened to Me", was published on 20 October 1930. Waugh's conversion, like that of Newman, Chesterton and Eliot, was rooted in tradition. The "essential issue" facing European civilization, he wrote, was "between Christianity and Chaos." Waugh's contemptuous dismissal of "talking cinemas and tinned food" as having any significance to civilization was indicative of a deep mistrust of scientism and technolatry, that is, the worship and idolization of technological "progress".

A year after the publication of Waugh's *Vile Bodies*, a novel that captured and encapsulated the author's disgust with the vulgar elements of modernity at the time of his conversion, a work in similar vein was published by the poet Roy Campbell. *The Georgiad* was a merciless verse satire of the wealthy party-set, centered around Harold Nicolson and Vita Sackville-West, of which Campbell and his wife had at one time been an integral part. *The Georgiad* steers a *via media* between Eliot and Waugh in its rejection of a modern wasteland, populated by vile bodies and hollow men. Largely to escape the decadence of their life in England, the Campbells moved to Provence and then to Spain, where they were received into the Catholic Church in 1935. Perhaps Campbell's most enduring contribution to Christian literature would be his masterful translation of the poems of Saint John of the Cross.

Besides Evelyn Waugh, the other leading Catholic novelist to emerge during the interwar years was Graham Greene. With *Brighton Rock* in 1938 and *The Power and the Glory* two years later, Greene made Catholic doctrine and religious dilemma the dominant force in his fiction. After the war, the increasingly heterodox nature of works such as *The Heart of the Matter*, *The End of the Affair* and *A Burnt Out Case* alarmed many Catholics, including Waugh, and some critics began to question whether Greene had lost his faith. Nonetheless, his biographer, Norman Sherry, believed that he "remained a strong Catholic until his death". Whether this is so, the fact remains that the enigma of both Greene and his novels rests in the presence of an uncomfortable sense of doubt. Yet he and they seemed to perceive that to be anything other than a Catholic would mean becoming something less than a Catholic, a passing from inexplicable and doubtful depths to inane and dubious shallows. There was no escape from a truth that couldn't be proved.

Ironically, considering the Allied victory over the Nazis, the same sense of pessimism accompanied the end of the Second World War as had greeted the end of the first. In part, this arose from the horror that many people felt about the dropping of the atom bombs on Hiroshima and Nagasaki and the realization that a new and horrific weapon had emerged. The dawn of the nuclear age coincided with the world's lurch from a world war into a cold war, in which the future was as bleak as it was uncertain. This spirit of gloom and despondency was captured most memorably in Orwell's *Animal Farm* and *Nineteen Eighty-Four*, but there were a host of other literary creations born of a similar anxiety, many of which were imbued with Christian disdain for the nihilism of postwar materialism.

Ronald Knox' *God and the Atom* set the cautionary tone with its warnings about the dire consequences of the triumph of scientific materialism. Edith Sitwell had been so shocked by an eyewitness account of the immediate effect of the atomic bomb upon Hiroshima that she composed her poem *The Shadow of Cain*, the first of her "three poems of the Atomic Age".

The horrors of Hiroshima also inspired Siegfried Sassoon, writer of some of the finest poetry of the previous war, to new heights of creativity. In 1945 he wrote "Litany of the Lost", a verse that echoed the concerns expressed by Sitwell and that employed similar resonant religious imagery as a counterpoise to postwar pessimism and alienation. By the middle of the following decade, these concerns had led both Sassoon and Sitwell into the arms of the Catholic Church. In common with Graham Greene and the many converts who had preceded them, they were longing for depth in a world of shallows, permanence in a world of change and certainty in a world of doubt.

In the same year that Sitwell and Sassoon were expressing their nuclear reactions, Waugh's *Brideshead Revisited* was published. Written over a year before the bomb was dropped but not published until 1945, Waugh's novel of hope among the ruins of a vanishing civilization was nonetheless animated by the same postwar pessimism and anxiety that permeated the poetry and prose of Sitwell, Sassoon and Knox. It sold exceedingly well on both sides of the Atlantic. In England, the *Tablet* acclaimed it as "the finest of all his works, a book for which it is safe to prophesy a lasting place among the major works of fiction". In America, *Time* described Waugh as a stylist unexcelled among contemporary novelists.

The praise was tempered by a vociferous minority who disliked *Brideshead Revisited* on both political and religious grounds. It was deemed politically incorrect for its nostalgic swan-songing of a rapidly vanishing aristocratic way of life, and Waugh was vilified for being a reactionary and a snob. Meanwhile, other critics, such as Edmund Wilson, had criticized the religious dimension.

With the publication of *Brideshead Revisited*, Waugh completed the metamorphosis from ultramodern to ultramontane and also invited comparisons between the works of Waugh and those of the disappearing old guard of the Catholic literary revival. Certainly, the influence of Chesterton on the writing of *Brideshead Revisited* is patently obvious. The combination of Catholicism and aristocratic high society in *Brideshead* also invites comparisons with the novels of Maurice Baring, who died in the year of the novel's publication. Less obvious but probably as powerful was the subliminal influence of Hilaire Belloc, who had been one of Waugh's heroes since Waugh's days as a schoolboy at Lancing. Waugh was attracted to Belloc's militantly aggressive and traditional approach to Catholicism but was equally impressed by the matter-of-fact, almost humdrum, way in which he practiced his faith. It was the simple unaffected faith of cradle Catholics like Belloc, as distinct from the *arriviste* zeal of converts, that shaped the characterization of the Flytes in *Brideshead*. Another Catholic writer who probably influenced aspects of the writing of *Brideshead Revisited* was Compton Mackenzie, whose evocative description of life in Oxford in *Sinister Street*, a book that Waugh had read and enjoyed at Lancing, found resonant echoes in Waugh's own atmospheric treatment of Oxford undergraduate life. Thus, in one novel, one can witness the full plethora of influences that had animated the Christian literary landscape in the previous forty years.

Another novel that displayed an orthodox Christian response to the dilemmas posed by postwar modernism was C. S. Lewis' *That Hideous Strength* published in July 1945. At the time of its publication, Lewis' friend J. R. R. Tolkien was in the midst of writing *The Lord of the Rings*, and there are certain distinct similarities between the two books. Lewis' ascribing of demoniac powers to the men of science in *That Hideous Strength* bore more than a marked resemblance to Tolkien's treatment of the same issue. Indeed, Lewis' description of *That Hideous Strength* to an American correspondent in 1954 could almost serve as a description of *The Lord of the Rings*: "I think *That Hideous Strength* is about a triple conflict: Grace against Nature and Nature against Anti-Nature (modern industrialism, scientism and totalitarian politics)". This triple conflict between the supernatural, natural and unnatural was arguably the key to both books, and it is an indictment of the ignorance of the postwar world that many of Tolkien's millions of readers remain entirely ignorant of the orthodox Catholic theology at the heart of his subcreation.

Unfortunately, the Church's ability to win converts through the power of tradition seems to have been undermined in recent decades by the efforts of a new generation of modernists hell-bent, seemingly, on tampering with Catholicism's timeless beauties and mysteries. The danger was perceived by Evelyn Waugh, who wrote in 1964 that "throughout her entire life the Church has been at active war with enemies from without and traitors from within". To his great distress Waugh began to feel that the "traitors" within the Church were working to deliver the faithful into the hands of the "enemies" without. The Church Militant was being betrayed to a modern world seemingly triumphant. Alarmed at developments, Waugh devoted a great deal of his time during the last few years of his life to opposing the modernist tendency in the Church.

In a postscript to his biography of Waugh, Christopher Sykes endeavored to put his friend's obstinate opposition into context. "His dislike of the reform-movement", Sykes wrote,

> was not merely an expression of his conservatism, nor of aesthetic preferences. It was based on deeper things. He believed that in its long history the Church had developed a liturgy which enabled an ordinary,

sensual man (as opposed to a saint who is outside generalisation) to approach God and be aware of sanctity and the divine. To abolish all this for the sake of up-to-dateness seemed to him not only silly but dangerous ... He could not bear the thought of modernized liturgy. "Untune that string" he felt, and loss of faith would follow ... Whether his fears were justified or not only "the unerring sentence of time" can show.

Perhaps the unerring sentence has not yet been passed, but it was certainly the case that Waugh was not by any means the only person who held these views. On 6 July 1971 *The Times* published the text of an appeal to the Vatican to preserve the Latin Mass. The appeal was signed by a host of well-known Catholics, as well as many non-Catholic dignitaries and celebrities, including Harold Acton, Vladimir Ashkenazy, Lennox Berkeley, Maurice Bowra, Agatha Christie, Kenneth Clark, Nevill Coghill, Cyril Connolly, Colin Davis, Robert Graves, Graham Greene, Joseph Grimond, Harman Grisewood, Rupert Hart-Davis, Barbara Hepworth, Auberon Herbert, David Jones, Osbert Lancaster, F. R. Leavis, Cecil Day Lewis, Compton Mackenzie, Yehudi Menuhin, Nancy Mitford, Raymond Mortimer, Malcolm Muggeridge, Iris Murdoch, John Murray, Sean O'Faolain, William Plomer, Kathleen Raine, William Rees-Mogg, Ralph Richardson, Joan Sutherland, Bernard Wall, Patrick Wall and E. I. Watkin.

A moderate but nonetheless critical view was offered by Robert Speaight, actor, writer and Catholic convert, in his autobiography, published in 1970. Although he had sympathized with the reforms of the Council, he complained that much had happened "far beyond the intention of the Conciliar fathers":

> The psychology of adherence to Catholicism has subtly changed; authority is flouted; basic doctrines are questioned ... The vernacular Liturgy, popular and pedestrian, intelligible and depressing, has robbed us of much that was numinous in public worship; there is less emphasis on prayer and penitence; and the personal relationship between God and man ... is neglected in favour of a diffused social concern.

Ultimately, Speaight's frustration with the modernists was linked to their evident contempt for tradition: "What exasperates me in the attitude of many progressives is not their desire to go forward or even to change direction, but their indifference to tradition which is the *terra firma* from which they themselves proceed".

Alec Guinness was another thespian convert who found his initial enthusiasm for reform tempered by subsequent abuses of the Council's teaching. "Much water has flown under Tiber's bridges, carrying away splendour and mystery from Rome, since the pontificate of Pius XII", he wrote in *Blessings in Disguise*, his autobiography. Yet he remained confident about the future, rooted in the belief that the essential traditions of Catholicism "remain firmly entrenched":

> The Church has proved she is not moribund. "All shall be well," I feel, "and all manner of things shall be well", so long as the God who is worshipped is the God of all ages, past and to come, and not the Idol of Modernity, so venerated by some of our bishops, priests and miniskirted nuns.

Guinness quoted one of Chesterton's "most penetrating statements" as a prelude to his discourse on the reform of the Church. "The Church", wrote Chesterton, "is the one thing that saves a man from the degrading servitude of being a child of his own time." Perhaps he may also have added that tradition, as guarded and guided by dynamic orthodoxy, is the one thing that saves the Church herself from being a child of her own time. Certainly Chesterton had something similar in mind when he employed the imagery of the Church as a heavenly chariot "thundering through the ages, the dull heresies sprawling and prostrate, the wild truth reeling but erect". It was this vision of a militant and dynamic tradition combating error down the ages that had inspired the host of converts from Newman to Chesterton, and from Waugh to Sitwell and Sassoon. If the flow of high-profile literary converts has been more noticeable by its absence than by its presence in the last quarter of the twentieth century, perhaps it has something to do with the loss of that vision of tradition amid the fogs of fashion. No matter. Fogs pass and the clarity of day reasserts itself.

Tradition remains. It not only remains, it also retains its power to win converts; for, as Chesterton also said, what is needed is not a Church that can move with the world but a Church that can move the world.

2

TWENTIETH-CENTURY ENGLAND'S CHRISTIAN LITERARY LANDSCAPE

T HE TURN OF THE TWENTIETH century was accompanied by the death of two figures, Friedrich Nietzsche and Oscar Wilde, who were the products of the century that had just expired and who would epitomize the spirit of the century that had just been born.

Friedrich Nietzsche, who died, after twelve years of insanity, in the opening months of the new century, was the most outspoken philosophical foe of Christianity to emerge in the late nineteenth century. Convinced that Christianity was bankrupt, he proclaimed Arthur Schopenhauer's "will to power" and emphasized that only the strong ought to survive. He maintained that Christian charity served only to perpetuate the survival of the weak and contraposed the idea of the superman or overman (the *Übermensch*), who would overcome human weakness and vanquish the meek. (In Tolkien's mythical world, Nietzsche's shadow emerges in the "will to power" of the Enemy, most specifically in the designs of Sauron and Saruman but also in the pathetic ambition of Boromir and Gollum.)

Oscar Wilde, who died on 30 November 1900, was the inheritor of the dark and decadent romanticism of Byron and Baudelaire. He flouted traditional morality and was sentenced to two years' imprisonment as a result of his homosexual affair with Lord Alfred Douglas, the sordidness of which scandalized late Victorian society.

Nietzsche's pride found deadly "fruition" in the Nazi death camps and in the rise of the abortion clinics. Wilde's prurience found its sterile "fruition" in the sexual "liberation" of the 'sixties, the AIDS epidemic of the 'nineties and, yes, in those same abortion clinics. Nietzsche died impenitent, insane and, one would imagine, condemned for his sins; Wilde was received into the Catholic Church on his death-bed, died as a penitent and, one would hope, was forgiven his sins.

The pernicious influence of Nietzsche and Wilde on the secular culture prompted a healthy reaction among many of the Christian literati in England, so much so that their influence would help to shape the Christian literary landscape of the century that followed their deaths.

G. K. Chesterton, the most important figure in the Christian liter-ary revival in the early years of the century, had fallen under the spell of Wilde and the Decadents as a young man at London's Slade School of Art during the early 1890s but had very quickly recoiled in horror from the moral implications of the Decadent position. Much of his early work, particularly his early novel, *The Man Who Was Thursday*, was an attempt to clear the Wildean fog of the 1890s with the crisp clean air of Christian clarity. Chesterton also crossed swords with Nietz-sche, most particularly in his refutation of the neo-Nietzschean ram-blings of George Bernard Shaw and H. G. Wells. "Nietzsche's Superman is cold and friendless", Chesterton wrote in *Heretics*. "And when Nietz-sche says, 'A new commandment I give to you, *be hard*', he is really saying, 'A new commandment I give to you, *be dead*.' Sensibility is the definition of life." In the light of the "hardness" of the Nazis and the communists during their mass extermination of millions of "dis-sidents" and "undesirables", Chesterton's words, written more than ten years before the Bolshevik Revolution and almost thirty years before Hitler's rise to power, resonate with authenticated prophecy.

Chesterton's influence on the Christian literary revival was so cen-tral and catalytic that only the giant figure of John Henry Newman in the previous century matches him in terms of stature and importance. Those literary figures who have expressed a specific and profound debt to Chesterton as an influence on their conversions include C. S. Lewis, Ronald Knox, Dorothy L. Sayers and Alfred Noyes. Thus, without Chesterton, it is possible that the world would have never seen the later Christian poetry of Noyes, the subtle satire of Knox, the mas-terful translation of, and commentary on, Dante by Sayers, and the multifarious blossoming of Lewis' prodigious talents. Clearly we, as the inheritors of this cultural treasure trove, have much for which to thank Chesterton.

If Chesterton, along with his friend Hilaire Belloc, was the giant figure of the Christian literary revival during the first twenty years of the century, the figure to emerge as a Christian literary giant and inspirational catalyst in the next twenty years was undoubtedly T. S. Eliot.

Eliot's *The Waste Land*, published in 1922, is probably the most important poem of the twentieth century, and arguably the greatest. Although grotesquely misunderstood and misinterpreted by modernist and postmodernist critics, *The Waste Land* is profoundly Christian in its deepest layers of meaning and profusely traditionalist in its inspiration. Eliot's reaction to Decadence is rooted in the same sense of disgust as that which had animated Chesterton, but his mode of expression is starkly different. Whereas Chesterton alluded to the "diabolism" of Decadence, Eliot exposed its putrid corpse to the cold light of day, dragging it whimpering from its furtively seedy den.

The Waste Land's depiction of modernity as utterly vacuous and sterile is reiterated as the central theme of Eliot's next major poem, "The Hollow Men", published in 1925. Following his open profession of Christianity in 1928, Eliot's poems become more overtly religious, more didactic and "preachy" and perhaps less accomplished as poetry—though it should be stressed that a relatively unaccomplished Eliot poem is considerably more accomplished than the finest efforts of most of his contemporaries.

Eliot exerted a considerable influence on the writers of his generation. One such writer was the young novelist Evelyn Waugh, who rose to prominence following the publication of his first novel, *Decline and Fall*, in 1928. Two years later Waugh was received into the Catholic Church, and thereafter, his darkly sardonic and satirical novels could be described as prose reworkings of the fragmented imagery of *The Waste Land*. Waugh's novel *A Handful of Dust* even took its title from a line in *The Waste Land*, and its plot could be seen as a tangential commentary on the disgust at Decadence that Eliot had expressed with such lurid eloquence in his great poem.

If Chesterton and Belloc could be said to have dominated the first twenty years of the twentieth century, and Eliot and Waugh the next twenty years, the middle years of the century belong to C. S. Lewis and J. R. R. Tolkien. These two giants are perhaps the "dynamic duo" at the very heart of the Christian literary landscape of the twentieth century (though one could certainly argue that Chesterton and Eliot are of equal or perhaps even greater stature—such an argument is, however, beyond the scope of the present essay).

Lewis' manifold and multifarious talents covered the spectrum of the peripatetically purgatorial *Pilgrim's Regress* and *The Great Divorce*, space travel and children's stories, and works of straightforward Christian apologetics. Tolkien, for the most part, channeled his own considerable gifts in one direction only. The subcreation of Middle Earth, through the weaving of *The Lord of the Rings* within the larger tapestry of *The Silmarillion*, was, for Tolkien, the labor of a lifetime. In his mythical epic we see the Nietzschean "will to power" countered by the humility of the meek, and we see the poison of Wildean decadence healed by the purity of relationships in which eros is bridled by the charity of chastity.

Tolkien's mythical masterpiece is the pinnacle of achievement at the highest and most beautiful point on the Christian literary landscape of the twentieth century. In the same landscape is to be found the most important poem of the century (Eliot's *The Waste Land*) and the century's finest novel (Waugh's *Brideshead Revisited*). Quite clearly, the twentieth century, like the preceding nineteen centuries, owes a great deal to the munificence and magnificence of its Christian heritage.

PART TWO

THE CHESTERBELLOC

3
———

THE CHESTERBELLOC

Examining the Beauty of the Beast

Wells has written ... about Chesterton and Belloc without stop-
ping to consider what Chesterton and Belloc is. This sounds like
bad grammar; but I know what I am about. Chesterton and Belloc
is a conspiracy, and a most dangerous one at that. Not a viciously
intended one: quite the contrary. It is a game of make-believe of
the sort which all imaginative grown-up children love to play ...

Now at first sight it would seem that it does not lie with me to
rebuke this sort of make-believe. The celebrated G.B.S. [George
Bernard Shaw] is about as real as a pantomime ostrich. But it is less
alluring than the Chesterton-Belloc chimera, because as they have
four legs to move the thing with, whereas I have only two, they can
produce the quadrupedal illusion, which is the popular feature of
your pantomime beast.

GEORGE BERNARD SHAW's affectionate attack on G. K. Chesterton
and Hilaire Belloc, in an article entitled "The Chesterbelloc: A
Lampoon", gave birth to a duomorph destined to find its place in
literary legend. Chesterton and Belloc were seen so synonymously,
said Shaw, that they formed "a very amusing pantomime elephant".

Shaw's lampoon, like a well-guided harpoon, struck home. Thereafter, the popular imagination could not conjure up an image of Chesterton's whalelike girth without perceiving the shadow of Belloc in
the background. Similarly, Belloc's bellicose bombast was always accompanied by the counterpoint of Chesterton's gesticulating jollity. For
good or ill, George Bernard Shaw, as a latter-day Victor Frankenstein,

had created a monster that had developed a life of its own. The Chesterbelloc was born.

Having been born, the duomorph has refused to die. More than a century after its two component parts had first met, and almost a century since Shaw had first melded them into a mythological whole, the Chesterbelloc strides across the decades in defiance of the deteriorating landscape of fads and fashions that have passed it by. As C.S. Lewis quipped, fashions are always coming and going, but mostly going. The peripheral departs; the perennial remains.

The Chesterbelloc remains. It remains, not in the sense of the remains of a corpse or the reminiscence of a memory, but as a reminder of the Permanent Things. If, however, it remains, it remains as something of a riddle. What exactly *is* the Chesterbelloc? Is it merely a meaningless amalgam of its two components, a good Shavian joke but nothing more; or does it represent something that transcends the individual personalities that give it life? Is there something about the Chesterbelloc that is larger than life, or, rather, larger than the lives of Chesterton and Belloc? Is it, in some mystical sense, greater than the sum of its parts? If it is true that two's company but three's a crowd, is it true of the Chesterbelloc that two's a friendship but one's an army? In order to answer these questions or riddles, it becomes necessary to dissect the beast. Such an operation is required in spite of the uncomfortable knowledge that, since the beast is alive, the dissection constitutes vivisection. Thankfully, the beast is immortal and cannot be harmed by the experience.

Perhaps the dissection should commence with a discussion of which of the two halves is more important. Who is the greater, Chesterton or Belloc? In the considered opinion of the two halves themselves, the other half is superior. Chesterton believed that Belloc was the better writer, Belloc that Chesterton was "the Master". In his autobiography, Chesterton was characteristically diffident as to his own literary powers but effusively laudatory as regards the literary merit of his friend. "It occurs to me", Chesterton wrote, "that the best and most wholesome test, for judging how far mere incompetence or laziness ... has prevented me from being a real literary man, might be found in a study of the man of letters I happen to know best; who had the same motives for producing journalism, and yet has produced nothing but literature." Belloc, begging to differ, insisted that "Chesterton expresses everything so much better than I do" and wrote that Chesterton's poem "Lepanto" was the "summit of high rhetorical verse in all our generation".

It seems that subjecting our judgment to the subjective judgment of our subjects does not get us very far. It is necessary, therefore, to consider their relative merits ourselves.

Both writers were prolific in terms of the quantity of their work and prodigious in terms of its versatility. They were what can be termed, in the truest sense, men of letters. They were poets, novelists, essayists, biographers, historians, satirists, political and economic commentators, journalists, critics, humorists, Catholic apologists and controversialists. Refusing to kowtow before the specious boast of the specialist, they proceeded with merry abandon to trample down the delineations of genre. If we are to discern their relative merits, and the relative superiority of one over the other, we must follow them on their adventurous journey through the jungle of genres through which they strayed.

In terms of verse, both men have bequeathed to posterity a body of work that places them among the *illustrissimi* of twentieth-century poets. Chesterton's "The Rolling English Road" and "The Donkey" continue to be resurrected regularly—and rightfully—in popular anthologies, but their appearance only highlights the sin of omission implicit in the exclusion of other poems of at least equal merit. Why, one wonders, is "The Secret People" seldom included in these populist volumes? Why is his lovingly plaintive "Hymn", "O God of earth and altar", so seldom seen and so hardly ever heard? Why are the whimsically sublime merits of "The Fish" or "The Skeleton", so similar to "The Donkey" in style and design and at least its equal in stature, rarely noted? In spite of the hostility of modish modernity, *The Ballad of the White Horse* remains as a permanent monument to heroic verse in an age that hates heroism. Ultimately, however, Chesterton deserves to be remembered as the poet who gifted the world with a poem of the stature of "Lepanto". This was, as we have seen, the considered judgment of Belloc. It is also the considered judgment of the present writer. If Chesterton is remembered for nothing other than being the poet who reached, in "Lepanto", the "summit of high rhetorical verse in all our generation", he will have earned himself a place among the immortals. Thankfully, he is remembered for much more.

It would appear that, as a poet, Chesterton is a hard act to follow. Belloc, however, is not only capable of following Chesterton, he actually succeeds in stealing the show. For all Chesterton's achievement in verse, Belloc is the superior craftsman. For sheer rambunctiousness, Chesterton cannot match the riotous invective of "Lines to a Don", Belloc's vituperative riposte to the don "who dared attack my Chesterton"; for sheer indefatigable vigor, Chesterton has no answer to the romp and stomp of Belloc's "The End of the Road"; for a doom-laden sense of "the ruines of time", Chesterton's knell must kneel before the toll of Belloc's "Ha'nacker Mill"; for the mystical sense of the exile of life, Chesterton cannot match the Yeatsian yearning betwixt faith and faerie that Belloc evokes in "Twelfth Night"; for sheer ingenuity of meter and scansion, Chesterton's regularly beating drum has no answer to the hip, hop, clap of Belloc's scintillating "Tarantella".

In the realm of comic verse or the ribaldry of their drinking songs, Belloc's bellowing voice does not always succeed in drowning out the more dulcet tones of Chesterton. A comparison between the songs embedded in Chesterton's novel *The Flying Inn* and those that punctuate Belloc's "farrago", *The Four Men*, illustrates that Chesterton could sometimes match Belloc as a composer of fine and funny lyrics. The hilariously irrepressible and unforgettable verse in *The Flying Inn* equals the best of Belloc's efforts in his farrago. Who but Chesterton could compose a poem about Saint George, entitled "The Englishman", in which "dragon" is rhymed with "flagon" in the first four lines; who but Chesterton, in "Wine and Water", could write about Noah that he didn't care where the water went "if it doesn't get into the wine"? Who but Chesterton could believe that "God made the wicked Grocer" as "a mystery and a sign" so that men would shun their "awful shops / And go to inns to dine"? As though these were not enough, Chesterton delights us with much more of the same before the novel's end: "The Rolling English Road", "The Song of Quoodle", "The Logical Vegetarian", "The Saracen's Head", "Me Heart" and "The Song of the Strange Ascetic", among others. It is no wonder that *The Flying Inn* is remembered more for its poems than for its plot.

Belloc is not easily outdone, however, and *The Four Men* responds to Chestertonian jollity with Bellocian bumptiousness. The very title of one of the poems in Belloc's "farrago" conveys an irrepressibility of spirit typical of the author. The poem in question rejoices in the following title: the "Song of the Pelagian Heresy for the Strengthening of Men's Backs and the Very Robust Out-Thrusting of Doubtful Doctrine and the Uncertain Intellectual". How can one fail to fall in love with a writer who has the pure and unadulterated audacity to compose a poem that warrants such a title? *The Four Men* also contains the notorious (and delightful!) "Sailor's Carol", which is full of faith and hope though precious little charity! Unlike *The Flying Inn*, however, *The Four Men* is not eclipsed by the verse contained therein. *The Four Men* carries the poetry easily and comfortably, as a natural outgrowth from the organic development of its storyline.

If Chesterton almost succeeds in matching Belloc, chuckle for chuckle, in respect of the comic verse he composed, he is finally defeated in mirth by Belloc's composition of the incomparable *Cautionary Tales for Children*. Chesterton's claim to supremacy as a humorist in verse is finally killed by the kindergarten army of Matilda, who told such dreadful lies; Jim, who ran away from his Nurse and was eaten by a Lion; and Algernon, who played with a loaded gun and, on missing his sister, was reprimanded by his father.

Having examined the position of the two halves of the Chesterbelloc as poets, we can proceed to their relative merit as novelists.

Nobody was more dismissive of Chesterton's merit as a novelist than was Chesterton himself. "My real judgment of my own work", he confessed in his autobiography, "is that I have spoilt a number of jolly good ideas in my time":

> I think *The Napoleon of Notting Hill* was a book very well worth writing; but I am not sure that it was ever written. I think that a harlequinade like *The Flying Inn* was an extremely promising subject, but I very strongly doubt whether I kept the promise. I am almost tempted to say that it is still a very promising subject—for somebody else. I think the story called *The Ball and the Cross* had quite a good plot ... but I am much more doubtful about whether I got a great deal out of it ... Considered as novels, they were not only not as good as a real novelist

would have made them, but they were not as good as I might have
made them myself, if I had really even been trying to be a real novelist.

It would be easy, and tempting, to dismiss this self-criticism as a
further example of Chesterton's charming humility. The temptation
should, however, be resisted. At the commencement of the appraisal
of his own value as a novelist, Chesterton specifically dismisses any
notion that his self-deprecation is the result of "mock modesty". There
is, therefore, no escaping the uncomfortable conclusion that Chesterton really believed that his novels were failures.

The key question is not whether Chesterton believed himself to be a
failure as a novelist but whether we agree with him. The present writer
is not in the habit of disagreeing with Chesterton. It is a bad habit! Nonetheless, such a sweeping dismissal of his own work leaves his admirers
with little option but to ask themselves awkward questions. If they had
previously admired his novels they might conclude, if Chesterton's judgment is correct, that they have been deluded as to the merits of his fiction. The alternative, that Chesterton is woefully wrong in his judgment,
is scarcely more reassuring to those accustomed to accepting his judgment as the epitome of both salience and sagacity. Thankfully, however,
this is not the only alternative available. It is possible to believe that Chesterton was correct in his judgment without the necessity of becoming
dismissive as to the merits of the novels themselves. There is little doubt
that the three novels he mentions suffer from a looseness of composi-
tional structure and what might be called a slapdash approach to plot con-
sistency and character development. These are, as Chesterton rightly
surmised, serious deficiencies, literarily speaking. He is also correct, however, in his appraisal of the novels as being "well worth writing" and
"extremely promising" in their initial inspiration. Each of the Chestertonian ideas that were the launching-pad for the novels contained a kernel of kinetic energy that the author let loose to run riot across the pages
of his stories. The lack of control might constitute a "failure", according to purely literary criteria, but who can resist the sheer exhilaration
of a roller-coaster ride in the presence of such a mind playing with
unabashed abandon with such ideas?

It is intriguing, and probably significant, that Chesterton failed to
make any mention of his finest and most successful novel, *The Man Who*

Was Thursday, in his self-deprecatory remarks. This particular novel, though it suffers from the same deficiencies, contains and conveys such an abundance of purest profundity that it demands a place among the most important novels of the twentieth century. Imagine an amalgam of Dickensian caricature, Stevensonian adventure and Wildean nightmare, injected with Thomist insight and infused throughout with Franciscan mysticism. Imagine! Seldom has a single novel plumbed such depths, reached such heights and conveyed such color. For this novel alone, if for nothing else, Chesterton deserves to be considered one of the most important fiction writers of the twentieth century.

Belloc, by comparison, has little to show in terms of fiction of enduring stature, and like Chesterton, he had a low opinion of his own work. In his own estimation, his novels were not as memorable as the illustrations by Chesterton with which they were adorned. As with Chesterton, however, there are exceptions—even if they are exceptions that tend to prove the rule. In the same way in which Chesterton had rather intriguingly, and possibly significantly, excluded his finest novel from those that he derided, Belloc believed that his own late novel, *Belinda*, was the one work of fiction with which he could feel satisfied. Certainly *Belinda* displays a delicacy and lightness of touch that is missing from the ponderous plod of his earlier satirical novels. It also exhales an exuberance of fun and frivolity that is rare in his later work. Seldom, in the wake of his wife's death in 1914 and the death of his son on active service with the Royal Flying Corps four years later, had Belloc reproduced the humor that had been one of the most attractive characteristics of his earlier work. *Belinda* emerges, therefore, as a breath of freshness amid the somber propriety of much of Belloc's later work. It is, however, much more than that. "Of all Belloc's works in prose *Belinda* is the most perfect, the most original, the most timeless, and therefore perhaps the most secure", wrote Robert Speaight, Belloc's biographer. He continued by stating that it was "also the most difficult to define":

> If we call it "pastiche", we realize at once that we have employed too light and artificial a word. Artificial in a sense it is, and no one could describe it as heavy; but deep feeling underlies the artifice and the humour has the weight of Belloc's own *gravitas*. The book grinds no

axe and proves no point. It is a gratuitous, disinterested and quite impersonal essay in romantic irony. Small in scale and purposely conventional
in subject, it still leaves an impression of grandeur; fine, not finicky;
hard as a diamond and delicate as wrought iron.

If, as Speaight maintains, *Belinda* can be called an essay in romantic
irony, there is an amusing irony in the fact that it appears to contradict
what Belloc had written in his essay "On Irony" almost twenty years
earlier. "Irony is a sword, and must be used as a sword", he had written. In *Belinda* irony is not wielded as a weapon, but flourished like a
feather. It is not used to bludgeon its victim senseless but to tickle
him with an affectionate sensibility. It is not an irony that is iron-shod
and hardened by its own heartlessness, but one that is fleet of foot and
on a flight of fancy.

Belinda is for Belloc what *The Man Who Was Thursday* is for Chesterton; it is the one literary achievement in fiction that ensures him a
place among the great novelists of his day. Perhaps, however, one should
not leave a discussion of Belloc's purely literary merit in prose without alluding to those two wonderful books, *The Path to Rome* and *The
Four Men*. Neither book can be categorized as fiction, though the
latter presents an assemblage of imaginary characters worthy of any
novel; nor can either book be dismissed as a mere work of nonfiction,
in the arid sense in which the word is usually taken. *The Path to Rome*
and *The Four Men* are, first and foremost, great works of literature
meriting their place in the literary canon of the twentieth century. If
Belloc had not written a single word of fiction, these two works would
have ensured him a place among the literary giants of his day.

We have lingered on the purely literary status of the Chesterbelloc,
principally because it is through its artistic achievement that the beauty
of the beast is most clearly evident. Nonetheless, no examination of
the beast would be complete without a discussion of its position as a
powerful commentator on socioeconomic and political issues, nor would
any examination be considered adequate without due attention being
given to its role as a fearless defender of the Faith. A full examination
is not possible within the parameters of a solitary essay of this length,
so we shall have to content ourselves with a short summary of the
Chesterbelloc's importance in these areas.

As socioeconomic and political commentators, Chesterton and Belloc have bequeathed to posterity an invaluable iteration of the social teaching of the Church. The sociopolitical creed dubbed "distributism" by the Chesterbelloc is merely the social doctrine known as "subsidiarity" in the *Catechism of the Catholic Church*. Chesterton bowed to Belloc's preeminence as a disseminator of the ideas of distributism, declaring Belloc the master in relation to whom he was merely a disciple. "You were the founder and father of this mission", Chesterton wrote. "We were the converts but you were the missionary ... You first revealed the truth both to its greater and its lesser servants ... Great will be your glory if England breathes again." In fact, of course, Belloc was merely the propagator and the popularizer of the Church's social doctrine as expounded by Pope Leo XIII in *Rerum novarum*, a doctrine that would be restated, reconfirmed and reinforced by Pope Pius XI in *Quadragesimo anno* and by Pope John Paul II in *Centesimus annus*. Belloc's key works in this area were *The Servile State* and *An Essay on the Restoration of Property*, whereas Chesterton's *The Outline of Sanity* and his late essay "Reflections on a Rotten Apple", published in *The Well and the Shallows*, represent the most salient and sapient contribution of the other half of the Chesterbelloc to the cause of subsidiarity. It should also be noted that Chesterton's novel *The Napoleon of Notting Hill* is essentially a distributist parable.

Chesterton is perhaps perceived as a greater Catholic apologist than Belloc, largely due to the enormous influence that his two important works, *Orthodoxy* and *The Everlasting Man*, exerted on several generations of converts to the Faith. Without wishing to understate the importance of either of these works, or indeed other works of apologetics by Chesterton, it is necessary to raise a small plaintive voice in praise of Belloc's seminal work, *Survivals and New Arrivals*. This sadly neglected work needs to be rediscovered. In essence it sets out the intellectual history of the past two thousand years, delineating the areas of heresy and illustrating the perennial truth and wisdom of the Church. Its style is more cumbersome and perhaps less exhilarating than Chesterton's *Orthodoxy* or *The Everlasting Man*. Chesterton takes our breath away with his vision of the Church as a heavenly chariot. Belloc, in *Survivals and New Arrivals*, makes us gasp in amazement as we perceive the Church as an unstoppable tank trundling over the horizon onto the landscape of history, relentlessly overpowering the impotent defense of her enemies. Whether one prefers the pyrotechnic prose of Chesterton, where the dazzling words serve as swords to cut down the enemy—wordplay as swashbuckling swordplay, wordsmanship as swordsmanship—or whether one prefers Belloc's battering rams and heavy artillery, the defense of the Faith is as successful in both cases.

Having spread the Chesterbelloc on the operating table, we feel that we have failed to dissect the beast as we had hoped. On the contrary, we feel that, far from making incisive inroads into the anatomy of the beast, we have barely scratched its surface. A whole book would be needed to study the nature of the Chesterbelloc with anything like the meticulousness that the subject requires. Perhaps the book will one day be written. In the meantime, this short exploratory operation has at least enabled us to see that both halves of the Chesterbelloc are indispensable. Chesterton's childlike and whimsical genius is enhanced by the balance of Belloc's *gravitas*; Belloc's bellicosity and bombast is softened by the counterpoise of Chesterton's charity. Perhaps we have at least discovered enough to confirm that the Chesterbelloc, as a mystical and mythological beast, is greater than its component parts. Perhaps we can truly infer that, as far as this particular beast is concerned, two is indeed a friendship but one's an army.

Since our end is our beginning, as Mary Stuart proclaimed and as T. S. Eliot never ceased to remind us, we shall end as we began. We commenced with a playfully plaintive comment by one of the Chesterbelloc's most illustrious enemies; we shall end in the same fashion. We began with Shaw; we shall end with Wells.

Wells complained that "Chesterton and Belloc have surrounded Catholicism with a kind of boozy halo." Wells, as usual, was wrong. As amusingly attractive as is the image he successfully presents, he fails to convey the magnitude of the truth he fails to perceive. The Church is not in need of a halo, boozy or otherwise. As the Mystical Body of Christ, she has her halo enshrined within her very being. The Chesterbelloc's value to the Church, and consequently its value to the world, is as a sometimes boozy defender of that halo. All sons and daughters of Christendom should, in the name of the halo of holiness, raise their glasses to the Chesterbelloc. May we always rejoice in the "boozy" beauty of the beast,

> And thank the Lord
> For the temporal sword,
> And howling heretics too;
> And whatever good things
> Our Christendom brings,
> But especially barley brew!

4

CHESTERTON AND SAINT FRANCIS

C HESTERTON ENJOYED a lifelong friendship with Saint Francis of Assisi. As a small boy, long before he had an inkling of the nature of Catholicism, Chesterton was read a story by his parents about a man who gave up all his possessions, even the clothes he was wearing on his back, to follow Christ in holy poverty. From the moment the wide-eyed Gilbert first heard the story of Saint Francis, he knew he had found a friend. As such, long before he had submitted to the reason of Rome, Chesterton had succumbed to the romance of Assisi.

Perhaps inevitably, childlike wonder was followed by adolescent doubt. As Chesterton groped toward manhood during the early 1890s, he succumbed temporarily to the beguiling power of the Decadents. Under the charismatic and iconoclastic seduction of Oscar Wilde, the world of Chesterton's youth seemed under the mad and maddening influence of those who preferred the shadows of sin and cynicism to the light of virtue and verity. Romance itself had donned the mask of darkness. It was in this gloom-laden atmosphere that the young Chesterton wrote a poem on Saint Francis of Assisi, published in November 1892. The questions it asks were a quest for answers in a world of doubt.

> Is there not a question rises from his word of "brother, sister",
>   Cometh from that lonely dreamer that today we shrink
>   to find?
> Shall the lives that moved our brethren leave us at the
> gates of darkness,
>   What were heaven if ought we cherished shall be wholly
>   left behind?
>
> Is it God's bright house we dwell in, or a vault of dark
> confusion ... ?

This poem, dedicated to the "lonely dreamer" of Assisi, illuminates the darkness of Chesterton's adolescence. The young poet, seeking to make sense of the conflicting visions of reality vying for his allegiance, was beginning to perceive that the Decadents had cast out Brother Sun so that they could worship Sister Moon. Within three years of the publication of this poem, Wildean Decadence had decayed in the squalor of the police courts. Wilde himself would repent and would be received into the Catholic Church on his deathbed. In his conversion, he was merely following many of the other Decadents, both in England and France, who, having dipped their toes in the antechambers of hell, had decided, prudently, that it wasn't somewhere they wished to spend eternity. Baudelaire, Verlaine, Huysmans, Beardsley, Johnson and Dowson had all followed the "Decadent path to Christ", repenting of their sin and embracing the loving forgiveness to be found in Mother Church. Paradoxically, the path to Christ was always to be found in the implicit Christian morality of much of the art of the Decadents, particularly, and most memorably, in Wilde's masterpiece, *The Picture of Dorian Gray*.

Chesterton's own response, and riposte, to the Decadence of the 1890s can be found in his novel *The Man Who Was Thursday*. Whereas the Decadents—taking their own perverse inspiration from the dark romanticism of Byron, Shelley and Keats—had stripped the masks off "reality" and discovered darkness, Chesterton stripped the masks off "reality" (from the "anarchists" in his novel) and discovered light. By the dawn of the new century, Chesterton had emerged from the sub-real dream of Decadence into the real awakening of a Christian perception of the cosmos. In this journey from darkness to light, he had as his constant ally and companion the "lonely dreamer" of Assisi. On 1 December 1900, the day after Wilde had died a Catholic in Paris, Chesterton, not yet a Catholic, was singing the praises of Saint Francis in an article published in *The Speaker*.

> To most people ... there is a fascinating inconsistency in the position of Saint Francis. He expressed in loftier and bolder language than any earthly thinker the conception that laughter is as divine as tears. He called his monks the mountebanks of God. He never forgot to take pleasure in a bird as it flashed past him, or a drop of water as it fell from

his finger: he was, perhaps, the happiest of the sons of men. Yet this man undoubtedly founded his whole polity on the negation of what we think the most imperious necessities; in his three vows of poverty, chastity, and obedience, he denied to himself and those he loved most, property, love, and liberty. Why was it that the most large-hearted and poetic spirits in that age found their most congenial atmosphere in these awful renunciations? Why did he who loved where all men were blind, seek to blind himself where all men loved? Why was he a monk and not a troubadour? These questions are far too large to be answered fully here, but in any life of Francis they ought at least to have been asked; we have a suspicion that if they were answered we should suddenly find that much of the enigma of this sullen time of ours was answered also.

These words, which could have served as the introduction to Chesterton's biography of Saint Francis published twenty-three years later, indicated that the saint had served as an antidote to the poison of the previous decade.

In 1902, in *Twelve Types*, Chesterton again lauded Saint Francis with the lucidity and faith that had been almost wholly absent in the questioning ambivalence of his poem of ten years earlier.

In July 1922 Chesterton was finally received into the Catholic Church. Eight weeks later he received the sacrament of confirmation, choosing Francis as his confirmation name. It would, perhaps, be easy to suggest that the obvious motive for the choice was a desire to show love and respect for Frances, his wife. It was, however, hardly surprising that he should have chosen the saint who had been the friend of his childhood, the ally in his confused adolescence and the companion in his approach to the Faith. In any case, the two motives are not mutually exclusive. In pleasing his wife, he was also pleasing himself.

At the time of his reception into the Church, Chesterton was already planning a full-length biography of Saint Francis that would be published in the following year. Confirming the saint's importance, he wrote that the figure of Saint Francis "stands on a sort of bridge connecting my boyhood with my conversion to many other things". With these words in mind, it is not difficult to imagine that Chesterton took on the writing of *Saint Francis of Assisi* so soon after his conversion as an act of thanksgiving to the saint who, above all others, had accompanied him on his journey to the Faith.

The admiration that Chesterton felt toward Saint Francis was inextricably bound up with his belief in the superiority of childlike innocence over all forms of cynicism. Saint Francis and his followers were called the Jongleurs de Dieu because of the innocence of their jollity and the jollity of their innocence. "The jongleur was properly a joculator or jester; sometimes he was what we should call a juggler." It was this mystical synthesis of laughter and humility, a belief that playing and praying go hand in hand, which was the secret of the saint's success. Ultimately, however, the laughter and the humility were rooted in gratitude because, as Chesterton discerned with characteristic and Franciscan sagacity, "there is no way in which a man can earn a star or deserve a sunset".

Chesterton's life of Saint Francis was destined to be one of the most commercially and critically successful of all his books. Typical of the enthusiastic response of the critics was that of Patrick Braybrooke, who described the book as "astoundingly brilliant": "The Catholic Church has found in Mr. Chesterton the greatest interpreter of her greatest saint." Ultimately, however, the book's brilliance shone from the blurring of the distinction between the Chestertonian and the Franciscan. It is, at times, difficult to distinguish between Chesterton's exposition of the Franciscan spirit and his elucidation of Chestertonian philosophy. Throughout the pages of the book, Chesterton chases the saint, complaining that all explanations of the saint's enigmatic character were "too slight for satisfaction". The book unravels like a heaven-sent game of hide-and-seek, similar to the plot of *The Man Who Was Thursday*, with the Man who was Francis remaining as difficult to pin down as the Man who was Sunday. Yet, as with the plot to the novel, there is something thrilling in the chase.

Whatever the book's shortcomings as an entirely satisfying explanation of the saint, it remains an emphatically successful romp and romance in the true Franciscan and Chestertonian spirit. From start to finish, Chesterton plays cat and mouse with the Jongleur de Dieu. And, in keeping with the poetry of the saint, it doesn't really matter that sister cat fails to catch brother mouse. The charm is in the chase. For those reading Chesterton's *Saint Francis of Assisi* for the first time, you are in for a rare treat. Prepare to be charmed. Enjoy the chase!

5

SHADES OF GRAY IN THE
SHADOW OF WILDE

THE DISCOVERY OF a "new" novel by G.K. Chesterton, sixty-five years after his death, has sent ripples of excitement through the literary world. It is, of course, not a new novel in the literal sense of the word but, as the cover of this attractively produced volume proclaims, "a first novel, previously unpublished". It was also, prior to publication, a first novel, previously untitled—a fact that its discoverer, Denis J. Conlon, has rectified. *Basil Howe: A Story of Young Love* is, however, far more exciting as a detective story than as a love story, and far more alluring as a barely concealed portrait of the young Chesterton than as an inadequately revealed portrait of "Basil Howe". It is the character of the author, not the character in the novel, who emerges from its fascinating pages.

Like all good detective stories, *Basil Howe* seduces the reader with tantalizing clues. Conlon, as both a dedicated Chestertonian and as a diligent academic, has uncovered many of these clues in the course of his work in preparing the manuscript for publication. We learn how the manuscript was discovered among Chesterton's notebooks "which had long lain forgotten under articles of clothing in an old box trunk"; we discover how the notebooks themselves had been saved from the municipal tip (or garbage can, for our American readers) by Dorothy Collins, Chesterton's secretary; we are taken through the painstaking process by which Professor Conlon assembled separated sections of the manuscript so that the novel could begin to emerge from the fragments. This, in itself, is an intriguing yarn—and we are still only on the first pages of Professor Conlon's introduction, long before we get to the novel itself.

Most importantly, Professor Conlon is convinced, and is pretty convincing in his conviction, that the novel was probably written in late 1893 or early 1894, when Chesterton was only nineteen years old. If this is so, the plot really thickens.

On 6 October 1893 Chesterton began his studies at University College in London and the Slade School of Art. It was at Slade, by his own admission, that he had temporarily fallen under the spell of the Decadents "and their perpetual hints of the luxurious horrors of paganism". Chesterton's "decadence" was short-lived, but if his own account is to be believed, it was very real while it lasted. "I deal here", he wrote in his autobiography, "with the darkest and most difficult part of my task; the period of youth which is full of doubts and morbidities and temptations; and which, though in my case mainly subjective, has left in my mind for ever a certitude upon the objective solidity of sin." In *Orthodoxy*, a book he wrote in 1908, he confessed that "I was a pagan at the age of twelve, and a complete agnostic by the age of sixteen". In 1893, at the age of nineteen and at the time he was apparently writing his first novel, he had regressed further:

> I am not proud of believing in the Devil. To put it more correctly, I am not proud of knowing the Devil. I made his acquaintance by my own fault; and followed it up along lines which, had they been followed further, might have led to devil-worship or the devil knows what.

In truth, Chesterton did not "know" the Devil at the age of nineteen any more than he was a pagan at twelve or an agnostic at sixteen. He had not formulated a final view in any of these areas at any of these ages. He was still searching, groping, exploring. He was asking the questions but, as yet, had not received the answers. Catholicism, Protestantism, paganism, agnosticism, socialism and spiritualism were all influences to varying degrees at varying times. During these formative years he caught these influences for short periods much as a man catches influenza. Each was a passing fancy, a temporary aberration battling for supremacy. None was accepted as definitive fact; all were fed on as fads that faded away, one by one, until the truth emerged from the remnants.

Nonetheless, Chesterton *did* have, so it seems or so he claimed, a decadent or devilish phase in his intellectual and emotional development, and this novel was written at the very height, or depth, of its influence upon him. It is this aspect of *Basil Howe* that is most intriguing and most fascinating.

The circles in which Chesterton moved at the Slade School of Art were very much under the spell of the Decadents and, in particular, under the beguiling influence of Oscar Wilde, whose novel *The Picture of Dorian Gray* had been published three years earlier. It is inconceivable that Chesterton had not read Wilde's controversial book, and there is evidence, albeit subliminal, in the pages of *Basil Howe* that he had done so. The fact that Chesterton named his heroine, the object of Basil Howe's affections, Gertrude Grey, is no doubt entirely coincidental, but there is more than a hint in Chesterton's characterization of Howe to suggest the powerful, if invisible, presence of Dorian Gray.

The effects of Wilde's worldly influence on the otherworldly Chesterton are laughably absurd, and it is hardly surprising that Chesterton's naïve teenage efforts to make his hero sophisticated in the Wildean sense are never convincing. He is convivial even when he is trying to be maudlin; chivalrous when he claims to be a charlatan; a gentleman when he protests that he is a cad. Basil Howe wears the masks of Wildean sophistication about as convincingly, as comfortably and as comically as a six-year-old child might wear her mother's makeup and shoes.

Chesterton is more convincing when his characters cease to imitate the Wildean with any sort of reverential deference and are allowed to mimic it mockingly instead. Most memorable in this respect is the discourse by the character Valentine Amiens on the legacy of classical Greece. "The Athenians ... selected as wives decent and hardworking women and called them by one name which I forget. They then locked them in a kind of everlasting kitchen and told them to do the housekeeping. Then they had another set of women, about whom the less said the better, and called them another name I forget. These women were very clever and amusing and said all sorts of funny things. They also dressed well, I believe. So you see the enlightened Athenians went to the bad women when they wanted wit, and went to the good ones when they wanted dinner.

"But Athens", Valentine concluded, with a conundrum that is paradoxical in the Wildean and not the Chestertonian sense, "was the mother of civilization. We owe a great deal to Athens."

Evidently bemused by this line of reasoning, Valentine's friend, Lucien, "beginning to think that genius was to madness near allied", asked his friend to explain himself. What follows, in Valentine's reply, is an early flourishing of the true Chestertonian wit that would delight readers a decade later and a clear indication that the nineteen-year-old Chesterton had already seen through the transparent spirit of the Decadents.

> We are a good deal too Athenian in our method with women. The *Alruna wives* of our teutonic ancestors and the mothers in Israel of Semitic moralism were alike in this that they were great through goodness: and the combination of the two produced the Queen of Love and Beauty of mediaeval chivalry. But the curse of our modern man of the world-ism is that we court the women we disapprove and despise the women we respect: we talk of a good woman lightly, like an old household chattel, and forget that her price is above rubies. We are not lowest on our knees before the pure and tender woman, but before two eyes and half a dozen diamonds. I am sick of all this *fin de siècle* sniggering over wit and culture and the rest of it. Did wit bring us into the world? Did culture bear pain that we might live? Did they love us in our silly fractious childhood and have no thought on earth but us? Can they comfort us, or kindle or sustain? ... No, indeed: beauty is deceitful, and favour is vain: but a woman that feareth the Lord she shall be praised: give her the portion that is due to her, and let her works praise her in the gates!

Later, a stimulating dialogue between Valentine Amiens and Basil Howe serves as a wonderfully penetrating insight into the conflicting philosophies battling for supremacy in the young Chesterton. The idealized medievalism of the Pre-Raphaelites, championed by Valentine, is countered by Howe's championing of Chaucer as being representative of medieval realism. More perplexingly intriguing, in the light of Chesterton's later traditionalist stance, is the way in which Valentine's antimodern reaction is met with Howe's faith in "progress".

We see in the characters of Valentine Amiens and Basil Howe the heart and the head of the postadolescent Chesterton; we see, in fact, a heart and a head that were hardly in harmony but that were nonetheless in creative conflict, colliding with the clash of symbols. With youthful precocity, Chesterton was struggling to give his head its head, though his heart was never fully in it. Over the following decade the

Basil-Howeism would emerge in Chesterton's political radicalism and in his brief flirtation with Christian socialism; the spirit of Valentine Amiens would gestate more slowly but would bear fruit more fulsomely in the birth of Chesterton's Christian spirituality and its fulfillment in his later conversion to Catholicism. Eventually, of course, the two apparent antitheses would unite in the powerful synthesis of dynamic orthodoxy, the indissoluble marriage of the head and the heart, of Rome and romance, with which Chesterton would do battle with the enemies of faith and reason.

Basil Howe is not a great—or even a good—work of literature. How could it be? Its author was only a teenager. As such, those hoping to be carried away by Basil Howe's "story of young love" will be disappointed. The novel does, however, offer a priceless insight into a great mind. First and foremost it is a portrait of the author as a young man—and, more specifically, a portrait of a young man trying to make up his own mind. Those who wish to discover more about the mind of Chesterton will be enthralled.

6

FIGHTING THE EURO FROM BEYOND THE GRAVE

The Ghost of Chesterton Haunts Lord Howe

C HESTERTON, the "jolly journalist" who became one of the finest prose stylists of the twentieth century, is suddenly, it seems, very much *en vogue*. A century after his paradoxes and his good-natured wit first delighted the reading public, he is once more being praised and lauded by the great and the good. Among the literati, those best-selling fantasists J. K. Rowling and Terry Pratchett have both paid homage to the man who blazed his own fantastic trail across Edwardian and Georgian England with novels such as *The Napoleon of Notting Hill*, *The Man Who Was Thursday* and *The Ball and the Cross*.

It is, however, among politicians that Chesterton is now considered to be particularly chic. Ken Clark is known to be an aficionado, as is Lord David Alton. William Hague, meanwhile, came out as a closet Chestertonian by declaring during his heady days as Leader of the Opposition that Chesterton was one of the most underrated writers and thinkers of the previous century.

The latest politician to nail his colors to the Chestertonian mast is Lord Howe, former Chancellor of the Exchequer and present-day champion of European federalism. As the subject of Radio Four's broadcast of "Great Inspirations", Lord Howe nominated Chesterton's *The Napoleon of Notting Hill* as the book that had most inspired his early life.

I was asked to participate in the program, presumably due to my authorship of a recent biography of Chesterton, and thus it was that I sat in the BBC's Westminster studio, both agape and aghast, as Lord Howe made out a bizarrely incredible case for Chesterton's posthumous membership of the "Britain in Europe" campaign. Seldom

85

have I witnessed such a brazen display of Orwellian "double-think" or "newspeak", even from the mouth of a politician, and I recalled with grim irony that Chesterton's futuristic fantasy had been set, like Orwell's darker fantasy, in nineteen eighty-four.

Somehow, Lord Howe managed to weave into his discussion of Chesterton and *The Napoleon of Notting Hill* some rather rickety logic in support of his own personal hobbyhorse of increased European integration with the implication that Chesterton would have agreed with him. Thus the bizarre statement that "you can't lose sovereignty like losing virginity—you have it, then you don't" was uttered in the manner of a Chestertonian epigram. Similarly, Lord Howe accused those who wished to halt the further erosion of sovereignty as wishing to erect "a cardboard curtain" around the United Kingdom, implying, by describing Chesterton explicitly as "a good European", that Chesterton would have agreed with his own Eurocentrist views.

Thankfully, Chesterton is able to reply to Lord Howe from beyond the grave, issuing devastating ripostes in the very words of the novel that Howe was holding up as his "inspiration". Above all, *The Napoleon of Notting Hill* is a powerful parable on the rights of small nations to preserve their identity in the face of the cosmopolitan encroachments of imperialism. Its principal theme was expounded in the words of "the President of Nicaragua", a mysterious figure who makes one fleeting but hugely significant appearance before "bowing profoundly" and disappearing into the fog. Before taking his bow, he neatly sets the scene for what is to follow. "Nicaragua has been conquered like Athens. Nicaragua has been annexed like Jerusalem", he exclaims passionately. "The Yankee and the German and the brute powers of modernity have trampled it with the hoofs of oxen. But Nicaragua is not dead. Nicaragua is an idea." He continues by delivering a spirited defense of the cultural integrity of small nations, and a damning indictment against the forces of imperialism.

> That is what I complain of in your cosmopolitanism. When you say you want all peoples to unite, you really mean that you want all peoples to unite to learn the tricks of your people. If the Bedouin Arab does not know how to read, some English missionary or schoolmaster must be sent to teach him to read, but no one ever says, "This school-

master does not know how to ride on a camel; let us pay a Bedouin to teach him." You say your civilisation will include all talents. Will it? Do you really mean to say that at the moment when the Esquimaux has learnt to vote for a County Council, you will have learnt to spear a walrus?

The scene thus set, the plot unfolds until Adam Wayne, the "Napoleon" of the novel's title, declares war in the name of Notting Hill to defend his beloved borough against plans by the central powers to develop parts of it against the wishes of the local people. Adam Wayne's local patriotism was epitomized by the proclamation that a place, however small, "which is large enough for the rich to covet ... is large enough for the poor to defend."

Not surprisingly, perhaps, *The Napoleon of Notting Hill* was the favorite book of Michael Collins, the Sinn Fein leader who was largely responsible for negotiating the treaty with Britain in 1921. It is said that Lloyd George, hearing of Michael Collins' literary taste, presented a copy of *The Napoleon of Notting Hill* to every member of his cabinet prior to their meeting with the Irish delegation so that they might better understand the Irish leader's mind.

There is little doubt that Collins' interpretation was closer to the spirit of Chesterton's novel than Lord Howe's, though it seems a little perverse that the Irish, having fought so dearly for their freedom from England, should subsequently sell it off so cheaply to the European Union. It is also more than a little surreal that the Welsh and Scottish Nationalists should seek to escape from the arms of hated uncle Albion into the grasp of Big Brother Brussels. It is almost as though imperialism is evil if advanced by force of arms but praiseworthy if achieved by sleight of hand.

As though remembering, perhaps too late, the principles of Michael Collins and other early Nationalists, the recent vote by the Irish to reject the Treaty of Nice had more than a touch of *The Napoleon of Notting Hill* about it. Significantly, however, the Eurocentrists were not about to allow the one small squeak of a solitary nation to stand in the way of the next giant leap of European expansion. With utter contempt for the right of democratic self-determination, the wishes of the Irish were dismissed as irrelevant.

"The modern world ... is on the side of the giants", complained Chesterton in an attack on H. G. Wells in his book *Heretics*. Wells was a "heretic", according to Chesterton, because his novel *The Food of the Gods* was "the tale of Jack the Giant-Killer told from the point of view of the giant". In Chesterton's eyes, "Jack" represented the small nation fighting for its independence against the giants of imperialism, or the small businessman fighting for his existence against the giants of multinational commerce. To side with the giant against Jack was to betray humanity. Surely, if the ghost of Chesterton were to return, it would point an accusing finger at Lord Howe and number the former chancellor among the latter-day "heretics".

And as for Howe's peculiar reading of *The Napoleon of Notting Hill*, one is reminded of Chesterton's observation, made in a letter to his friend Maurice Baring, that it was "extraordinary how the outer world can see everything about it except the point ... I find that if I make the point of a story stick out like a spike, they carefully go and impale themselves on something else."

Lord Howe did at least attribute one thing to Chesterton correctly. In calling him "a good European", he was stating a sublime truth. Chesterton, like his Anglo-French friend, Hilaire Belloc, loved the "Europe of the Faith" with its noble traditions and its unity with the concept of Christendom. Yes, Chesterton is every inch a "good European", and, like all good Europeans, he is, and has to be, a Eurosceptic. That's why his ghost still has the power, through the books he has left as a legacy, to fight the euro from beyond the grave. In taking on Chesterton's "Napoleon", Lord Howe has met his Waterloo.

7

CATHOLICISM AND "DEMOCRACY"

A review of

Catholic Intellectuals and the Challenge of Democracy
by Jay P. Corrin[†]

T HERE IS MORE THAN A LITTLE IRONY—albeit unintentional—in the
title of Jay P. Corrin's study of the volatile relationship of the
Catholic intelligentsia with the turbulent politics of the twentieth century. The irony resides in the author's failure to rise to the challenge
he sets himself. Dr. Corrin, indubitably an intellectual and presumably
a Catholic, fails to achieve his purported objective because he insists
on subjecting the object of his study to his own subjective agenda.

Dr. Corrin betrays himself in the language of his introduction. In
the very first sentence he divides "Catholic intellectuals" into two
simplistically convenient categories: the "progressive" and the "reactionary". Immediately we know that the heroes are those whom the
author places in the former category, whereas the villains are condemned to the ignominy of the latter. Thus, from the outset, we are
reduced to the dialectic of the stereotype. The "progressives" are enlightened, reasonable, up-to-date, in tune with the times, "with it". The
reactionaries are unenlightened, unreasonable, out-of-date, behind the
times and very much "without it". The former are to be praised, the
latter condemned—or, perhaps, if we are feeling charitable, patted
patronizingly and platitudinously on the head with self-assured and
self-righteous smugness.

[†] Notre Dame, Ind.: University of Notre Dame Press, 2002.

This, of course, is the language of the liberal secularist, the inheritor of the "progressive" philosophy of the superciliously self-named
"Enlightenment". It is the language of those who believe that human
society is forever "progressing" from the primitive past to the enlightened
future. It is the language of those condemned by G. K. Chesterton
and C. S. Lewis as the "chronological snobs" who contemptuously
kick down the ladder by which they've ascended. Unfortunately, it is
also the language employed by Dr. Corrin. Thus he states glibly that
the Second Vatican Council "called upon Catholics to broaden their
historical perspectives, move beyond a static theology fixed to the past,
and embrace the kinds of changes that would allow the Church to be
more in step with contemporary society" (1). Really? Did Vatican II
call upon the faithful to abandon the faith of their fathers; did it suggest that the anchor of tradition be cut free so that the Church can
drift freely with the tides of time, going with the flow of the present
rather than being "fixed" to the lessons of the past? Is it the duty of
the Church to move "in step with contemporary society"? Certainly
G. K. Chesterton didn't think so. Chesterton, one of the "intellectuals" scrutinized in Corrin's book, responded to those who made similarly glib statements in his own day with the riposte that we did not
need a Church that will *move with* the world but a Church that will
move the world. The Church is called to lead society, not to be led
by it.

In reality, the much-vaunted *aggiornamento* of Vatican II had nothing to do with surrendering to modernity. On the contrary, it had
everything to do with enabling the Church to engage modernity, to
respond to it, to *react* to it. Paradoxically, one of the earliest fruits of
aggiornamento was Pope Paul VI's encyclical *Humanae vitae*. It was a
perfect example of the Church's response to what Dr. Corrin called
the "challenge of resolving the conflicting demands of religion and
modernity by aggiornamento" (1).

The spirit of Vatican II, truly understood, had precious little to do
with opening the windows to let in the malodorous scent of modernity. It had everything to do with opening the windows so that the
scent of incense within the Household of Faith might waft more freely
into the world beyond. Needless to say, the world has often been
incensed by the incense.

Even more incredibly, Dr. Corrin complains that, prior to Vatican II, the intellectual and spiritual life of the Church "had become rigidified by tradition", whereas "Protestantism, on the other hand, had centuries of experience trying to accommodate itself to the culture of modernity" (1). Is Dr. Corrin seriously asking us to take this seriously? The compromise of Protestantism with the zeitgeist, its unholy marriage with modernity, has merely resulted in a "progressive" theological fragmentation and fading. Today there are thousands of Protestant sects preaching thousands of mutually contradictory views. Those that are most "accommodating" to modernity simply fade away into shades of agnostic gray; those that are least "accommodating" to modernity, and are in fact reacting against it, such as the Fundamentalists, are flourishing. If there is a lesson to be learned from Protestantism's "centuries of experience", it is that the zeitgeist devours its suitors.

Dr. Corrin's introduction serves as the key to understanding his misunderstanding of the issues upon which he focuses. Quite simply, he is too prejudiced to judge. His obsession with stereotypes and the overly simplistic labeling of "friends" and "enemies" is irritatingly irrational. One becomes tired of the criticism of "tradition-bound clerics" seeking "a return to a hierarchical age of paternalistic authoritarianism" in defiance of "an imaginative, progressive, and carefully reasoned Catholic response" (2–3).

At times Dr. Corrin's labels become almost libelous. His woeful demonizing of Hilaire Belloc betrays a superficial and selective reading of the facts. Anyone who has studied the life of the mercurial and oft-times bellicose Belloc will know that he defies the straitjacket of simplistic categorization with which Dr. Corrin endeavors to constrain him. Belloc is beyond Dr. Corrin's comprehension of him, or lack thereof.

Similarly, Dr. Corrin's inability to see beyond the "liberal" labels of the Spanish civil war results in a distorted and contorted view of historical realities. Catholics who supported the Nationalists in that fratricidal conflict were not, ipso facto, "fascists" or fellow travelers, as Dr. Corrin insinuates. Many despised fascism but felt, nonetheless, that it was their duty to oppose the rabid atheism of the communists and anarchists. We should never forget that during the Spanish civil war 12 bishops, 4,184 priests, 2,365 monks and about 300 nuns were murdered.

In order to understand the motives of the vast majority of Catholics who opposed the communists and supported Franco, however reluctantly, we might posit a simple question: Were the British and Americans during the Second World War "fellow travelers" or quasi communists because of their alliance with Stalin's Soviet Union? Surely not. Only McCarthyism would suggest otherwise. In essence, Dr. Corrin's tarring of Catholics with the fascist brush is akin to an inverted McCarthyism.

The great tragedy of Dr. Corrin's book is that it could and should have been much better. The subject itself is fascinating, and the compendium of facts that he assembles is a fitting testimony to the considerable historical research he has undertaken. As a historical document it has much to offer. The history is, however, marred by the author's philosophy. One wonders, for instance, why Pope John Paul II's encyclical *Centesimus annus* fails to warrant a single mention in a study of the Church's social doctrine, such as this purports to be. Written on the centenary of Pope Leo XIII's *Rerum novarum*, the document that, in many ways, was the springboard for distributism, the political creed that is at the center of Dr. Corrin's book, the present Pope's reiteration of the Church's social teaching would have been an appropriate place to conclude such a study. This particular sin of omission is exacerbated by the failure to mention the teaching on subsidiarity in the *Catechism of the Catholic Church*, a teaching that not only answers "the challenge *of* democracy" but that serves as a challenge *to* the plutocratic macrodemocracies that hold sway in most of the world today. Perhaps these omissions are due to the fact that the encyclicals and *Catechism* were written by "tradition-bound clerics" not deemed sufficiently "progressive" to qualify for favorable treatment.

Catholic Intellectuals and the Challenge of Democracy is a book that needed to be written. Unfortunately, after the shoddiness of this particular effort, it is a book that still needs to be written.

8

FASCISM AND CHESTERTON

I T COMES AS A DISAPPOINTMENT to learn that Chesterton is once more the victim of gossip. The gossip is not new. In fact, it is an old chestnut that has been hauled out at regular intervals. Chesterton is tarred with a Fascist brush. If not a Fascist in the strict sense of the word, he is described at least as a fellow traveler, besmirched by association with the creed of Mussolini, Hitler and Franco. The charge is not really worth serious consideration. It has, however, been leveled, and the case for the defense must be mounted.

One should start with essentials. Before the innocence of Chesterton, the defendant, can be established, we must consider the nature of the crime. Exactly what is Fascism? This is not an easy question to answer. There is the *precise* definition, the *not-so-precise* definition, the *too-imprecise* definition and, then, there is the generally *accepted* definition. The *precise* definition of "Fascism" in *The Concise Oxford English Dictionary*[1] is "principles and organisation of the patriotic and anti-communist movement in Italy started during the 1914–18 war, culminating in the dictatorship of Benito Mussolini and imitated by Fascist or blackshirt associations in other countries." Chesterton could possibly be accused of sympathizing with this Fascism for a time during the 1920s before finally declaring his opposition to it. He had met Mussolini in 1929 and came away with, at best, ambivalent and, at worst, positive impressions of the Italian dictator, *as a man*. Yet in his account of the meeting in *The Resurrection of Rome*, he was at pains to point out his concern that his views "may be mistaken for a defence

---

[1] Fifth edition, 1964.

of Fascism".[2] One might acquit Chesterton of the allegations of Fascism on that statement alone. Yet Chesterton is at least partly responsible for misapprehensions because his analysis of Mussolini's Fascism is uncharacteristically incoherent. He appeared to prefer Fascist syndicalism to either the capitalist or Communist alternatives but saw it nonetheless as only the least objectionable of this pernicious bunch, not necessarily desirable in itself, and certainly not as praiseworthy as distributism. At worst, Chesterton painted the blackshirts less dark than they deserved because he felt that almost anything was preferable to multinational plutocracy. At his best, he rejected the authoritarian stance of Mussolini:

> I think there is a case for saying that this revolution is too much of a reaction. I mean it in the psychological sense of a recoil; that he does sometimes recoil so much from anarchy as to talk only of authority; that he does recoil from mere pacifism as to seem to endorse mere militarism; that he does recoil so much from the babel of tongues talking different heresies and contrary forms of nonsense as to make his own moral thesis a little too much on one note.[3]

That Chesterton had no time for Mussolini's moral thesis was owing to his allegiance to the other man with whom he had an audience during his visit to Rome in 1929, Pope Pius XI. Ultimately, however, he appears to have rejected Mussolini's politics as well as his philosophy:

> I am well aware that two black shirts do not make a white. But I assure the reader that I am not, in this case, in the least trying to prove that black is white. I wish there were in the world a real white flag of freedom, that I could follow, independently of the red flag of Communist or the black flag of Fascist regimentation. By every instinct of my being, by every tradition of my blood, I should prefer English liberty to Latin discipline.[4]

By instinct, Chesterton was against any form of dictatorship and eventually arrived at the "logical case against Fascism", which is, in itself, a wonderful example of Chestertonian wit and wisdom: "The

[2] G. K. Chesterton, *The Resurrection of Rome* (London, 1930), 242.
[3] Ibid., 273.
[4] Ibid., 283

intellectual criticism of Fascism is really this; that it appeals to an appetite for authority, without very clearly giving the authority for the appetite." [5] In this epigram Chesterton not merely rejected Fascism but gave it a brilliant and pithy putdown. He ended his discussion of Italian Fascism by stating that his remarks should be taken as "a warning against Fascism, as a wise man in the early eighteenth century might have uttered a warning against the French Revolution." [6]

One can hardly see how the allegation that Chesterton was a Fascist, in the precise definition of the word, can be maintained. Far from supporting it, he was responsible for its most precise, succinct and effective condemnation.

The worst Chesterton could be accused of is an initial naïveté in accepting an audience with Mussolini. One thinks of Shaw and Wells, both of whom had audiences with Josef Stalin, a tyrant who murdered thousands for every one murdered by Mussolini. And yet no one brands them Stalinists. Furthermore, Chesterton saw the error of Mussolini's actions and condemned them, whereas Shaw and Wells, blinded by their own utopianism, obstinately refused to recognize Stalinist tyranny.

We can proceed to a discussion of the *not-so-precise* definition of Fascism. It can be taken to encompass any right-wing totalitarianism but, for the present purpose, will be limited to Hitler's National Socialist regime in Germany and Franco's Fascist regime in Spain. With regard to National Socialism, no defense of Chesterton is necessary because there is no case against him. Almost as soon as Hitler had become chancellor of Germany in January 1933, Chesterton began to condemn the evils for which he stood. In one of his articles for the *Illustrated London News*, later collected and published in *Avowals and Denials* (1934), Chesterton likened Hitler's rise to "the Return of the Barbarian": "ever since Herr Hitler began to turn the beer-garden into a bear-garden, there has been an increasing impression on sensitive and intelligent minds that something very dangerous has occurred. A particular sort of civilisation has turned back towards barbarism." [7] By the end of 1933 Chesterton had become as preoccupied with the

---

[5] Ibid., 286.
[6] Ibid., 345.
[7] G. K. Chesterton, *Avowals and Denials* (London: Methuen, 1934), 37.

Nazis in Germany as he had been with the Fascists in Italy four years earlier. He condemned Hitler's return to "the stale theories of Eugenics; the talk of compulsory action to keep the breed in a certain state of bestial excellence; of nosing out every secret of sex and origin, so that nobody may survive who is not Nordic; of setting a hundred quack doctors to preserve an imaginary race in its imaginary purity." [8] From this imaginary purity the Nazis had resurrected an imaginary deity: "Mythology has returned; the clouds are rolling over the landscape, shutting out the broad daylight of fact; and Germans are wandering about saying they will dethrone Christ and set up Odin and Thor." [9]

On 20 April 1933 Chesterton had already written in *G.K.'s Weekly* on "The Heresy of Race":

> In the lands of the new religions, rapidly turning into new irreligions, there had already sprung up a number of new tests and theories; of which the most menacing was the new theory of Race ... that a modern science of ethnology revealed a superior Teutonic type, spread everywhere from prehistoric times, and wherever that type could be recognised (by square heads, saucer blue eyes, hair like tow or other signs of godhood) there the new German Kaiser would stamp his foot crying, "This is German land."
>
> I think this wild worship of Race far worse than even the excessive concentration on the nation, which many Catholics rightly condemn. Nationalism may in rational proportion help stability, and the recognition of traditional frontiers. But Anthropology gone mad, which is the right name for Race, means ever-lastingly looking for your own countrymen in other people's countries.

In the following edition of *G.K.'s Weekly*, Chesterton resumed the attack. Hitler had built a successful career "by raving against Catholicism and hounding the Jews like rats" and by "making his great speeches about Race":

> Oh those speeches about Race! Oh the stewed staleness and stupidity of the brains of a thousand boiled owls, diluted and filtered through

[8] Ibid., 135.
[9] Ibid., 187.

the brains of a thousand forgotten Prussian professors! The German is not only a German. He is an Aryan. His heart leaps up when he beholds a Swastika in the sky; because Professor Esel found it carved on quite a number of prehistoric stones in Northern Europe. The Jew, on the other hand, is not an Aryan. Most of us imagined that it was enough for general common sense, that he was a Jew; but, alas, he is a Semite. Show him a Swastika and he remains cold ... Need even a new Religion fall back on anything quite so faded and threadbare as the notion that nobody is any good but a Teuton?

Although the tone of the article was somewhat softened with satire, this was Chesterton in an unusually savage mood. He concluded by branding the Nazism of Hitler as "one huge and howling Heresy: a Heresy run quite wild and raving: Race and the pride of Prussia."

One positive result of Chesterton's abhorrence of Hitler's regime was the softening of his attitude toward the Jews. For Chesterton the whole issue was tied up with questions of justice. He had criticized Jews when he believed that they were the perpetrators of injustice, particularly in the wake of the Marconi Scandal of 1913, when he felt that his brother had been unjustly attacked by his Jewish adversaries; but as soon as he saw that the Jews had themselves become the victims of persecution, he was swift in their defense. As early as 1923 Chesterton had expressed misgivings about the rise of crude anti-Semitism in Fleet Street newspapers. Newspapers that had been talking nothing but nonsense about Bolshevism, he said, were not likely to begin talking sense about Jews.[10] There was certainly an element of both irony and paradox in the fact that the final reconciliation between Chesterton and the Jews came about as a direct result of Hitler's anti-Semitism. The Jews forgave Chesterton his earlier indiscretions because, in the words of Rabbi Wise, "he was one of the first to speak out with all the directness and frankness of a great and unabashed spirit" when Hitlerism came.[11] Meanwhile, Chesterton altered his attitude toward the Jews because he was horrified at the hardening of attitudes in Germany and its results. In 1989 two British Jews, Anthony Read and David Fisher, wrote *Kristallnacht: The Nazi Night of Terror*, in which

[10] *G.K.'s Weekly*, 13 April 1923.
[11] Maisie Ward, *Gilbert Keith Chesterton* (London: Sheed & Ward, 1944), 228.

they documented the opening of the Nazi campaign of anti-Semitic persecution. In it they wrote:

> Belloc, like his friend Chesterton, like so many of the English middle class, was prejudiced against Jews. He did not like them. Nevertheless, he was not anti-Semitic—certainly not in the Nazi sense and the idea of employing physical brutality against a single Jew would have appalled him. He was an honourable man, uneasily aware that there was something going on in Germany of which, in conscience, he could not approve.[12]

Toward the end of his life, Chesterton echoed these sentiments:

> In our early days Hilaire Belloc and myself were accused of being uncompromising anti-Semites. Today, although I still think there is a Jewish problem, I am appalled by the Hitlerite atrocities. They have absolutely no reason or logic behind them. It is quite obviously the expedient of a man who has been driven to seeking a scapegoat, and has found with relief the most famous scapegoat in European history, the Jewish people. I am quite ready to believe now that Belloc and I will die defending the last Jew in Europe.[13]

Perhaps it is now safe to assume that Chesterton can be cleared of any sympathy with Nazi Germany, and indeed that he can be cleared of the charge of anti-Semitism. There still remains, however, the specter of the other regime that falls within the boundaries of the not-so-precise definition of Fascism, namely that of General Franco in Spain.

The charge that Chesterton was a supporter of Franco is as unfounded as saying that he was a supporter of Hitler. In this case, however, his defense lies not in what he did say but in what he failed to say. Chesterton was notably silent about General Franco. Yet, before the thought police of political correctness insinuate that his silence condemns him, that there was something suspicious in his failure to speak out against the Spanish dictator, perhaps one should be aware of his alibi. By the time that Franco had become dictator of Spain, Chesterton was dead.

---

[12] Anthony Read and David Fisher, *Kristallnacht: The Nazi Night of Terror* (London, 1989), 183.

[13] Quoted in the *Sunday Times*, 18 August 1957.

One may dismiss autopsies that imply that Franco would have been supported by Chesterton if Chesterton hadn't died. The fact is that Chesterton escapes the charge by the simple expedient of having expired before it was committed.

More may be said, however, about Franco and the Spanish civil war. The fact is that *if* Chesterton had lived and if he had failed to support Franco's side in the civil war, he would have been out of step with most of his Catholic contemporaries around the world. This prompts an important question: Does the fact that the majority of Catholics supported Franco indicate that they were Fascists?

Some words Chesterton wrote in a Christmas article at the end of 1935, six months before his death, will serve as an appropriate place to begin a discussion on this subject:

> We live in a terrible time, of war and rumour of war ... International idealism in its effort to hold the world together ... is admittedly weakened and often disappointed. I should say simply that it does not go deep enough ... If we really wish to make vivid the horrors of destruction and mere disciplined murder we must see them more simply as attacks on the hearth and the human family; and feel about Hitler as men felt about Herod.[14]

These words were prophetic in more ways than one. Within less than a decade, the concentration camps and the slaughter of the innocents really did cast Hitler in the role of Herod. But—and this is central to the present question—many Catholics regarded the anti-Franco forces in the Spanish civil war exactly as Chesterton had Hitler. The Communists and the anarchists who made up the bulk of the Republican forces, fanatically anticlerical and anti-Christian, were responsible for the murders of numerous priests, monks and nuns and for the burning and looting of hundreds of churches throughout Spain. George Orwell recorded of Barcelona, "almost every church had been gutted and its images burned." Priests had their ears cut off, monks had their eardrums perforated by rosary beads being forced into them, and the mother of two Jesuit priests had a rosary forced down her throat. How else could Catholic Christians regard such outrages than as "attacks on

[14] Ward, *Gilbert Keith Chesterton*, 540.

the hearth and the human family" and feel about the murderers of priests and nuns what "men felt about Herod"?

Arnold Lunn, Alfred Noyes, Ronald Knox, Christopher Hollis, Christopher Dawson and a host of other Catholic writers came out in support of the Nationalists, even though many found Hitler's support for Franco disquieting. Evelyn Waugh spoke for many Catholics when, in 1937, he replied to a questionnaire sent to writers in the British Isles asking them to state their attitude toward the war in Spain. In answer to the question "Are you for, or against, the legal government and the people of republican Spain? Are you for, or against, Franco and Fascism?" Waugh replied:

> I am no more impressed by the "legality" of the Valencia government than are English Communists by the legality of the Crown, Lords and Commons. I believe it was a bad government, rapidly deteriorating. If I were a Spaniard I should be fighting for General Franco ... I am not a Fascist nor shall I become one unless it were the only alternative to Marxism. It is mischievous to suggest that a choice is imminent.[15]

The word that best describes Catholic motives during the Spanish civil war is, ironically, the German word *real-politik*, roughly interpreted as the necessity of putting one's own survival before theoretical niceties. Certainly Catholics, in their implicit support for Franco, found it unfortunate, even embarrassing, to be on the same side as Hitler, even on this one issue alone. Yet five years later, Churchill, in his war with Hitler, found himself on the same side as Josef Stalin, who by the most conservative estimates murdered at least five times as many people as Hitler and millions more than Franco. Does *real-politik* make Catholics Fascists or Churchill a Communist?

The sort of woolly-mindedness that could lead to allegations that Churchill was a "bolshie" or many Catholics were "Fascist" leads to the next definition of Fascism. The *too-imprecise* definition gives Fascism such a broad meaning that the term becomes meaningless, a mere expletive with which to insult anyone with whom one disagrees. A brilliant depiction of this too-imprecise use of the word was given by Evelyn Waugh in a letter to the *New Statesman* on 5 March 1938:

[15] Louis Aragon, ed., *Authors Take Sides on the Spanish War* (London, 1937).

There was a time in the early twenties when the word "Bolshie" was current. It was used indiscriminately of refractory school children, employees who asked for a rise in wages, impertinent domestic servants, those who advocated an extension of the rights of property to the poor, and anything or anyone of whom the speaker disapproved. The only result was to impede reasonable discussion and clear thought.

I believe we are in danger of a similar, stultifying use of the word "Fascist". There was recently a petition sent to English writers ... asking them to subscribe themselves, categorically, as supporters of the Republican Party in Spain, or as "Fascists". When rioters are imprisoned it is described as a "Fascist sentence"; the Means Test is Fascist; colonisation is Fascist; military discipline is Fascist; patriotism is Fascist; Catholicism is Fascist; Buchmanism is Fascist; the ancient Japanese cult of their Emperor is Fascist; the Galla tribes' ancient detestation of theirs is Fascist; fox-hunting is Fascist ... Is it too late to call for order?

This *reductio ad absurdum* of labeling everyone and everything either "bolshie" or "Fascist" was finding tragicomic expression in Spain itself even as Waugh wrote. As the war began to swing in Franco's favor, the Communists and the anarchists in the Republican forces began to turn their guns on each other, each accusing the other of being "Fascist". In such circumstances it *was* "too late to call for order" because order itself was deemed "Fascist". Interestingly, the socialist subeditors at the *New Statesman* headed Waugh's letter "Fascist", evidently as a juvenile gibe intended to annoy their hostile correspondent. They were only reinforcing his point.

The allegation that Chesterton was a Fascist in this too-imprecise definition of the word is the hardest to defend him against. It is too intangible to touch, too airy to grasp, too vacant to engage. It is the enthronement of meaninglessness by the assassination of meaning. The triumph of the trite. Alas, on this level, and this level alone, we must admit defeat and confess that Chesterton is indeed a "Fascist". The only consolation is the knowledge that so is everyone else.

Apart from the above-mentioned definitions, there is also what could be called the generally *accepted* definition of Fascism. This is the definition popularized brilliantly by George Orwell in *Animal Farm* and *Nineteen Eighty-Four*. Orwell cut through the cant of what has been called "that damn-fool dichotomy of Left and Right", deliberately refraining from specifying whether the totalitarian regimes he was describing were "Fascist" or "Communist". The point was that, to all intents and purposes, it didn't matter. Regardless of the theory that gave them theoretical justification, they were the perpetrators of injustice. Certainly, there are deliberate parallels in *Animal Farm* to Stalin's machiavellianism and Trotsky's murder, but the story is just as applicable to Hitler's machiavellianism and the killing of Ernst Rohm and Gregor Strasser in the Night of the Long Knives. Meanwhile, the image of Big Brother, omnipresent, omnipotent and omniscient, in *Nineteen Eighty-Four* has impressed itself upon the public imagination to such a degree that the most powerful dictators—Hitler, Stalin, Mussolini, Mao—are synthesized in the name of Big Brother. This, then, is the public perception of totalitarianism, the practically and generally *accepted* definition of Fascism, and indeed of Communism, that most people have today.

Of course, as neither of Orwell's books had been written at the time of Chesterton's death, the general perceptions of Fascism then were different from those of today. To Chesterton and his contemporaries, Fascism was defined by one or other of the three definitions already discussed. Nonetheless, because allegations of Chesterton's Fascism continue today, it is necessary to address the current practically accepted definition of the word.

Big-Brother Fascism involves an increase of state power and state control over everyday life; it believes in the right of government to exercise control over the private property of individuals; it believes in strong central government at the expense of local or regional authority; it promotes intolerance of its opponents, whether on the grounds of race, creed or politics; it is characterized by a xenophobic chauvinism and a contempt for foreigners; it is militarist and often has imperialist aspirations. On each of these components, Chesterton is anti-Fascist according to the modern conception of the word. For the sake of anyone who does not know Chesterton's work, one or two brief examples may be given.

On numerous occasions, Chesterton attacked the creeping encroachment of the state into the lives of ordinary people, and particularly into the family, which was to Chesterton the bastion of freedom in any civilized society. More specifically, he was an outspoken opponent of Prohibition in the United States, partly because it was undesirable in itself but also because it was state interference in the civil liberties of individuals. The creed of distributism, distilled by Belloc from the social teaching of the Catholic Church as expounded by Pope Leo XIII, was a central tenet of Chesterton's socioeconomic thinking. He believed in the sanctity, in the restoration and the preservation of small, widely distributed private property. These views were the antithesis of economic centralism, whether by state-run nationalized industries or by privately owned monopolies. He was the defender of small property from both big business and Big Brother, an early exponent of the creed of "Small is Beautiful" as espoused in the 1970s by E. F. Shumacher.

His views on devolved power, liberated from central government,. infused *The Napoleon of Notting Hill*, which is, in its own way, as much a call for freedom from Big Brother as is *Nineteen Eighty-Four*. Chesterton's novel was set in 1984; perhaps Orwell chose that year as a tribute to Chesterton's earlier work. I prefer this to the more prosaic suggestion that Orwell simply reversed the numbers of the year in which it was written, 1948.

Chesterton cannot be accused of intolerance of his opponents. Almost unique among writers, he spent a lifetime arguing with everyone but quarreling with no one, a man with no enemies although he had numerous opponents. Chesterton is an icon of tolerance in an intolerant world. He was a Little Englander who loved his country without denigrating anyone else's country, with one exception: that of Germany in its expansionism and militarism under both the kaiser and the führer. Throughout his life, he never accepted the right of one country to impose itself upon another, an anti-imperialist stance that dates to the days of the Boer War (1899–1902).

In short, Chesterton stands acquitted of the charge of Fascism in the generally accepted definition of the word even more than in the other senses. Far from being a Fascist, he seems to be the quintessential anti-Fascist. By a bizarre Chestertonian paradox, he is often accused of Fascism by means of the stereotypes, smears, superficiality and prejudice that one normally associates with Fascism itself.

A postscript may be appropriate. Speaking as one who was once attracted to Fascism, I can testify that Chesterton more than anyone rescued me from the intolerant world into which I had strayed. Reading his words, I was gradually awakened, as if from a bad dream, into the world of wisdom and innocence that Chesterton inhabited. I have more reason than most to be thankful for the fact that Chesterton was not a Fascist.

I met at a recent meeting of the Chesterton Society in Sussex a clergyman who had been a member of both the Communist Party and the International Marxist Group. Earlier we would have despised each other, but now we were united by love for Christ . . . and for Chesterton. If, as Chesterton believed, faith alone is not enough but must be accompanied by good works, it is clear for all who have eyes to see, that both Chesterton's faith and his good works continue to work wonderfully and efficaciously across the generations.

9

G. K. CHESTERTON

Champion of Orthodoxy

C HESTERTON'S REPUTATION as one of the key figures in Christian literature during the twentieth century is linked inextricably with the concept of "orthodoxy". His book of that title, published in 1908, was, according to Wilfrid Ward, a major milestone in the development of Christian thought.

Wilfrid Ward was certainly not alone in his flattering praise of Chesterton's book. The book's influence on the intellectual development of a whole generation was summed up by Dorothy L. Sayers. She had first read *Orthodoxy* as a schoolgirl when her faith had been threatened by adolescent doubt. In later years she confessed that its "invigorating vision" had inspired her to look at Christianity anew and that if she hadn't read Chesterton's book, she might, in her schooldays, have given up Christianity altogether. "To the young people of my generation," Sayers wrote in 1952, "G.K.C. was a kind of Christian liberator."

In stressing firm and fixed foundations for the concept and teachings of Christianity, Chesterton had turned "orthodoxy" into a battle cry—a rapier-sharp reply to the heresies of the age. His approach would be very influential on C. S. Lewis, and there are obvious and unmistakable parallels between Chesterton's populist approach to "orthodoxy" and Lewis' "mere Christianity".

There is also a clear similarity between Chesterton's approach to orthodoxy and that of T. S. Eliot. In *Notes towards the Definition of Culture*, Eliot captured the spirit of the Christian literary revival, of which he and Chesterton were part, in his last appeal ... to the men of letters of Europe, who have a special responsibility for the preservation and transmission of our common culture ... We can at least try to save something of the goods of which we are the common trustees; the legacy of Greece, Rome and Israel, and the legacy of Europe throughout 2,000 years. In a world which has seen such material devastation as ours, these spiritual possessions are also in imminent peril.

For Eliot, and for Chesterton, this inheritance was not merely something old-fashioned that could be shrugged off and discarded in favor of new fads. It was a sacred tradition, the custodian of eternal verities that spoke with inexorable authority to every new and passing generation. The beauty of great literature resided in its being an expression of a common culture, which was itself the fruit of the preservation of learning, the pursuit of truth and the attainment of wisdom. The highest function of art, therefore, was to express the highest common factors of human life and not the lowest common denominators—life's loves and not its lusts. This was the mindset at the very core of the literary revival of which Chesterton was part.

In the wake of the publication of *Orthodoxy*, Chesterton was no longer tolerated as a young and precocious writer but was considered provocative and a threat to the agnostic status quo. Chesterton was acutely aware of this change in attitude:

> Very nearly everybody ... began by taking it for granted that my faith in the Christian creed was a pose or a paradox. The more cynical supposed that it was only a stunt. The more generous and loyal warmly maintained that it was only a joke. It was not until long afterwards that the full horror of the truth burst upon them; the disgraceful truth that I really thought the thing was true.
> ... Critics were almost entirely complimentary to what they were pleased to call my brilliant paradoxes; *until* they discovered that I really meant what I said.

It says something about the scintillating cynicism of our age that, in the eyes of his contemporaries, Chesterton's greatest sin was his sincerity. This thought was certainly in Chesterton's mind in the months following the publication of *Orthodoxy* and was one of the principal inspirations behind his novel *The Ball and the Cross*, published in February 1910. "The theme in Mr. Chesterton's new novel", wrote a reviewer in the *Pall Mall Gazette*, "is largely the same that he treated in *Orthodoxy* ... The story is concerned with the effort of the two honest men to fight a duel on the most vital problem in the world, the truth of Christianity."

Although the truth of Christianity may have been the object of *The Ball and the Cross*, its subjects were two men—one a Catholic, the other an atheist—whose sincerity scandalized their cynical contemporaries. There is little doubt that Chesterton had intended the novel as a light-hearted, entertaining response to those who had criticized his defense of Christianity in *Orthodoxy*. It was also a thinly disguised parable on his relationship with George Bernard Shaw, one of the literary figures discussed by Chesterton in his earlier book *Heretics*. Like the two adversaries in *The Ball and the Cross*, Chesterton and Shaw disagreed passionately on most of the issues of the day but remained good friends. Their relationship was a living embodiment of the command to "love thine enemy".

If Chesterton's *Orthodoxy* had been born out of debates with "heretics" such as Shaw, his other great work of Christian apologetics, *The Everlasting Man*, would be born out of a protracted and bad-tempered debate between Hilaire Belloc and H. G. Wells. Initially, Belloc had objected to the tacitly anti-Christian stance of Well's *Outline of History*, which had given less space to Christ than to the Persians' campaign against the Greeks. Yet Belloc's principal objection was the materialistic determinism that formed the foundation of Wells' *History*, and this prompted him to write a series of articles exposing Wells' errors.

Chesterton's own contribution to the debate was *The Everlasting Man*, intended as a refutation of Wells' case, but written in a wholly different tone from that of the bombastic bellicosity that characterized Belloc's articles. In essence, *The Everlasting Man* was Chesterton's own attempt at an "outline of history".

Perhaps the importance of *The Everlasting Man*, as with the importance of *Orthodoxy*, is best judged by its impact on others.

Ronald Knox was "firmly of the opinion that posterity will regard *The Everlasting Man* as the best of his books", a view echoed by Evelyn Waugh, who wrote that Chesterton was "primarily the author of

The Everlasting Man", which he described as "a great, popular book, one of the few really great popular books of the century; the triumphant assertion that a popular book can be both great and popular."

Perhaps the literary figure who was affected most profoundly by *The Everlasting Man* was C. S. Lewis. Although Lewis was already an admirer of Chesterton when *The Everlasting Man* was published in 1925, he could not accept Chesterton's Christianity. "Chesterton had more sense than all the other moderns put together," Lewis wrote, "bating, of course, his Christianity ... Then I read Chesterton's *Everlasting Man* and for the first time saw the whole Christian outline of history set out in a form that seemed to me to make sense."

Lewis, of course, would go on to become arguably the most influential Christian apologist of the twentieth century, with the possible exception of Chesterton himself. The fact that Lewis owed his own conversion to Christianity in large part to Chesterton is a living testament to the latter's enduring importance.

Yet the importance of Chesterton to the subsequent development of the Christian literary revival goes much deeper. He influenced the conversion of Evelyn Waugh and inspired, at least in part, the original conception of *Brideshead Revisited*. He indirectly influenced the conversion of Graham Greene, who converted following discussions with his future wife—who had previously converted through the avid reading of Chesterton's books. Chesterton had nurtured to full recovery the ailing faith of both Ronald Knox and Dorothy L. Sayers during periods of adolescent doubt. This, in itself, would constitute a laudable testament to Chesterton's importance. Yet even this tells only a tiny part of the story, the tip of the evangelical iceberg. How many others, less well known, have had their faith either restored or germinated by Chesterton's genius and his genial expositions of orthodoxy?

Dr. Barbara Reynolds, friend and biographer of Dorothy L. Sayers, has described the interchange and interplay of ideas between Christian writers as a network of minds energizing each other. In this network of minds, few have done more "energizing" than Gilbert Keith Chesterton.

10

HILAIRE BELLOC IN A NUTSHELL

Hilaire Belloc was born at La Celle Saint Cloud, twelve miles outside Paris, on 27 July 1870. His birth coincided with the outbreak of the Franco-Prussian War, and his parents were forced to evacuate the family home a few weeks later. They fled to Paris to escape the advancing Prussian army, and as the Prussians prepared to lay siege to the French capital, the Bellocs managed to catch the last train to Dieppe, on the Normandy coast, from whence they sailed to the safety of England.

Belloc was educated in the benevolent shadow of the aging Cardinal Newman at the Oratory School in Birmingham and at Balliol College in Oxford. As an undergraduate, his considerable presence and oratorical prowess gained him a degree of preeminence among his peers that culminated in his election to the presidency of the Oxford Union. In June 1895 he crowned his exceptionally brilliant career at Oxford with a first-class honors degree in history.

Even before going to Oxford, the young Belloc had commenced his wanderlustful perambulations, tramping through his beloved France and traveling across the United States. The latter was undertaken in an endeavor to persuade Elodie Hogan, a young Irish American girl whom he had met in London, to marry him. Having traveled the breadth of the United States, he arrived in California to be informed that his beloved was intent on trying her vocation with the Sisters of Charity. Returning broken-hearted and empty-handed to Europe, he enlisted for national service in the French army.

Belloc never lost touch with his apparently lost love in America, and in the summer of 1896, he returned to California, marrying Elodie at Saint John the Baptist Church in Napa on 15 June of that year. The newlyweds returned to England, where they would be blessed with five children before Elodie's tragic death in 1914.

The commencement of Belloc's married life coincided with the commencement of his literary career. In 1896 his first two books were published, *Verses and Sonnets* and *The Bad Child's Book of Beasts*. The latter became an instant popular success, prompting more of the same, including *More Beasts (for Worse Children)* in 1897 and *Cautionary Tales for Children* ten years later. Although these books for children (of all ages) are indubitably charming and enduringly funny, it is perhaps unfortunate that, for many, Belloc is remembered primarily for these relatively trivial sorties into children's literature rather than for the vast body of work, transcending several genres, that represents his true and lasting legacy.

His first biography, *Danton*, was published in 1899, and, thereafter, Belloc would continue to write biographies of historical figures, specializing particularly, though by no means exclusively, in the figures of the English Reformation. These included studies of Cromwell, James II, Wolsey, Cranmer, Charles I and Milton. He also published panoramic studies of the whole period, such as *How the Reformation Happened* and *Characters of the Reformation*, as well as a four-volume *History of England*. His motivation for this prodigious output of what might be termed historical revisionism was a personal crusade to fight the "enormous mountain of ignorant wickedness" that constituted "tom-fool Protestant history".[1]

Belloc was also interested in questions of politics and economics and was a resolute and vociferous champion of the social teaching of the Catholic Church as espoused by Pope Leo XIII in the encyclical *Rerum novarum* (1891). His principal works in this area are *The Servile State* (1912) and *An Essay on the Restoration of Property* (1936). Belloc should also be remembered for his works of apologetics, particularly perhaps for his late masterpiece *Survivals and New Arrivals* (1929), a much-underrated book that rivals in lucidity and potency the much better-known apologetic works of G. K. Chesterton, such as *Orthodoxy* (1908) and *The Everlasting Man* (1925).

---

[1] Joseph Pearce, *Old Thunder: A Life of Hilaire Belloc* (San Francisco: Ignatius Press, 2002), 230.

As a novelist, Belloc was prolific, though not always particularly adept. Most of his excursions into fiction were bogged down by stolid prose and stagnant storylines. The one notable exception, *Belinda* (1928), fulfilled his potential as a novelist, which had, hitherto, been frustrated. He was far more successful as an essayist and as the writer of what might be termed (inadequately) farragoes. These farragoes, such as *The Path to Rome* (1902), *The Four Men* (1912) and *The Cruise of the "Nona"* (1925) are among the most loved and most popular of all his work. It was, however, as a poet that Belloc achieved true greatness in the literary sphere. "Tarantella", "Ha'nacker Mill", "Lines to a Don", "The End of the Road" and several of his sonnets guarantee his place among the *eminenti* of twentieth-century English poets.

Lastly, Belloc must be remembered for the gargantuan nature of his personality. In his case, to an extraordinary degree, it is the man himself who breathes life and exhilaration into his work. When he is writing at his best, every page exudes the charisma of the author, spilling over with the excess of exuberance for which the man was famous among his contemporaries. From his legendary and fruitful friendship with G. K. Chesterton to his vituperative enmity toward H. G. Wells, Belloc always emerges as the sort of man who is often described as being larger than life. Strictly speaking, of course, no man is larger than life. In Belloc's case, however, perhaps more than almost any other literary figure of his generation, the man can be considered truly greater than his oeuvre. As such, his greatest works are those that reflect his personality to the greatest degree. Whether he is loved or loathed—and he is loved or loathed more than most—he cannot be easily ignored.

I I

———

BELLOC'S *THE PATH TO ROME*

B ELLOC CONSIDERED *The Path to Rome*[1] to be perhaps his finest work. Six years after its publication, he wrote in his own personal copy of the book the final wistful lines of a ballade, the first part of which was presumably never written:

> Alas! I never shall so write again!

> *Envoi*
> Prince, bow yourself to God and bow to Time,
> Which is God's servant for the use of men,
> To bend them to his purpose sublime.
> Alas! I never shall so write again.[2]

It could be considered a trifle presumptuous to assume that these lines of verse prove that Belloc thought that he never wrote so well thereafter. After all, he wrote a great deal thereafter. The lines were written in 1908, before he wrote *The Four Men* and many years before he wrote *Belinda*. Writing of the latter to his friend Maurice Baring, Belloc stated that it was "the only thing I ever finished in my life and the only piece of my own writing that I have liked for more than 40 years" (*Old Thunder*, 234). Belloc informed another friend, however, that *Belinda* was "certainly the book of mine which I like best since I wrote *The Path to Rome*" (*Old Thunder*, 234). These words, written in 1930, would appear to confirm the lines inscribed in his own copy of

---

[1] Hilaire Belloc, *The Path to Rome* (San Francisco: Ignatius Press, 2003).

[2] Joseph Pearce, *Old Thunder: A Life of Hilaire Belloc* (San Francisco: Ignatius Press, 2002), 84.

The Path to Rome twenty-two years earlier. It is clear, therefore, that in the opinion of the author himself, and regardless of the dissenting views of some of his admirers, the "best of Belloc" is to be found on the path to Rome.

At its most basic, *The Path to Rome* is an account of the author's pilgrimage to Rome in 1901. He sets off from Toul, in France, and journeys through the valley of the Moselle, heading for Switzerland and then, traversing the Alps, to Italy. The book itself, though ostensibly an account of the author's pilgrimage, is much more. In its pages we see Europe at the turn of a new century through the eyes of a poet besotted with its beauty. We see it through the lens of a historian who understands the living majesty of Europe's past. We see it through the faithful heart of a Catholic who beholds a vision of the Europe of the present in vibrant communion with the Europe of the past. We see it in the transcendence of all these visions united in one mystical flesh; the poet and the historian and the Catholic forming a united trinity beholding something greater than itself. As such, it is a work of humility and awe, of gratitude and hope, of faith and love. Yet it is more, and less, than this. It is incarnational. Its flesh, mystically communing with, and exiled from, heaven, is also rooted in the earth. It is pithy and earthy, anecdotal and tangential; it is both prayerfully reverent and playfully irreverent, at one and the same time. It is a faith loved and lived within the constraints of the fallible and fallen nature of the author.

From the pregnant poignancy of Belloc's superb preface, with its delightful combination of the wistful and the whimsical, to the dash and dare of the wonderful poem that serves as the book's, and the pilgrim's, conclusion, *The Path to Rome* takes the reader on a journey into himself and out of himself, a voyage of discovery in which home and exile are interwoven in a mystical dance of contemplation. In its pages we discover the Europe of the Faith, which was, and is, the heart of Christendom, and the Faith of Europe, which was, and is, the heart of all.

And as for Belloc's motivation for writing *The Path to Rome*, the inscription in his own personal copy of the book, dated 29 March 1904, says it all: "I wrote this book for the glory of God" (*Old Thunder*, 84).

MAJOR THEMES

The Path to Rome is both a travelogue and a farrago, which is to say
that it is, at one and the same time, a linear narrative connected to a
journey, and a seemingly random dispersal of anecdotal thoughts and
musings. Its overriding structure is, therefore, animated by the tension
between the forward momentum maintained by the author's account
of his pilgrimage and the inertial force of the tangential interruptions.
This singular literary combination constitutes a distinct literary genre,
and one in which Belloc excelled. Having experimented with what
may be dubbed the "travel-farrago" in the writing of *The Path to Rome*,
he would return to it with great success in *The Four Men* and *The
Cruise of the "Nona"*.

Perhaps the best way of discussing the major themes in a work of
this sort is to follow the line of the narrative, while pausing at need to
study the ponderable, and sometimes ponderous, interruptions with
which Belloc punctuates his narrative. In other words, it is not the
intention to analyze the work thematically but, rather, to study the
themes as they emerge from the narrative in the order in which they
are presented to the reader. To put the matter succinctly, we shall
follow the author along the route of his pilgrimage and shall not attempt
to remain aloof by dissecting it thematically from a disengaged distance.

Belloc begins his narrative by recounting an unexpected encounter
with the valley of his birth. He is surprised to see "the old tumble-
down and gaping church" that he had loved in his youth renovated so
that it appeared "noble and new" (*Path to Rome*, xvii). This pleased
him "as much as though a fortune had been left to us all; for one's
native place is the shell of one's soul, and one's church is the kernel of
that nut" (xviii). At the very outset, therefore, Belloc has laid the
foundations of what might be termed the "theology of place". This
concept, which can be said to be truly at the heart of Belloc's work,
is quintessentially incarnational. A sense of "place" is linked to the
love of home, and the love of home is itself salted by the home's
temporary absence or unattainability. Paradoxically, it is the sense of
exile that gives the love of home its intensity and its power. The theology of place is therefore rooted in the earth and yet reaches to heaven.
It is expressed most sublimely in the *Salve Regina*, in which the "poor

banished children of Eve" lost in "this vale of tears" hope that, "after this our exile", we might behold the Blessed Fruit of our Mother's womb. Heaven is our haven, Jesus is our home. And where Jesus is at home, in his Mother's arms and in her womb, we shall be at home also. One's earthly home, or "native place", is "the shell of one's soul" because it is an incarnated inkling of the home for which we are made and toward which we are mystically directed. It is for that reason that·"one's church is the kernel of that nut".

Nowhere has Belloc encapsulated the theology of place better than in a letter he wrote to Katherine Asquith:

> The Faith, the Catholic Church, is discovered, is recognized, triumphantly enters reality like a landfall at sea which first was thought a cloud. The nearer it is seen, the more it is real, the less imaginary: the more direct and external its voice, the more indubitable its representative character, its "persona", its voice. The metaphor is not that men fall in love with it: the metaphor is that they discover home. "This was what I sought. This was my need." It is the very mould of the mind, the matrix to which corresponds in every outline the outcast and unprotected contour of the soul. It is Verlaine's "Oh! Rome—oh! Mère!" And that not only to those who had it in childhood and have returned, but much more—and what a proof!—to those who come upon it from the hills of life and say to themselves, "Here is the town." [3]

This theology of place is such a recurrent theme in Belloc's work that it could be said to be almost omnipresent. Few writers have felt so intensely the sense of exile, and hence the love of home, to the degree to which it is invoked by Belloc. From the love of Sussex evoked in *The Four Men* and in poems such as "Ha'nacker Mill" or "The South Country", to the love of Europe in general, and France in particular, evoked in *The Path to Rome* and in poems such as "Tarantella", his work resonates with the love of earth as a foreshadowing of the love of heaven.

Seen in this light, the renovation of the church in his native valley, which Belloc proclaims as the very "kernel of that nut" that is his soul, takes on metaphorical, and therefore metaphysical, significance.

---

[3] Quoted in Joseph Pearce, *Literary Converts: Spiritual Inspirations in an Age of Unbelief* (San Francisco: Ignatius Press, 1999), 319.

Is the church itself a metaphor for Belloc's soul? Is its renovation a symbol of the renewal of the author's spirit inherent in his pilgrimage to Rome? Is the church of home (the soul of the author) retracing its source, its meaning and its purpose, to the Church of Rome (the Mystical Body of Christ)? Is home paying homage to Home?

Those intent on a strictly two-dimensional reading of the text might insist that this metaphorical interpretation goes too far. Isn't the book simply a straightforward factual account of the author's pilgrimage to Rome in the late spring and early summer of 1901? Certainly there is ample documentation, particularly in the contemporaneous correspondence with his wife, to verify that Belloc actually followed the route recounted in the book, yet the factual foundation does not exclude the metaphorical ascent into higher levels of meaning. On the contrary, if we accept that facts are physical whereas truth is metaphysical, it follows that facts serve the truth and that metaphor or allegory are the means by which the applicability of physical facts to metaphysical truth is conveyed. Indeed, these were the very principles upon which Saint Augustine and Saint Thomas Aquinas built their understanding of scriptural exegesis. Belloc, as a lifelong practicing Catholic educated by the Oratorians, would have been well versed in such concepts. It is, therefore, hardly controversial to insist that Belloc perceived that the facts of his pilgrimage served the truth toward which the pilgrimage was directed. As Belloc insisted, the book itself was written "for the glory of God".

Perhaps the best way of illustrating Belloc's employment of metaphor in *The Path to Rome* is to compare it with *The Four Men*. These two books are remarkably similar in style and structure. Both are travel-farragoes recounting a journey by the author, on foot, through land that he loves. In *The Four Men*, the men in question are Grizzlebeard, the Sailor, the Poet and Myself. It seems likely that each character was not an individual whom Belloc had actually met en route but that they were in fact, or in truth, allegorical representations of the various facets of Belloc's own character. It can be seen, therefore, that Belloc was not averse to the use of allegory and metaphor but that, on the contrary, he employed them liberally throughout his work.

Having ascertained the meaning of the initial metaphor that, in turn, is the key to understanding the deeper meaning of the work, the reader can proceed with the author along the path to Rome.

Inspired by the vision of the renovated church in his native valley, Belloc makes a prayerful vow "to go to Rome on Pilgrimage and see all Europe which the Christian Faith has saved" (xviii). Furthermore, he pledges that he will set off from Toul, the garrison town in which he had served in the army; that he will walk all the way and take advantage of no wheeled thing; that he will sleep rough, cover thirty miles a day and hear Mass every morning; and that he will arrive in Rome in time to attend high Mass in Saint Peter's on the Feast of Saint Peter and Saint Paul. As the narrative unfolds, we see that he breaks many of these vows, one by one. He sets off as he intended from the French garrison town of Toul, but he does not sleep rough every night, he does not attend Mass daily and he eventually succumbs to the temptation of "wheeled things". Again, the parallels with the life of the proverbial Everyman are obvious. We set out with good intentions and with a set goal in mind but fail to live up to the standards we set for ourselves. The author's pilgrimage to Rome is a microcosmic metaphor for Everyman's pilgrimage through life.

The metaphor recurs at various times and in various guises as, for instance, in Belloc's description of the Moselle near its source. The young river was "full of the positive innocence that attaches to virgins":

> There was about that scene something of creation and of a beginning, and as I drew it, it gave me like a gift the freshness of the first experiences of living and filled me with remembered springs. I mused upon the birth of rivers, and how they were persons and had a name—were kings, and grew strong and ruled great countries, and how at last they reached the sea. (84–85)

Belloc's portrayal of the people he encounters is always engaging and displays a genuine love for mankind. In the Ballon d'Alsace he finds his prejudiced presuppositions against those of Germanic culture challenged by the experience of meeting a German-speaking family. Having described "the Germanies" as "a great sea of confused and dreaming people, lost in philosophies" (93), he is humbled by the civilized customs of his Germanic hosts: "In good-nights they had a ceremony; for they all rose together and curtsied. Upon my soul I believe such people to be the salt of the earth. I bowed with real contrition, for at several moments I had believed myself better than

they" (98). He is also graphically effective in his depiction of
pain, describing how his feet "were so martyrised that I doubted if I
could walk at all on the morrow". In the morning, as he "fearlessly
forced" (99) his boots onto his feet, the reader almost winces in sympathy, especially if he has also experienced the pain of a protracted
perambulation.

Possibly the most subtle metaphoric suggestiveness in the whole
work emerges following the author's musing upon the nature of the
human soul, which was "a puzzling thought, very proper to a pilgrimage". What exactly is it? he wonders. Describing himself as knowing nothing of "pleasures ... in which my senses have had no part",
he is baffled by the saints and the mystics who speak of the pleasures
of the spirit as being distinct from, and superior to, the pleasures of
the flesh.

> As I was pondering on these things in this land of pastures and lonely
> ponds ... (my pain seemed gone for a moment, yet I was hobbling
> slowly)—I say as I was considering this complex doctrine, I felt my
> sack suddenly much lighter, and I had hardly time to rejoice at the
> miracle when I heard immediately a very loud crash, and turning half
> round I saw on the blurred white of the twilit road my quart of Open
> Wine all broken to atoms. My disappointment was so great that I sat
> down on a milestone to consider the accident and to see if a little
> thought would not lighten my acute annoyance. Consider that I had
> carefully cherished this bottle and had not drunk throughout a painful
> march all that afternoon, thinking that there would be no wine worth
> drinking after I had passed the frontier.
>
> ... I rose to go on into the night. As it turned out I was to find
> beyond the frontier a wine in whose presence this wasted wine would
> have seemed a wretched jest, and whose wonderful taste was to colour
> all my memories of the Mount Terrible. It is always thus with sorrows
> if one will only wait.
>
> So, lighter in the sack but heavier in the heart, I went forward to
> cross the frontier in the dark. (117–120)

In this short passage Belloc's use of metaphor becomes a parable. Having described himself as a sensualist, Belloc discovers that the immediate objects of his senses, both the painful and the pleasurable, are

taken away. First his pain "seemed gone", and then his pleasure, the quart of wine, is "broken to atoms". If the wine is taken as a symbol of worldly pleasures, being those that hinder the pleasures of the soul, the wine's destruction or removal becomes a symbol for pain or suffering and, ultimately, death. He had cherished it on the assumption that it would be unavailable once he had "passed the frontier". The frontier is itself a symbol for the moment of suffering, or the point of death, and, though he couldn't know it at the time, he was destined to discover that the unknown wine over the frontier would make his cherished possession on this side of the frontier seem "a wretched jest". "It is always thus with sorrows if one will only wait." The allegorical intent is also demonstrated by other uses of religious imagery. His burden becomes miraculously light; he crosses the frontier "in the dark"; and his destination over the frontier is Mount Terrible, surely an allusion to Purgatory, particularly in relation to the following sentence, in which Belloc speaks of the healing of sorrows "if one will only wait". The fact that these events, presumably, happened in actuality in the manner in which Belloc describes them does not, in the least, negate the allegorical interpretation of the parable. It merely indicates a providential connection between the experience of life and its deeper meaning, the apprehension of which is something "very proper to a pilgrimage". As J. R. R. Tolkien once remarked, life is a study for eternity for those so gifted. Clearly Belloc is one so gifted.

Throughout *The Path to Rome*, Belloc continually bestows upon the reader the fruits of his considerable wisdom. Thus he informs us that "economics are but an expression of the mind and do not (as the poor blind slaves of the great cities think) mould the mind": "What is more, nothing makes property run into a few hands but the worst of the capital sins, and you who say it is 'the modern facility of distribution' ... are like men who should say that their drunkenness was due to their drink, or that arson was caused by matches" (131). The insistence that economics is merely a derivative of philosophical presumptions, coupled with an exposé of the folly of deterministic analyses of economic "laws", foreshadows the work of the Catholic economist E. F. Schumacher, whose million-seller, *Small Is Beautiful*, was destined to reiterate these very same conclusions seventy years later.

An intermittent recurrence throughout the narrative of *The Path to Rome* is the dialogue between the Author ("Auctor") and the Reader ("Lector"). Apart from Belloc's use of the Lector as a foil, he is also employed as a symbol of modernity. Whenever the discussion strays into the area of philosophy or religion, the Lector invariably acts as the voice of shallow scepticism or agnostic indifference. He is a child of his age, a slave to intellectual fashion. "I see that all the religion I have stuck into the book has no more effect on you than had Rousseau upon Sir Henry Maine. You are as full of Pride as a minor Devil" (162). Thus does the Auctor upbraid the Lector, berating his superficiality.

Whereas the Lector plods, clod-laden, unable to lift his mind and heart above the "see" level of ground zero, the lowest-common-denominator-world of presumed materialism, the Auctor rises to the heights of mysticism, never more so than in his first vision of the Alps:

> Their sharp steadfastness and their clean uplifted lines compelled my adoration. Up there, the sky above and below them, part of the sky, but part of us, the great peaks made communion between that homing creeping part of me which loves vineyards and dances and a slow movement among pastures, and that other part which is only properly at home in Heaven. (180)

Once again the theology of place places the mysticism of the alpine vision into the vision of home. And once again the very vision of nature resplendent inspires the author's prose to metamorphose into metaphor:

> Since I could now see such a wonder and it could work such things in my mind, therefore, some day I should be part of it. That is what I felt.
>   This it is also which leads some men to climb mountain-tops, but not me, for I am afraid of slipping down. (181)

The mountain summits having become a celestial vision, the saints have become mystical mountaineers whose abilities to attain the spiritual heights outstrip the Auctor's backsliding and earthbound spirituality: "For it is the saddest thing about us that this bright spirit with which we are lit from within like lanterns, can suffer dimness. Such frailty makes one fear that extinction is our final destiny, and it saps us with numbness, and we are less than ourselves" (190). The days in which the author suffers such "dimness" are described as days "without salt", days in which the pilgrimage becomes a "trudge", days in which "the air was ordinary, the colours common; men, animals, and trees indifferent". On such days "something had stopped working". The "salt" to which Belloc is referring is the joy of surprise; an energy from God: "I say our energy also is from God, and we should never be proud of it as though it were from ourselves, but we should accept it as a kind of present, and we should be thankful for it; just as a man should thank God for his reason" (193–94). On such days it is only "Duty" that keeps the pilgrim resolutely on his path to Rome (191). Again, it is difficult not to see autobiographical parallels between the author's present journey and his life's journey, parallels that are, of course, equally applicable to the lives of his readers.

Once the sense of gratitude for the salt of life is lost, the salt itself is soon lost. Thereafter, the unsalted lapse into intellectual pride, "than which no sin is more offensive to the angels":

> What! here are we with the jolly world of God all round us, able to sing, to draw, to paint, to hammer and build, to sail, to ride horses, to run, to leap; having for our splendid inheritance love in youth and memory in old age, and we are to take one miserable little faculty, our one-legged, knock-kneed, gimcrack, purblind, rough-skinned, underfed, and perpetually irritated and grumpy intellect, or analytical curiosity rather (a diseased appetite), and let it swell till it eats up every other function? Away with such foolery. (234–35)

By contrast, the words of the Creed contain "a power of synthesis that can jam all their analytical dust-heap into such a fine, tight, and compact body as would make them stare to see" (235). Here Belloc might indeed have descended to the level of bombast, but it is not the bombast of relativism, the bombast of mere opinion, sanitized by self-righteousness, but the bombast of absolutes, the bombast of certitude, sanctified by servitude to the objective righteousness beyond the self.

The high point, literally and literarily, of *The Path to Rome* is Belloc's description of his foolhardy attempt to cross the Alps in a snow-storm, an attempt that ended in heroic failure. In these pages the prose soars as loftily as the peaks it describes and as powerfully as the elements that beat him back in sullen defeat. Again, the whole episode resonates with moral applicability. His proud and self-willed determination to conquer the peaks ends in the sort of humiliation that points to humility. "Indeed it is a bitter thing to have to give up one's sword" (249).

The other high point, literarily, is not prose but poetry; it is the verse with which Belloc chooses to conclude his book and his pilgrimage. "The End of the Road" is effectively a summary of the whole book distilled into thirty-four energy-charged lines. Although deceptively simple in structure, it exhibits masterful metrical acrobatics. At the outset, it surges and soars, filled with the freshness of the first days of the pilgrimage; it marches, pants, swings and dashes. Slowly it slows, plodding, hobbling, trudging and sauntering to a standstill. There is a pregnant pause, followed by a parenthetical penitential prayer orated bilingually in Latin and English, leading into a confession of broken vows. Finally, it glides unhurriedly to its destination. Throughout the length of the poem, the metrics are controlled by an ingenious combination of iambic dexterity, variations in scansion and, equally important, the dynamics of the verbs employed in the text itself. Rarely has Belloc achieved such heights in verse; indeed, rarely are such heights reached by any poet. And, of course, the ascent from prose to poetry, especially when executed so expertly, represents the perfect finishing touch to the work of literature, a finish with finesse. A climax.

With characteristic humor hinting at a more serious intention, Belloc describes the poem as a "dithyrambic epithalamium or threnody". It is certainly dithyrambic, reeling wildly and ecstatically, almost drunkenly, toward its destination; but can anything be both an epithalamium *and* a threnody? Can one sing of marriage and death in the same breath? Aren't nuptial bliss and the *Nunc dimittis* unacceptable bedfellows? Clearly Belloc is concluding his path to Rome with a provocative paradox, but the apparent contradictions point profoundly to a greater truth. His arrival in Rome resonates with the joy of the marriage bed. The Church is both the Mystical Body of Christ, and at the same time, she is the Bride of Christ. The pilgrim, at his most Christlike, is mystically married to the Bride; he is wedded to the Church; he is at one with her. At the same time, as a loyal and suppliant member of the Church, he is mystically married to Christ. More soberly and somberly, the arrival in Rome, the end of the pilgrimage, also signifies death, the end of our earthly pilgrimage. Ultimately the marriage bed and the grave represent a consummation. The joys and sorrows of life and death find their true consummation in the glory of eternity, represented symbolically in *The Path to Rome* by the Eternal City itself.

> Drinking when I had a mind to,
> Singing when I felt inclined to;
> Nor ever turned my face to home
> Till I had slaked my heart at Rome.

SURVEY OF CRITICISM

The Path to Rome was published in April 1902. It would eventually sell more than 100,000 copies and is still reprinted regularly today. Something of its spirit, and perhaps part of the secret of its success, was captured by G. K. Chesterton in a review for *The World* in which Chesterton contrasted Belloc's rambunctious *joie de vivre* with the ennui of the Decadents:

> *The Path to Rome* is the product of the actual and genuine buoyancy and thoughtlessness of a rich intellect ... The dandies in *The Green Carnation* stand on their heads for the same reason that the dandies in Bond Street stand on their feet—because it is the thing that is done; but they do it with the same expression of fixed despair on their faces, the expression of fixed despair which you will find everywhere and always on the faces of frivolous people and men of pleasure. He will be a lucky man who can escape out of that world of freezing folly into the flaming and reverberating folly of *The Path to Rome*. (*Old Thunder*, 83–84)

Other critics were also as fulsome in their praise. Reviewers in periodicals as diverse as the *Athenaeum*, the *Literary World*, the *Daily Chronicle*, the *Manchester Guardian* and the *New York Times* queued up to salute the arrival of an exciting new author, comparing his creative credentials to writers as rare and distinguished as Burton, Butler, Cobbett, Heine, Rabelais, Sterne, Stevenson and Walton. More recently, Dom Philip Jebb, former abbot of Downside and Belloc's grandson,

opined that the descriptive passages of the Alps in *The Path to Rome*
confirm Belloc's status as a genuine mystic (*Old Thunder*, 83).

Nobody has summed up the importance of this classic work better
than Belloc's friend, admirer and biographer, Robert Speaight:

> More than any other book he ever wrote, *The Path to Rome* made Bel-
> loc's name; more than any other, it has been lovingly thumbed and
> pondered. It was a new kind of book, just as Belloc was a new kind of
> man. It gave a vital personality, rich and complex, bracing and abun-
> dant, to the tired Edwardian world. Above all, it brought back the sense
> of Europe, physical and spiritual, into English letters. Vividly and per-
> sonally experienced, the centuries returned. (*Old Thunder*, 84)

A CHIP OFF THE OLD BELLOC

Bob Copper in Memoriam

MARCH 2004 SAW THE PASSING of Bob Copper, one of the last of the Old Bellocians. Although he will be remembered with fondness by all who had the immeasurable pleasure of knowing him, he will be remembered with especial affection by all those who shared his passionate love for Hilaire Belloc. To the wider world he will be remembered as one of the pioneers of the English folk music revival, but to those of us who knew him through the Hilaire Belloc Society, he will be always present to our minds and our hearts as a "chip off the old Belloc", a link to the very world that Belloc had himself inhabited.

It was not merely that Bob Copper was a child of the South Country who shared Belloc's love for the very soil of Sussex, it was as though he *belonged* in Belloc's world and was only a sojourner in ours. My mind's eye, gazing wishfully across the chasm of the Atlantic and wistfully across the abyss of the years, sees Bob Copper as I last saw him. He is standing by an open fire in an oak-beamed pub near Horsham in Sussex, a pub that Belloc himself frequented and wrote about. The surroundings are snug, the ceiling is low and Bob's face is aglow with a Chestertonian rambunctiousness accentuated by the flickering flames of the hearth. In his hand is a flagon of the finest English ale. Then, as the company is hushed in pregnant anticipation, he begins to sing the strains of Belloc's "Ha'nacker Mill", unaccompanied except by the powerful presence of the fallen silence. The tune is Belloc's own setting of his poem to music, and one can almost imagine Belloc himself lamenting the loss of Sally, the destruction of the mill and the demise of England. To me, however, Bob seemed to be an apparition of one of the ghosts of Belloc's imagination. As I watched him singing of a Sussex long deceased, his gray beard swaying with the melody and his old-young eyes glinting with the melancholy of long-lost moments, I was haunted by a vision of Grizzlebeard, the voice of sagacious virtue in Belloc's *The Four Men*. For that fleeting moment Bob Copper *was* Grizzlebeard, and I had been magically transported into the pages of Belloc's book. Fleeting moments pass away in the wisp of a whisper, but the memory lingers on persistently, and I have never managed to think of Bob Copper since without the shade of Grizzlebeard passing like a shadow across the landscape of my imagination. Bob Copper *was* Grizzlebeard for an elusive moment but *is* Grizzlebeard forever in the realm of the Permanent Things.

The last time I heard Bob Copper's voice, he was not physically present at all. In fact, as I was shocked to discover, he was already dead. His ghostly presence had floated across the Atlantic on the air-waves of the BBC, courtesy of the Internet. My ears had pricked to attention when I heard a master of ceremonies announce that he was being honored with a special award for a lifetime of achievement in the field of English folk music. Accepting the award to rapturous applause, Copper explained how important family tradition was to him and his music. He explained that he still sang songs that had been taught to him by his grandfather, who had been taught them by his own grandfather, that is, Copper's great-great-grandfather, who had learned them in the 1780s. He had since taught the same songs to his own children and grandchildren, who performed them with him as the Copper Family, one of the most respected names on the English folk music scene. Furthermore, all these generations had lived in the one small Sussex coastal town of Rottingdean, rooted in the soil and soul, and in the life and traditions, of Belloc's beloved Sussex. "One with our random fields we grow," as Belloc had said:

> because of lineage and because
> The soil and memories out of mind
> Embranch and broaden all mankind.

Like Belloc, Bob Copper was a living incarnation of the theology of place, one who lived in mystical union and communion with the land and culture that had nurtured and nourished him. In our rootless age of fungoid cosmopolitanism, such men are the breath of fresh air blowing through the branches of the Grizzlebeards and Treebeards of Permanence.

Bob Copper was quite simply a true giant among men, exuding a true gentleness and a giant humility. As my Grizzlebearded memory of him flashes across my consciousness, I am reminded of the words of Chesterton: "All roads point at last to an ultimate inn, where we shall meet Dickens and all his characters: and when we drink again it shall be from the great flagons in the tavern at the end of the world." I cherish the hope, and the prayer, that, along with Dickens and all his characters, I shall also meet once more Bob Copper and that I shall find him drinking to the eternal health of those others gathered around the table: Belloc and Chesterton, along with Grizzlebeard and the Sailor, and the Poet and Myself. For the tavern at the end of the world is where everlasting men commune everlastingly.

In the meantime, I can console myself with some timely words by Hilaire Belloc that will serve as a timeless epitaph to the late and greatly missed Bob Copper.

> He does not die that can bequeath
> Some influence to the land he knows,
> Or dares, persistent, interwreath
> Love permanent with the wild hedgerows;
>   He does not die, but still remains
>   Substantiate with his darling plains.
>
> The spring's superb adventure calls
> His dust athwart the woods to flame;
> His boundary river's secret falls
> Perpetuate and repeat his name,
>   He rides his loud October sky:
>   He does not die. He does not die.

MAURICE BARING

In the Shadow of the Chesterbelloc

T HE TWO GIANTS OF THE CATHOLIC LITERARY REVIVAL in the first
third of the twentieth century were, without doubt, G. K. Chesterton and Hilaire Belloc. They were seen so synonymously in the
eyes of the reading public that they were the butt of the caricaturist's
humor and the satirist's wit. Max Beerbohm, a friend of both men,
drew a famous caricature depicting Belloc and Chesterton seated at a
table, each holding a tankard of foaming beer, with the former lecturing the latter on "the errors of Geneva". George Orwell, in the
satirical attack on the literati in the opening chapter of his novel *Keep
the Aspidistra Flying*, went one step further than other humorists by
bestowing an honorary ordination on the Chesterbelloc, describing
"Father Hilaire Chestnut's latest book of R.C. propaganda".

The literary legend surrounding the figure of the Chesterbelloc has
cast such a long and enduring shadow that the less-known figure of
Maurice Baring has been almost eclipsed by it. This is unfortunate
and unjust. As a man of letters, and as a man of faith, Baring deserves
to emerge from the shadow of his two illustrious friends. He deserves,
in fact, to take his place beside them as he did in the famous painting
The Conversation Piece by Sir James Gunn. This large group portrait,
now displayed in London's National Portrait Gallery, depicts Baring,
Belloc and Chesterton assembled around a table. The three literary
figures, whom Chesterton, with characteristic humor, labeled "Baring, over-bearing and past-bearing", represented more than a mere
assemblage of friends. By the 1920s, after Baring had established a
reputation as a Catholic novelist, he was seen in the eyes of the read-

ing public as the third person, alongside Belloc and Chesterton, in a
Catholic literary trinity. Sharing not only a common friendship, but a
common philosophy and a common faith, Baring, Belloc and Chesterton might not have been as indivisible as the Holy Trinity, but they
were certainly seen by many as being as indomitable as the Three
Musketeers.

Baring was born in 1874, the same year as Chesterton and four
years after Belloc. A younger son of the first Lord Revelstoke, and an
heir to the Baring international banking dynasty, he enjoyed all the
trappings of privilege. As a child, he was looked after by a succession
of nannies and governesses in the sprawling opulence of England's great
country houses or in the dignified splendor of town houses in London. His autobiography, *The Puppet Show of Memory*, evokes a world
of wealth and cultured comfort, a world furnished with servants and
characterized by a *savoir vivre* that would be beyond the reach of following generations. It is invaluable as an elegy and as a eulogy to a
dying world and as a testament to a blissfully carefree childhood.

Baring's schooldays at Eton are also remembered in *The Puppet Show
of Memory* and are re-created atmospherically in his novel *Friday's Business*. From Eton he went to Hildesheim, near Hanover, to learn German, adding to the French he had learned in the nursery and to the
Latin and Greek in which he had excelled at school. Later, he would
become fully conversant in Italian, Russian and the Scandinavian languages. After a period in Florence, he went to Trinity College in
Cambridge, where he first came into contact with the fashionable scepticism of the 1890s. He met Bertrand Russell, Robert Trevelyan and
other "intellectuals" who sought to convince him that he should
not go to chapel because "Christianity was exploded, a thing of the
past" and that "nobody believed in it really among the young and the
advanced".

> I remember thinking that although I was much younger in years than
> these intellectuals, and far inferior in knowledge, brains, and wits, no
> match for them in argument or in achievement, I was none the less
> older than they were in a particular kind of experience—the experi-
> ence that has nothing to do either with the mind, or with knowledge,
> and that is independent of age, but takes place in the heart, and in

which a child may be sometimes more rich than a grown-up person. I do not mean anything sentimental. I am speaking of the experience that comes from having been suddenly constrained to turn round and look at life from a different point of view. So when I heard the intellectual reason in the manner I have described, I felt for the moment an old person listening to young people. I felt young people must always have talked like that. It was not that I had then any definite religious creed. I seldom went to Chapel.

Although the "dogmatic disbelief" of these intellectuals remained "intolerable", the "religious tenets" of his own lukewarm Protestant faith were equally unsatisfactory. Eventually his insecurely held faith, the remnants of childhood, "just dropped away ... as easily as a child loses a first tooth". By the winter of 1893 he was an avowed agnostic, ceasing all church attendance and declaring to friends that he "didn't believe in a Christian faith". This was his state of heart and mind when, in 1897, he first made the acquaintance of Belloc.

Having witnessed one of Belloc's pyrotechnic displays at the Oxford Union, Baring described him as "a brilliant orator and conversationalist ... who lives by his wits". At their first meeting, Belloc confronted Baring's agnostic arguments with the uncompromising riposte that he would "most certainly go to hell". Evidently finding Belloc's dogmatic belief more tolerable than the dogmatic disbelief of Bertrand Russell's intellectual coterie in Cambridge, Baring concluded from "the first moment I saw him" that Belloc was "a remarkable man".

In spite of their differences, Belloc's and Baring's friendship was cemented by mutual respect. "I like him immensely and think him full of brilliances and delightful to be with", Baring wrote of Belloc three years later. At this stage, however, Baring did not feel tempted to succumb to the allure of Belloc's faith. When Baring's friend Reggie Balfour informed him in the autumn of 1899 that he "felt a strong desire to become a Catholic", Baring was "extremely surprised and disconcerted". Until that moment, he had only known two converts— his sister Elizabeth, who had married the Catholic Earl of Kenmare, and an undergraduate who had explained his motive merely as a need to have all or nothing. He was "amazed" that his friend should consider such a step and sought to discourage him, arguing that the Christian religion "was not so very old, and so small a strip in the illimitable series of the creeds of mankind".

Out of loyalty to his friend, or simple curiosity, or both, Baring accompanied Balfour to a Low Mass. He was pleasantly surprised. "It impressed me greatly ... One felt one was looking on at something extremely ancient. The behaviour of the congregation, and the expression on their faces impressed me too. To them it was evidently real."

Soon after their attendance at Low Mass, Balfour sent Baring an epitaph that he had come across in the church of San Gregorio in Rome.

> Here lies Robert Peckham, Englishman and Catholic, who, after England's break with the Church, left England not being able to live without the Faith and who, coming to Rome, died not being able to live without his country.

This epitaph, and its underlying tragedy, produced a marked and lasting effect on Baring's whole view of the Reformation and probably had as much to do with his eventual conversion as anything he might have discussed with Belloc. The epitaph itself would haunt him to such a degree that, thirty years later, it would reemerge as the inspiration for his novel *Robert Peckham*, which, alongside R. H. Benson's classic, *Come Rack! Come Rope!* is perhaps the finest historical novel ever written about the bloody legacy of the English Reformation.

Baring entered the diplomatic service and was posted, between 1899 and 1904, to Paris, Copenhagen and Rome. Becoming disillusioned with life as a diplomat, and simultaneously becoming enamored of Russia, its language and its people, he resigned from the diplomatic service and arrived in Saint Petersburg shortly after Christmas 1904. It was from here, in January 1906, that he had written excitedly to a friend about the books of Chesterton, particularly Chesterton's first novel, *The Napoleon of Notting Hill*, and his controversial book of essays entitled *Heretics*, stating emphatically that "I like his *ideas*".

Considering that Baring and Chesterton had both been good friends of Belloc since the turn of the century, it is perhaps surprising that they did not become acquainted with each other until 1907. Indeed, as late as March 1908, Baring was writing to Chesterton from Moscow requesting a greater intimacy in their relationship, asking whether he might "call you by your Christian name" and adding his hope that "you & I & Hilaire may meet". The slow development of their friendship was probably due principally to Baring's long absences from England, but, once formed, their affection for each other grew stronger as the years passed. Frances Chesterton was to say, many years later, that "of all her husband's friends" there was none he loved more than Maurice Baring.

It is not clear whether Chesterton's *Orthodoxy*, published on 25 September 1908, had any direct influence on Baring's conversion, but considering Baring's admiration for Chesterton's earlier works and his growing fondness for the author, it would be surprising if he had not read Chesterton's hugely influential volume in the months immediately preceding his reception into the Church on 1 February 1909.

Describing his reception as "the only action in my life which I am quite certain I have never regretted", Baring sought to elucidate the forces at work in his conversion in the admirable sonnet sequence "Vita Nuova". Divided into a chronological trinity, the first sonnet deals with the initial approach to conversion: "I found the clue I sought not, in the night, / While wandering in a pathless maze of gloom".

The second sonnet describes the act of conversion itself, the desire to linger no longer "in a separated porch" and the sudden realization that the fire was "ablaze beyond the gate". He knocked, "and swiftly came the answering word" inviting him to enter into his own estate, where "my broken soul began to mend".

> I knelt, I knew—it was too bright to see—
> The welcome of a King who was my friend.

The final sonnet centers on the hope for eternity beyond the grave, where the "tranquil harbour shines and waits".

Explaining his reasons for conversion more prosaically, he wrote that once "I came to the conclusion *inside* that life was for me divine, and that I had inside me an immortal thing in touch with an Eternal Spirit, there was no other course open to me than to become a Catholic". He told the composer Ethel Smyth, who was a close friend and confidante, that his faith was a fusion of want and need. "I feel that human life which is almost intolerable as it is, would be to me quite intol-

erable without this which is to me no narcotic but food, air, drink".
These words, so candidly self-perceptive, offer a key not only to Baring's conversion but to the motivation behind so many of his novels,
in which his stoically self-sacrificial heroes and heroines cope with the
exile of life, its trials and sufferings, with the help of the consolation
offered by their faith. "One has to *accept* sorrow for it to have any
healing power, and that is the most difficult thing in the world", says
one of the characters in his final novel, *Darby and Joan.* "When you
understand what *accepted* sorrow means, you will understand everything. It is the secret of life."

Ethel Smyth described Baring's conversion as "the crucial action of
his life", and when she had been informed of the event, she "had the
feeling that the missing piece of a complicated puzzle, or rather the
only key wherewith a given iron safe could be unlocked, had at
last been found". A similar view was held by the French writer Raymond Las Vergnas in his critical study of Chesterton, Belloc and Baring, translated into English by the Jesuit C. C. Martindale. Baring's
Christian faith was, wrote Las Vergnas, the "powerful unifying force"
responsible for "harmonising the complex tendencies" in his artistic
temperament.

Belloc, who had observed his friend's slow but steady spiritual progress
for more than a decade, greeted his conversion with jubilation. "It is
an immense thing", he wrote to Charlotte Balfour, who had herself
been received into the Church in 1904. "They are coming in like a
gathering army from all manner of directions, all manner of men each
bringing some new force: that of Maurice is his amazing accuracy of
mind which proceeds from his great virtue of truth. I am profoundly
grateful!"

Baring also brought a depth of culture that few of his generation
could equal. Although still only thirty-four years old, he had traveled
widely throughout Europe as a diplomat, journalist and man of leisure. He knew Latin, Greek, French, German, Italian, Russian and
Danish, and he was widely read in the literature of all these languages.
He was the quintessential European. As such, Belloc's words in *An
Open Letter on the Decay of Faith*, published in 1906, would have struck
Baring with a particular resonance and poignancy as he made his final
approach to the Church:

I desire you to remember that we are Europe; we are a great people. The faith is not an accident among us, nor an imposition, nor a garment; it is bone of our bone and flesh of our flesh: it is a philosophy made by and making ourselves. We have adorned, explained, enlarged it; we have given it visible form. This is the service we Europeans have done to God. In return He has made us Christians.

At the time of his reception, Baring had only scratched the surface of his own literary potential. He had written several books, most notably on his experiences in Russia, and also a translation of Leonardo da Vinci's *Thoughts on Art and Life*. He had also published, in 1906, a volume of poetry, *Sonnets and Short Poems*, which had not received the critical acclaim it deserved. Sadly, today, as in his own day, Baring's position as a poet of considerable merit continues to go largely unnoticed. Several sonnets inspired by his experience as a war correspondent during the Russo-Japanese War in 1904, particularly "The Dead Samurai to Death" and "The Dying Reservist", warrant a place in any anthology of war poetry. The place warranted is, however, seldom granted. Similarly, several sublimely beautiful sonnets inspired by his love for Russia, most notably "Harvest in Russia", and by his love for the arts, particularly his trilogy of sonnets on "Beethoven", "Mozart" and "Wagner", remain unread and completely unknown to modern readers. His poem "Candlemas", written alongside the sonnet sequence "Vita Nuova" as a commemoration and celebration of his reception into the Church, is one of the finest religious sonnets of the twentieth century.

Further books on Russia followed in the wake of his reception into the Church, along with a number of genre-defying humorous volumes, *Diminutive Dramas*, *Dead Letters* and *Lost Diaries*, in which subtle pastiche, mischievous satire and sheer farce are combined in equal measure. It was, however, as a novelist that he would finally receive the literary recognition commensurate with his superlative gifts.

Baring's career as a novelist was relatively short, commencing with the publication of *Passing By* in 1921 and ending prematurely fifteen years later with the onset of the debilitating effects of Parkinson's disease. In between he left his claim to posterity in the form of several novels of outstanding grace. *C*, published in 1924, was highly praised by the French novelist André Maurois, who wrote that no book had given him such pleasure since his reading of Tolstoy, Proust and certain novels by E. M. Forster. If anything, Baring was to enjoy greater success in France than in England. Ten of his books were translated into French, with one—*Daphne Adeane*—going through twenty-three printings in the edition of the Librairie Stock. Others were translated into Czech, Dutch, German, Hungarian, Italian, Spanish and Swedish.

Not surprisingly, Baring's greatest literary champions in England were Belloc and Chesterton. Belloc considered *Cat's Cradle*, published in 1925, "a great masterpiece ... the best story of a woman's life that I know". He also greatly admired *Robert Peckham*. "The style," Belloc wrote, "which is characteristically yours, is even better in *Robert Peckham* than in any of the other books ... Where you triumph unusually is in the exact valuation of characters which do not differ in black and white, but in every shade. You do it better in this book, I think, than in any other, even than in *Cat's Cradle* ... It seems to me to have a more permanent quality than any other ... All those who count will unite in its praise, except those who do not feel a subtle thing at the first shock."

In 1929, shortly after Baring's novel *The Coat without Seam* had been published, Chesterton wrote that he had been "much uplifted" by his friend's latest book:

> It is, as you say, extraordinary how the outer world can see everything about it except the point. It is curiously so with much of the very good Catholic work now being done in literature, especially in France. The Protestant English, who prided themselves on their common sense, seem now to be dodging about and snatching at anything except the obvious ... But there are plenty of people who will appreciate anything as good as *The Coat Without Seam*.

If Baring could rely on Belloc and Chesterton to appreciate the subtleties of grace and providence that he had sought to weave throughout the fabric of his novels, he could count on the "dogmatic disbelief" of the Bloomsbury group to miss the point entirely. Virginia Woolf dismissed what she perceived as the "superficiality" of Baring's novels. Baring's riposte to what he himself perceived to be the superficiality of such criticism was expressed plaintively in his last book, *Have You Anything to Declare?*

It is utterly futile to write about the Christian faith from the outside. A good example of this is the extremely conscientious novel by Mrs. Humphry Ward called *Helbeck of Bannisdale*. It is a study of Catholicism from the outside, and the author has taken scrupulous pains to make it accurate, detailed and exhaustive. The only drawback is that, not being able to see the matter from the inside, she misses the whole point.

If Baring felt frustrated at being misunderstood by those who were exiled in ignorance from the Faith that breathed life into his novels, he was "too moved to speak" when he learned that François Mauriac had a deep admiration for his work. "What I most admire about Baring's work", Mauriac had told the Catholic actor-writer Robert Speaight, "is the sense he gives you of the penetration of grace."

Speaight himself described *Have You Anything to Declare?* as "the best bedside book in the English language". The extensive nature of Baring's knowledge of European literature was displayed in this anthology, which was inspired by the author's imagined arrival on the banks of the Styx and his being asked by Charon to declare his literary luggage. His selection, gleaned from the literature of many of the languages in which he was conversant, displays an extraordinary catholicity of taste and reminds one of the description of a character in his novel *The Coat without Seam*: "Everything about him ... gave one the impression of centuries and hidden stores of pent-up civilisation." Baring's selection exhibited a particular love for Homer and Virgil, and a deep devotion for Dante:

> Scaling the circles of the *Paradiso*, we are conscious the whole time of an ascent not only in the quality of the substance but in that of the form. It is a long perpetual crescendo, increasing in beauty until the final consummation in the very last line. Somebody once defined an artist ... as a man who knew how to finish things. If this definition is true—and I think it is—then Dante was the greatest artist who ever lived. His final canto is the best, and it depends on and completes the beginning.

Ironically, this book of excerpts from the works of Baring's favorite authors became better known than all his other books. Such neglect of his literary achievement does both the man and his work an injustice.

In our uncivilized age, it is perhaps inevitable that Baring's star should have been eclipsed by the polluting smog of mediocrity. For as long as the light of civilization dwindles, so will the reputation of this most civilized of writers. Ultimately, however, his future position in the ranks of the great novelists of the twentieth century is ensured. As the Permanent Things reassert themselves and as civilization rises from the ashes of burned-out nihilism, so the works of Maurice Baring will enjoy their own resurrection. The facile and the fashionable will fade, and the peripheral will pass away; but Baring, or at least the best of Baring, will remain.

14

R. H. BENSON

Unsung Genius

ROBERT HUGH BENSON WAS LAUDED in his own day as one of the
leading figures in English literature, yet today he is almost completely forgotten outside Catholic circles and is sadly neglected even
among Catholics. Few stars of the literary firmament, either before or
since, have shone quite so brightly in their own time before being
eclipsed quite so inexplicably in posterity. Almost a century after his
conversion, Benson has become the unsung genius of the Catholic
literary revival.

It was not always so.

Robert Hugh Benson was born in 1871, the youngest son of E. W.
Benson, a distinguished Anglican clergyman. In 1882, when Benson
was eleven years old, his father became Archbishop of Canterbury.
Following in his father's footsteps, Benson took Anglican orders in
1894. When, two years later, his father died, he read the litany at the
funeral in Canterbury Cathedral. Everything seemed to suggest that
the son would continue to follow dutifully in the illustrious steps of
his father. Providence had, however, woven another pattern.

After a torturously conscientious self-examination, the details of which
were elucidated masterfully in his autobiographical apologia, *Confessions of a Convert*, Benson was received into the Catholic Church in
1903. His unexpected conversion caused a sensation and sent shock
waves through the Anglican establishment. No conversion since Newman's, almost sixty years earlier, had caused such controversy.

There is no doubt that the new convert belonged to a remarkable
family. Apart from his father's rise to ecclesiastical prominence as head

of the Church of England, both of Benson's brothers became leading members of the Edwardian literati. A. C. Benson, his eldest brother, was master of Magdalene College in Cambridge and built a reputation as a fine biographer, diarist and literary critic, writing acclaimed studies of Rossetti, Fitzgerald, Pater, Tennyson and Ruskin. His other brother, E. F. Benson, wrote prolifically and is best known to posterity for his satirical Mapp and Lucia novels, which have been successfully adapted for television.

The youngest Benson was not destined to live in the literary shadow of his famous brothers. On the contrary, his first novel, *The Light Invisible*, was quickly followed by a string of other novels, all of which were commercially successful. In the meantime, he was ordained in 1904, and upon his return from Rome that same year, he moved to Cambridge, where he served as a curate. Thereafter he became as popular for his preaching and his fiery oratory as he was for his novels. He was, according to Brian Masters, author of a biographical study of the three Benson brothers, "a preacher with fire in his voice": "Whenever Monsignor Hugh Benson was due to preach one could be sure the hall, no matter how big, would be sold out months in advance ... Hugh gave a *performance* in the pulpit as certainly as Sarah Bernhardt gave one on stage."

The Light Invisible was published in 1903 and written when he was in the midst of the convulsive throes of spiritual conversion. The book is awash with a veritable confusion of emotive mysticism—a confession of faith amid the confusion of doubt. Once he had gained the clarity of Catholic perception, Benson looked upon his first novel with a degree of scepticism. In 1912 he commented that its subsequent popularity appeared to be determined by the religious denomination of those who read it. It was "rather significant" that it was popular among Anglicans, whereas Catholics appreciated it to "a very much lesser degree": "most Catholics, and myself among them, think that *Richard Raynal, Solitary* is very much better written and very much more religious."

Richard Raynal, Solitary evokes with beguiling beauty the spiritual depth of English life prior to the rupture of the Reformation, as Benson seamlessly weaves the modern storyteller's art with the chivalrous charm of the Middle Ages. It succeeds, principally, as a work that conveys the medieval spirit. The reader, if he allows himself to be carried thither, will find himself transported to the early fifteenth century. He will find himself at home in Richard Raynal's England and will rejoice in the presence of the colorful character of "Master Richard" himself. At times he will be reminded of *The Little Flowers of Saint Francis*, but he will never be able to forget, nor will he wish to forget, that this is Catholic England, not Catholic Italy. He will find himself in the presence of a hermit on a God-given mission. Above all, he will find himself in the presence of holiness and will find himself at home in its presence. *Richard Raynal, Solitary* is Christian literature at its most beautiful, at once both edifying and efficacious. Its power is purgatorial. It purges. It cleanses. It makes whole. Ultimately it serves as a timely reminder that the roots of romance are in Rome.

Hilaire Belloc was so impressed by Benson's historical novels that he wrote enthusiastically of him to A. C. Benson in 1907 that it was "quite on the cards that he will be the man to write some day a book to give us some sort of idea what happened in England between 1520 and 1560." In fact, prompted by his anger and frustration at the Protestant bias of the Whig historians, Belloc would write several books of his own on this subject, including studies of key sixteenth- and seventeenth-century figures such as Wolsey, Cromwell, James I, Charles II and Cranmer. Belloc's *How the Reformation Happened*, published in 1928, was an endeavor to put the whole period into context.

Benson, however, achieved in his fiction what Belloc was striving to achieve in his nonfiction. In *Come Rack! Come Rope!*, possibly the finest of Benson's historical novels, the whole period of the Reformation is brought to blood-curdling life. With a meticulous approach to period detail, *Come Rack! Come Rope!* leaps from the page with historical realism. The reader is transported to the time of persecution in England when priests were put to a slow and tortuous death. The terror and tension of the tale grips the reader as tightly as it grips the leading characters, who courageously witness to their faith in a hostile and deadly environment. Few novels have so successfully brought the past so potently to life. This is not to say that the work is flawless. Far from it. Belloc, who for the most part was a great admirer of Benson's historical novels, complained that the description of daily life in *Come*

Rack! Come Rope! was inaccurate, resembling life in the eighteenth, not the sixteenth, century.

Perhaps the clearest evidence of Benson's genius is to be found in the ease with which he crossed literary genres. Aside from his historical romances, he was equally at home with novels with a contemporary setting, such as *The Necromancers*, a cautionary tale about the dangers of spiritualism, or with futuristic fantasies, such as *Lord of the World*. The latter novel is truly remarkable and deserves to stand beside Huxley's *Brave New World* and Orwell's *Nineteen Eighty-Four* as a classic of dystopian fiction. In fact, though Huxley's and Orwell's modern masterpieces may merit equal praise as works of literature, they are clearly inferior works of prophecy. The political dictatorships that gave Orwell's novel-nightmare an ominous potency have had their day. Today his cautionary fable serves merely as a timely reminder of what has been and what may be again if the warnings of history are not heeded. Benson's novel-nightmare, on the other hand, is coming true before our very eyes.

The world depicted in *Lord of the World* is one where creeping secularism and godless humanism have triumphed over religion and traditional morality. It is a world where philosophical relativism has triumphed over objectivity; a world where, in the name of tolerance, religious doctrine is not tolerated. It is a world where euthanasia is practiced widely and religion hardly practiced at all. The lord of this nightmare world is a benign-looking politician intent on power in the name of "peace", and intent on the destruction of religion in the name of "truth". In such a world, only a small and shrinking Church stands resolutely against the demonic "Lord of the World".

If Benson's literary output encompassed multifarious fictional themes—historical, contemporary and futuristic—he also strayed into other areas with consummate ease. His *Poems*, published posthumously, displayed a deep and dry spirituality, expressed formally in a firmly rooted, if sometimes desiccate, faith. The same deep and dry spirituality was evident in *Spiritual Letters to One of His Converts*, also published posthumously, which offers a tantalizing insight into a profound intellect. A series of sermons, preached in Rome at Easter 1913 and later published as *The Paradoxes of Catholicism*, illustrates why Benson was so popular as a public preacher, attracting large audiences wherever he spoke. Particularly remarkable is Benson's masterly *Confessions of a Convert*, which stands beside John Henry Newman's *Apologia pro Vita Sua* and Ronald Knox' *A Spiritual Aeneid* as a timeless classic in the literature of conversion.

In *A Spiritual Aeneid*, Knox confessed candidly that Benson's influence was crucial to his own conversion: "I always looked on him as the guide who had led me to Catholic truth—I did not know then that he used to pray for my conversion." The other great influence on Knox' conversion was G. K. Chesterton, and it is perhaps no surprise that Benson was a great admirer of Chesterton. Benson's biographer, the Jesuit C. C. Martindale, who was himself a convert, wrote that Benson's *Papers of a Pariah* were "noticeable" for their "Chestertonian quality": "Mr. G. K. Chesterton is never tired of telling us that we do not see what we look at—the one undiscovered planet is our Earth ... And Benson read much of Mr. Chesterton and liked him in a qualified way."

Further evidence of Chesterton's influence on Benson is provided by Benson's admiration of Chesterton's *Heretics*. "Have you read", he inquired of a correspondent in 1905, "a book by G. K. Chesterton called *Heretics*? If not, do see what you think of it. It seems to me that the spirit underneath it is splendid. He is not a Catholic, but he has the spirit ... I have not been so much moved for a long time ... He is a real mystic of an odd kind." Chesterton was not a Catholic in 1905, but *Heretics* was a first evidence that, as Benson put it, he "had the spirit".

If links of affinity with Chesterton are less than surprising, Martindale's assertion that there is a "disconcerting affinity" between Benson's *Papers of a Pariah* and Wilde's *De Profundis* are more intriguing.

> Benson had, and Wilde was resolving, so he thought, to get, that direct eye for colour, line, and texture that the Greeks possessed ... In his direct extraction of natural emotion from simple and beautiful elements, like fire and wax, as in his description of the Easter ceremonies, [Benson] reaches, sometimes, an almost word-for-word identity with Wilde.

A further affinity with Wilde could be detected in Benson's love for the theater. He was a keen theater-goer and had lectured on the theme

of the Church and the stage. In 1914 he became particularly fascinated by Chesterton's *Magic*, which was being staged on both sides of
the Atlantic. During a visit to the United States, he was regularly to
be found behind the scenes at rehearsals of the play. Benson appeared
to be at the very height of his power and popularity, and one might
have expected that he would have enjoyed considerable success as a
playwright were he to have turned his creative talents in that direction. It was not to be. Before the end of the year, his life would come
to an abrupt and unexpected end. The cause of death was pneumonia.
He was only forty-three years old.

On 20 October 1914, the morning after his death, *The Times* carried the following tribute:

> Well known as a preacher, he had a yet larger following as a novelist.
> His first book, *The Light Invisible*, was recognised at once by good judges
> as remarkable for a peculiar charm of mind and manner ... Consider-
> ing the number of novels that he wrote, the wonder is that they should
> be as good as they are ... Undoubtedly he had great gifts.

Why, one wonders, has a writer of Benson's popularity become so
eclipsed by posterity? Why has a writer possessed with such "great
gifts" failed to hold his own in the presence of lesser talent? The answer,
perhaps, can be found in his militant and uncompromising defense of
the Faith, a militancy and a lack of compromise that became strangely
suspect in the age of "ecumenism". In the decades after his death,
Benson was attacked for exhibiting "triumphalism" (as if the Church
Militant was not always mystically united to the Church Triumphant).
Even among Catholics, his energetic proselytizing and uncompromising zeal led to criticism. "Most 'cradle Catholics' and many converts
dislike those jibes at Anglicans", opined the Catholic publisher and
biographer Maisie Ward. "Moreover, along with the jibes at Anglicanism were attacks upon Catholic complacency." Why, one is tempted
to ask, is it reprehensible to criticize the complacency of the faithful—
or, more correctly, the not-so-faithful—in the context of the Great
Commandment of Christ that we should love God with all our heart,
with all our soul and with all our mind? And as for the alleged "jibes
at Anglicanism", his attitude was expressed in his autobiographical *Confessions of a Convert*, published in 1913. Toward the end of the book,

Benson asserted "that to return from the Catholic Church to the Anglican would be the exchange of certitude for doubt, of faith for agnosticism, of substance for shadow, of brilliant light for sombre gloom, of historical, worldwide fact for unhistorical, provincial theory". This is certainly strong language, especially from the pen of a son of the Archbishop of Canterbury, but does it constitute a gibe? At worst, it could be said to display a tactless candor; at best, it shows a refreshingly sincere statement of belief. "I do not know how to express myself more mildly than that," Benson continued, "though even this, no doubt, will appear a monstrous extravagance, at the least, to the sincere and whole-hearted members of the Anglican communion".

The harshness, or "triumphalism", of Benson's words is best judged within the context of his belief in the objective truth and rectitude of the teaching of the Catholic Church. This belief was expounded with eloquence in an essay on the future of Catholicism published in 1910:

> The modern thinkers take their rise, practically, from the religious upheaval of the sixteenth century ... Little by little there came into existence the view that "true religion" was that system of belief which each individual thought out for himself; and, since these individuals were not found to agree together, "Truth" finally became more and more subjective; until there was established the most characteristically modern form of thought—namely that Truth was not absolute at all, and that what was true and imperative for one was not true and imperative for another.

To illustrate his belief in the ultimate insanity of subjectivism, Benson quoted Chesterton that "the man who believes in himself most consistently, to the exclusion of cold facts, must be sought in a lunatic asylum". Benson had no doubt that this subjectivism was an anarchy of antitheses, a *reductio ad absurdum* to which the objective authority of the Church was the only solution: "To the Catholic it appears ... certain that the crumbling of all systematic authority down to that of the individual ... is the death sentence of every attempt to find religious Truth outside that infallible authority to whose charge, he believes, truth has been committed."

Are such words the product of "harshness"? Do they constitute a "jibe" against non-Catholics? Or are they, rather, the words of one who retains a refreshing sense of intellectual honesty? Are they, to echo Chesterton, the words of one who knows the difference between an argument and a quarrel? An argument, as Chesterton and Benson knew from their possession of more than a modicum of Latin, was a positive force for good, a *polishing* of perception. A quarrel, on the other hand, is a dispute that, lacking charity, can produce only enmity and, in consequence, a negation of perception. Arguments, *ipso facto*, are good and should be pursued with diligence; quarrels, *ipso facto*, are bad and are to be avoided wherever possible. And herein lies the secret of Benson's falling from favor in the age of "ecumenism". It was simply his misfortune to know the difference between an argument and a quarrel in an age that was blinded by the belief that they were synonymous.

Take "ecumenism", for instance. Benson subscribed to the view that ecumenism, ultimately, should be translated as "you-come-in-ism". Is this triumphalism? Perhaps so; but only in the sense that he desired that everyone should triumph over sin and death by entering into the fullness of Truth that Catholicism offered. Is it wrong to want what is best for others—even if it necessitates argument? Benson thought not. Perhaps, indeed, he was, and is, correct. The preference for dilution, as opposed to dilation, of the Truth has had harmful consequences. It is, in fact, only a short and dangerous step from dilution to delusion. It was, at least, a step that Benson could never be accused of taking.

15

MAISIE WARD

Concealed with a Kiss

The truth is that the modern world has a mental breakdown; much more than a moral breakdown. Things are being settled by mere associations because there is a reluctance to settle them by arguments.

G. K. Chesterton, *The Thing*

T HERE ARE SEVERAL WAYS of approaching the writing of someone else's life. The most commendable approach, and the approach that is so rarely achieved even when attempted, is to seek for perfect empathy in the pursuit of objective truth. This involves the subjugation of the self in the service of the subject and the quashing of any temptation to squeeze the subject into the ill-fitting clothes of one's own prejudices and preconceptions. In short, the biographer must be subject to his subject and not make his subject subject to him. This is far easier said than done.

If a biographer succumbs to the temptation to make his subject dance to his own tune, or to the tune of the times in which he is living, he is in danger of presenting only a marionette to the reader. His desire to control his subject becomes a barrier to the truth. At one extreme, the desire to present one's subject in the best possible light leads to hagiography, in which the biographer plays the role of a disciple paying homage to his master; at the other extreme, the desire to present one's subject in the worst possible light leads to hackiography, or the hatchet-job, in which the biographer plays the role of the supercilious high priest demanding crucifixion. There is, however, another approach, which is motivated by the desire to paint one's subject in one's own image, or in the image of the latest prevailing fad to which one currently subscribes. In this case, the biographer plays the role of Judas, betraying his subject with a kiss. None of these approaches is satisfactory. In each case, the desire of the biographer has distorted the subject. Desire has become destroyer.

Unfortunately, in *The Living of Maisie Ward*, Professor Dana Greene has opted for the last of the approaches cited above. She has succumbed to the temptation to paint her subject in the colors of her own choosing with little regard for Ward's true colors as a staunch and resolute defender of Catholic orthodoxy against modernism. She writes sympathetically of her subject, always couching her arguments in the language of praise so that the truth is concealed with a kiss. Suspicions are aroused at first perusal of the jacket notes, which bemoan the fact that in the mid-decades of the twentieth century, "very few Catholic women were able to define themselves beyond the traditional roles of wife and mother". Maisie Ward was one of these noble exceptions because she "managed to elude the powerful constraints of her upbringing to make a unique contribution to Catholicism". Since her upbringing was thoroughly Catholic and economically comfortable, one can only assume that the "powerful constraints" arose from the expectation that she should become a wife and mother, which, had she not "managed to elude" this dreadful fate, would presumably have prevented her making "a unique contribution to Catholicism". The assertion is even more puzzling since Ward seems to have accepted the traditional roles of wife and mother with dutiful complaisance and with the utmost joy.

Having demeaned the role of motherhood, the jacket notes conclude with a few biographical details about Dana Greene herself. As associate provost for faculty and professor of history at Saint Mary's College of Maryland, she is the author of five books on women and religious history. Presumably, Professor Greene is a Catholic, though her general tone throughout suggests that she is very much a disaffected one. The tone is set in her introduction, in which Ward is held up as a feminist icon in spite of the fact that the author admits that Ward was never a feminist:

When she gave voice in her writing and lecturing to the latent desire
for transformation in Catholicism, she did so as a traditional woman,
wife, and mother. While offering no feminist critique, her life would
nonetheless belie the traditional rhetoric about woman's place. To women,
the most dedicated and numerous participants in the Catholic revival,
Maisie Ward offered an example; articulate and committed, she gave
them liberty to think and act independent of clergy and with or without husbands.

Throughout her biography, Greene's feminism is combined with half-
digested Freudian and Marxian assumptions so that Maisie Ward is
explained, or explained away, in terms that Ward would have angrily
rejected. Thus, for instance, Ward's birth into a prominent and devout
Catholic family is not depicted as a blessing, but as a burden. As the
firstborn daughter of Wilfrid Ward, the well-known intellectual and
biographer, and of Josephine Hope Ward, novelist and relative of the
Duke of Norfolk, she was inhibited by "a narrow Catholic upbringing": "Unbelief was not an option for Maisie. Her experience was too
narrow, and Catholic doctrine and family culture too emotionally tena-
cious for her to reject them. Her only options were commitment or
tepidity, and Maisie was incapable of the latter."

Leaving aside the theologically dubious assumption that faith is fixed
by heredity and not by grace, freely given and freely accepted, one
wonders what Professor Greene means by "a narrow Catholic upbringing". Is she saying that Catholicism is not really catholic? Is she saying
that the world outside the Church is broader than the Mystical Body
of Christ? If so, she must realize, though she certainly doesn't admit as
much in her book, that Maisie Ward would have disagreed with her
wholeheartedly. As Ward's tireless work for the Catholic Evidence Guild
clearly demonstrates, she believed that the Church's teaching in its full
and orthodox beauty was infinitely greater and eternally more relevant than the "broad church" of modernism with its enslavement to
philosophical materialism and intellectual fashion. She would have dismissed as self-evidently absurd any suggestion that her upbringing could
have been broadened in any meaningful or beneficial sense by the
influx of non-Catholic or anti-Catholic influences. Such a suggestion
would be akin to saying that something is gained by diluting the pure
wine of truth with the stagnant water of secularism.

The antagonism toward Catholic tradition in Professor Greene's approach is betrayed by the title that she gives to the first chapter of her study. Maisie's Catholic inheritance is discussed under the title "The Ties That Bind" as though, rather than providing the roots that impart life, the Catholic faith was something from which she had a duty to escape. Indeed, there is a sense in which Greene appears to be reprimanding Ward when she writes that "Maisie admitted that she was a conformist child who obeyed the dictates of parents and culture." It is almost as though Maisie needs to confess publicly her failure to rebel.

Maisie's grandfather, William George Ward, a Tractarian and colleague of Newman, represented, according to Professor Greene, "the most conservative wing" of Roman Catholicism because he believed "that the church embodied the principles of right and truth and as such was a bulwark against the corrosive currents of modern thought." According to such criteria, every Pope since Saint Peter and all the doctors of the Church down the ages can be marginalized as members of "the most conservative wing"! Incidentally, it is interesting that "the church" is relegated to the lowercase throughout Greene's book, as indeed is "the pope", whereas "Liberal" and "Modernist" warrant aggrandizement into the uppercase. So, for instance, the paragraph that precedes the assertion that William Ward is an extremist for believing that the Church is the embodiment of truth concludes by stating that he used his position as editor of the *Dublin Review* "to forward his views on strong papal authority against Liberals such as Acton." Whether this is a deliberate literary ploy, or merely a subconscious slip of the pen, it illustrates clearly where Professor Greene's sympathies lie.

The most striking example of the author's liberal bias is displayed in her evident support for the modernists, who were condemned by Pope Saint Pius X in 1906. The intellectual contortions and distortions to which she descends in order to insinuate that Maisie's father, Wilfrid Ward, was a would-be fellow traveler with the modernists is frankly laughable—and thoroughly reprehensible in its dishonesty. Maisie's parents were both resolute in their loyalty to the teaching of the Church and were united in their condemnation of modernism, as Maisie herself demonstrated in her biographical study, *The Wilfrid*

Wards and the Transition. Similarly, Professor Greene's co-opting of Cardinal Newman into the modernist camp is tenuous beyond belief. We are told at one point that Ward's attempts to show deference to the authority of the Church while at the same time defending New-man was intellectually "untenable", as though support for Newman and support for papal authority are incompatible. Tellingly again, this discussion has "the church" and "the pope" rendered impotent in the lowercase while "Modernism" is accentuated into the full potent glory of the uppercase.

The author alludes to the importance of R. H. Benson on Maisie's intellectual and spiritual development without, apparently, knowing anything about the deeply traditional nature of Benson's spirituality or his art. The merest cursory glance at Monsignor Benson's *Spiritual Letters*, his *Poems* or his autobiographical *Confessions of a Convert* will illustrate the profoundly orthodox nature of his influence on Maisie. Similarly, Benson's novels, which Maisie most certainly would have read and which her biographer evidently has not, depict the Church as very much the embodiment of the principles of right and truth, which Professor Greene finds "most conservative".

Professor Greene is evidently embarrassed by Maisie's loyalty to the "aggressive style" of Chesterton and Belloc and is quick to point out that their "triumphalism" was "challenged" in the late 1920s by apparently more acceptable Catholic literary figures such as Christopher Dawson, E. I. Watkin and David Jones. Evidently she is unaware of the deep concerns that each of these authors expressed with regard to the impact of the new modernism on the Church in the 1960s. Dawson lamented "the pro-Lutheran utterances in the Catholic press", failing to comprehend "how they reconcile this with their liturgical principles". In 1969, in a tribute to Dawson on the occasion of his eightieth birthday, Watkin defended his friend's position:

> In too many Catholic quarters ... Dawson and his teaching have been discarded as outdated, without value or even significance for the contemporary Catholic. Some who were foremost in his welcome and in the display of their regard for his work have turned away to a religious and cultural (more truly anticultural and radically irreligious) avant-gardism.

As for David Jones, he spoke of the importance of the Greek and Latin languages and called on the leaders of the Church to guard her heritage, which was "saturated with the sacral": "It's not a matter of knowledge but of love. It's a terrible thought that the language of the West, of the Western liturgy, and inevitably the Roman chant, might become virtually extinct."

Professor Greene appears to be blissfully unaware that the modernism that she espouses was rejected by the very intellectuals whom she praises, each of whom echoed Evelyn Waugh's disdain for those "modernists who wish to give the Church the character of our own deplorable epoch". Yet she is forced to admit that Maisie Ward, along with her husband Frank Sheed, expressed grave doubts of their own about the direction in which the Church seemed to be moving in the years after the Second Vatican Council. A year after the Council, Sheed declared that "chaos is staring us in the face", citing the example of a priest in Australia who had taken a Rosary apart in the pulpit and thrown the beads into the congregation with the remark, "That's the end of that nonsense." Professor Greene's study similarly misunderstands and misinterprets Maisie's lifelong commitment to the social teaching of the Church. The rich social heritage passed down through the papal encyclicals of Leo XIII, Pius XI and John Paul II and preached through the works of Belloc, Chesterton, Father McNabb, Eric Gill and others is lost on Professor Greene, who seems to be able to see political ideologies solely in the myopically stale formulae of "Left" and "Right".

There are a few redeeming features in *The Living of Maisie Ward*, but they are overshadowed and eclipsed by its shortcomings. There is no getting away from the fact that Professor Greene has written a muddled account of a life enlightened by the clarity of orthodox doctrine. Maisie Ward once referred to the Catholic intellectual revival, of which she was a small but significant part, as the "antidote" to modernism. As such, the "antidote" to Professor Greene's study is to be found in Maisie Ward's own works. If *The Living of Maisie Ward* prompts any of its readers to return to Maisie Ward's books, it will have provided the antidote to its own poison.

Apart from her best-selling life of Chesterton, Maisie Ward's finest book was her two-volume family history, *The Wilfrid Wards and the*

Transition. The second volume, published in 1987, was entitled *Insurrection versus Resurrection*. This work dealt with the "insurrection" of the modernist and the "resurrection" of the Church. It is, therefore, more than a little perverse that Maisie's life should be retold and "defended" in the language of the insurrection that she condemned and not the resurrection that she preached. She has been betrayed with a kiss.

16

JOHN SEYMOUR

Some Novel Common Sense

I F THE CHESTERBELLOCIAN CREED of distributism is still alive as our misguided world begins the third millennium, it has as much to do with John Seymour as with any other person. In the last third of the twentieth century, only E. F. Schumacher, author of the neodistributist classic *Small Is Beautiful*, has done as much as John Seymour to propagate Chesterton's "outline of sanity".

Perhaps Seymour is best known for *The Complete Guide to Self-Sufficiency*, a practical approach to one aspect of distributist life that has sold more than 650,000 copies in Britain alone. Since its first publication more than a quarter of a century ago, this book has inspired countless people to "drop in" to an improved quality of life.

In a recent interview in *Country Living* magazine, Seymour made it clear that he disliked being referred to as a "guru", but I hope he will forgive me if I say that he was, in my case, not so much a guru as a mentor. Along with Chesterton and Belloc, he was a beacon of common sense that enabled me to grope my way toward a clearer understanding of society's ills. Indeed, the key books in my own progress, sociopolitically speaking, were Chesterton's *The Outline of Sanity*, Belloc's *Essay on the Restoration of Property* and *The Servile State* and Seymour's *Bring Me My Bow*. All these books left an indelible mark.

There is, however, one notable difference that sets Seymour apart from my other two mentors. Unlike the two halves of the Chesterbelloc, he is still alive. Whereas I cannot hope to meet Chesterton or Belloc in the flesh, at least not while I am marooned this side of the grave, I still live in hope of meeting Seymour, hopefully on his farm in Ireland over several pints of his home brew! (Now there's a vision almost as celestial in its beauty as a meeting with GKC beyond the grave—well, almost!) In any case, although I have not met Seymour yet, I have corresponded with him on several occasions and can confirm that he is a great admirer of both Chesterton and Belloc and the distributism that they espoused. As a young man, however, he had admired H. G. Wells and was even a member of the H. G. Wells Society. Yet, as he put it, "Long before Wells had reached the end of his tether I had reached the end of mine." It was then that he began to perceive the distributist alternative to Wells' technolatry.

I mention all this as a preamble to Seymour's *Retrieved from the Future*, which is, I believe, his first foray into fiction. In its pages one sees the distant shadow of Wells in the fact that the novel is set in the future, but although the form is Wellsian, the substance is decidedly Chestertonian. It is a cautionary tale of the collapse of consumerism and the emergence of distributism in its wake. Yet it is not a tale of Orwellian gloom but of Chestertonian rambunctiousness filled to the brim with characters spilling over with Bellocian bombast. Certainly one could make many technical criticisms, but it is enough that this novel exudes common sense to a world in dire need of more of the same.

In this age of pulp fiction, to speak of a modern novel exuding common sense sounds so incongruous that it almost has a ring of Chestertonian paradox about it. So be it. I love Chestertonian paradox, and I enjoyed this novel.

PART THREE

THE WASTELAND

17

ENTRENCHED PASSION

The Poetry of War

IN THE SPHERE OF LITERATURE, the modern world has precious little to teach the Middle Ages. It is, therefore, refreshing to find that, in the sphere of war poetry at least, the twentieth century has something of real value to offer. It has something to say of enduring value. In fact, it has something to say that has seldom been said as evocatively in any of the preceding centuries. In the poetry of war, if in very little else, the twentieth century has a place of honor.

In days of yore, the poetry of war was punctuated with pomp and pomposity and executed with the excitement and exhilaration of battle. We hear in the Norse sagas how King Harald Sigurdsson's "war-seasoned heart never wavered in battle".

> Norway's warriors were watching
> The blood-dripping sword
> Of their courageous leader
> Cutting down their enemies.

Similarly, the *Orkneyinga Saga* recounts with relish the blood spilled at the battle of the Menai Strait.

> On shields the arrow-storm
> Spattered; as men fell,
> deftly the lord of Hordar
> dealt the Earl's death-blow.

The bloodlust of the Viking versifiers was shared by the poets of England. Michael Drayton's triumphal depiction of the English victory over the French at the battle of Agincourt glories unashamedly in the gore of battle. Shakespeare, in *King Henry V*, also waxes lyrical over the English victory at Agincourt, though with greater subtlety than Drayton. Before the battle, the king tells his outnumbered troops that they are destined for immortality.

> This story shall the good man teach his son;
> And Crispin Crispian shall ne'er go by,
> From this day to the ending of the world,
> But we in it shall be remembered—
> We few, we happy few, we band of brothers;
> For he to-day that sheds his blood with me
> Shall be my brother.

Great military blunders could be made as glorious as great military victories. Tennyson immortalized the disastrous Charge of the Light Brigade during the battle of Balaclava in the Crimean War with a eulogistic elegance that turns the blunder to wonder. With a graceful flourish of his pen, mightier by far than the sword, Tennyson makes the blood of the butchered glow as gloriously as that of the martyrs.

> Not tho' the soldier knew
> Some one had blundered:
> Theirs' not to make reply,
> Theirs' not to reason why,
> Theirs' but to do and die:
> Into the valley of Death
> Rode the six hundred.

By the twentieth century, attitudes to war had changed. Rupert Brooke's "The Soldier", written shortly before the poet's death in 1915, was the last glorious swan song of the poetry of War Glorified.

> If I should die, think only this of me:
> That there's some corner of a foreign field
> That is for ever England.

Attitudes to war had changed because war itself had changed. No longer was war a trial of strength between man and man but between man and machine, or even, and increasingly, between machine and machine—with man in the middle. There was nothing glorious about going "over the top" to certain death in a hail of machine-gun fire; nothing glorious about poison gas or barbed wire; nothing glorious about trench fever or dysentery. War was no longer about warriors but about killing machines and killing fields. War was now about machine as victor and man as victim. Fate and fatality had been replaced by fatuous futility.

Under the new conditions of modern warfare, the weapons of the warrior were as redundant as the warrior himself. Swords, sabers, scimitars and shields would gather dust or turn to rust. Now, more than ever, the pen was indeed mightier than the sword. From the filth and futility of the First World War emerged a generation of poets more potent than their predecessors in expressing the grim realities of warfare. Two, in particular, emerged phoenix-like from the ashes of the conflict. Siegfried Sassoon and Wilfred Owen wrote with a realism that shocked and shamed their compatriots out of their indifference to the suffering of the trenches. Sassoon's "Fight to a Finish", "The General" and "Golgotha", and Owen's "Spring Offensive", "Exposure" and "Dulce et Decorum Est" changed the public's perception of the war. In Germany, the grim power of Otto Dix' gruesome paintings, depicting limbless victims condemned to a postwar life of squalor, confronted and still confront the complacency of the voyeuristic noncombatant. In the Second World War, Solzhenitsyn's disturbing poem "Prussian Nights", with its ruthlessly unremitting realism, its depiction of mass rape, arson and murder, stands as a morbid monument to the terrors of Stalinism and to the inhumanity of the Soviet regime.

Wilfrid Owen and Rupert Brooke never survived the war. Sassoon and Solzhenitsyn not only survived but surfaced from their sufferings resurgent in spirit. In both men, the suffering of war prefigured the resurrection of the spirit and the peace it heralds. In their conversion to orthodox Christianity, Sassoon and Solzhenitsyn are witnesses to the greater Peace that war can never destroy.

18

WAR POETS

Cutting through the Cant

F OR THOSE WHO FEEL ACUTELY the stultifying staleness of so much
modern literary criticism, Bernard Bergonzi's new book will arrive
as a breath of fresh air. Its title, though strictly accurate, tells only half
the story—less than half. The war poets are the subject of only a third
of the essays in the book so that the "other subjects" predominate.
War Poets and Other Subjects is divided into three distinct parts: "Writers and War", "Modern Masters" and "Catholics". In each section,
Professor Bergonzi, professor emeritus of English at the University of
Warwick, exhibits a masterful control of his subject and an ability to
cut through the cant of modern literary fads with a firm but gentle
touch. He is never clumsy or heavy-handed and always gives those he
criticizes a fair hearing. The subtle dexterity may cause some to feel
that he suffers fools a little too gladly. He does not.

Bergonzi's ability to fathom folly is most apparent in the first section of the book. His dissection of Pat Barker's *Regeneration Trilogy*, a
quasi-fictional account of Siegfried Sassoon's friendship with Wilfred
Owen, culminates in a complaint that Barker's approach is marred by
her lack of concern for historical truth. He reads it with "admiration
but also with unease". She is more concerned with placing her historical figures in straitjackets constructed out of certain modern
preoccupations—"gender roles . . . feminism, psychotherapy, false memory syndrome, the sexual abuse of children". Bergonzi's unease with
historical inaccuracy resurfaces in an essay entitled "The Great War
and Modern Criticism" in which he questions the assumption that
nationalism was a nineteenth-century invention. He alludes to the

aggressive patriotism of the eighteenth century, the Englishness of Shakespeare's history plays, and Michael Drayton's *Battle of Agincourt*. He could, of course, have mentioned the battle of Agincourt itself and the nationalist mythology that grew up in its wake, or similar nationalist myths in Scotland, Ireland, Wales and countless other nations, all of which predate nineteenth-century "capitalism" by many centuries. In the same essay, he exposes the critic Adrian Caesar for the transparent shallowness of his approach, complaining that "he seems to be located beyond absolute pacifism, in a perspective where suffering has no place of any kind". In contrast, Bergonzi praises Douglas Kerr for drawing parallels between Owen's poetry and Dante's *Inferno*, highlighting the perennial relevance of their respective approaches to the psychology of suffering.

The section on "Modern Masters" includes a discussion of Anthony West's book about his parents, H. G. Wells and Rebecca West. The son's bitterness toward the selfishness of his parents, particularly that of his mother, had created a love-hate triangle from which the son was powerless to escape. Other "modern masters" discussed include Aldus Huxley, George Orwell and, most notably, T. S. Eliot.

The section on Catholics features two superb essays on Gerard Manley Hopkins, an essay on Chesterton and, bravest of all, an attempt to get to grips with David Jones' complex and often contradictory idea of art. Particularly enjoyable is an essay on "The Other Mrs. Ward". Bergonzi's treatment of Mrs. Wilfrid Ward's almost forgotten novel, *One Poor Scruple*, is a poignant reminder of the neglected gems of the Catholic literary revival. I was left wishing that Bergonzi would turn his attention to the novels of R. H. Benson or Maurice Baring or to the deeper spiritual verse, as opposed to the satire, of Roy Campbell.

Unfortunately, the book ends on something of an anticlimactic note. The last two essays focus on Graham Greene and David Lodge, the first of whom described himself as a "Catholic agnostic" while the second prefers to be known as an "agnostic Catholic". Bergonzi prefers to overlook these contradictions posing as paradoxes. In consequence, these essays lack the incisiveness that is so present in the rest of the book. But ultimately, *War Poets and Other Subjects* confirms Bergonzi's place at the forefront of literary criticism.

19

SIEGFRIED SASSOON

Poetic Pilgrimage

S IEGFRIED SASSOON is *arguably* the greatest of the War Poets. Arguably, but not indisputably. Many critics, begging to differ with such
a judgment, would argue that Sassoon's friend, Wilfred Owen, was
more gifted and could boast a superior achievement in verse. Yet, if
they are right, Sassoon becomes, if not the greatest, then certainly the
most important of the War Poets. Sassoon was Owen's mentor, without whom Owen would probably have never written the acerbically
assonant verse for which both men are celebrated. Furthermore, it
was Sassoon who edited Owen's poems, following the latter's death,
introducing the public to his verse. Without Sassoon there would not
have been an Owen.

Owen was killed in action on the western front in 1918, one of the
final victims of the dying embers of the First World War. As such, he
remains cocooned in the incorruptible image of eternal youth, a slaughtered lamb, butchered before his gifts could develop. Sassoon, on the
other hand, lived to a ripe old age, growing ever closer to Christ and
His Church. His life, and the poetry that was its expression, would be
one long and contemplative search for truth, a poet's pilgrimage.

Sassoon enjoyed, or rather endured, a controversially meteoric and
mixed military career, his war service making him both famous and
infamous, hero and villain. In June 1916 he was very much the hero,
being awarded the Military Cross for gallantry in battle after he had
brought in under heavy fire a wounded lance corporal who was
lying close to the German lines. This and other acts of bravery earned
him the nickname of "Mad Jack". Robert Graves, a fellow officer in

the Royal Welch Fusiliers who would himself become a poet and novelist of some distinction, remembered Sassoon calmly reading a newspaper shortly before going "over the top" during the crucial attack at
Fricourt. In 1917, after capturing some German trenches in the Hindenburg Line single-handedly, he remained in the enemy position reading a volume of poems, seemingly oblivious of the danger. This particular
act of cavalier gallantry earned him a recommendation for the Victoria Cross, the highest honor attainable in the British army.

Having been wounded in the fighting on the Hindenburg Line,
Sassoon was invalided home. It was then that he began to reflect upon
the human butchery he had witnessed, endured and inflicted. From
these moments of reflection the hero hatched the villain. The perfect
soldier became the pacifist rebel. "Siegfried's unconquerable idealism
changed direction with his environment", wrote Robert Graves. "He
varied between happy warrior and bitter pacifist."

In July 1917 his "Soldier's Declaration", addressed ostensibly to his
commanding officer but published or quoted in several newspapers,
gained him notoriety. It was made "as an act of wilful defiance of
military authority" and attacked those in power who were willfully
prolonging "the sufferings of the troops ... for ends which I believe
to be evil and unjust." He also complained about "the callous complaisance with which the majority of those at home regard the con-
tinuance of the agonies which they do not share and have not sufficient
imagination to realise".

Sassoon's contempt for his commanding officers, expressed prosaically in his declaration, would be exemplified poetically in verses such
as "Base Details" and "The General", whereas his anger at the jingoism of politicians and the press would be captured bitterly in "Fight to
a Finish". His plaintive reaction against the "callous complaisance" of
"those at home" was immortalized with gruesome realism in "Glory
of Women".

In a further gesture of defiance, Sassoon threw his Military Cross
into the River Mersey, and his notoriety reached new heights when
his declaration was read in the House of Commons. Many expected
that such open acts of rebellion would lead to Sassoon's court-martial,
but in true Orwellian fashion, he was declared mentally overwrought
and not responsible for his actions. He was sent to Craiglockhart military

hospital in Edinburgh to be treated for psychological shell shock. It was here that he met and befriended Wilfred Owen.

In the midst of Sassoon's lurid descriptions of the "base details" of war was an intrepid introspection that saw Golgotha amid the hell. Religious imagery, albeit sometimes overlaid with the irony of anger, is discernible in much of his war poetry and detectable in the very titles of many of the poems. "Absolution", "Golgotha", "The Redeemer" and "Stand-To: Good Friday Morning" all testify to a soul haunted by Christ even when the spirit was spurned. The spirit was most apparent in "Reconciliation", a poem written in November 1918, the month the war finally ended. In only eight intensively potent lines, Sassoon asks his compatriots, even as they mourn their own dead, to remember the German soldiers who were killed.

> In that Golgotha perhaps you'll find
> The mothers of the men who killed your son.

With the war ended, Sassoon, like many of his contemporaries, found himself lost in, and alienated by, the nihilistic no-man's land, or Eliotic "wasteland", of postwar England. Apart from the solace sought in the writing of his own verse, Sassoon gained consolation in the poetry of others. He defended the provocative modernity of Edith Sitwell, writing an article defending her work in the *Daily Herald* under the combative title "Too Fantastic for Fat-Heads". He also found solace in music, defending the provocative modernity of Stravinsky in one of his finest poems, "Concert-Interpretation", in which the Russian composer's controversial *Le sacre du printemps* inspires the English poet to muse with ambient ambivalence that the "polyphony through dissonance" of Stravinksy's work reminds him of a "serpent-conscious Eden, crude but pleasant". A different spirit pervades "Sheldonian Soliloquy", possibly Sassoon's best known postwar poem, in which his feelings of elation during a recital of Bach's Mass in B Minor are expressed with delightful and cathartic whimsy.

> *Hosanna in excelsis* chants the choir
> In pious contrapuntal jubilee.
> *Hosanna* shrill the birds in sunset fire.
> And Benedictus sings my heart to Me.

Written in 1922, there is in "Sheldonian Soliloquy", as in many of his war poems, a tantalizing glimpse of an embryonic Christianity that would have a further thirty-five-year gestation period. In the interim, Sassoon became as respected for his prose as for his poetry. His semi-fictitious autobiography, *The Complete Memoirs of George Sherston*, published in 1937, was begun with *Memoirs of a Fox-Hunting Man* in 1928, continued with *Memoirs of an Infantry Officer* in 1930 and concluded with *Sherston's Progress* in 1936. Truly autobiographical works followed. *The Old Century* was published in 1938, *The Weald of Youth* in 1942 and *Siegfried's Journey 1916–20* in 1945.

Neither the "journey" of Siegfried nor the "progress" of Sherston ended in 1945, the year in which the last of his autobiographical works of prose was published. On the contrary, the ending of the Second World War marked a new beginning for the poet. In spite of the success of the prose volumes, the most profound autobiography of the poet was to be found in his poems. Arranged chronologically, they offer an impressionistic picture of a heart's journey toward God and that heart's progress through the trials and tribulations of life.

The dropping of the atomic bomb on Hiroshima inspired Sassoon to the same heights of horrified creativity as had inspired Sitwell in the composition of her "three poems of the Atomic Age". Sassoon's "Litany of the Lost" employed resonant religious imagery as a counterpoint to the postwar pessimism and alienation engendered by the descent from world war to cold war. As with the previous war, the world had emerged from the nightmare of conflict into the desert of despair, transforming "wasteland" to nuclear waste.

The ending of the second of the century's global conflagrations marked the beginning of Sassoon's final approach to the Catholic faith. Influenced to a degree by Catholic friends such as Ronald Knox and Hilaire Belloc, but to a far greater degree by the experience of his own life, Sassoon was received into the Church in September 1957, shortly after his seventy-first birthday. After a lifetime of mystical searching, he had finally found his way Home.

During his first Lent as a Catholic, Sassoon wrote "Lenten Illuminations", a candid account of his conversion that invites obvious comparisons with T. S. Eliot's "Ash Wednesday". The last decade of his life, like the last decades of the Rosary he came to love, was a quiet meditation on the glorious mysteries of faith. As ever, his meditations were expressed in memorable verse, particularly in the peaceful mysticism of "A Prayer at Pentecost", "Arbor Vitae" and "A Prayer in Old Age".

In 1960 Sassoon selected thirty of his poems for a volume entitled *The Path to Peace*, which was essentially an autobiography in verse. From the earliest sonnets of his youth to the religious poetry of his last years, Sassoon's intensely personal and introspective verse offered a sublime reflection of a life's journey in pursuit of truth. These, and not his diaries, his letters or his prose, are the precious jewels of enlightenment that point to the soul within the man.

20

EMERGING FROM THE WASTELAND

The Cultural Reaction to the Desert of Modernity

M UCH OF WHAT COULD BE CALLED "Old Europe" was killed off by the First World War. I am aware that, to a degree, this is an oversimplification. If Hilaire Belloc's assertion that "Europe is the Faith, and the Faith is Europe" is to be taken seriously, and I think that it should be, much of Old Europe was killed off by the Reformation four hundred years earlier. (Incidentally, Belloc was not suggesting in this statement that the Faith was *only* European—indeed, he publicly and stringently denied that he had meant this when someone suggested that this had been his meaning. He meant that Europe, properly understood, was *only* the Faith—in the sense that the concept of Europe was bound up with the concept of Christendom. Take away Christendom as the unifying principle and the whole edifice of Europe begins to crumble.) If this is so, and as I have said, I believe that it is, Europe has been crumbling since the heresies of Luther and Calvin undermined its unifying principle.

This is the theme of Chesterton's epic poem, "Lepanto", written in 1912, two years before the start of the First World War. Europe in the sixteenth century is being overwhelmed by Protestant heresy and undermined by late-Renaissance decadence. This poison from within is being exacerbated by the Muslim threat from without. A weakened Europe is in danger of being overthrown by a resurgent Islam. (The more things change, the more they remain the same!)

They have dared the white republics up the capes of Italy,
They have dashed the Adriatic round the Lion of the Sea,

And the Pope has cast his arms abroad for agony and loss,
And called the kings of Christendom for swords about the Cross,
The cold queen of England is looking in the glass;
The shadow of the Valois is yawning at the Mass;
From evening isles fantastical rings faint the Spanish gun,
And the Lord upon the Golden Horn is laughing in the sun.

. . .

The North is full of tangled things and texts and aching eyes
And dead is all the innocence of anger and surprise,
And Christian killeth Christian in a narrow dusty room,
And Christian dreadeth Christ that hath a newer face of doom,
And Christian hateth Mary that God kissed in Galilee,
But Don John of Austria is riding to the sea.

. . .

King Philip's in his closet with the Fleece about his neck
(Don John of Austria is armed upon the deck.)
The walls are hung with velvet that is black and soft as sin,
And little dwarfs creep out of it and little dwarfs creep in.
He holds a crystal phial that has colours like the moon,
He touches and it tingles, and he trembles very soon,
And his face is as a fungus of a leprous white and grey
Like plants in the high houses that are shuttered from the day,
And death is in the phial and the end of noble work,
But Don John of Austria has fired upon the Turk.

The poem concludes thus:

> *Vivat Hispania!*
> *Domino Gloria!*
> Don John of Austria
> Has set his people free!

Cervantes on his galley sets the sword back in the sheath
(Don John of Austria rides homeward with a wreath.)
And he sees across a weary land a straggling road in Spain,
Up which a lean and foolish knight forever rides in vain,
And he smiles, but not as Sultans smile, and settles back the blade . . .
(But Don John of Austria rides home from the Crusade.)

Chesterton's concluding lines are curious. As a climax they are curiously anticlimactic. Why is this? Historically speaking, Miguel Cervantes fought at Lepanto and was severely wounded in his chest and arm during the battle. This is the fact of the matter. Chesterton, however, is using the fact only as a launchpad to the truth it represents. "Not facts first, truth first" was one of Chesterton's maxims. What, then, is the truth that Chesterton is trying to convey? He is telling us that the Christian victory at Lepanto in 1571 saved European civilization and European culture from destruction. An Islamic victory would have meant the destruction of Christendom—the Europe of the Faith—and all that it represents. In short, if Don John of Austria had not set his people free, Cervantes would never have written *Don Quixote*. And here *Don Quixote* is a symbol of all the Christian culture that followed: Shakespeare, Calderon de la Barca, Manzoni, Newman, Hopkins, Eliot, Tolkien—yes, even Chesterton himself!

Although Chesterton's poem is about a battle fought in the sixteenth century, it is awash with cultural references to his own time. The battle for Christendom—for orthodoxy—was still being fought; the war against the heretics was still being waged. It was indeed no surprise that Chesterton had written books entitled *Orthodoxy* and *Heretics* a few years before writing "Lepanto". Also, the allusions to Decadence in the poem were very close to home. Chesterton had grown to maturity in the fungoid atmosphere of the *fin de siècle*. Much of his work in the first decade of the twentieth century was, in fact, a reaction against the Decadence of the previous decade. In fact, the ennui, pessimism and cynicism of the 1890s had been replaced in the years from 1900 to 1914 by an overriding sense of excitement, optimism and romance. Decadence had been exorcised by a resurrected sense of the adventure of life.

On the one hand, you had the counter-Decadent defiance of the dynamic orthodoxy propounded by Chesterton and Belloc—the excitement of a Crusade, the optimism of the *vita nuova* and the sheer romance of Rome. On the other hand, you had the counter-Decadent superciliousness of the dynamite idealism expounded by Shaw and Wells—the excitement of Socialism, the optimism of the New Age and the sheer romance of Revolution. Pilgrims or "Progress"—that was the question; Pilgrims or "Progress"—that was the choice. This almost

universal sense of optimism would be blown apart by the utter carnage of the First World War, leaving only a wasteland of shattered
dreams and broken images.

The world entered the war with jingoistic optimism, besotted with
the ideal of heroism. These early months of the war have been called
the "Rupert Brooke period" after the poet of that name who marched
to his death in 1915 having left as an epitaph to himself the haunting
lines of his poem "The Soldier":

> If I should die, think only this of me:
>   That there's some corner of a foreign field
>   That is for ever England.

Soon, however, after the war had become bogged down in the
entrenched nightmare of no-man's-land, and after the combatants had
been butchered, or had witnessed their comrades being butchered, in
battle after endless battle, the jingoistic optimism began to make way
for the jungles of despair. In Germany, the horrifically graphic depiction of hideously deformed and limbless war veterans by the artist
Otto Dix encapsulated the despair and desolation of that nation's defeated
army. The angst and anger of postwar Germany, captured so luridly
on canvas by Dix, was the breeding ground of the hatred that festers
and fosters revolution. The result was the rise of a certain Adolf Hitler.

So much for the Weimar Wasteland.

In England the artistic reaction against what Tolkien called the "animal horror" of the war was most graphically expressed not on canvas
(though C. R. W. Nevinson and John Singer Sargent produced some
gruesomely realistic paintings) but in poetry. In particular, the poetry
of Siegfried Sassoon and Wilfred Owen conveyed the growing sense
of disillusionment and resentment. This was the poetry of protest, and
Sassoon and Owen were pulling no punches.

In Sassoon's bitter verse invective "Fight to a Finish", the poet dreams
luridly of a Revolution of Revenge in which the returning troops
would turn their guns and bayonets on the politicians and the press.
Such a revolution would never materialize in England, although of
course it became all too real in Russia, where the Bolshevik Revolution of 1917 heralded seventy years of Marxist wasteland. Fueled with

the fading dreams of the French Revolution and inflamed with the passions aroused by the bloodbath of the war, the Russians took the elusive and illusory vision of *liberté, égalité et fraternité* and turned it into the three steps on the path toward their own enslavement, the three steps—or perhaps that should be steppes—toward the Gulag Archipelago from which Solzhenitsyn would emerge like a phoenix from the ashes. In Germany the Revolution of Revenge would take the form of the seeking of a scapegoat on which to enact the revenge: in Russia, the wasteland of the Gulag Archipelago; in Germany, the wasteland of Auschwitz and Dachau. Never in the long and bloody field of human history had there been an Inquisition as diabolical as the KGB or the Gestapo. Oh, how the gurus of modernity, Hegel, Marx and Nietzsche, had ushered in a brave new world of mass murder and genocide!

So much for the Revolution of Revenge and the wasteland that followed in its wake. England would not follow such a path, though she would emerge into her own more insipid wasteland.

Let's return to England ...

Having heard Sassoon's poetry of protest, let's now turn to the poetry of his friend and comrade in arms, Wilfred Owen. Perhaps Owen's best-known—and perhaps indeed his best—poem is "Dulce et Decorum Est". Describing how from behind the safety of his gas mask he had watched another soldier "drowning" in the "green sea" of gas, the poet concludes in plaintive rage:

> If in some smothering dreams you too could pace
> Behind the wagon that we flung him in,
> And watch the white eyes writhing in his face,
> His hanging face, like a devil's sick of sin;
> If you could hear, at every jolt, the blood
> Come gargling from the froth-corrupted lungs,
> Obscene as cancer, bitter as the cud
> Of vile, incurable sores on innocent tongues,—
> My friend, you would not tell with such high zest
> To children ardent for some desperate glory,
> The old Lie: Dulce et decorum est
> Pro patria mori.

Does one not sense that the bitter conclusion of Owen's poem is a deliberate riposte to the naïve jingoism of Rupert Brooke's rosy portrait of the dignity of heroism, written at the beginning of the war before its full "animal horror" was known? Rupert Brooke was killed in 1915 and was laid to rest in some corner of a foreign field that is, presumably, "forever England". Owen would be killed in the last few days of the war and, in consequence, was not part of the "music of returning feet" of those "who'd refrained from dying" of whom Sassoon had written.

Belloc lost a son in the war, and Chesterton lost his beloved brother. Such was the collective desolation, if not despair, that gripped England in the wake of the war that even the usually upbeat and optimistic Chesterton, mourning his brother, descended to the level of the protest poem. A year or so after the war's end, Chesterton poured forth his anger in his "Elegy in a Country Churchyard", the very title of which conveyed a bitterly ironic allusion to the peaceful tranquility of Thomas Gray's eighteenth-century poem of the same name.

> The men that worked for England
> They have their graves at home:
> And bees and birds of England
> About the cross can roam.
>
> But they that fought for England,
> Following a falling star,
> Alas, alas for England
> They have their graves afar.
>
> And they that rule in England,
> In stately conclave met,
> Alas, alas for England
> They have no graves as yet.

Chesterton, like Belloc, had been a jingoistic supporter of the war at its outset; by its end, he was singing the same tune as Owen and Sassoon.

It was in this death-laden and doom-laden atmosphere that T. S. Eliot emerged as the voice of what became known as the Wasteland generation.

Eliot's poem *The Waste Land*, published in 1922, four years after the war had ended, is probably the most influential and controversial poem of the twentieth century. Its appearance was at once a revelation and a revolution, polarizing opinion. It bemused and beguiled its admirers and irritated and infuriated its detractors. The avant-garde gazed in awe at its many layers; the old guard claimed that the layers were an illusion and that the emperor had no clothes. The pessimism of its language and the libertine nature of its form both added to the controversy. The war of the Waste Land was joined.

Almost half a century later, the obituary to Eliot in *The Times* perceived the heated reaction to the poem with a detached perspective that few at the time, caught in the heat of the fray, could achieve:

> Its presentation of disillusionment and the disintegration of values, catching the mood of the time, made it the poetic gospel of the post-war intelligentsia: at the time, however, few either of its detractors or its admirers saw through the surface innovations and the language of despair to the deep respect for tradition and the keen moral sense which underlay them.

It is certainly true that few, at the time, understood Eliot's purpose in writing *The Waste Land*. Lack of understanding led to misunderstanding so that battle lines were drawn according to erroneous preconceptions. On the one side, the "moderns" hailed it as a masterpiece of modern thought that had laid waste traditional values and traditional form. On the other side, the "ancients" attacked it as an iconoclastic affront to civilized standards. Both sides had made the grave and fundamental error of mistaking Eliot's pessimism toward the wasteland of modern life for a cynicism toward tradition. In fact, the philosophical foundations of Eliot's thought were rooted in classical tradition and found expression in a deep disdain for modern secular liberalism and the heedless hedonism that was its inevitable consequence.

The real key to understanding Eliot's message in *The Waste Land*, and his motive for writing it, is to be found in his devotion to Dante. Eliot upheld the "philosophy of Aristotle strained through the schools", that is, strained, particularly, through the thought of Saint Thomas Aquinas, and Dante was, of course, the poetic master of the Thomist school. Scarcely two years before *The Waste Land* was published, Eliot had written:

> You cannot ... understand the *Inferno* without the *Purgatorio* and the *Paradiso*. "Dante", says Landor's Petrarch, "is the great master of the disgusting." ... But a disgust like Dante's is not hypertrophy of a single reaction: it is completed and explained only by the last canto of the *Paradiso* ... The contemplation of the horrid or sordid or disgusting, by an artist, is the necessary and negative aspect of the impulse toward the pursuit of beauty.

The fact is that modernity is more at home in hell than in Purgatory and paradise. It is where it wants to be. It is where it has condemned itself to be by its perverse desire. As post-Reformation puritanism had stressed the punishment of hell in Dante and had ignored the "papist" parts about Purgatory and paradise, so postwar cynicism had stressed the negative aspects of Eliot's wasteland and had ignored the "impulse toward the pursuit of beauty" that had led Eliot to the positive conclusion pointing to a "resurrection". A world without faith, basking self-indulgently in its self-proclaimed futility, could understand the ugliness of the wasteland, sympathize with the souls in the inferno, see the Crucifixion and perhaps even weep for itself as the victim on the Cross; but it could not perceive the cleansing fires of Purgatory, the sanctified bliss of paradise or the glory and significance of the Resurrection. Ignited by the indignation of its own ignoble desires, it could not perceive perfection, nor the nobility that is its cultured servant.

Eliot responded to the sheer vacuity of those who could not perceive the beauty beyond the ugliness in *The Waste Land* in his next major poem, "The Hollow Men". Here, the doyens of modernity are depicted as the hollow, empty-headed inhabitants of the postwar no-man's-land: the anticultural no-man's-land in which reside the no-men who refuse the call to manhood. Thus the poem begins:

> We are the hollow men
> We are the stuffed men
> Leaning together
> Headpiece filled with straw. Alas!

It ends with a prophecy of the self-destructive doom that awaits those who dwell in the anticultural abyss of nihilistic self-indulgence:

This is the way the world ends
This is the way the world ends
This is the way the world ends
Not with a bang but a whimper.

Put simply, Eliot's poetry might have been a reaction to the "animal horror" of the war, but it was much more than that. Ultimately, it was not so much a reaction to the war as a reaction to the reaction. The destruction and desolation of the war had led to the cynicism and nihilism of the postwar generation; Eliot's depiction of the hollow men who live in the wasteland of modernity was a reaction against this abysmal slide into the nihilistic inferno.

Seen in this light, Eliot's conversion to Anglo-Catholicism is scarcely surprising. Paradoxically, he had perceived the light of heaven through a deep penetration into the light of the fires burning in the infernal soul of postwar modernity. He, at least, had no intention of ending with a whimper.

Eliot's conversion sent shock waves through the self-proclaimed avant-garde of the British literary establishment. How could the ultra-modern poet have embraced the ultratraditional creed of Catholic Christianity? It was all too much for Virginia Woolf, who greeted the news with horror. "I have had a most shameful and distressing inter-view with dear Tom Eliot," she wrote to a friend, "who may be called dead to us all from this day forward. He has become an Anglo-Catholic believer in God and immortality, and goes to church . . . There's something obscene in a living person sitting by the fire and believing in God." (It is difficult to resist the temptation to retort that it is better than sitting *in* the fire by not believing in God!)

One is tempted, in fact, to treat the comparison between T. S. Eliot and Virginia Woolf as a parable of our singularly corrupt age. Eliot is still considered suspect in modernist circles for his "reactionary" embrace of Catholicism, whereas Virginia Woolf is lionized as a "progressive" soul who has much to say to the modern world. The Hollywood film *The Hours* has restored her status as one of the leading literary lights of the twentieth century. Indeed, in the wake of the film's success, Woolf's novel, *Mrs. Dalloway*, made the U.S. bestseller lists. What are her credentials for such laudatory treatment? She was an active homosexual who, as we have seen, detested traditional Christianity. In the end, her "enlightened" views brought her to despair, and she committed suicide. Thus, in our perverted age, Eliot, who preached the Gospel of Life, "may be called dead to us all" (to reemploy Woolf's own words), whereas Woolf, as a prophet of the culture of death, is declared immortal for the "martyrdom" of taking her own life. It is easy to detect the satanic inversion at work in such a state of affairs. Hell on earth, or at least a foretaste of it.

Appropriately, Eliot's first major poem following his conversion was the penitential "Ash Wednesday", and he went on to produce several major works of Christian literature, notably the religious plays *The Rock* and *Murder in the Cathedral*, and the long, mystically sublime poem *Four Quartets*. Taken as a whole, one can see Eliot's major work paralleling that of his master, Dante. *The Waste Land* and "The Hollow Men" were his *Inferno*, "Ash Wednesday" and *The Rock* were his *Purgatorio*, and *Four Quartets* was his vision of *Paradise*. What a legacy he has bequeathed to posterity!

One cannot conclude a reflection on the cultural reaction to the wasteland of modernity without paying respect, at least in passing, to several other major figures who followed in Eliot's footsteps. Most notably, Evelyn Waugh should be considered "the T. S. Eliot of prose fiction". His early satirical novels parodied the "bright young things" of the Wasteland generation in much the same terms as had Eliot in his early verse. Waugh's novel *A Handful of Dust* even took its title from Eliot's *The Waste Land*. Waugh's conversion to Roman Catholicism in 1930 caused as much of a sensation as had Eliot's conversion two years earlier. In avant-garde circles, Waugh was hailed as the "ultramodern novelist" just as Eliot had been the "ultramodern poet". The fact that both had embraced Catholicism served as a salutary shock to the supercilious presumptions of modernity and as a source of salvific inspiration to the Christian literati.

Interestingly, a similar "reaction to the reaction" occurred at the end of the Second World War. On that occasion, as the world lurched from world war to the wasteland of the cold war, many great works of Christian literature emerged phoenix-like from the ashes—or perhaps, in keeping with the metaphor, emerged not from the ashes but from the ice. Edith Sitwell, having written her wonderful protest poem, "Still Falls the Rain", during the Blitz in 1940, wrote *The Shadow of Cain*, the first of her "three poems of the Atomic Age", which, inspired by the horror of Hiroshima, lamented "the fission of the world into warring particles, destroying and self-destructive" and prophesied "the gradual migration of mankind ... into the desert of the Cold". Edith Sitwell was received into the Catholic Church a few years later.

In the same year, 1945, Waugh published *Brideshead Revisited*, possibly the finest novel of the century; Lewis published his timeless indictment of modernity, *That Hideous Strength*; and Tolkien was putting the finishing touches to *The Lord of the Rings*, which is the greatest literary achievement of the century. And so we see that, emerging from the wasteland, the cultural reaction to the desert of modernity had produced the greatest poet of the century, T. S. Eliot; the greatest novelist, Evelyn Waugh; and one of the greatest epics not merely of the twentieth century, but of all time, Tolkien's *The Lord of the Rings*.

It was also in 1945 that our old friend, Siegfried Sassoon, who had come to prominence during the First World War for his poetry of protest, emerged once again with a poem of protest about the wasteland that followed the Second World War. It was titled "Litany of the Lost":

> In breaking of belief in human good;
> In slavedom of mankind to the machine;
> In havoc of hideous tyranny withstood,
> And terror of atomic doom foreseen;
> *Deliver us from ourselves.*
>
> Chained to the wheel of progress uncontrolled;
> World masterers with a foolish frightened face;
> Loud speakers, leaderless and sceptic-souled;
> Aeroplane angels, crashed from glory and grace;
> *Deliver us from ourselves.*
>
> In blood and bone contentiousness of nations,
> And commerce's competitive re-start,
> Armed with our marvelous monkey innovations,
> And unregenerate still in head and heart;
> *Deliver us from ourselves.*

Unlike his previous poems of protest, this time the poem was also a prayer. The prayer was answered. Several years later, like Sitwell, Sassoon was received into the peaceful arms of Mother Church.

The final words should belong not to Sassoon, the war poet, but to Eliot, the poet of the wasteland. Significantly and appropriately, the words, published in 1944, are not words of protest but words of praise. Ultimately these writers, Sassoon, Sitwell, Lewis, Waugh and Eliot himself, emerged from the infernal wasteland of modernity into the purgatorial conversion to traditional Christianity, which carries with it the paradisal promise of eternal life. Eliot ends his *Four Quartets*, as Dante ends his *Divine Comedy*, with a vision of the eternal Home that awaits the faithful soul in this vale of tears, this land of exile, this wasteland:

> And all shall be well and
> All manner of thing shall be well
> When the tongues of flame are in-folded
> Into the crowned knot of fire
> And the fire and the rose are one.

21

EDITH SITWELL

Modernity and Tradition

E DITH SITWELL WAS A SHOCK TROOPER of the poetic avant-garde, a champion of modernity who reveled in the use of shock tactics to push the boundaries of poetry, angering traditionalists in the process. Perhaps, therefore, she would seem an unlikely convert to the creed and traditions of the Catholic Church. Yet, like her friend "the ultra-modern novelist" Evelyn Waugh, she would come to realize that the liberating power of orthodoxy could transfuse tradition with the dynamism of truth.

Born into privilege, as the daughter of Sir George Sitwell and Lady Ida Sitwell of Renishaw Hall in Derbyshire, and as the granddaughter of Lord Londesborough, Sitwell would also seem to be an unlikely revolutionary. Yet, from the appearance of her first published poem, "Drowned Suns", in the *Daily Mirror* in 1913, she had sent tremors through the landscapes of literary convention. The tremors grew to seismic levels between the years of 1916 and 1921 with her editorship of *Wheels*, an annual anthology of new verse. The poetry selected by Sitwell for these anthologies was not only self-consciously modern in style but was superciliously contemptuous of the flaccid and idyllic quietism of the so-called Georgian poets.

In 1922 Sitwell published *Façade*, her most controversial poem to date, which, accompanied by the music of William Walton, was given a stormy public reading in London. In the same year, the publication of Eliot's *The Waste Land* had polarized opinion still further between the "ancients" and the "moderns". A reviewer in the *Manchester Guardian* called *The Waste Land* "a mad medley" and "so much waste paper", whereas a more sympathetic review in the *Times Literary Supplement* spoke of Eliot's "poetic personality" as being "extremely sophisticated" and his poem as being an "ambitious experiment". Clearly, the battle lines were being drawn for a very uncivil war of words between the forces of modernity and those of tradition. Poetry was in commotion.

G. K. Chesterton was critical of some of the modern trends in poetry, and the young C. S. Lewis was hostile to what he referred to contemptuously as "Eliotic" verse. It was, however, in the person of Alfred Noyes, a respected poet of the old guard, that Sitwell and Eliot found their most formidable foe.

Noyes had found himself out of favor and out of fashion in the atmosphere created by the moderns, and Sitwell had dismissed his poetry as "cheap linoleum". Unprepared to take such abuse lightly, Noyes came out fighting, throwing down the gauntlet of tradition in defiance of modern trends.

The first blows were struck at a public debate held at the London School of Economics, at which Noyes and Sitwell were to discuss "the comparative value in old poetry and the new". Edmund Gosse, who had agreed to chair the discussion, asked Noyes not to be too hard on his opponent. "Do not, I beg of you, use a weaver's beam on the head of poor Edith." Noyes, for his part, believed that he might become the victim of Sitwell's vociferous supporters and could "suddenly be attacked by a furious flock of strangely coloured birds, frantically trying to peck my nose".

Noyes' quip was an act of sartorial sarcasm aimed at Sitwell's flamboyant taste in clothes. She arrived for the debate dressed in a purple robe and gold laurel wreath, contrasting clashingly with Noyes' sober American-cut suit and horn-rimmed spectacles. The contrast was sublimely appropriate, the dress addressing the issue.

The debate began uneasily when Edith asked if her supporters might sit on the platform with her. Noyes agreed but took advantage of the situation by telling the audience that he wished he could bring his supporters along as well, naming Virgil, Chaucer, Shakespeare, Dante and others. The riposte was effective, if a trifle unfair. Sitwell had not renounced any of these poets, and T. S. Eliot, the other "ultramodern" poet, was steeped in poetic tradition and was deeply devoted to Dante. Nonetheless, the *coup de théâtre* had the desired effect, and Sitwell shamefacedly sat alone on the platform with Noyes and Gosse.

Paradoxically, the debate proceeded with Sitwell defending innovation from a singularly traditionalist perspective. "We are always being called mad", she complained. "If we are mad ... at least we are mad in company with most of our great predecessors ... Schumann ... Coleridge and Wordsworth were all mad in turn." She might have added that the romanticism of Coleridge and Wordsworth, considered very "modern" and avant-garde in its day, spawned the reaction against the "progressive" scientism of the anti-Catholic Enlightenment and was influential in the resurrection of medievalism in England in the form of the Gothic revival and the Oxford movement.

Equally paradoxically, Noyes defended tradition from the perspective that it was always "up-to-date", declaring with the great French literary critic Sainte-Beuve that "true poetry is a contemporary of all ages". Thus, there was, it seemed, a unity in their apparent division that neither poet perceived at the time.

This higher reality, or true realism, was largely lost in the increasingly vitriolic war of words that followed the much-publicized debate. In the furious controversy that raged in the press throughout the 1920s, the prevailing bias was in favor of the moderns. Eliot and Sitwell were popularly perceived as marching "hand in hand ... in the vanguard of progress", whereas the ancients, as the agents of reaction, merely sought to turn back the tide. Tides turn on their own, of course, but it was true at the time that the waves of sympathy were flowing, for the most part, with the moderns.

"Certain things are accepted in a lump by all the Moderns", Chesterton complained in a review of a book by Noyes, "mainly because they are supposed (often wrongly) to be rejected with horror by all the Ancients." Taking the example of Edgar Allan Poe, Chesterton remarked that the moderns hijacked their favorite ancients, bestowing honorary modernity on them. Poe had been "set apart as a Modern before the Moderns", whereas he was "something much more important than a Modern ... he was a poet."

Noyes wrote that Chesterton was one of the few who "completely understood my defence of literary traditions, as well as my criticism of them". Perhaps so. Yet Noyes had singularly failed to perceive that

Sitwell, like Eliot, was "something much more important than a Modern ... she was a poet".

In 1929 Sitwell published *Gold Coast Customs*, a vision of the horror and hollowness of contemporary life that not only echoed Eliot in its purgatorial passion but that served as an early indication that she was on the road to religious conversion. Her sublimely sorrowful "Still Falls the Rain", depicting the bombing of London during the Blitz in 1940, resonated with the bitter imagery of Christ's Crucifixion and humanity's perennial culpability,

> Blind as the nineteen hundred and forty nails
> Upon the Cross.

Most memorable, perhaps, were her "three poems of the Atomic Age", inspired darkly by eyewitness descriptions of the dropping of the atomic bomb on Hiroshima in 1945. "The Shadow of Cain", the first of the poems, was about "the fission of the world into warring particles, destroying and self-destructive. It is about the gradual migration of mankind, after that Second Fall of Man ... into the desert of the Cold, towards the final disaster, the first symbol of which fell on Hiroshima." The poem's imagery was, she explained, "partly a physical description of the highest degree of cold, partly a spiritual description of this".

Sitwell's desire, spiritually, to come in from the cold drew her, ever more surely, to the warm embrace of the Church.

Another, more personal, influence on her slow progress toward Christianity was her admiration for the convert-poet Roy Campbell. She looked upon Campbell not only as a friend but as one of the few people who would defend her from her critics. "Roy Campbell represented a great deal to her", recalled Elizabeth Salter in her memoir of Sitwell. "Not only was he a poet whom she greatly admired, but he was that rare thing in her life, a champion ... and she responded to Roy Campbell's championship with an entirely feminine gratitude." The fact that her knight in shining armor also happened to be a vocal champion of the Church Militant had not gone unnoticed.

Edith Sitwell was finally received into the Catholic Church in August 1955. She asked Evelyn Waugh to be her godfather, and he recorded in his diary how she had appeared on the day of her reception "swathed in black like a sixteenth-century infanta". Another guest, the actor Alec Guinness, who was soon to be received into the Church himself, remembered "her tall figure, swathed in black, looking like some strange, eccentric bird ... She seemed like an ageing princess come home from exile."

The happiest irony of all resided in the fact that Alfred Noyes, her bitterest enemy, had also been received into the Church many years earlier. In their reconciliation in the same spiritual communion, they had, symbolically and poetically, united modernity and tradition—the unity of ancient and modern in something greater than both.

22

ROY CAMPBELL

Bombast and Fire

Roy Campbell was considered by many of his peers, most notably T. S. Eliot, Dylan Thomas and Edith Sitwell, as one of the finest poets of the twentieth century. Why then, one wonders, is he not as well known today as many lesser poets? The answer lies in his robust defense of unfashionable causes, both religious and political, but also, and more regrettably, in his unfortunate predilection for making powerful enemies. Seldom has a life been more fiery, more controversial and more full of friendship and enmity than that of this most mercurial of men.

Born in South Africa in 1901, Campbell learned to speak Zulu almost as soon as he had learned to speak English. "The Zulus are a highly intellectual people", Campbell recorded in his first volume of autobiography. "They have a very beautiful language, a little on the bombastic side and highly adorned. Its effect on me can be seen in *The Flaming Terrapin* ... They take an enormous delight in conversation, analysing with the greatest subtlety and brilliance."

It seems that Campbell's own conversation conveyed more than a hint of this Zulu influence. Following his arrival at Oxford in 1919, his contemporaries were both bemused and beguiled by his tales, "a little on the bombastic side and highly adorned", of the African bush. He soon earned himself the nickname of "Zulu", and his reputation as a wild colonial boy was immortalized by his friend Percy Wyndham Lewis, who modeled the character of Zulu Blades in his novel *The Apes of God* on Campbell's image at Oxford.

The African influence was also to the fore in the long, vibrant and colorful poem that established Campbell's reputation. *The Flaming Terrapin*, published in 1924, was, according to one critic, "like a breath of new youth, like a love-affair to a lady in her fifties".

"Among a crowd of poets writing delicate verses he moves like a mastodon with shaggy sides pushing through a herd of lightfoot antelopes", wrote George Russell in the *Irish Statesman*. "No poet I have read for many years excites me to more speculation about his future, for I do not know of any new poet who has such a savage splendour of epithet or who can marry the wild word so fittingly to the wild thought."

Commenting on the "energy and flamboyance" of *The Flaming Terrapin*, the poet David Wright remarked that "its verve and extravagance burst like a bomb in the middle of the faded prettiness of the 'Georgian' poetry then in vogue". Campbell's "flamboyant imagery, drawn from his memories ... of his native Africa, exploded with an almost surrealist proliferation of exoticism."

Almost overnight, Roy Campbell, still only twenty-two years old, was rocketed into the ranks of the *illustrissimi* of English letters, his work being discussed in the same breath, and with the same reverence, as that of T. S. Eliot. The comparison between Campbell and Eliot, whose hugely influential *The Waste Land* had been published eighteen months prior to the appearance of *The Flaming Terrapin*, is singularly appropriate. Both poets, and both poems, were displaying an embryonic rebellion against the prevailing cynicism, born out of postwar angst, which afflicted the younger generation in the years following the carnage of the First World War. Eventually both poets would reject the superficiality and shifting sands of modern cynicism for the sure foundation of traditional Christianity.

Apart from his African roots, the other great influence on Campbell's work was that of the great Elizabethan dramatists. He was an avid admirer not only of Shakespeare and Marlowe but of lesser Elizabethans, such as Chapman, Peele and Dekker.

By Jove they are marvellous poets ... Their poetry is so living and fresh it makes even the greatest work of Keats and Shelley seem just a little bit artificial ... When you come back you'll find us ranting long passages of bombast and fire ... I am absolutely drunk with these fellows. They wrote poetry just as a machine-gun fires off bullets ... They don't even stop to get their breath. They go thundering on until you forget everything about the sense and ... end up in a positive debauch of thunder and splendour and music ... They are raw, careless, headstrong, coarse, brutal. But how vivid they are, how intoxicated with their own imagination.

In this intoxicated and intoxicating letter, Campbell had unwittingly described many of the characteristics of his own work. The flamboyance of the Elizabethans had colored the imagery of *The Flaming Terrapin* with a vivid sharpness that distinguished it from most other contemporary verse in much the same way as the vivid sharpness of the Pre-Raphaelites had stood out from the monochrome subtleties of impressionism. In describing the "bombast and fire", the writing of poetry "just as a machine-gun fires off bullets", the failure to stop to catch one's breath, Campbell could have been describing his own satires. These too could be "raw, careless, headstrong, coarse, brutal" and would be written in a breathless stream of invective, in stark contrast to the measured and meticulous care that he always took with his lyrical verse.

In the spring of 1931 Campbell informed Wyndham Lewis that he was "just finishing a long satire, the Georgiad". This was a scathing attack on the Bloomsbury group, the sexually promiscuous and implicitly anti-Christian literary set who exerted a fashionably iconoclastic and culturally subversive influence in the years between the two world wars. Campbell attacked the Bloomsburys as "intellectuals without intellect" whose hate

> dribbles, week by week,
> Like lukewarm bilge out of a running leak.

The vitriolic attacks on Vita Sackville-West, Virginia Woolf and other members of the Bloomsbury group were spoiled by Campbell's vindictiveness and lack of charity. Yet, embedded between the vitriol, mounted like pearls of wisdom in the basest of metal, were instances of a deep yet inarticulate yearning for faith. *The Georgiad* confirmed Campbell's rejection of postwar pessimism and its nihilistic ramifications and placed him beside others, such as Eliot and Waugh, who were similarly seeking glimmers of philosophical light amid the prevailing gloom.

Desiring an escape from the world of the "intellectuals without intellect", Campbell moved with his wife, Mary, and their two daughters to Provence and, later, to Spain. Throughout this period, he and Mary found themselves being slowly but irresistibly drawn toward the Catholic faith. The seemingly somnambulant process of conversion was charted by Campbell in a sonnet sequence entitled *Mithraic Emblems*, which shows the progress of a soul in transit. The earliest sonnets, written in Provence, show the poet groping with an uncomprehended and incomprehensible paganism, relishing the irrational, the *obscurum per obscurius*—the obscure by the still more obscure. It is Mithraic "truth" whispered with Masonic secrecy—the affirmation of faith without reason. In the later sonnets, written after Campbell's arrival in Spain, Christianity emerges triumphant, not so much to vanquish Mithraism as to make sense of it. In these later sonnets, the sun is no longer a god to be worshiped, but only a symbol of the Son, the true God, who gives the sun its meaning and its purpose.

> Oh let your shining orb grow dim,
> Of Christ the mirror and the shield,
> That I may gaze through you to Him,
> See half the mystery revealed.

Roy and Mary Campbell, together with their daughters, were received into the Catholic Church in the Spanish village of Altea in June 1935.

They had chosen a dangerous time and place to profess their faith. In the following year, Spain was plunged into a fratricidal civil war. By its end, 12 bishops, 4,184 priests, 2,365 monks and about 300 nuns had been murdered by the anti-Catholic Republican forces. Details of these atrocities horrified Catholics around the world. Father Gregorio, the parish priest of Altea, who had described the day in which he had received the Campbells into the Church as the best day of his life, was murdered by Republican militiamen only a year later. The Campbells, too, narrowly escaped with their lives, escaping from Spain only days after their friends the Carmelite monks of Toledo had been murdered in cold blood.

The horrors of the Spanish civil war would inspire some of Campbell's finest verse. In much the same way that the sonnet sequence *Mithraic Emblems* had been the outpouring of a poetic baptism of desire, so the poems inspired by the Spanish war would be the outpouring of a poetic baptism of fire.

> The towers and trees were lifted hymns of praise,
> The city was a prayer, the land a nun:
> The noonday azure strumming all its rays
> Sang that a famous battle had been won,
> As signing his white Cross, the very Sun,
> The Solar Christ and captain of my days
> Zoomed to the zenith; and his will was done.

23

ROY CAMPBELL

Religion and Politics

I T IS ONE OF THE TRITE ASSUMPTIONS of modern life that the subjects of religion and politics should not be discussed in public. Somehow it is considered impolite or indecorous to broach either topic in a social setting. The result, of course, is that the art of conversation either stagnates in the swamps of trivia or else descends to the level of the banal or the profane. Thankfully, this social stricture has been wholeheartedly ignored by the key literary figures of the past century. Writers as diverse as George Orwell and Graham Greene, G. K. Chesterton and George Bernard Shaw, H. G. Wells and Hilaire Belloc, T. S. Eliot and W. H. Auden, and Evelyn Waugh and J. R. R. Tolkien, have spiced their lives, their conversation, their correspondence and their works with a healthy cocktail of the religious and the political. Few, however, have employed the spice of religion and politics as robustly or as candidly as Roy Campbell. It would, in fact, be true to say that Campbell, more perhaps than any other writer of his generation, is *defined* by his religion and his politics. This being so, any failure to understand Campbell's religious or political stance is a failure to understand Campbell himself and, therefore, a failure to understand, or fully appreciate, his work. Sadly, many of Campbell's critics have been unfailing in their failure in this regard, so much so that it has been Campbell's fate to be misunderstood, again more perhaps than any other writer of his generation, by those who lack either empathy or sympathy with his politics or his faith. Put simply and succinctly, he has been judged by the prejudiced.

If, therefore, we are to understand Campbell *objectively*, leaving our subjective presumptions aside, we must come to terms with, and get to grips with, his core beliefs. In order to do this, it is essential to begin at the beginning, through an examination of the earliest influences in his life.

Taken collectively, the politics, culture and religion of Campbell's childhood constituted a conundrum of contradictions. His mother's Jacobite romanticism, passed on to her son in the singing of old Scottish ballads, conflicted with her dourly lackluster Presbyterianism. Similarly, the songs of Jacobite rebellion reverberated discordantly with the unquestioning acceptance of British imperialism and resonated in uneasy and unusual counterpoint to the jingoism of empire. Finally, the family's privileged position as white colonials in the heart of black South Africa added to the political and cultural tension. These diverse and divisive forces fought for supremacy in the youthful Campbell's mind and heart. The Highland Catholicism of the Jacobites jostled with the Lowland Presbyterianism of the family's lukewarm faith; the Scottish nationalism thumbed its nose at the pomp and circumstance of the British Empire; and the prestige and privilege of the colonial looked down its imperious and impervious nose at the presumed "inferiority" of the nonwhite natives. The overall effect was that Campbell had inherited from his family the psychology of both the oppressed and the oppressor, the legacy of defeat and the spoils of victory.

"The Theology of Bongwi, the Baboon", one of Campbell's earliest poems, probably written prior to his arrival in Oxford in 1919 or very shortly thereafter, indicates that he had sought to resolve the religious contradictions inherent in his family by an escape into agnosticism. With youthful impatience at the centuries-old conflict between the Catholic thesis and its Protestant antithesis, he rejected dialectic in favor of diversion, or even derision. Possibly inspired by Yeats' poem "An Indian upon God", "The Theology of Bongwi, the Baboon" is, in spite of its playful theological subversion, utterly devoid of the cynical world-weariness of so much iconoclastic, antireligious satire. On the contrary, its jovial tone has much in common with the satirical verse of G. K. Chesterton, as becomes instantly apparent if Campbell's poem is compared with Chesterton's "Race Memory (by a dazed Darwinian)".

The cultural and political conflicts at the heart of Campbell's upbringing came to creative fruition in two more early poems, "Zulu Girl" and "The Serf", in which he exhibits, simultaneously, both sympathetic admiration for, and suppressed fear of, the native Africans, the contradictory emotions clashing in tensile creativity. Ironically, Campbell would be given the nickname "Zulu" upon his arrival in Oxford, finding himself a misfit, a wild colonial boy, who rejected, and was rejected by, the mother culture. This rejection of, and rejection by, the elitist atmosphere of the English public school, which was all-pervasive in the hallowed halls of Oxbridge in the years following the First World War, not only reawakened the latent antagonism to Anglo-Saxondom inherent in the Jacobite romanticism of Campbell's boyhood but placed him, culturally, in a similar position to that of the Zulus in South Africa. Thus the psychology of the oppressor was eclipsed by that of the oppressed.

In *The Flaming Terrapin* (1924), the long and ambitious poem that established his reputation, Campbell reacted against the prevailing pessimism and nihilism of postwar England and against the hedonism of the "bright young things" with whom he had flirted and from whom he had recoiled. Although awash with remnants of a confused and confusingly heterodox Christianity, *The Flaming Terrapin* regards postwar politics and culture more through the prism of Nietzsche, Darwin and Einstein than through the teaching of Christ. The idealization of the Nietzschean "strong" and the Darwinian "fittest" provides the first inkling of a protofascism. There is also an implicit aversion to communism as the product of postwar demoralization and stagnation and the hope that it might be countered by those who, refusing to become demoralized or stagnant, are instead "ennobled" by the sufferings of war. Beneath the surface of the poem, submerged and potent as the terrapin itself, is the sublime influence of Eliot's subliminally cathartic tour de force, *The Waste Land*, published eighteen months earlier. A pose-modern *cri de coeur* exuding postwar angst and superficial cynicism, Eliot's hidden agenda pointed, paradoxically, toward the resurrection of Christian tradition. Campbell's *Terrapin* lacked the profound philosophical coherence of *The Waste Land* but shared intuitively the latter's traditionalist aspirations, albeit inarticulately. Certainly, with the wisdom of hindsight, it can be seen that both poems—and both poets—were grappling with the same issues and groping toward the same, ultimately religious, goal.

Following the publication of *The Flaming Terrapin*, Campbell enjoyed a brief period of fashionable celebrity. He was seen by many of his contemporaries as the finest poet of his generation, with the exception of the universally lauded Eliot. He was, however, to fall from favor following his vicious attack on the Bloomsbury group in the long satirical poem *The Georgiad* (1931). Written in the manner of Dryden and Pope, this merciless broadside against the self-styled elite of England's literati would render him anathema in the eyes of many of the contemporaries who, a few years earlier, had praised him for his achievement. *The Georgiad* is a vituperative invective, "venomous with truth" [1], against the Freudian gospel of self-gratification in general and against the sexual mores of the Bloomsbury group in particular. Campbell's poem rests on the premise that sexual "liberation", so-called, leads to a culture of death, devoid of joy. Sex was not a subject for morbid fascination, Campbell argued, but was a glorious mystery to be enjoyed in the purity of passion. As such, every attempt to strip it of its mystery strips it of its higher meaning. All that remains when sex is removed from the glory of its romantic heights is a gaudy remnant festering in the furtive frustrations of its sterile depths. Sex, as preached and practiced in Bloomsbury, was the omnipotence of impotence. Such is the leitmotif of *The Georgiad*. Androgyno, the poem's hero, is so shocking to the puritanically prurient sensibilities of Bloomsbury because he flouts their adolescent furtiveness in an unrestrained fertility rite. Androgyno is the shamelessly potent vanquisher of psychosexual impotence, the exorciser of Bloomsbury's perverse spirit.

Although it is an uncompromising attack on "modern" attitudes to sex, the spirit and language of *The Georgiad* is neither puritanical nor prudish but, on the contrary, is a passionate and prudent response to prurience.

As with so much of Campbell's satire, *The Georgiad*'s invective is too vindictive. It is spoiled by spite. The result is that the abuse obscures the truth Campbell is seeking to convey. Embedded between the attacks

[1] Roy Campbell, "To a Pet Cobra", in *Selected Poems*, ed. Joseph Pearce (London: Saint Austin Press, 2001), 7.

on Bertrand Russell, Marie Stopes, Vita Sackville-West, Virginia Woolf and a host of other Bloomsburys and Georgians are classically refined objections to the prevailing philosophy of scepticism, mounted like pearls of wisdom in the basest of metal. "Nor knew the Greeks, save in the laughing page, the philosophic emblem of our age". This age's "damp philosophy" is "the fountain source of all [the] woes" of modern man, who is left "damp in spirit" by his adherence to it. His nihilism is self-negating. It is the philosophy of the self-inflicted wound.

Whatever its objective merits, and objectionable flaws, *The Georgiad* clearly displays a soul utterly alienated from the society and philosophy of his contemporaries and peers.[2] Escaping from such an inhospitable environment, Campbell fled to Provence. It was here, perhaps for the first time in his turbulent life, that he found a degree of peace.[3]

> Rest under my branches, breathe deep of my balm
> From the hushed avalanches of fragrance and calm,
> For suave is the silence that poises the palm.
> The wings of the egrets are silken and fine,
> But hushed with the secrets of Eden are mine.[4]

Why, one wonders, did Campbell find such peace in Provence whereas he had found nothing but emotional turmoil in England and during his abortive return to South Africa in the mid-twenties? The answer, if the witness of his poetry is to be taken as authoritative, is to be found in the rustic culture that he discovered there and into which he submerged himself wholeheartedly. For Campbell, the peasant had always

[2] I am, of course, aware of the personal reasons for Campbell's enmity toward the Bloomsbury group and for his "escape" to Provence, namely, his wife's passionate affair with Vita Sackville-West. Those wishing to know more of this episode in Campbell's life should see my biography, *Bloomsbury and Beyond: The Friends and Enemies of Roy Campbell* (London: HarperCollins, 2001). It is, however, my contention that Campbell's philosophical objections to Bloomsbury are a genuine reflection of his intellectual opposition to the "damp philosophy" of its members and that such objections transcend any personal enmity he might have held against certain individuals.

[3] With the possible exception of the "honeymoon" period with his wife in Wales, shortly after their wedding, during which time he wrote *The Flaming Terrapin*.

[4] Roy Campbell, "The Palm", in *Collected Poems* (London: The Bodley Head, 1949), 1:50.

represented the permanent. Civilizations rise and fall. Only the peasant remains.

> The timeless, surly patience of the serf
> That moves the nearest to the naked earth
> And ploughs down palaces, and thrones, and towers.[5]

Akin to the permanence of the peasant was the permanence of the
peasants' religion. In Provence, for the first time, Campbell found himself immersed in a Catholic culture. From this time, his poetry begins
to proliferate with Catholic imagery. It is, however, Catholic imagery
without Catholic faith, as is exemplified most poignantly in the tranquil agnosticism of "Mass at Dawn". There are, however, hints of a
faith desired, if not necessarily attained, in the final verses of "Saint
Peter of the Three Canals", a poem that transforms itself beguilingly
from the apparently faithless frivolity of the early verses to the tacit
acceptance of faith in its invocatory finale.

It is not, however, until the poet's arrival in Spain in 1933 that the
Faith finally claims the poet, or, at least, that the poet finally acclaims
the Faith,

> under the stretched, terrific wings,
> the outspread arms (our soaring King's)—
> the man they made an Albatross![6]

Campbell's conversion was charted in the sonnet sequence *Mithraic
Emblems*, the earliest of which were written in Provence and the last
of which were written in Spain. Taken as a whole, they display a soul
in transit. The early sonnets show the poet groping with an uncomprehended and incomprehensible paganism, relishing the irrational, the
obscurum per obscurius—the obscure by the still more obscure. The poet
makes an affirmation of faith without reason, whispering Mithraic
"truth" with Masonic secrecy. In the later sonnets, Christianity emerges
triumphant, not so much to vanquish Mithraism as to make sense of
it. *Fides* is now married to *ratio*, faith to reason. In the final sonnets,
the sun is no longer a god to be worshiped, but only a symbol of the

---

[5] Roy Campbell, "The Serf", in *Selected Poems*, 5.
[6] Roy Campbell, "Mithraic Emblems: Mithras Speaks 2", in *Selected Poems*, 45.

Son, the true God, who gives the sun its meaning and purpose. The Mithraic emblem is transformed by Christian typology and becomes Christ transfigured.

> Oh let your shining orb grow dim,
> Of Christ the mirror and the shield,
> That I may gaze through you to Him,
> See half the miracle revealed.[7]

Campbell's reception into the Catholic Church on 24 June 1935 confirmed him in his love for Spain, which he later described as "a country to which I owe everything as having saved my soul".[8] As with his rustic experience of Provence, he felt a deep admiration for the Spanish peasants, whose lives and traditions were centered solely on the feasts of the Church and the changing seasons of the year. He never ceased to find their ordered lives, which resembled what might be termed a life-dance, absorbingly interesting, whereas the frantic lives of modern people, which resembled a race against time, was inimical to the flourishing of the human spirit. In this, of course, he was rekindling his affinity with Eliot, who had waxed contemptuously about the "unreal" and "time-kept city" in *The Waste Land*.

Campbell's conversion would also accentuate still further his alienation from the secularist ascendancy in British literature. The reaction of his former friends and present enemies among the British literati to the news of his conversion can be gauged by Virginia Woolf's horrified response to Eliot's embrace of Anglo-Catholicism several years earlier.

> I have just had a most shameful and distressing interview with dear Tom Eliot, who may be called dead to us all from this day forward. He has become an Anglo-Catholic believer in God and immortality, and goes to church. I was shocked. A corpse would seem to me more credible than he is. I mean, there's something obscene in a living person sitting by the fire and believing in God.[9]

---

[7] Roy Campbell, "To the Sun", in *Selected Poems*, 46.

[8] Quoted in Matthew Hoehn, OSB, ed., *Catholic Authors: Contemporary Biographical Sketches 1930–1947* (Newark, N.J.: Saint Mary's Abbey Press, 1947), 104.

[9] Quoted in Walter Hooper, *C. S. Lewis: A Companion and Guide* (London: Fount/HarperCollins, 1996), 25.

There is little doubt that Campbell's submission to Rome would have elicited similar sneers of contempt. Already dead in the eyes of Bloomsbury, he could now be considered well and truly buried.

His conversion would also place a catechetic chasm between himself and the new generation of left-wing poets, such as Stephen Spender, W. H. Auden, Louis MacNeice and Cecil Day-Lewis. Campbell's faith was inextricably linked to politics—and his politics became increasingly linked to, and colored by, his love for Spain. With the Spanish civil war looming, Campbell would find himself on the opposite side to these young atheist and socialist poets.

Few of his contemporaries would understand his stance during the Spanish civil war, but of the few who did understand, few would understand better than his friend Lawrence Durrell. Unlike so many others, Durrell understood the importance to Campbell of the potent trinity of influences—religious, cultural and political—with which his life in Spain was entwined. Durrell explained that he was "simultaneously happy and saddened" when he discovered that Campbell had become a Catholic: "happy for him, sad because I myself could not participate ... But Roy had taken from Spain the brocades and the dust of the bull-ring and how can anyone penetrate to the heart of Spain without embracing the faith which animates its brutal vivid life? It was totally right for him—'a second motherland'." [10]

Durrell was wrong, however, when he wrote that "his politics became a faith". It would be much truer to say that Campbell's faith became his politics. In being received into the Church, he had grafted himself onto Catholic Spain, and his politics thereafter would be determined by his desire to defend Catholic Spain from her enemies. In fundamental political terms, he perceived the Church as the defender of the integrity of the family against those "rebels", anarchist or communist, who sought the family's disintegration. For Campbell, the "Heart of Rome" and "hearth and home" were one and indivisible.

In March 1936 the anticlerical contagion spreading across Spain reached the streets of Toledo, the ancient city in which the Campbells had made their home. Churches were burned in a series of violent

[10] Alister Kershaw, ed., *Salute to Roy Campbell* (Francestown, N.H.: Typographeum, 1984), 26.

riots in which priests and monks were attacked. During these bloody disturbances, Roy and Mary Campbell sheltered in their house several of the Carmelite monks from the neighboring monastery. In the following weeks, the situation worsened. Portraits of Marx and Lenin were posted on every street corner, and horrific tales began to filter in from surrounding villages of priests being shot and wealthy men being butchered in front of their families. Toledo's beleaguered Christians braced themselves for the next wave of persecution, and the Campbells, in an atmosphere that must have seemed eerily reminiscent of the clandestine gatherings of early Christians in the catacombs of Rome, were confirmed in a secret ceremony, before dawn, by Cardinal Goma, the elderly Archbishop of Toledo and Primate of Spain.

In July 1936 the civil war erupted onto the streets of Toledo, heralded by the arrival in the city of communist militiamen from Madrid. With no one to defend them, the priests, monks and nuns fell prey to the hatred of their adversaries. The seventeen monks from the Carmelite monastery were rounded up, herded into the street and shot. Campbell discovered their murdered bodies, left lying where they fell. He also discovered the bodies of other priests lying in the narrow street in which the priests had been murdered. Swarms of flies surrounded their bodies, and scrawled in their blood on the wall was written, "Thus strikes the Cheka".[11] It should also be noted that Father Gregorio, the simple parish priest who had received Roy and Mary Campbell into the Church, was also murdered in cold blood by communist militiamen.

Having witnessed the cold-blooded murder of his friends and acquaintances, it was not likely that Campbell was going to support the cause of the perpetrators. Bearing these horrific facts in mind, it is clearly a gross oversimplification to dismiss Campbell's stance in the Spanish civil war as evidence that he was a fascist. Such an obvious mitigating circumstance was, however, almost universally overlooked by Campbell's detractors in England, all of whom appended the "fascist" label to his person, employing it, and the accompanying stereotypical effluvia with which such an epithet is associated, with the cynical glee of seasoned character assassins.

[11] Anna Campbell Lyle, *Son of Valour*, unpublished manuscript, 111.

The overriding irony of the misnomer with which he was shack-
led is that the protofascist tendencies evident, to a limited degree, in
early poems such as *The Flaming Terrapin* were actually softened, or
perhaps even exorcised, by his embrace of Catholic Christianity. His
admiration for the cult of Mithras, the religion of the warrior, had
been moderated by his acceptance of Christianity, the religion of the
slave. The Nietzschean philosophy of "might is right" had been conquered by the Christian concept of the rights of the meek. Thereafter, far from being a believer in totalitarianism, Campbell's politics
reflected the social vision of the Catholic Church, particularly in
relation to the Church's teaching on "subsidiarity", the sociopolitical
belief that the family should be the most powerful institution in society and that, in consequence, small government and small business is
preferable to big government and big business. Subsidiarity emphasizes that power should be devolved upward from the family, not
imposed downward by the state. This, surely, is the very antithesis
of, and antidote to, "fascism" in either its national socialist or international socialist variations.

Campbell encapsulated his adherence to subsidiarity in his invention of a humorously apposite neologism: "fascidemocshevism".[12]
Coined as a criticism of the whole concept of the postwar vision of
the welfare state, Campbell insisted that such unwarranted state intervention in people's lives constituted a combination of fascism and bolshevism under the guise of democracy. It can be seen, therefore, that,
far from being a fascist, Campbell deserves a place of honor among
those other writers of the twentieth century who have espoused the
cause of the political liberty of the family against the encroachments
of the state. Others who shared Campbell's subsidiarist vision include
Eliot, Tolkien, C. S. Lewis, Chesterton, Belloc, Waugh, Orwell and
Solzhenitsyn, all of whom, with the exception of Orwell, shared Campbell's Christian religion as well as his Christian politics. Campbell is,
therefore, in illustrious company. He is not, however, a pygmy among
giants. On the contrary, he deserves to be seen as a giant in his own
right. Few artists, even among those just named, have more successfully united the art of politics with the politics of art. Few artists have

[12] Roy Campbell, "The Beveridge Plan", in *Selected Poems*, 93.

shown more successfully the subservience of politics and art to religion. Few artists of such stature have been so maligned and treated so unjustly. Few artists that have shone so brightly have been eclipsed so shamefully. An eclipse is, however, a transitory phenomenon. It is to be hoped that this great poet of the sun will emerge from the shadow of lesser lights and that, having done so, his art, his religion and his politics will shine forth more brightly than ever.

24

CAMPBELL IN SPAIN

Outside, it froze. On rocky arms
Sleeping face-upwards to the sun
Lay Spain. Her golden hair was spun
From sky to sky. Her mighty charms
Breathed soft beneath her robe of farms
And gardens: while her snowy breasts,
Sierras white, with crimson crests,
Were stained with sunset.[1]

M ORE THAN MOST MEN, more even than most poets, Roy Campbell was a paradox. He was at once rooted and rootless; at home
and in exile. These apparent contradictions were, however, not in conflict. On the contrary, they were in creative and harmonious tension,
the apparent rootlessness of his wanderlusting spirit serving merely to
emphasize the rootedness of his creative imagination. Enigmatically,
and sometimes ironically, the counterpoise was the very cause of his
muse's counterpoint.

Although Campbell's multifarious roots were always being uprooted,
they were never discarded or left to decay in soilless and soulless iso-
lation. Instead, they were taken with him on his wanderings and
replanted in whatever new soil he happened to find himself. What,
then, were Campbell's roots?

Born into the culturally exotic catalyst of Durban in South Africa,
he imbibed the Celtic legacy of his family's Scottish ancestors, the
colonial privileges of his family's social status and the tribal traditions
of his family's African servants. From thence, enamored of the colonial predilection for the motherland, he drifted from Africa to England
and, disillusioned, drifted back again. Then, having rebelled against
the white South Africa of his birth, he rebounded back once more to

[1] Roy Campbell, "Posada", in *Collected Poems* (London: The Bodley Head, 1949),
1:158.

England. His disillusionment with all things Anglo-Saxon was soured still further by his disgusted rejection of the psychosexual babble of the Bloomsbury circle, and retreating to the rustic simplicity and sanity of Provence, he discovered, for the first time, Catholic Europe. Here, for a while, his restive spirit found rest. It was not, however, until he arrived in Spain in November 1933 that the poet finally felt that he had found a true home.

"The impact of Spain on Roy was profound", wrote Campbell's daughter, Anna Campbell Lyle. "He was quite unprepared for this impact, this deep new experience, and it had a lasting effect. The romantic in his personality was stirred and awakened".[2] To take issue with the last part of Mrs. Campbell Lyle's statement, it is patently untrue that Campbell's romantic personality had not been stirred and awakened long before his arrival in Spain. His African poems, such as "The Serf" and "The Sisters", resonate and ripple with romantic intensity, whereas the Provençal poetry overflows with the stirrings of a fully awakened romantic personality, most notably perhaps in "Mass at Dawn", "Autumn" and "Choosing a Mast". Yet his daughter's observations are true in the sense that the impact of Spain on Campbell's psyche was more profound and more permanent than any of his previous experiences. The romantic in his personality had never been *as* stirred, nor had it been *as* startlingly awakened. Take, for instance, the erotically charged imagery of "Posada", a sensual hymn of praise to a supine seductress of superlative beauty, reclining in primeval splendor. Seldom has a Spanish lady been courted so eloquently. Yet the object of this particular hymn of praise is no ordinary Spanish lady but Lady Spain herself. It is a hymn in homage to Campbell's adopted home.

How, then, did this love affair begin? It began, perhaps unpromisingly, in an atmosphere of surreal uncertainty accentuated by real and threatened violence. Roy and Mary Campbell arrived in Barcelona at the height of the anarchist unrest that followed the right-wing victory in the recent elections. The abortive "revolution" was at its most violent in the Barrio Chino, the prostitutes' quarter of the city, where the Campbells had found rooms in a tenement. "The worst part of the 'revolution' was in this and the adjoining street", Campbell reported

---

[2] Anna Campbell Lyle, *Son of Valour*, unpublished manuscript, 77.

to his friend C. J. Sibbett soon after their arrival. "Machine guns were posted at every corner and we had to keep indoors after dark." [3] At the height of the violence, a bomb exploded about two hundred yards from where the Campbells were staying, shaking the doors and windows of their apartment. "The anarchists have made their bombs so badly that they either were duds or when they did go off it was generally during their manufacture—blowing up a posse of anarchists, which discouraged them rather. The only serious tragedy was the derailment of the Seville express by a bomb." [4]

This baptism of fire seemed to have inflamed Campbell's passion for Spain and its people. In a letter to Wyndham Lewis, he described Barcelona as "a fine place ... full of dancing girls". [5] To Sibbett he wrote that it was "the strangest town I have seen, the most extraordinary clash of modern and ancient". The city was "seething with politics and strikes ... For the Catalonians, as with the Irish, politics is a national industry." [6] Yet, if politics was their national industry, the national religion of the Catalonians, as with the Irish, was Catholicism. Thus the "extraordinary clash of modern and ancient" was a clash between modern ideologies, such as communism, anarchism and fascism, and the ancient faith of the Spanish people. The impact of the latter on Campbell and his family was exemplified by Anna Campbell Lyle's memories of her first impressions of Barcelona:

> The quantity of churches was a surprise and the fact that they were usually full at least twice a day. Their bells were a delight. Such a variety ringing for so many different services. Such a variety of different tolls and pitches ringing all through the day for Mass, for Benediction, for the dead and for the Angelus. The Angelus ringing every six hours in memory of Our Lady and to venerate her with a short prayer was especially beautiful, especially when heard in the country at some distance from the church when the ringing of the bell was

[3] Joseph Pearce, *Bloomsbury and Beyond: The Friends and Enemies of Roy Campbell* (London: HarperCollins, 2001), 153.
[4] Ibid., 153.
[5] Ibid.
[6] Ibid.

wafted across the fields giving one an ineffable sense of peace and age-old civilization.[7]

These words, written many years later and colored by subsequent experience, illustrate nonetheless the real impact that Catholic Christianity exerted on the whole family following their arrival in Spain. The "sense of peace and age-old civilization", wafting across the fields with the bells of the Angelus, was evocative of the Church at prayer. Its peaceful potency, encapsulated so timelessly in Millet's famous painting, would prove to be a powerful stimulus to the imagination of both Roy and Mary as Spain seeped ever more deeply into their psyches.

It is perhaps significant that, in his autobiography, *Broken Record*, which he wrote in great haste following his arrival in Barcelona, Campbell refers to himself for the first time as a Catholic, although it seems that he does so more as a means of thumbing his nose at English Protestantism than as an affirmation of his own belief in Christian orthodoxy.

> Protestantism is a cowardly sort of Atheism, especially in the anglo-Oxfordish-Henry VIII sense. It has even betrayed great minds like Milton's, who in *Comus* attacks female virtue, reducing it to lawcourt, technical terms and destroying the idea of virtue as "value", charm or valour, in a manner that would make Sappho, Sulpicia, Heloise and the holy Saint Teresa ... turn somersaults in their graves.
> To read a few pages of Saint Teresa and then turn to this unholy onslaught makes one regret the wreck of the Armada and the loss of the Inquisition.[8]

As with so much of his satire, the shrillness of tone and the desire to shock or offend dulls the sharpness of the point he seeks to make, but Campbell's evident preference for pre-Reformation thought, or what on the following page he terms "traditional human values", is clear enough. Clearly, in the "clash of modern and ancient", he is siding resolutely with the latter.

---

[7] Campbell Lyle, *Son of Valour*, 75.
[8] Roy Campbell, *Broken Record* (London: Boriswood, 1934), 157.

If the impact of his arrival in Spain had signaled more clearly than ever Campbell's break with intellectual modernism, he still had no ordered or coherent philosophy with which to counter it. Having diagnosed the disease, he was still uncertain of the cure and was left groping, with little more than fragments of a truth only dimly discerned, with elusive shadows. This groping after the shadows of truth found expression in *Mithraic Emblems*, a sequence of sonnets that serves to illustrate his spiritual quest from its tentative beginnings in Provence to its final fulfillment under the protective mantle of Lady Spain.

Campbell's interest in Mithraism was ignited by his arrival in Provence, a region awash with relics of this ancient religion that, for a time during the declining centuries of the Roman Empire, had struggled with Christianity for the hearts and minds of Europeans. As a religion that valued strength and nobility over meekness and humility, Mithraism was seen as the religion of the soldier, whereas Christianity was seen as the religion of the slave. For Campbell, who greatly admired Julius Caesar and the martial spirit of Rome Triumphant, Mithraism seemed a more natural home than Christianity. Interwoven with his preference for the faith of the warrior was his attraction to the myth, rooted in tauromachy, which lay at the heart of Mithraism. The forces of life in Mithraism are symbolized by a wild bull, by which sacrifice Mithras brought forth all the fruits of the earth. In Campbell's fertile imagination, the courage of the arena took on a mystical transcendence, a ritualistic reenactment of the sacrificial miracle of life. The bullfight was more than a mere sport: it was a spiritual sacrifice.

This potent imagery, reinforced by the Mithraic worship of the light- and life-giving power of the sun, combined to form the catalytic inspiration for the sonnets. The sense of obscurantism and obliqueness that pervades the sonnets is heightened by the overlaying of other Mithraic emblems, such as the image of the raven as a messenger of the Sun God, and the snake and the scorpion as images of the hateful designs of the Evil One. To complicate matters still further, Campbell christens his Mithraism with specifically Catholic imagery, such as the "seven sorrowful swords" that pierced the heart of the Blessed Virgin during the Passion of her Son.

The towering influence of Saint John of the Cross, the great Spanish poet, mystic and doctor of the Church, emerges as a herald of divine revelations, a surrogate Saint John the Baptist preparing the way for the coming of Christ. At the end of the sequence, Mithras himself speaks, confessing that he, the god identified with the sun, is but a servant of the one true God.

> We work for the same Boss
> though you are earth and I a star,
> and herdsmen both, though my guitar
> is strung to strum the world across!

He, Mithras, serves the same God as does the poet, the God who won His victory on the Cross. In the final sonnet, addressed "To the Sun", the poet affirms his unequivocal embrace of Christian faith.

The twenty-three sonnets that comprise the *Mithraic Emblems* clearly represent the story of a spiritual conversion. Beginning with the seeds of Mithraic uncertainty planted in Provence, the soul's transformation would finally bear Christian fruit in the fertile, faithful soil of Spain. The sonnets serve as living proof that the arrival of Roy and Mary Campbell in Spain was crucial to their conversion.

Years later, with the advantage of hindsight, Campbell rationalized, in typically uncompromising style, the nature of Spain's importance to him and his wife.

> Protestants go to these countries for spiritual fresh air, yet ... they ascribe the attraction, which is really that of the Church and the people who have not been amputated from the Church by force of tyrants like Henry VIII, or crooks like Calvin and Luther—to the climate or the landscape, or to anything else save in the culture and civilization which hold them spellbound ... They would sooner join with atheists and diabolists ... than with anything straightforwardly European or Roman, though they will hang around a place like Spain for whatever by-products of the Catholic faith they can pick up buck-shee, without any responsibilities—the courtesy, hospitality, and nobility of the people.
>
> From the very beginning my wife and I understood the real issues in Spain. There could be no compromise ... between the East and the West, between Credulity and Faith, between irresponsible innovation

... and tradition, between the emotions (disguised as Reason) and the intelligence.[9]

It is clear from this robust defense of the Catholic faith that Campbell considered Catholicism to be the antidote to the "psychic miasma" that he had sought to confront, somewhat inarticulately, in *Broken Record* and in his earlier verse satire *The Georgiad*. The Church to which he was to offer his allegiance was very much the Church Militant, waging war on the intellectual modernism that he despised. Until their arrival in Spain, he and Mary had been "vaguely and vacillatingly Anglo-Catholic ... but now was the time to decide whether ... to remain half-apathetic to the great fight which was obviously approaching—or whether we should step into the front ranks of the Regular Army of Christ".[10] Their final decision to be received into the Catholic Church was made in the small village of Altea, squeezed between the mountains and the sea, not far from Alicante. "I don't think that my family and I were converted by any event at any given moment", Campbell wrote later. "We lived for a time on a small farm in the sierras at Altea where the working people were mostly good Catholics, and there was such a fragrance and freshness in their life, in their bravery, in their reverence, that it took hold of us all imperceptibly."[11] Presenting themselves to Father Gregorio, the village priest, Roy and Mary requested instruction for themselves and for their two daughters, Teresa and Anna. According to Teresa, the decision had "a profound influence on our lives and filled an abysmal vacuum".[12]

It is significant that many of the later, and specifically Christian, sonnets in the *Mithraic Emblems* sequence were written in Altea at around the time of Campbell's conversion. It was also during this period that he wrote "The Fight", one of his finest poems, in which he pours out the fervor of his Christian conversion and describes the interior

[9] Roy Campbell, *Light on a Dark Horse* (London: Hollis & Carter, 1951), 316–17.

[10] Ibid., 317.

[11] Quoted in Matthew Hoehn, O.S.B., ed., *Catholic Authors: Contemporary Biographical Sketches 1930–1947* (Newark, N.J.: Saint Mary's Abbey Press, 1947), 104.

[12] Teresa Campbell, unpublished memoirs; quoted in Pearce, *Bloomsbury and Beyond*, 164.

struggle that led him to it. "The fight" is being waged for the poet's soul in the militant and militaristic imagery of an aerial dogfight.

> One silver-white and one of scarlet hue,
> Storm-hornets humming in the wind of death,
> Two aeroplanes were fighting in the blue
> Above our town: and if I held my breath,
> It was because my youth was in the Red
> While in the White an unknown pilot flew—
> And that the White had risen overhead.

Clearly the struggle is not merely between belief and unbelief but between the poet's new and previous self. His youth, scarlet with sinfulness and red with the political atheism he had rejected, was at war with a new force in his life—the "white", symbolic of the Mithraic unity of the spectral colors and also of the transfigured purity of Christ, the "unknown pilot". The red craft, the former self, is finally shot down so that the white can emerge triumphant, a "white phoenix" rising from the ashes of "his scarlet sire". The final verse is a joyous hymn of thanksgiving for the poet's deliverance, paying homage to the victory of the "Solar Christ", the Sun and Son Ascendant.

> The towers and trees were lifted hymns of praise,
> The city was a prayer, the land a nun:
> The noonday azure strumming all its rays
> Sang that a famous battle had been won,
> As signing his white Cross, the very Sun,
> The Solar Christ and captain of my days
> Zoomed to the zenith; and his will was done.

Campbell's passion for Spain, which he later described as "a country to which I owe everything as having saved my soul", was inflamed still further by the ancient city of Toledo, the city to which the family moved in June 1935. "Good Lord, kid," Campbell exclaimed to Mary when they first arrived, "this town is fabulous! I never imagined it would be so marvelous! Let's stay here for the rest of our lives." [13]

---

[13] Campbell Lyle, *Son of Valour*, 90.

Toledo was bulging with religious buildings, including two cathedrals, and because the great fortress of the Alcazar served as one of Spain's leading military academies, every other person seemed to be a monk, nun, priest, seminarian or soldier. Mrs. Campbell Lyle recalled that her father was "almost too enthusiastic over the town", soaking up the atmosphere of military and religious discipline that permeated every aspect of its life. "Its strong, nostalgically evocative historical and literary associations overwhelmed him." [14] Clearly Toledo had cast its spell on Campbell, who dubbed it "a sacred city of the mind", [15] and one can imagine his echoing the words of the Austrian lyric poet Rainer Maria Rilke, who had been similarly intoxicated by the city's mystical beauty. "My God," Rilke had enthused, "how many things have I loved because they tried to be like this, because they had a drop of this blood in their hearts ... Can I bear it?" [16]

"But it was not only Toledo itself that had this effect on my father," wrote Mrs. Campbell Lyle, "it was the whole of Spain—its architecture, its painting, its language."

> What affected him most profoundly was to find a country where tradition still exercised a civilizing force on the population. He was deeply affected by the mystery and spiritual strength of this surprising country. Obviously in Toledo he was suffering from culture-shock. Spanish culture had opened up a vast new vein of gold in the fabulous mine of the arts, and he found it intoxicating ... He was immersed in the works of Gongora, Quevado, Calderon, Lopa de Vega, Fray Luis de Leon, Teresa of Avila and John of the Cross; immersed also in the paintings of Goya, Velazquez (his favourite) and El Greco—who lived and died in Toledo. [17]

Campbell was also fascinated by the ordinary Spanish people with whom he imbibed wine in the local cafes, intoxicated by their conversation, "so prolific in proverbs, puns, irony and fatalism". [18] His gratitude and

[14] Ibid., 93.
[15] In his poem "Toledo, July 1936".
[16] Quoted in Campbell Lyle, *Son of Valour*, 93.
[17] Ibid., 94.
[18] Ibid.

love for those who populated the sacred city of his mind was expressed effusively in his poem "Driving Cattle to Casas Buenas".

> The church, with storks upon the steeple,
> And scarcely could my cross be signed,
> When round me came those Christian people
> So hospitably clean, and kind.
> Beans and Alfalfa in the manger—
> Alfalfa, there was never such!
> And rice and rabbit for the stranger.
> Thank you very much!

Little could Campbell have known during those halcyon days in Toledo in 1935 that his bliss would soon be blistered by a fratricidal civil war in which the Spanish people would expose their dark and murderous underbelly.

In March 1936 the anticlerical contagion spreading across Spain reached the streets of Toledo. Churches were burned in a series of violent riots in which priests and monks were attacked. During these bloody disturbances, Roy and Mary Campbell sheltered in their house several of the Carmelite monks from the neighboring monastery. These anticlerical riots shattered Campbell's perception of Toledo as a pastoral paradise beyond the ravages of time. It seemed that even the sacred city had succumbed to secularism and that he and Mary, refugees from modernity, were once more without refuge.

By bribing some militiamen, the family managed to escape from Toledo in the back of a truck used for conveying corpses. Eventually, by long and tedious stages, they made their way to Madrid and then to Valencia. In every village en route they saw burned or burning churches, a grim reminder of the madness gripping the country they had learned to love but were now being forced to flee. On 9 August 1936 Roy and Mary Campbell, together with their two daughters, boarded HMS *Maine* bound for Marseilles. The Campbells had spent less than three years of their torrid and turbulent lives in Spain, but those three years were the most important and most potently significant days of their lives. Life after Spain would never be the same.

EVELYN WAUGH

Ultramodern to Ultramontane

Conversion is like stepping across the chimney piece out of a
Looking-Glass world, where everything is an absurd caricature,
into the real world God made; and then begins the delicious
process of exploring it limitlessly.

THESE WORDS OF EVELYN WAUGH, written in "intense delight" to
Edward Sackville-West after the latter had informed him of his
intention to be received into the Catholic Church, represent perhaps
the most succinct and sufficient description of the process of conversion ever written. Waugh's own conversion from the "absurd caricature" of ultramodernity to the "real world" of Catholic orthodoxy
was greeted with astonishment by the literary world and caused a sensation in the media.

Waugh's reception into the Church on 29 September 1930 prompted
bemused bewilderment in the following morning's edition of the *Daily
Express*. It seemed incomprehensible that an author notorious for his
"almost passionate adherence to the ultra-modern" could have joined
the Catholic Church. In the gossip columns, his latest novel, *Vile Bodies*, had been dubbed "the ultra-modern novel". How could the pur-
veyor of all things modern have turned to the pillar of all things ancient?

The paradox was both perplexing and provocative, prompting the
Express to publish two lead articles on the significance of Waugh's
decision. Finally, three weeks after Waugh's controversial conversion,
Waugh's own contribution to the debate, entitled "Converted to Rome:
Why It Has Happened to Me", was published. It was given a full-
page spread, boldly headlined.

Waugh's article was so lucid in its exposition that it belied any suggestion that he had taken his momentous step lightly, or out of ignorance. He dismissed the very suggestion that he had been "captivated

by the ritual" of the Church or that he wanted to have his mind made up for him. Instead, he insisted that the "essential issue" that had led to his conversion was a belief that the modern world was facing a choice between "Christianity and Chaos":

> Today we can see it on all sides as the active negation of all that western culture has stood for. Civilization—and by this I do not mean talking cinemas and tinned food, nor even surgery and hygienic houses, but the whole moral and artistic organization of Europe—has not in itself the power of survival. It came into being through Christianity, and without it has no significance or power to command allegiance. The loss of faith in Christianity and the consequential lack of confidence in moral and social standards have become embodied in the ideal of a materialistic, mechanized state ... It is no longer possible ... to accept the benefits of civilization and at the same time deny the supernatural basis upon which it rests.

Waugh concluded by stating his belief that Catholicism was the "most complete and vital form" of Christianity.

The debate continued in the next day's edition of the *Express* with the publication of an article by a Protestant member of Parliament, which was followed, a day later, with an article by Father Woodlock, a Jesuit, entitled "Is Britain Turning to Rome?" Three days later, an entire page was given over to the ensuing letters. Seldom has a religious conversion prompted such a blaze of national publicity.

Part of the reason for the extensive interest in Waugh's conversion, apart from his own celebrity status as a fashionable young author of best-selling satirical novels, was the growing awareness that his reception into the Church was only the latest of a long and lengthening list of literary converts to the Catholic faith. On 8 October 1930 the *Bystander* observed of Waugh's conversion that "the brilliant young author" was "the latest man of letters to be received into the Catholic Church. Other well-known literary people who have gone over to Rome include Sheila Kaye-Smith, Compton MacKenzie, Alfred Noyes, Father Ronald Knox and G. K. Chesterton". The list was impressive but far from exhaustive. By the 1930s the tide of converts had become a torrent, and throughout that decade there were some twelve thousand converts a year in England alone.

A similar mood prevailed in the United States. A few weeks after the controversy in the *Daily Express*, a debate between G. K. Chesterton and the famous Chicago lawyer Clarence Darrow on the question "Will the World Return to Religion?" attracted an audience of four thousand to the Mecca Temple in New York. At the close of the debate, a vote was taken. The result was 2,359 for Chesterton's point of view and 1,022 for Darrow's.

Waugh's particular path to Rome had been influenced by a number of the literary converts who had preceded him, particularly by Chesterton and Knox, the latter of whom would be the subject of a biography by Waugh published in 1959. When Waugh was only eleven, his father had read Knox' antimodernist satire *Reunion All Round* and was "dazzled" by its brilliance. "Since then," Waugh wrote to Knox years later, "every word you have written and spoken has been pure light to me." In 1924 Waugh had been impressed by Knox' oratorical prowess at the Oxford Union. On that occasion, Knox had been among several well-known speakers to debate the proposition "that civilization has advanced". In Waugh's opinion, Knox had stolen the show by showing that "we were rapidly approaching the civilization of the savage". In Waugh's public confession of faith in the *Express*, there are clearly discernible echoes of Knox' brilliant oratory from six years earlier.

The most striking example of Chesterton's influence on Waugh is to be found in the way that Chesterton inspired *Brideshead Revisited*, arguably the finest of Waugh's novels and undeniably one of the greatest novels of the twentieth century. The novel's central theme of the redemption of lost souls by means of "the unseen hook and invisible line ... the twitch upon the thread" was taken from one of Chesterton's *Father Brown* stories. Waugh told a friend that he was anxious to obtain a copy of the omnibus edition of the *Father Brown* stories at the time he was putting the finishing touches to *Brideshead*, and a memorandum he wrote for MGM studios when a film version of the novel was being considered confirmed the profundity of Chesterton's influence:

> The Roman Catholic Church has the unique power of keeping remote control over human souls which have once been part of her. G. K. Chesterton has compared this to the fisherman's line, which allows the fish the illusion of free play in the water and yet has him by the hook;

in his own time the fisherman by a "twitch upon the thread" draws the fish to land.

The Chestertonian metaphor was not lost on Ronald Knox when he first read *Brideshead Revisited*: "Once you reach the end, needless to say the whole cast—even Beryl—falls into place and the twitch upon the thread happening in the very bowels of Metroland is inconceivably effective".

In many respects, Waugh's finest novel is a reiteration of the theme in his article for the *Daily Express*. It is a tale of hope among the ruins of a vanishing civilization in which the light of Christianity shines out amid the Chaos.

Brideshead Revisited sold exceedingly well on both sides of the Atlantic. In England, the *Tablet* acclaimed it "a book for which it is safe to prophesy a lasting place among the major works of fiction." In America, *Time* described Waugh as a stylist unexcelled among contemporary novelists.

The praise was tempered by a vociferous minority who disliked *Brideshead Revisited* on both political and religious grounds. In particular, the American critic Edmund Wilson criticized the religious dimension in the novel. "He was outraged (quite legitimately by his standards) at finding God introduced into my story", Waugh replied. "I believe that you can only leave God out by making your characters pure abstractions." Modern novelists, Waugh continued, "try to represent the whole human mind and soul and yet omit its determining character—that of being God's creature with a defined purpose. So in my future books there will be two things to make them unpopular: a preoccupation with style and the attempt to represent man more fully, which to me means only one thing, man in his relation to God."

With the publication of *Brideshead Revisited*, Waugh completed the metamorphosis from ultramodern to ultramontane and in so doing passed from fashion to antifashion. As with so many of the other converts at the vanguard of the Catholic literary revival, his work was an act of sub-creation reflecting the glory of Creation itself. As Waugh himself put it: "There is an Easter sense in which all things are made new in the risen Christ. A tiny gleam of this is reflected in all true art." What is true of art is as true of the artist. In the works of Waugh, as in the works of the other literary converts, a tiny gleam of Christ is always reflected.

26

BEYOND THE FACTS OF LIFE

Douglas Lane Patey's Biography of Evelyn Waugh[†]

"NOT FACTS FIRST Truth first." These words, scrawled by G. K. Chesterton into a notebook sometime around 1910, should be pinned in a prominent position above the desk of anyone writing biographies. The principal concern of a biographer should be to discover who someone is, rather than what someone did. The latter represents the facts of life, whereas the former embodies its underlying truth. The facts are merely indicators, the tools by which the truth can be discerned. It is the failure to adhere to, or to comprehend, this golden rule that has led to the failure of many modern biographers to shed light on their subjects. This deep-rooted problem is most evident in the failure of agnostic or secularized biographers to understand the Christianity of their subjects. The books may be well researched, but the facts bestow only knowledge, not understanding, and, still less, wisdom.

"It is utterly futile to write about the Christian faith from the outside", wrote Maurice Baring.

> A good example of this is the extremely conscientious novel by Mrs. Humphry Ward called *Helbeck of Bannisdale*. It is a study of Catholicism from the outside, and the author has taken scrupulous pains to make it accurate, detailed and exhaustive. The only drawback is that, not being able to see the matter from the inside, she misses the whole point.

What is true of Christianity in general is true of Christian writers in particular. So often they are misunderstood by their biographers to

---

[†] *Life of Evelyn Waugh: A Critical Biography* (Oxford: Blackwell, 2001).

such an extent that their portraits are two-dimensional at best or, at worst, are misleading caricatures. Few Christian writers knew this better than Evelyn Waugh, who considered that all life outside the Faith was itself "an absurd caricature".

The paramount importance of Waugh's conversion and his Christian faith are evident from this succinctly sublime sentence, and any biographer of Waugh should have this epigraph attached securely beside Chesterton's before daring to proceed. Unfortunately, few have paid it due attention. Martin Stannard's two-volume study was full of facts but largely devoid of truth, so that its claim to be "definitive" was a mockery. It failed to define Waugh's being in any way that Waugh himself would have countenanced and failed to understand the metaphysical realities that were the prime movers and motivators in Waugh's life and art. It is, therefore, refreshing that the jacket notes to Douglas Lane Patey's new *Life of Waugh* claim that Professor Patey "explores the nature of Waugh's Catholicism and examines how his religious beliefs began to guide his novelistic practice." It is also encouraging that the notes insist that Patey's book "works to redress the bias against its subject that is so representative of Stannard's two-volume study."

After being suitably encouraged by the promise of the cover blurb, it was even more refreshing to discover that the book itself largely lives up to its billing. Patey possesses a firm grasp of the philosophical foundations upon which Waugh built his life and places these metaphysical realities at the center of his study. Whereas other studies would have lingered on Waugh's evident love for gossip, Patey considers it more significant to point out, for example, that Waugh took Jacques Maritain's *Introduction to Philosophy* and a volume of Aquinas as reading matter during a trip to British Guiana in 1932. According to Patey, the choice of such reading material "attests a desire not only to educate himself in his faith but also to clarify his stance as a writer." The extent to which Waugh became *au fait* with the Church's philosophy can be gauged from an essay entitled "Sloth" that he wrote in 1962 for a series in the *Sunday Times* on the seven deadly sins. Again, it is significant that Patey considers this particular essay worthy of quotation:

> What then is this Sloth which can merit the extremity of divine punishment? St. Thomas's answer is both comforting and surprising: *tristitia*

de bono spirituali, a sadness in the face of spiritual good. Man is made for joy in the love of God, a love which he expresses in service. If he deliberately turns away from that joy, he is denying the purpose of his existence. The malice of Sloth lies not merely in the neglect of duty (though that can be a symptom of it) but in the refusal of joy. It is allied to despair.

Patey is also good at placing Waugh within a wider network of minds. The influence of Belloc, R. H. Benson and Christopher Dawson is discussed, and Waugh's concept of Christendom and his initial attraction to Belloc's Europe of the Faith are considered at length. Other important figures in the Christian literary revival also figure prominently as influences on Waugh, including the Jesuits Philip Caraman and Martin D'Arcy, Ronald Knox, T. S. Eliot and, of course, Chesterton.

Patey is to be commended on the whole for his treatment of Waugh's alleged reactionary politics. Patey quotes Roy Campbell, another writer who has been vilified for his political views, who complained that "anyone who was not pro-Red in the Spanish War automatically became a fascist." This was echoed by Waugh, who wrote of the Spanish civil war that he was "not in the predicament of choosing between two evils." Unfortunately, Patey's otherwise temperate discussion of this potentially volatile area is marred by an insinuation that Chesterton was a fascist or at least a fellow traveler. The insinuation arises from a selective quotation from Chesterton's *The Resurrection of Rome* that overlooks the explicitly antifascist conclusion that Chesterton eventually arrives at elsewhere in the same volume. After stating his own preference for "a real white flag of freedom" in opposition to "the red flag of Communist or the black flag of Fascist regimentation", Chesterton gives "the logical case against fascism", namely, "that it appeals to an appetite for authority, without very clearly giving the authority for the appetite". In this pyrotechnic epigram he not only rejects fascism but gives, in a flash of inspiration, the most brilliant and pithy putdown of fascism imaginable.

Apart from this one faux pas, Patey's study excels—particularly in placing Waugh within the wider context of the Christian literary revival. This revival spawned numerous works that were acts of subcreation reflecting the glory of Creation itself. As Waugh himself put it: "There is an Easter sense in which all things are made new in the risen Christ. A tiny gleam of this is reflected in all true art." What is true of art is true of the artist. Any biographer who fails to understand this bedrock reality will fail not only to understand the life he is writing but, more crucially, will fail to understand the life he is himself living. Thankfully, Patey is very much alive and, in consequence, so is his subject.

27

IN PURSUIT OF THE GREENE-EYED MONSTER

The Quest for Graham Greene

M ORE THAN A CENTURY after the birth of Graham Greene, questions remain as to his enduring legacy. Although few would question his place as one of the most influential and enigmatic writers of
the twentieth century, it is equally true that few would agree as to the
exact nature of his influence or as to the peculiar quality of his enigma.
The fact remains that Greene is not only one of the most important
writers of his generation but is also one of the most elusive. Indeed, it
was Greene's view that one cannot understand a man without understanding "the man within". As such, the quest for Graham Greene
involves a pursuit of the Greene-eyed monster that haunted his luridly
vivid imagination. Greene's novels, and the characters that adorn them,
are riddled with angst and anger. Simultaneously confused and confounded by a deep sense of guilt and failure, his characters are informed
and sometimes deformed by a deeply felt religious sensibility. The
oppressive weight of the real presence of Christian faith, or the terrible emptiness of its real absence, turn Greene's novels into a fascinating and unforgettable conflict between the fertile and the furtive.
The depiction of a drunken priest in *The Power and the Glory* and also
in the play *The Potting Shed* exudes Greene's morbid preoccupation
with human folly and failure, as well as exhibits his belief in the remnants of human dignity even amid the deepest degradation. At other
times, as in *The Comedians*, he squirms amid the squalor of sin and
cynicism, or, as in *Brighton Rock*, he squeals in the sadistic self-
indulgence of the psychopath.

Greene's fiction is gripping because it grapples with faith and dis-illusionment on the shifting sands of uncertainty in a relativistic age. His tormented characters are the products of Greene's own tortured soul, and one suspects that he was more baffled than anyone else at the contradictions at the core of his own character and, in conse-quence, at the heart of the characters that his fertile and fetid imag-ination had created.

From his earliest childhood, Greene exhibited a world-weariness that at times reached the brink of despair. In large part this bleak approach may have been due to a wretched childhood and to the traumatic time spent at Berkhamsted School, where his father was headmaster. His writing is full of the bitter scars of his schooldays. In his autobiographical *A Sort of Life*, Greene described the panic in his family after he had been finally driven in desperation to run away from the horrors of the school: "My father found the situation beyond him ... My brother suggested psycho-analysis as a possible solution, and my father—an astonishing thing in 1920—agreed."

For six months the young, and no doubt impressionable, Greene lived at the house of the analyst to whom he had been referred. This episode would be described by him as "perhaps the happiest six months of my life", but it is possible that the seeds of his almost obsessive self-analysis were sown at this time. Significantly, he chose the follow-ing words of Sir Thomas Browne as an epigraph to his first novel, *The Man Within*: "There's another man within me that's angry with me."

In later years, the genuine groping for religious truth in Greene's fiction would often be thwarted by his obsession with the darker recesses of his own character. This darker side is invariably transposed onto all his fictional characters, so that even their goodness is warped. Greene saw human nature as "not black and white" but "black and grey", and he referred to his need to write as "a neurosis ... an irresistible urge to pinch the abscess which grows periodically in order to squeeze out all the pus". Such a tortured outlook may have produced entertaining novels but could not produce any true sense of reality. Greene's novels were Frankenstein monsters that were not so much in need of Freud-ian analysis as they were the products of it.

Greene's conversion in 1926, when he was still only twenty-one years old, was described in *A Sort of Life*, in which he contrasted his

own agnosticism as an undergraduate, when "to me religion went no
deeper than the sentimental hymns in the school chapel", with the
fact that his future wife was a Roman Catholic:

> I met the girl I was to marry after finding a note from her at the
> porters lodge in Balliol protesting against my inaccuracy in writing,
> during the course of a film review, of the "worship" Roman Catholics
> gave to the Virgin Mary, when I should have used the term "hyper-
> dulia". I was interested that anyone took these subtle distinctions of an
> unbelievable theology seriously, and we became acquainted.

The girl was Vivien Dayrell-Browning, then twenty years old, who,
five years earlier, had shocked her family by being received into the
Catholic Church. Concerning Greene's conversion, Vivien recalled that
"he was mentally converted; logically, it seemed to him ... It was all
rather private and quiet. I don't think there was any emotion involved".
This was corroborated by Greene himself when he stated in an interview that "my conversion was not in the least an emotional affair. It
was purely intellectual."

A more detailed, though hardly a more emotional, description of
the process of his conversion was given in his autobiography. "Now it
occurred to me ... that if I were to marry a Catholic I ought at least
to learn the nature and limits of the beliefs she held." He walked to
the local "sooty neo-Gothic Cathedral", which "possessed for me a
certain gloomy power because it represented the inconceivable and
the incredible" and dropped a note requesting instruction into a wooden
box for inquiries. His motivation was one of morbid curiosity and
had precious little to do with a genuine desire for conversion. "I had
no intention of being received into the Church. For such a thing to
happen I would need to be convinced of its truth and that was not
even a remote possibility."

His first impressions of Father Trollope, the priest to whom he would
go for instruction, had reinforced his prejudiced view of Catholicism:
"At the first sight he was all I detested most in my private image of
the Church". Soon, however, he was forced to modify his view, coming to realize that his initial impressions of the priest were not only
erroneous but that he was "facing the challenge of an inexplicable
goodness". From the outset, he had "cheated" Father Trollope by fail-

ing to disclose his irreligious motive in seeking instruction, and he did not tell the priest of his engagement to a Catholic. "I began to fear that he would distrust the genuineness of my conversion if it so happened that I chose to be received, for after a few weeks of serious argument the 'if' was becoming less and less improbable".

The "if" revolved primarily on the primary "if" surrounding God's existence. The center of the argument was the center itself or, more precisely, whether there was any center:

> My primary difficulty was to believe in a God at all . . . I didn't disbelieve in Christ—I disbelieved in God. If I were ever to be convinced in even the remote possibility of a supreme, omnipotent and omniscient power I realized that nothing afterwards could seem impossible. It was on the ground of dogmatic atheism that I fought and fought hard. It was like a fight for personal survival.

The fight for personal survival was lost, and Greene, in losing himself, had gained the Faith. Yet the dogmatic atheist was only overpowered; he was not utterly vanquished. He would reemerge continually as the devil, or at least as the devil's advocate, in the murkier moments in his novels.

The literary critic J. C. Whitehouse has compared Greene to Thomas Hardy, rightly asserting that Greene's gloomy vision at least allows for a light beyond the darkness, whereas Hardy allows for darkness only. Chesterton said of Hardy that he was like the village atheist brooding over the village idiot. Greene is often like a self-loathing sceptic brooding over himself. As such, the vision of the divine in his fiction is often thwarted by the self-erected barriers of his own ego. Only rarely does the glimmer of God's light penetrate the chinks in the armor, entering like a vertical shaft of hope to exorcise the simmering despair.

Few have understood Greene better than his friend Malcolm Muggeridge, who described him as "a Jekyll and Hyde character, who has not succeeded in fusing the two sides of himself into any kind of harmony". There is more true depth and perception in this one succinct observation by Muggeridge than in all the pages of psychobabble that have been written about Greene's work by lesser critics. The paradoxical union of Catholicism and scepticism, incarnated in Greene and his work, had created a hybrid, a metaphysical mutant, as fascinating as Jekyll and Hyde and perhaps as futile. The resulting contortions and contradictions of both his own character and those of the characters he created give the impression of depth; but the depth was often only that of ditch water, perceived as bottomless because the bottom could not be seen. Greene's genius was rooted in the ingenuity with which he muddied the waters.

It was both apt and prophetic that Greene should have taken the name of Saint Thomas the Doubter at his reception into the Church in February 1926. Whatever else he was or wasn't, he was always a doubter par excellence. He doubted others; he doubted himself; he doubted God. Whatever else might be puzzling about this most puzzling of men, his debt to doubt is indubitable. Ironically, it was this very doubt that had so often provided the creative force for his fiction. Perhaps the secret of his enduring popularity lies in his being a doubting Thomas in an age of doubt. As such, Greene's Catholicism becomes an enigma, a conversation piece—even a gimmick. Yet, if his novels owe a debt to doubt, their profundity lies in the ultimate doubt about the doubt. In the end, it was this ultimate doubt about doubt that kept Graham Greene clinging doggedly, desperately—and doubtfully—to his faith.

28

CROSS PURPOSES

Greene, Undset and Bernanos

A review of J. C. Whitehouse's

Vertical Man: The Human Being in the Catholic Novels of Graham Greene, Sigrid Undset and Georges Bernanos[†]

TOWARD THE BEGINNING of this thought-provoking study of three of the last century's most prominent Catholic novelists, Dr. Whitehouse claims that their work was informed by "that older Catholic view of man as a creature of enormous individual worth, living in a special and dynamic relationship with his Creator, taught by the Church Christ founded and moving gradually towards salvation or damnation". Rather incongruously, he then adds that such a view "no longer seems quite relevant to the newer, post-Council and conciliatory Catholic world of community and communications". This alleged schism between the pre- and post-conciliar Church runs through Dr. Whitehouse's book and mars what is otherwise an intriguing study.

The vision of "vertical man", who is principally concerned with his relationship with God, and the vision of "horizontal man", who sees himself as part of society or the community, are perceived as distinct. The Second Vatican Council is seen as guilty of promoting the latter vision of man as opposed to the former. Perhaps, however, Dr. Whitehouse is guilty of praising vertical man to the detriment or even exclusion of horizontal man. Surely the two great commandments of Christ, that we love the Lord our God *and* that we love our neighbor, place the two visions in equilibrium. We cannot truly do the one

---

[†] London: Saint Austin Press, 1999.

without the other. They are inseparable. The vertical and the horizontal meet in the love of Christ and, in so doing, form the cross of our salvation.

Apart from this reservation, Dr. Whitehouse's study of the vertical aspects of the fiction of Greene, Undset and Bernanos is fascinating. Of the three, Undset emerges as possibly the most profound, particularly in the poignant depiction of the soul as a fathomless sea at the bottom of which is its Creator. "Fear and uneasiness and indignation might chase each other on the surface. But love was felt as something heavy which sank down and down." Such a view is rooted in perennial Christian mysticism. The problem arises when this is confused with, or confounded by, post-Freudian self-analysis. There are dangers in Bernanos' view that life is an elaborate masquerade. If everyone adopts a persona that deceives as much as it reveals, there is nothing left but relativism. The lie is enshrined as the individual's personal truth. At this stage, the perceived depths are an illusion. It is a case not of fathoming the depths of the soul but of muddying the shallows of the self.

Nowhere is this confusion more evident than in the novels of Graham Greene, a fact that Dr. Whitehouse prefers to overlook so that he can concentrate instead on the theological aspects of Greene's work. The genuine groping for religious truth in Greene's fiction is always thwarted by his obsession with the darker side of his own character. As such, his vertical vision only rarely escapes beyond his own ego. It is only at such moments that the glimmer of God's light penetrates the chinks in the armor, a vertical shaft of hope.

The last words belong not to Greene but to his long-suffering wife. "Many of the later Catholic writers had a dark view, whereas Chesterton had high spirits. The later writers seemed depressed in comparison. Perhaps it had something to do with what was happening in the world." Perhaps indeed . . .

29

MUGGERIDGE RESURRECTED

A review of

Malcolm Muggeridge: A Biography
by Gregory Wolfe[†]

STRICTLY SPEAKING, GREGORY WOLFE's biography of Muggeridge is not a new volume. It was first published in 1995 by Hodder and Stoughton in the United Kingdom and, two years later, by Eerdmans in the United States. At the time of its first publication, I was living in England and was putting the finishing touches to my own first biography, a life of G. K. Chesterton, which was to be published by Hodder and Stoughton a year later. I recall that Wolfe's biography appeared at the same time that HarperCollins published another life of Muggeridge, by Richard Ingrams. The two volumes even had very similar titles. Wolfe's was entitled *Malcolm Muggeridge: A Biography*, whereas Ingrams' volume was called, more boldly, *Muggeridge: The Biography*. The boldness of the latter sprang from the fact that Ingrams was a well-known journalist and television celebrity and a long-standing friend of Muggeridge, whereas Wolfe was a young and unknown debutant. Ingrams had a sufficient degree of *gravitas* to claim the right to have written *the* biography of his friend. A similar claim by the young arriviste would have sounded not only absurdly precocious but absolutely preposterous. It would seem, therefore, that this battle of competing biographies was a somewhat one-sided affair. Ingrams was cast in the role of Goliath, whereas Wolfe was David. Surely there could be only one winner, as indeed there was. In conformity with the

[†]Wilmington, Del.: ISI Books, 2003.

tradition established by their archetypal forebears, David triumphed unexpectedly over Goliath.

Although both biographies were enjoyable and sympathetic, Ingrams' bore the mark of the tried and tested journalist, while Wolfe's bore the stamp of the true and trusty scholar. Ingrams waxed eloquently and entertainingly while barely paying lip service to scholarly standards of annotation and source citation; Wolfe wrote well, and with equal eloquence, without ever compromising the highest standards of scholarship. Ingrams was somewhat sketchy in his coverage of the full panorama of Muggeridge's multifaceted life, providing good coverage of some periods but inadequately patchy coverage of others; Wolfe covered every period with detailed dexterity and wove them all together into a perfectly proportioned tapestry. It is, therefore, a real boon for twentieth-century literary scholarship that ISI Books has resurrected Wolfe's wonderful work.

Wolfe sets the tone (if the obscure Irish pun can be forgiven!) in the very opening paragraph of the first chapter.

> In 1903, the year Malcolm Muggeridge was born, George Bernard Shaw published his play, *Man and Superman*. Malcolm's father, H. T. Muggeridge, would boast to his friends that he had published his own Superman in 1903 ... H.T.'s *bon mot* ... concealed a world of hopes and ambitions for his son. It foreshadowed nearly all of the conflicts and tensions that would be played out in Malcolm's life.

In these few lines, Wolfe succeeds in setting the scene for the whole of the life he is about to present to the reader. He sets the scene not merely physically but metaphysically. As Wolfe informs us, Shaw was not only "the leading socialist intellectual of the time", he also "symbolized everything that H.T. fervently admired". Shaw was the hero of Muggeridge's father's generation. He was the prophet of the Nietzschean notion of the superman. The young Muggeridge was born into a world that idolized the myth of "progress" and the perfectibility of mankind. Man, so the theory insisted, would outgrow the primitive superstitions of the past and would evolve into an advanced superintelligent being. Man would become superman. Muggeridge would spend the rest of his life unlearning these dogmas that dogged his childhood. Eventually, and progressively, he would see beyond the chimera of the Shavian "superman" and discover the reality of the essentially unchanging and everlasting "man" that predates and post-dates the Nietzschean nonsense of his father's generation. Eventually. And progressively. But it would take him a lifetime of soul-searching and intellectual probing to do so. This book takes us on that exhila-rating journey as we watch Muggeridge's Dantean progress from the hell of man's insurrection to the heaven of God's resurrection. From Fabian socialist to Roman Catholic convert, and all stops in between, we see the travels and travails of a soul in search of its source.

Muggeridge's journey, or perhaps we should say his pilgrimage, is also interesting for the people who accompanied him along the way. He was born in the same year as Evelyn Waugh and George Orwell, and a year before Graham Greene, and his relationship with these lit-erary giants, his exact contemporaries, is one of the most illuminating and engrossing aspects of his life. There is also a wonderful, if some-what voyeuristic, account of Muggeridge's encounter with the aging Winston Churchill and his sudden vision of Churchill as Shakespeare's King Lear, a pathetic figure, "imprisoned in the flesh, in old age, long-ing for a renewal of the disease of life, all passion unspent" (263).

I note, as a postscript, upon perusing my 1984 edition of *Chambers Biographical Dictionary*, that there is no entry for Muggeridge. It skips from Robert Mugabe to Ladowick Muggleton. The former, as the butcher and tyrant of Zimbabwe, needs no introduction, but who on earth is the latter? I know now, of course, because I have the dictio-nary open in front of me, but why, I wonder, does the obscure founder of an obscure seventeenth-century puritan sect called the Muggleto-nians take precedence over a writer as important as Malcolm Mug-geridge? Why indeed? I note upon further perusal that Muggeridge's aforementioned contemporaries—Greene, Orwell and Waugh—all merit reasonably sized entries in the selfsame dictionary. Perhaps this is fair enough. Perhaps it is true that Muggeridge has not bequeathed to posterity literary classics of the caliber of *Brighton Rock*, *Nineteen Eighty-Four* and *Brideshead Revisited*. His legacy is, however, of a different sort. Aside from his works of real literary merit, of which there are several, he was a pioneer of quality television in the days of the medi-um's infancy, and, more important, he was, and remains, a towering figure as a fearless dissident against the decadence of his age and ours.

As a prophet, his reputation stands secure. He is a modern-day Jeremiah, or, perhaps, England's answer to Solzhenitsyn. Either way, his reputation merits resurrection.

As a writer who has specialized in writing biographies of literary converts to Catholicism, I would have relished the challenge of writing a life of Malcolm Muggeridge. It is, however, too late. The challenge has already been met. The definitive biography has already been written. Indeed, my only complaint is that Gregory Wolfe's book has the wrong title. It is not "a biography"—it is *the* biography of Malcolm Muggeridge.

PART FOUR

J. R. R. TOLKIEN AND THE INKLINGS

30

INKLINGS OF GRACE

THE FIRST HALF of the twentieth century was marked by a battle for the very soul of English literature. The early years of that century were remarkable, principally, for the battle of wits and the war of words between the prophets of secularist "progress" and those of dynamic orthodoxy. In the former camp were the literary giants H. G. Wells and George Bernard Shaw, urged on by the "progressive" socialists of the Fabian Society; in the latter camp were giants of at least equal stature in the pyrotechnic personalities of G. K. Chesterton and Hilaire Belloc.

Two distinct literary "movements" were, in some respects, the inheritors of this struggle. On the side of those who shared Shaw's belief in the perfectibility of man into a mythical superman, and who shared Wells' faith in the benevolence of "progress" or at least his contempt for the past, were the small group of writers and artists that became known, collectively, as the Bloomsbury group. These included Virginia Woolf, Vita Sackville-West, Duncan Grant and, perhaps most notoriously, the archcynic and cultural iconoclast Lytton Strachey. The group's moral relativism, which found expression in a bland blend of subtle subversion and pathetic perversion, was a natural prerequisite for the nihilism of deconstructionism. The other group, far healthier in outlook and far closer to reality, was the Inklings, who included in their number J. R. R. Tolkien, C. S. Lewis and Charles Williams.

The cult of "deconstruction" now exerts a grip on the discipline of literary criticism that is vicelike, in both senses of the word. In fact, and ironically, "deconstruction" is best expressed through the deconstruction, anagrammatically, of the word itself. Deconstruction is the "destruction con". It is the confidence trick by which the edifying edifice of culture is destroyed in the name of "cultural" dissection. It is the destruction of art for "art's" sake. These cultural vivisectionists, practicing their "criticism" much as Josef Mengele practiced his "science", treat artistic works as objects on which to experiment with their existential prejudices. It is literary criticism as cultural abuse. Art as victim.

It was, I think, C. S. Lewis who wrote, no doubt with the cultural abusers in mind, that there are two types of people in the world, those who do things to books and those who allow books to do things to them. The Bloomsbury group and their relativist ilk represent those who do things to books, whereas the Inklings represent those who let books do things to them. The former abuse tradition, molding it into their own pathetically deformed image; the latter use tradition as a mold, forming themselves in the space it provides, enabling its light to shed illumination on both the self and the not-self, that is, on both the subjective and the objective. As such, the Inklings represent not only the antithesis of the Bloomsbury group but also the antidote to its poison. The Inklings represent the power of civilized reconstruction amid the barbaric wasteland of deconstruction. They offer inklings of grace to a sceptic-soiled world.

Lewis disliked those who did things to books, and not merely because what they did to the books was often unmentionable. Apart from the fact that such people were often vandals or vivisectionists, they were also depriving themselves, and those influenced by them, of the enormous benefit that the books could bestow on them. A good book enables the reader to enlarge his experience of life; it enables him to share the life experience and the wisdom of another, namely, the author. The better the book, or the author, the greater the benefit to the reader—but only if the reader is prepared to let the book be a teacher. If he approaches the book with the humility of receptivity, or the receptivity of humility, he will receive its riches in abundance. The book will provide metaphysical nourishment, and this spiritual nutrition will enable him to grow. It will enable him to ennoble himself. If, however, he insists on squeezing the square peg of the book into the round hole of his own preconceptions, he will be severely limiting his ability to benefit from the book's beauty or its wisdom. He will be too busy making the book small enough to fit into the narrow confines of his own prejudices to enjoy the nourishing fruits it has to offer. And there's the rub. In doing things to books, we prevent books from doing things to us, and for us. In the penury of our selfishness, we are depriving ourselves of the many riches to be derived from selflessness. And this is the paradox at the very heart of Lewis' statement. In humility there is reception; in pride there is only self-deception.

Thus, for instance, Wells' blind faith in scientism, the belief that "progress" is both inexorable and inexorably beneficent, led inexorably to his inability to view or value the treasures of the past or the accumulated wisdom of the ages. Thus Shaw's belief in man's perfectibility, that man can become superman, blinded him to the base and basic reality of man's weakness, and this in turn hardened his heart and hindered his ability to sympathize and empathize with beleaguered humanity. Thus Strachey's cynical prejudice against the Catholic Church rendered it impossible for him to understand the great mind and heart of that truly eminent Victorian Cardinal Manning. Prejudice prejudges, and one who prejudges is not fit to judge.

Of course, the secularists and deconstructionists will counter that the Christianity of Chesterton, Belloc and the Inklings meant that they were as prejudiced in their assumptions as were their enemies. Indeed, those secularists who, in spite of their prejudices, have read the Bible, might remind us—no doubt with a smile of triumphalism— that we should examine the plank in our own eye (perhaps, in fact, two planks hammered together in the shape of a cross) before pointing out the motes in the eyes of others. Our reply, of course, should be, "Of course!" It's our duty to remove these planks. They are merely a metaphor, a euphemism, for the pride that must be overcome with the paradoxical strength of meekness in order that the clarity of charity might be attained. If we do not remove the planks from our eyes, we will find ourselves doing things to books, not letting books do things to us. Planks impair vision!

The difference between Christians and secularists does not lie in the existence of the planks, which afflict the vision of believers and unbelievers alike, but in their attitude toward the planks. Christians know that the planks are a recurring problem, that we must be on our guard against their return, and that when we discover their return it is our duty to remove them so that we can restore the clarity of our vision. The problem that our opponents must overcome is much more serious. Many are not aware that planks are a problem. Indeed, many are blinded by the belief that the planks do not exist! If the planks are a euphemism for pride, those who fail to see that pride is a problem, still less a mortal sin, will hardly be bothered to remove them. Those who are proud of their pride are scarcely seeking humility. They might even cherish the plank in their eye as a precious possession and make it the prism through which they view "reality". This is, in fact, exactly what the deconstructionists are doing. They make themselves the sole arbiters of "reality". Their "truth", even if they admit reluctantly that it may not be the only "truth", is, they say, at least as valid as all the others. In subjecting truth to their own prejudices, they are denying, implicitly at least, the validity of objective criteria. The plank in their eye has become the touchstone of reality. Thus, we see (even if they don't) that prejudice is the product of pride. In this way, the cross, far from representing a plank (or two) in our eyes, serves rather as a telescopic sight enabling us to see more clearly.

Ultimately the cross is the very crux of the matter, in the sense that a paradox of cross purposes is at the center of the problem. It is, in fact, not only a paradox of cross purposes but a paradox of cross-beams. The beam in the eye of the proud can be removed only by the beam of light that enters the eye of the humble. The blindness of Bloomsbury is curable only through the inklings of grace.

31

FROM THE PRANCING PONY
TO THE BIRD AND BABY

Roy "Strider" Campbell and the Inklings

O N 3 OCTOBER 1944, during the final months of the Second World
War, J. R. R. Tolkien and Charles Williams called in at the Eagle
and Child pub in the center of Oxford for their customary pint of ale.
They and the other Inklings met on a regular basis in this particular
pub, which was known affectionately as the Bird and Baby. On this
occasion, however, Tolkien and Williams arrived at noon and were
surprised to find C. S. Lewis and his brother "already ensconced". The
conversation was "pretty lively", and Tolkien noticed "a strange tall
gaunt man half in khaki half in mufti with a large wide-awake hat,
bright eyes and a hooked nose sitting in the corner. The others had
their back to him, but I could see in his eye that he was taking an
interest in the conversation quite unlike the ordinary pained astonishment of the British (and American) public at the presence of the Lewises
(and myself) in a pub." The stranger reminded Tolkien of Strider in
The Lord of the Rings, the mysterious Ranger who eavesdropped on
the conversation of the hobbits at the Prancing Pony at Bree.

All of a sudden he butted in, in a strange unplaceable accent, taking up
some point about Wordsworth. In a few seconds he was revealed as
Roy Campbell ... Tableau! Especially as C.S.L. had not long ago vio-
lently lampooned him in the Oxford Magazine ... There is a good
deal of Ulster still left in C.S.L. if hidden from himself. After that things
became fast and furious and I was late for lunch. It was (perhaps) gratifying to find that this powerful poet and soldier desired in Oxford
chiefly to see Lewis (and myself).

The "violent lampoon" to which Tolkien referred was Lewis' poetic riposte to Campbell's long poem *Flowering Rifle*. Campbell's poem, published five years earlier, was a robust and often embarrassingly jingoistic eulogy to the victorious Nationalist forces in the Spanish civil war. In a poem entitled simply "To the Author of *Flowering Rifle*", published in *The Cherwell* magazine on 6 May 1939, Lewis had condemned Campbell's lack of charity, reminding him that "the merciful are promised mercy still". Campbell was a "loud fool" who had learned the art of lying from his enemies on the left,

> since it was from them you learned
> How white to black by jargon can be turned.

Lewis had retained his early admiration for Campbell's poetic powers, declaring that his verse "outsoars with eagle pride" the "nerveless rhythms" of the left-wing poets. Yet his "shrill covin-politics" and that of his enemies were "two peas in a single pod":

> —who cares
> Which kind of shirt the murdering Party wears?

Although Lewis' critique of Campbell's harshness and lack of charity in *Flowering Rifle* was justified, his simplistic approach to the religious and philosophical dynamics of the war in Spain exposed his own political näiveté. Campbell was actually living in Spain when the war began, and he and his family were lucky to escape with their lives. Many of their friends were not so lucky. The priest who had received Roy and Mary Campbell into the Church in 1935 was murdered in cold blood in the following year by communist militiamen, as were the Carmelite monks whom Roy and Mary had befriended in Toledo. In seeing the war in Spain as a fight to the death between traditional Christianity and secular atheism, Campbell was closer to reality than was Lewis with his simplified depiction of a battle between "left" and "right". The war was beyond politics. It was a struggle for the religious heart and soul of Europe.

Campbell had read Lewis' attack on him, but it seems, from Tolkien's rendition of events, that he had taken the criticism in good spirits and that it was Lewis who became aggressive during the "fast and furious" discussion in the Bird and Baby. In spite of their differences, Lewis invited Campbell to a gathering of the Inklings in Lewis' rooms in Magdalen College two days later. Again, it was Lewis who became aggressive. According to Tolkien, Lewis "had taken a fair deal of port and was a little belligerent". He insisted on reading out his lampoon again, but Campbell laughed the provocation aside.

If Lewis was belligerent toward Campbell, Tolkien was transfixed by him, listening intently, as the assembled Inklings "were mostly obliged to listen to the guest". Paradoxically, Tolkien felt that Campbell was "gentle, modest, and compassionate", even though he and the others spent most of the evening listening to Campbell's embellished and highly romanticized account of his own life. Tolkien's report of the biographical monologue is awash with the combined effects of Campbell's exaggeration and Tolkien's faulty memory.

> What he has done ... beggars description. Here is a scion of an Ulster prot. family resident in S. Africa, most of whom fought in both wars, who became a Catholic after sheltering the Carmelite fathers in Barcelona—in vain, they are caught & butchered, and R.C. nearly lost his life. But he got the Carmelite archives from the burning library and took them through the Red country. He speaks Spanish fluently (he has been a professional bullfighter). As you know he then fought through the war on Franco's side, and among other things was in the van of the company that chased the Reds out of Malaga ... But he is a patriotic man, and has fought for the B. Army since ... I wish I could remember half the picaresque stories, about poets and musicians etc. from Peter Warlock to Aldous Huxley ... However, it is not possible to convey an impression of such a rare character, both a soldier and a poet, and a Christian convert. How unlike the Left—the "corduroy panzers" who fled to America (Auden among them who with his friends got R.C.'s works "banned").

If Campbell had made a favorable impression on Tolkien, who thought him "old-looking", "war-scarred", and "limping from recent wounds", Lewis' attitude remained as combative as ever, much to Tolkien's evident chagrin.

> C.S.L.'s reactions were odd. Nothing is a greater tribute to Red propaganda than the fact that he (who knows that they are in all other subjects liars and traducers) believes all that is said against Franco, and

nothing that is said for him ... But hatred of our church is after all the real only final foundation of the C of E—so deep laid that it remains even when all the superstructure seems removed (C.S.L. for instance reveres the Blessed Sacrament, and admires nuns!). Yet if a Lutheran is put in jail he is up in arms; but if Catholic priests are slaughtered—he disbelieves it (and I daresay really thinks they asked for it). But R.C. shook him a bit.

Following the meeting, Lewis stated that he "loathed ... Roy Campbell's particular blend of Catholicism and Fascism, and told him so". His judgment was unfair. Campbell never considered himself a fascist, at least not in the sense in which it is usually understood, and his support for Franco's Nationalists was based on the simple and laudatory desire to defend traditional Christian culture from the destructive atheism of the communists. Having been received into the Church in the year before the outbreak of the war, he considered it his duty to defend the culture and traditions he had recently discovered and embraced. Furthermore, having witnessed the cold-blooded murder of his friends, it is scarcely surprising that Campbell was somewhat vociferous in his attacks on communism. He was, however, as vociferous in his attacks on Nazism. Before the Spanish war had started, he had made the acquaintance of two Norwegians, also living in Spain. One was a communist and the other a Nazi, but, Campbell observed, "they were both staunchly united in their hate of Christ and Christianity". "From the very beginning my wife and I understood the real issues in Spain", Campbell wrote on another occasion. "Now was the time to decide whether ... to remain half-apathetic to the great fight which was obviously approaching—or whether we should step into the front ranks of the Regular Army of Christ. Hitler himself had said, even by then, how much more easy the Protestants were to enslave and bamboozle than the Catholics." One can imagine Tolkien nodding sagely in agreement with Campbell's words, perceiving them as an example of Campbell's Strideresque wisdom in comparison with Lewis' naïve credulity.

Happily, the differences between Campbell and Lewis did not prevent the development of a genuine friendship. Campbell's respect for Lewis was illustrated by his request for Lewis' advice on which selections from Milton would be best suited for broadcasting on the BBC, where Campbell was working as a talks producer. Lewis, reciprocating the expression of respect, replied that Campbell was "quite as able as I to choose", though he proceeded to make suggestions nonetheless. "Oddly enough," Lewis wrote in the same letter, "we were all talking about you last night. Next term you must break away and spend a Thursday night with us in College. (I can do dinner, bed, and breakfast.)"

On 28 November 1946 Campbell returned to Oxford to attend another meeting of the Inklings at Lewis' rooms in Magdalen College. Lewis' brother recorded in his diary that Campbell was the main attraction of the evening. "A pretty full meeting of the Inklings to meet Roy Campbell ... whom I was glad to see again; he is fatter and tamer than he used to be I think." Lewis had also become somewhat tamer, and certainly far less belligerent. He seems, in fact, to have forgiven Campbell for *Flowering Rifle* and to have embraced him both as a friend and as a fellow Inkling. They still crossed swords at these lively literary gatherings, but they were now arguing as friends, not quarreling as enemies. The difference in their relationship can be perceived in the tone of another of Lewis' poems, "To Roy Campbell", in which he complained that Campbell was wrong to dismiss romantic poets such as Coleridge and Wordsworth merely because they were praised by untrustworthy critics. These poets, wrote Lewis, were "far more ours than theirs", indicating that Campbell was now accepted by Lewis as "one of us" in the battle against common literary foes.

One wonders, as Tolkien watched Lewis' slow acceptance of Campbell into the inner sanctum of the Inklings, whether he ever mused further on the parallels between Campbell and Strider. The parallels are certainly striking. The hobbits had regarded the Ranger with deep suspicion when they had first met him in the convivial yet threatening surroundings of the Prancing Pony at Bree; Lewis had regarded the arrival of the Stranger with the same suspicion when they had met in the equally convivial, though hardly threatening, surroundings of the Bird and Baby in Oxford. In both cases, the suspicions gave way to a warmhearted trust. Roy "Strider" Campbell had walked out of the Prancing Pony of Tolkien's imagination into the Bird and Baby of Lewis' world. He had stepped out of the Fellowship of the Ring into the ring of fellowship known as the Inklings.

32

J. R. R. TOLKIEN

Truth and Myth

J.R.R. TOLKIEN, AUTHOR of the world best seller *The Lord of the Rings*, qualifies, technically, as a "literary convert" because of his reception into the Church as an eight-year-old following his mother's conversion to the Faith. It could be said, therefore, that he joins the ranks of the literary converts by creeping in through the back door or, perhaps more correctly, through the nursery door. With beguiling ambiguity he is neither a cradle Catholic nor a full-blown convert, but a charming mixture of the two—a cradle convert.

Since, as Wordsworth reminds us, "the child is father of the man" and since, in Tolkien's case, this is particularly true, the eight-year-old's "cradle conversion" was destined to shape the remainder of his life in a profound manner. Indeed, it would not be an exaggeration to say that Tolkien's conversion was crucial to both the making of the man and to the shaping of the myth he created.

Following the death of her husband in February 1896, a few weeks after her son's fourth birthday, Mabel Tolkien began a new love affair that would soon estrange her from her family. She became passionately devoted to Christianity, taking her two sons every Sunday on a long walk to a "high" Anglican church. Then, one Sunday, they were taken by strange roads to a different place of worship. This was Saint Anne's, a Roman Catholic church amid the slums of Birmingham. She had been considering conversion for some time. During the spring of 1900, she received instruction and was duly received in June of the same year.

By her conversion, she incurred the immediate wrath of her family. Her father, who had been brought up as a Methodist but had since lapsed further from orthodoxy into Unitarianism, was outraged. Her brother-in-law withdrew the little financial help that he had provided since she had become a widow, plunging her and the children into poverty. She also met with considerable opposition from her late husband's family, many of whom were Baptists with strong anti-Catholic prejudices. The emotional strain affected her health adversely, but undaunted, she began to instruct her sons in the Faith.

Tolkien made his First Communion at Christmas 1903. The joy, however, was soon followed by tragedy. Less than a year later, his mother died, having lapsed into a coma caused by diabetes. In her will, Mabel Tolkien had appointed her friend, Father Francis Morgan, to be guardian of her two orphaned sons. He arranged for them to live with their Aunt Beatrice, not far from the Birmingham Oratory, but she showed them little attention, and the brothers soon began to consider the oratory their real home. Each morning they hurried round to serve Mass for Father Morgan at his favorite side altar in the oratory church. Afterward they would eat breakfast in the refectory before setting off for school. Tolkien remained forever grateful for all that Father Morgan did for him and his brother. "I first learned charity and forgiveness from him". The oratory was a "good Catholic home" that contained "many learned fathers (largely 'converts')" and where "observance of religion was strict".

The charity and forgiveness that Tolkien learned from Father Morgan in the years after his mother's death offset the pain and sorrow that her death engendered. The pain remained throughout his life, and sixty years later he compared his mother's sacrifices for her faith with the complacency of some of his own children toward the faith they had inherited from her:

> When I think of my mother's death ... worn out with persecution, poverty, and, largely consequent, disease, in the effort to hand on to us small boys the Faith, and remember the tiny bedroom she shared with us in rented rooms in a postman's cottage at Rednal, where she died alone, too ill for viaticum, I find it very hard and bitter, when my children stray away.

Tolkien always considered his mother a martyr for the Faith. Nine years after her death, he had wrote: "My own dear mother was a martyr indeed, and it was not to everybody that God grants so easy a way to his great gifts as he did to Hilary and myself, giving us a mother who killed herself with labour and trouble to ensure us keeping the faith."

Following Mabel Tolkien's death, Father Francis Morgan of the Birmingham Oratory became legal guardian to Tolkien and his brother. Father Morgan became a surrogate father to the two orphaned boys, so that Tolkien would describe him later as "a guardian who had been a father to me, more than most real fathers".

In June 1915 Tolkien achieved first-class Honors in English Language and Literature from Oxford University, the first significant milestone on his brilliant academic career at Oxford as a philologist and expert in Anglo-Saxon. He would later refer to his academic vocation as one of the "significant facts, which *have* some relation" to his work, stating that his academic pursuits had affected his "taste in languages" and that this was "obviously a large ingredient in *The Lord of the Rings*".

On 22 March 1916 Tolkien married his childhood sweetheart, Edith Bratt, and, two months later, left for what he described as the "carnage" and the "animal horror" of the battle of the Somme, surely one of the most brutal bloodbaths in human history.

Although Tolkien was at pains to insist that his war experience was not a major influence upon *The Lord of the Rings*, and although some critics have indeed overemphasized its influence, there is little doubt that his experience of the "animal horror" darkened his vision to such an extent that the shadow of the First World War always lingers, vulturelike, over his work. In particular, he retained a horror of the new weapons of mass destruction, crafted by sin-stained minds, with which men now killed each other with bloodlustful abandon. Machine guns and mustard gas became a metaphor for the mindless application of new technology—the triumph of the machine over humanity. In the years between the two world wars, Tolkien befriended other like-minded academics, most notably C. S. Lewis, with whom he formed probably the most important literary relationship of the twentieth century. Lewis was "a great encourager" of Tolkien's embryonic efforts at myth creation, and Tolkien confessed on one occasion that he might never have finished *The Lord of the Rings* if Lewis had not been there to encourage him and to cajole him to continue. Similarly, there is little doubt that Tolkien was the greatest single influence on Lewis' own literary oeuvre. Tolkien's philosophy of myth, by which Tolkien explained the deep-rooted relationship between God's Creation and human "subcreation", constituted the final coup de grace in Lewis' embrace of Christianity following a long discussion on the nature and supernature of mythology in September 1931.

Myths, Lewis had asserted during this discussion, were "lies and therefore worthless, even though breathed through silver".

"No", Tolkien replied. "They are not lies." On the contrary, they were the best way, sometimes the only way, of conveying truths that would otherwise remain inexpressible. We have come from God, Tolkien argued, and inevitably the myths woven by us, though they contain error, reflect a splintered fragment of the true light, the eternal truth that is with God. Myths may be misguided, but they steer, however shakily, toward the true harbor, whereas materialistic "progress" leads only to the abyss and the power of evil.

"In expounding this belief in the inherent *truth* of mythology," wrote Tolkien's biographer, Humphrey Carpenter, "Tolkien had laid bare the centre of his philosophy as a writer, the creed that is at the heart of *The Silmarillion*." It is also the creed at the heart of all his other work. His short novel *Tree and Leaf* is essentially an allegory on the concept of true myth, and his poem "Mythopoeia" is an exposition in verse of the same concept.

Building on this philosophy of myth, Tolkien explained to Lewis that the story of Christ was the true myth at the very heart of history and at the very root of reality. Whereas the pagan myths were manifestations of God expressing Himself through the minds of poets, using the images of their "mythopoeia" to reveal fragments of His eternal truth, the true myth of Christ was a manifestation of God expressing Himself *through* Himself, *with* Himself and *in* Himself. God, in the Incarnation, had revealed Himself as the ultimate Poet who was creating reality, the true poem or true myth, in His own image. Thus, in a divinely inspired paradox, myth was revealed as the ultimate realism.

Such a revelation changed Lewis' whole conception of Christianity, precipitating his conversion.

Lewis was one of the select group of friends known collectively as the Inklings who read the manuscript of Tolkien's timeless classic, *The Lord of the Rings*, as it was being written.

Tolkien began work in earnest on *The Lord of the Rings* during the dark years of the Second World War, and there is perhaps an element of irony that the war in which Tolkien did not fight is more potently present in his magnum opus than the war in which he did. It is indeed no coincidence that Sauron has been thought to represent Josef Stalin, who was described by Tolkien in 1943 as "that bloodthirsty old murderer", and Mordor, by implication, to represent the Soviet Union. Similarly, Saruman has been said to represent Hitler, and Isengard, with its racially charged emblem of the White Hand, to represent the Third Reich. "I have spent most of my life ... studying Germanic matters", Tolkien wrote to one of his sons in 1941, adding that he knew "better than most what is the truth about this 'Nordic' nonsense". The result was that he had "in this War a burning private grudge ... against that ruddy little ignoramus Adolf Hitler", adding that Hitler's ideology was the result of "demonic inspiration and impetus", a comment that takes on considerable significance considering Hitler's personification as Saruman in *The Lord of the Rings*. In this light, Saruman's scoffing dismissal of the difference between white and black, that is, between good and evil, declaring himself no longer Saruman the White but Saruman the many-colored, is a clear allusion to the Nietzschean boast that the "wise" must go "beyond good and evil", a boast that lay, and lied, at the cankered heart of the Third Reich.

Tolkien was still working on *The Lord of the Rings* when the world lurched uncertainly from world war to cold war, and, as such, there is more than a hint of Orwellian chill in the air of Middle Earth. It is, for instance, intriguing that the palantir stones, the seeing stones employed by Sauron, the Dark Lord, to broadcast propaganda and sow the seeds of despair among his enemies, are uncannily similar in their mode of employment to the latest technology in mass communications media. It is even more intriguing once one realizes that *palantir* translates from the elvish as *television*!

More perceptive than most, Tolkien had prophesied the future of globalization as early as 1943, opining about the likely triumph of Mammon over Marx in a letter to his son.

I wonder (if we survive this war) if there will be any niche, even of sufferance, left for reactionary back numbers like me (and you). The bigger things get the smaller and duller or flatter the globe gets. It is going to be all one blasted little provincial suburb. When they have introduced American sanitation, morale-pep, feminism, and mass production throughout the Near East, Middle East, Far East, U.S.S.R., the Pampas, el Gran Chaco, the Danubian basin, Equatorial Africa, Hither Further and Inner Mumbo-land, Gondhwanaland, Lhasa, and the villages of darkest Berkshire, how happy we shall be. At any rate it ought to cut down travel. There will be nowhere to go. So people will (I opine) go all the faster . . .

But seriously: I do find this Americo-cosmopolitanism very terrifying.

Perhaps it is more than a little encouraging that a work by a self-confessed "reactionary back number" should emerge as the most popular and influential work of literature of the twentieth century, continuing to win converts to its wisdom and charm fifty years after it was first published. Its power lies in the way that he succeeds, through myth, in making the unseen hand of providence *felt* by the reader. In his mythical creations, or subcreations as he would call them, he shows how the unseen hand of God is felt far more forcefully in myth than it is ever felt in fiction. It is paradoxical that fiction works with *facts*, albeit invented facts, whereas myth works with *truth*, albeit truth dressed in fancy disguises. Furthermore, since facts are physical and truth is metaphysical, myth, being metaphysical, is, in its very essence, spiritual.

The writer and poet Charles A. Coulombe concluded his essay "*The Lord of the Rings*: A Catholic View" with the following incisive assessment of Tolkien's importance. It was a fitting conclusion to his essay on the subject. It is a fitting conclusion to mine:

It has been said that the dominant note of the traditional Catholic liturgy was intense longing. This is also true of her art, her literature, her whole life. It is a longing for things that cannot be in this world: unearthly truth, unearthly purity, unearthly justice, unearthly beauty. By all these earmarks, *Lord of the Rings* is indeed a Catholic work, as its author believed: but it is more. It is this age's great Catholic epic, fit to stand beside the Grail legends, *Le Morte d'Arthur*, and *The Canterbury Tales*. It is at once a great comfort to the individual Catholic, and a tribute to the enduring power and greatness of the Catholic tradition, that JRRT created this work. In an age which has seen an almost total rejection of the Faith on the part of the Civilisation she created ... *Lord of the Rings* assures us, both by its existence and its message, that the darkness cannot triumph forever.

33

THE INDIVIDUAL AND COMMUNITY
IN TOLKIEN'S MIDDLE EARTH

T OLKIEN'S MAGNUM OPUS, *The Lord of the Rings*, has emerged as the
most popular work of literature of the twentieth century. Popularity aside, it is also, in my judgment and in the judgment of thousands of others who have registered their opinion in several national
opinion polls, the *greatest* work of the century. It is indeed unusual,
particularly in the midst of the junk culture regurgitated by modernity, to find that the most popular is also the best. This marriage of
quality and quantity, in which the best is also the best seller, is particularly gratifying because the work in question is so Catholic in its
inspiration and so traditionalist, and consequently antimodernist, in its
message.

Thankfully, much has been written in the past few years about the
underlying theology and philosophy of *The Lord of the Rings*. Tolkien's
assertion that "*The Lord of the Rings* is of course a fundamentally religious and Catholic work; unconsciously so at first, but consciously in
the revision" has served as the springboard for a number of excellent
studies of the spiritual dimension of Middle Earth. One aspect of this
spiritual dimension is that pertaining to the place and role of the individual within the community—or what may be termed the sociopolitical or sociocultural applicability of Tolkien's vision to the problems
facing the individual and the community in a secular age.

Bearing in mind Tolkien's assertion that his work was fundamentally Catholic, we should not be surprised to discover that the vision
of *communitas* in *The Lord of the Rings* was shaped by the social teaching of the Church, at least indirectly. This influence seems to have
come via the distributist social vision of G. K. Chesterton and Hilaire

Belloc, who in turn had distilled their distributism from Pope Leo XIII and from the social vision of Cardinal Manning.

In his essay "On Fairy Stories", Tolkien confesses the influence of what he terms "Chestertonian fantasy" on his own formulation of the nature, and supernature, of mythology. It is, indeed, no wonder that Chesterton should have been so important to the young Tolkien. The towering influence of the legendary Chesterbelloc upon the intellectual life of England in general, and upon the intellectual life of Catholics in England in particular, was at its most potent and profound in the years from 1900 until the outbreak of the First World War in 1914. This is significant because it coincides with Tolkien's youth and, presumably, with the most crucial years of his own intellectual and spiritual development. He was eight years old when Chesterton burst upon the literary and intellectual scene in 1900 and was twenty-two at the outbreak of the war. (Incidentally, although Chesterton's influence on Tolkien is well documented, there is little direct evidence of Belloc's importance—though for the reasons just stated, it can be deduced implicitly. It is, however, my belief that the graphic description of the blizzard on the heights of Caradhras in *The Fellowship of the Ring* is derived from Belloc's description of his near-fatal efforts to cross the Alps in *The Path to Rome*. Certainly Tolkien had no direct experience of hiking in mountains in such treacherous conditions, and his powerful evocation of the elemental power of nature bears a striking similarity to Belloc's treatment of the subject.)

Why, one might ask, is Chesterton's and Belloc's influence on Tolkien so relevant to a discussion of the individual and the community in Middle Earth? Put simply, it is my contention that Tolkien was greatly enamored of the distributist ideas of both these men and that this animated the sociopolitical and sociocultural vision of his work. Chesterton's distributist novel, *The Napoleon of Notting Hill*, and Belloc's seminal critique of sociopolitical history, *The Servile State*, were published during the formative years of Tolkien's life, the former in 1904, the latter in 1912. These works were themselves inspired by the social teaching of the Church, as expounded in Pope Leo XIII's celebrated encyclical *Rerum novarum*, published in 1891. The vision of society presented in these works, combined with their denunciation of the encroaching artificiality of industrialization, harmonized with Tolkien's romantic desire for what he called "a pre-mechanical age".

It must be stressed that the social teaching of Leo XIII and the distributism of Belloc and Chesterton are rooted in *philosophical* first principles. They do not subsist within the sphere of ideology; that is to say, they are not merely sociopolitical or sociocultural responses to other sociopolitical or sociocultural realities. The same is true of Tolkien's vision of *communitas* in Middle Earth. His position is that of a Catholic responding to the ills of society in accordance with the theological and philosophical principles of the Church. Thus, if we are to understand the vision of the individual and the community in his work, we need to understand the first principles from which that vision springs. The fundamental tenets of what may be termed Tolkien's "philosophy of myth", rooted as it is in the teachings of the Church, are to be found in three crucial though often overlooked works, namely, his essay "On Fairy Stories", his "purgatorial" allegory "Leaf by Niggle" and his poem "Mythopoeia". Essentially, Tolkien's philosophy is rooted in the principle that human beings are made in the image of God. Man is not merely *Homo sapiens*, he is *Homo viator*; that is to say, he is not merely created "wise", he is created with a purpose. Furthermore, he is created with free will, enabling him to obey or disobey the purpose for which he is created. This, in turn, means that he is responsible for his actions. He is responsible for his obedience and for his disobedience and must face the consequences of his choices. This mystical equation is thrown into turmoil by the Fall, the primeval act of disobedience for which we are still suffering the consequences. Thus, in his essay "On Fairy Stories", Tolkien writes of "the great mythical significance of prohibition ... Thou shalt not—or else thou shalt depart beggared into endless regret." Given our gift of freedom, this prohibition can either be heeded or ignored. Thus, says Tolkien, "the Locked Door stands as an eternal Temptation".

So where does this "locked door" fit into the relationship between the individual and the community? Quite simply, it shows the necessity of resisting temptation, the necessity of self-sacrifice. Our freedom is the key to the locked door. As such, the door will remain locked only if we choose not to use the forbidden key that is entrusted to us. The temptation is rooted in the fact that we have the freedom to break the rules but the duty to refrain from doing so. The applicability of this principle to the sphere of the sociopolitical is obvious and is perhaps best expressed in two paradoxically convergent political maxims. The first is a so-called liberal maxim by the Catholic historian Lord Acton: "Power tends to corrupt and absolute power tends to corrupt absolutely." The second is a so-called conservative maxim by Edmund Burke: "Liberty itself must be limited in order to be possessed." Put bluntly in the modern vernacular, the first of these could be translated as "power corrupts, and big power corrupts big time". No wonder E. F. Schumacher declared that small is beautiful! Similarly, Burke's maxim could be restated bluntly as a warning that unrestrained liberty, otherwise known as anarchy, would not result in widespread freedom but in the rule of the most brutal and the enslavement of everyone else. Imagine a world in which rapists, murderers and thieves were at liberty to do as they please. No wonder Solzhenitsyn insists that "self-limitation" is the key to a healthy society!

This is how Tolkien discussed this issue. He is speaking specifically about marriage, but, after all, the relationship between the individual and the community is the mystical "marriage" at the heart of Christ's Great Commandment that we should love our neighbor as ourselves. Think of the individual as the bridegroom, and the community, or his neighbor, as the bride. If this is done, Tolkien's advice to his son about marriage takes on great sociopolitical significance:

> The essence of a *fallen* world is that the *best* cannot be attained by free enjoyment, or by what is called "self-realisation" (usually a nice name for self-indulgence, wholly inimical to the realization of other selves); but by denial, by suffering. Faithfulness in Christian marriage entails that: great mortification.

In another letter, Tolkien discussed this principle of self-limitation or "abnegation" in the specific context of the allegorical treatment of the issue of Power in *The Lord of the Rings*:

> Of course my story is not an allegory of Atomic power, but of *Power* (exerted for Domination). Nuclear physics can be used for that purpose. But they need not be. They need not be used at all. If there is any contemporary reference in my story at all it is to what seems to me

the most widespread assumption of our time: that if a thing can be done, it must be done. This seems to me wholly false. The greatest examples of the action of the spirit and of reason are in *abnegation*. When you say A[tomic] P[ower] is "here to stay" you remind me that Chesterton said that whenever he heard that, he knew that whatever it referred to would soon be replaced, and thought pitifully shabby and old-fashioned. So-called "atomic" power is rather bigger than anything he was thinking of (I have heard it of trams, gas-light, steam-trains). But it surely is clear that there will have to be some "abnegation" in its use, a deliberate refusal to do some of the things it is possible to do with it, or nothing will stay! However, that is simple stuff, a contemporary & possibly passing and ephemeral problem. I do not think that even Power or Domination is the real centre of my story ... The real theme for me is about something much more permanent and difficult: Death and Immortality.

It is intriguing that Tolkien passes beyond the discussion of power, at least in its purely physical and secular sense, to the perennial questions of life itself: "death and immortality". Tolkien perceived, as all Christians must, that politics and economics are merely a derivative of theology and philosophy. Change the philosophy and you change the politics. If your philosophy has God as its first cause and center, His commandments will be obeyed and the locked door will remain secure. A belief in God *demands* self-limitation or "abnegation". Remove God, however, and the commandments will be ignored or ridiculed. The locked door will be opened, and like a Pandora's box, its woes will be released on a heedless and hedonistic humanity. No God means "no limits", and no limits leads to the anarchy, which leads in turn to the rule of the most ruthless: the political rapists, thieves and murderers known as dictators. The fact that Tolkien perceived these primary realities of sociopolitical life is evident from further comments that he made in the same letter as the one just quoted:

I am *not* a "democrat" only because "humility" and equality are spiritual principles corrupted by the attempt to mechanise and formalize them, with the result that we get not universal smallness and humility, but universal greatness and pride, till some Orc gets hold of a ring of power—and then we get and are getting slavery.

These words, written in 1956, were indeed written in an age when Orcs wielded the rings of power: the age of Lenin, Stalin, Hitler and Mao. These theoretical "socialists" of one sort or the other, national or international, were in practice moral anarchists whose wielding of the ring of power heralded not merely slavery but slaughter—tens of millions massacred in the bloodiest orgy of power-wielding in human history.

Perhaps we should clarify exactly what Tolkien meant by his not being a "democrat". He is voicing his contempt for the macrodemocracies of modern secular states with their tendency to centralize power in huge "democratically elected" political mechanisms that are increasingly distant from, and deaf to, the needs and aspirations of ordinary people. It is clear, however, that Tolkien's insistence on the "spiritual principles" of humility and equality illustrates his placing of the integrity of the individual and the family at the very heart and center of political life. It is clear, in fact, that his views are convergent with the distributism of the Chesterbelloc and with the creed of "small is beautiful" expounded by Schumacher, both of which are merely popular applications of the Church's teaching on subsidiarity.

Tolkien's insistence on the "spiritual principles" at the heart of all reality, including the sociopolitical and sociocultural, found expression in the way that he viewed Creation and creativity. His reasoning was as follows: since man is made in the image of God, and since we know that God is the Creator, man's own creativity must be a gift of God reflecting His "imageness" in us. Since, however, only God can create in the true or absolute sense by making something from nothing, our creativity is only subcreation in the sense that we make things from other things that already exist. Thus the potter molds his earthenware from clay; the artist paints his picture using oils or watercolors to bring to physical fruition his imaginative perception of a landscape or a human face or a still life; the storyteller or mythmaker uses words or possibly music as the means to bring to physical fruition his imaginative perception of the things, or images, about which he writes, recites, sings or plays. In each case our creativity employs real things, Creation, to subcreate something original yet subsistent upon the Creation itself. Thus, in Tolkien's view, there is a hierarchy of Creation. At the top is God, as Creator; then comes Creation, which is the direct fruit of

God's primal creativity; finally, there is subcreation, whereby man partakes of the image of the Creator through the gift of creativity.

The sociopolitical and sociocultural impact of such a belief in the hierarchy of Creation can be seen from Tolkien's discussion of true and false perceptions of life in his essay "On Fairy Stories":

> Not long ago—incredible though it may seem—I heard a clerk of Oxenford declare that he "welcomed" the proximity of mass-production robot factories, and the roar of self-obstructive mechanical traffic, because it brought his university into "contact with real life". He may have meant that the way men were living and working in the twentieth century was increasing in barbarity at an alarming rate, and that the loud demonstration of this in the streets of Oxford might serve as a warning that it is not possible to preserve for long an oasis of sanity in a desert of unreason by mere fences, without actual offensive action (practical and intellectual). I fear he did not. In any case the expression of "real life" in this context seems to fall short of academic standards. The notion that motor-cars are more "alive" than, say, centaurs or dragons is curious; that they are more "real" than, say, horses is pathetically absurd. How real, how startlingly alive is a factory chimney compared with an elm tree: poor obsolete thing, insubstantial dream of an escapist!

Tolkien is saying, of course, that a horse, as a living work of Creation—that is, having been made by God directly—is more real, more alive, than a car which, as a work of subcreation made by man, is lower in the hierarchy of creative value. Yet he is actually saying more than that. The car, as a product of "mass-production robot factories", is actually a machine made by a machine! The artificial in the service of the artificial. Worse, the human beings working in the mind-numbing robot factories are actually servicing the machines. The alive in the service of the dead. Reality sacrificed on the altar of virtual reality.

But Tolkien is saying even more than this. What does he mean by insinuating that centaurs and dragons are more "alive", and therefore within the hierarchy of creative value more "real", than cars? Well, for one thing, he is referring to the fact that centaurs and dragons are animate creatures, albeit animated only by the imagination! Yet I believe he is saying something even more potent and important. He is saying that there is even a hierarchy within the realm of subcreation. He is saying that subcreation in the service of beauty and truth is better than subcreation for purposes of power. Put simply, art is better than technology. But why is he saying this? To answer that particular question, we have to return to the hierarchy of created value. If God is at the top, His Creation next and subcreation at the bottom, does it not follow that subcreation, being a gift from God, should be at the service of its Giver, its Source? Since God *is* the Beautiful and the True, so much so that all beauty and all truth, properly understood, are a reflection of Him, isn't subcreation in the service of beauty and truth better than subcreation in the service of mere utility? Isn't the former, subcreation in the service of God, whereas the latter is subcreation in the service of man?

Here, perhaps, we should remind ourselves that art, within the context of this discussion, is meant in terms of the liberal arts. Theology is an art. She is queen of the arts as she is queen of the sciences. Philosophy is an art. History is an art. Literature is an art. Within this context, we can see that Tolkien is agreeing with Josef Pieper that leisure is indeed the basis of culture. If we do not have time to study, to enjoy and indeed to practice the arts, we will not be truly alive and therefore not fully real—in the sense of not being as real as we are meant to be, as real as God meant us to be. Heaven forbid that we should stand before the Judgment Seat and be told that we are only virtually real!

All of this has merely served as a preamble to discussing the individual and community in Middle Earth, Tolkien's subcreated world. There is not time to enter into the discussion itself. I thought it more important to provide the *key* by which we can enter Middle Earth and the tools by which we can apply the truths found therein to the truths we find in the created world in which we live. These principles, rooted in the author's Catholic faith, are the animus by which Tolkien asks, and answers, fundamental questions about the individual and his relationship with the community of neighbors he is commanded to love. Throughout *The Lord of the Rings*, the perennial tension between the selflessness and the selfishness in human nature is felt palpably on almost every page. Tolkien illustrates, as only a master storyteller can, that only if selflessness, born of humility, prevails can the individual and the community prosper, and not only prosper but, ultimately, survive. In practical terms this means that self-sacrifice, that is to say, heroism—heroic virtue—is absolutely necessary as the antidote to spiritual obesity, that is to say, hedonism. Heroism or hedonism, that is the question. To be or not to be. To be as we were meant to be, or not to be as we were meant to be. That is the question.

And there is much else besides. Central to any understanding of *The Lord of the Rings* or *The Silmarillion* is the power of tradition as both a guide and protector of the community. Faced with the dynamics of time, which is sometimes given the misnomer of "progress", tradition serves as both a steering wheel and a brake. Thus Middle Earth is strengthened by the knowledge of genealogy, by the longevity and immortality of the elves, and by the sheer "entishness" of the ents, who serve as the very quintessence of tradition—a tradition that is particularly applicable in terms of etymology and ecclesiology. Akin to the centrality of tradition is the nature of authority, both authentic and usurped, a question that is as central to, and therefore as applicable to, the liberal secularist world in which we live.

Ultimately, we should end with the ultimate—in the sense of the ultimate question to which all other questions owe their relevance and all other answers owe their rectitude. Toward the end of his life, Tolkien was asked by a young girl, "What is the purpose of life?" Tolkien's reply will serve as the ultimate rationale for his beliefs vis-à-vis the individual and the community. The extent of the duty of the individual to the community, and its limits, and the extent of the community's responsibility to the individual, and its limits, all spring from the duty of the one and the responsibility of the other to praise and love the One who gives meaning and life to both.

Enough of me. Here is Tolkien, answering the question "What is the purpose of life?"

So it may be said that the chief purpose of life, for any one of us, is to increase according to our capacity our knowledge of God by all the means we have, and to be moved by it to praise and thanks. To do as we say in the *Gloria in Excelsis*: Laudamus te, benedicimus te, adoramus te, glorificamus te, gratias agimus tibi propter magnam gloriam tuam. We praise you, we call you holy, we worship you, we proclaim your glory, we thank you for the greatness of your splendour.

And in moments of exaltation we may call on all created things to join in our chorus, speaking on their behalf, as is done in Psalm 148, and in The Song of the Three Children in Daniel II. PRAISE THE LORD ... all mountains and hills, all orchards and forests, all things that creep and birds on the wing.

34

RELIGION AND POLITICS IN
THE LORD OF THE RINGS

*T*HE *LORD OF THE RINGS* was, without doubt, the most popular book of the twentieth century. Now, at the beginning of the twenty-first century, the film adaptation of Tolkien's masterpiece has brought his work to a whole new generation of readers and movie-goers. Fifty years after its first publication, it is being read by more people than ever. It is, however, interesting that Tolkien's popular success has been greeted with scorn by the liberal secularist denizens of the self-styled literati.

Why, one wonders, was there such an abysmal gulf between the views of the reading public and those of the self-styled "experts"? Perhaps it has something to do with the religious and political content of *The Lord of the Rings*. Certainly Tolkien's stance, theologically and politically, was aeons removed from the position of his critics. He was a lifelong practicing Catholic and, as such, would elicit little sympathy from the ranks of the moral relativists who proliferate among the modern literati. Similarly, he was an opponent of socialism, in both its national and international guises, as well as a critic of the hedonism masquerading as capitalism, which is put forward as socialism's only alternative. As such, he would alienate the intelligentsia of both the socialist and the antisocialist camps. Furthermore, Tolkien's religious and political beliefs are made manifest in multifarious ways throughout his work, particularly in *The Lord of the Rings* itself.

Let's examine the religious and political dimension of "the greatest book of the twentieth century".

"*The Lord of the Rings* is of course a fundamentally religious and Catholic work; unconsciously so at first, but consciously in the revision." This was Tolkien's own judgment of his work. On another occasion, he wrote about a "scale of significance" in the relationship between himself, as author, and his work. At the very top of this scale of significance, enshrined as the most important of the "really significant" factors governing the nature of his work, was the fact that "I am a Christian (which can be deduced from my stories), and in fact a Roman Catholic".

In what way is *The Lord of the Rings* "fundamentally religious and Catholic"? Although it is too subtle to be read merely as a formal or crude allegory, it is, in fact, *so* religious and Catholic, and so fundamentally so, that it is impossible to enumerate the many instances of what Tolkien called the religious "applicability" of his work in an essay of this length. In brief, however, the salient Christian features in *The Lord of the Rings* can be sketched as follows.

On the literal level, "the Lord of the Rings" is Sauron, described by Tolkien in *The Silmarillion* as "the greatest of Melkor's servants". Since Melkor is, in fact, Satan, as is made apparent in the creation story at the beginning of *The Silmarillion*, Sauron is actually the greatest of *Satan's* servants and is, like his master, a fallen angel. As such, the evil in *The Lord of the Rings* is specifically and unequivocally *satanic* and demonic. There is, therefore, no moral relativism in Middle Earth. Followers of Sauron are quite literally going to hell.

On a deeper level, however, "the Lord of the Rings" is not Sauron at all. On the contrary, "the Lord of the Rings" is the same Lord that Tolkien worshiped as a Catholic, the one true God who reigns for all eternity. Samwise Gamgee, the hobbit, perceives as much when he affirms that "above all shadows rides the sun". Sauron and his evil forces are referred to as "the Shadow", whereas the sun is used by Tolkien, in *The Hobbit* as well as in *The Lord of the Rings*, as a symbol of God's presence and a sign of the rarely perceived but nonetheless omnipresent hand of providence. Sauron might believe that he is the Lord of the Rings, but the wise, of whom Samwise is a shining example, know better. Again, there is no room for relativism or agnosticism in Tolkien's world.

What, then, is the Ring? It is a symbol of sin in general and original sin in particular. The "one ring to rule them all and in the darkness bind them" is, in fact, the one sin to rule them all and in the darkness bind them: the original sin of Adam and Eve. How do we know this? It is revealed to us by Tolkien in one of the appendices to

The Lord of the Rings, in which he states that the Ring was destroyed or "unmade" on 25 March. This, of course, is the Feast of the Annunciation, the day on which the Word was made flesh in the womb of the Blessed Virgin Mary. The date of 25 March was also, according to medieval belief, when the Crucifixion took place. Taken together, the Annunciation and the Crucifixion destroyed or "unmade" original sin, signifying man's redemption from Satan's power.

If the Ring is sin, it follows that Tom Bombadil, as the only living being in Middle Earth who is unaffected by the Ring's power, represents unfallen Adam or unfallen Creation, a timely and timeless reminder of the way things could and should have been if we had remained obedient to the will of God. Similarly, the example of Gollum shows us the effect of falling into sin habitually. When we put on the ring, or commit sin, we become invisible to the eyes of the good world created by God and, simultaneously, more visible to the eyes of the infernal world inhabited by the forces of evil. Quite literally, when we put on the ring/sin, we enter Satan's world. If we leave it on, we stay there. If we leave it on long enough, we stay there forever. Gollum is fading and is in dire danger of falling into the infernal pit. The ringwraiths, once proud kings of men, have already done so.

The Lord of the Rings is so filled to the brim with an abundance of religious significance that it would be possible to write a whole book on the subject—as indeed I and others have done! Perhaps a few further examples, briefly listed, will whet the reader's appetite. Tolkien confessed that his characterization of Galadriel was inspired by his love for the Blessed Virgin; lembas, the elvish way-bread that possesses such remarkable power, has been likened to the Blessed Sacrament, not least because *lembas* translates from the elvish as "life-bread" or "bread of life"; the parallels between Denethor and Theoden represent a parable of pagan despair versus Christian hope; and the list goes on and on. There is so much more.

If much has been written on the religious significance of *The Lord of the Rings*, less has been written on its political significance—and the little that has been written is often erroneous in its conclusions and ignorant of Tolkien's intentions. There are exceptions, but alas, they are merely the exceptions that tend to prove the rule. Much more work is needed in this area, not least because Tolkien stated, implicitly at least, that the political significance of the work was second only to the religious in its importance.

I addressed the fundamental tenets of Tolkien's political philosophy in the essay entitled "The Individual and Community in Tolkien's Middle Earth", which precedes the present essay. This philosophy itself has far-reaching consequences on the purely political level. Significantly, it led Tolkien to reach the same conclusions as had Pope Leo XIII in his encyclical *Rerum novarum* and as had G. K. Chesterton and Hilaire Belloc in their advocacy of what became known as distributism. What Chesterton and Belloc called distributism is, to all intents and purposes, what the Catholic Church, in her *Catechism*, calls subsidiarity. *The Lord of the Rings* is, on the political level, a mythical exposition of these ideas of subsidiarity. The Shire is itself the model of a society in which subsidiarity is the established norm. It is a family-centered society rooted in human-scale communities living in harmony with the primary realities of nature. Hobbits shun the artificial accretion of unnecessary technology and resist the encroachment of the power of the machine. The Enemy, on the other hand, seeks domination through the power of technology and through the employment of the machine. Whereas hobbits, elves and men of good will have organically oriented minds and hearts, rooted in roots (tradition) and bearing fruit (wisdom), the evil forces have only "a mind of wheels" bent on the destruction of the natural order (civilization) and its replacement by the artificial (modernity).

The Ring itself has great political significance. It teaches us that the thing possessed possesses the possessor, or, as Christ put it, that where our treasure is, there our heart will be also. This is a sobering lesson, rooted in perennial wisdom. It is a lesson that our own meretricious and crassly materialistic age is in need of being reminded.

Perhaps we can now understand why the liberal secularist intelligentsia despises Tolkien's masterpiece. *The Lord of the Rings* is not merely a riposte to the agnosticism and hedonism of the proponents of modernism and modernity, it is an antidote to their poison. And, of course, as is proven by Tolkien's immense popularity, most people still prefer good old-fashioned Christian morality to new-fangled ideas of moral relativism. Purity is still preferable to poison. And that's a happy ending of which Tolkien himself would have approved.

35

QUEST AND PASSION PLAY:
J. R. R. TOLKIEN'S SANCTIFYING MYTH†

T HE PHENOMENAL POPULARITY of Tolkien's *The Lord of the Rings* continues to be greeted with anger and contempt by many self-styled literary "experts". Rarely has a book caused such controversy, and rarely has the vitriol of the critics highlighted to such an extent the cultural schism between the cliquish literary illuminati and the views of the reading public.

It is perhaps noteworthy that most of the self-styled "experts" among the literati who have queued up to sneer contemptuously at *The Lord of the Rings* are outspoken champions of cultural deconstruction and moral relativism. Most would treat the claims of Christianity in general, and of the Catholic Church in particular, with the same dismissive disdain with which they have poured scorn upon Tolkien. Indeed, their antagonism could be linked to the fact that Tolkien's myth is enriched throughout with inklings of the truths of the Catholic faith.

According to Tolkien's own "scale of significance", expressed candidly in a letter written shortly after *The Lord of the Rings* was published, his Catholic faith was the most important, or most "significant", influence on the writing of the work. It is, therefore, not merely erroneous but patently perverse to see Tolkien's epic as anything other than a specifically Christian myth. This being so, the present volume [Birzer's *J. R. R. Tolkien's Sanctifying Myth*] emerges as a valuable and timely reiteration of the profoundly Christian dimension in the work of the man who is possibly the most important writer of the twentieth century.

† An Introduction to *J. R. R. Tolkien's Sanctifying Myth*, by Bradley J. Birzer (Wilmington, Del.: ISI Books, 2002).

Professor Birzer grapples with the very concept of "myth" and proceeds to a discussion of Tolkien's philosophy of myth, rooted as it is in the relationship between Creator and creature, and, in consequence, the relationship between Creation and subcreation. In his rigorously researched and richly written study, Professor Birzer helps us understand the theological basis of the mythological world of Middle Earth and enables us to see that Tolkien's epic goes beyond mere "fantasy" to the deepest realms of metaphysics. Far from being an escapist fantasy, *The Lord of the Rings* will be revealed as a theological thriller.

Tolkien's development of the philosophy of myth derives directly from his Christian faith. In fact, to employ a lisping pun, Tolkien is a *mis*understood man precisely because he is a *myth*understood man. He understood the nature and meaning of myth in a manner that has not been grasped by his critics. It is this misapprehension on the part of his detractors that lies at the very root of their failure to appreciate his work. For most modern critics, a myth is merely another word for a lie or a falsehood, something that is intrinsically *not* true. For Tolkien, myth had virtually the opposite meaning. It was the only way that certain transcendent truths could be expressed in intelligible form. This paradoxical philosophy was destined to have a decisive and profound influence on C. S. Lewis, facilitating his conversion to Christianity. It is interesting—indeed, astonishing—to note that without J. R. R. Tolkien, there might not have been a C. S. Lewis, at least not the C. S. Lewis that has come to be known and loved throughout the world as the formidable Christian apologist and author of sublime Christian myths.

Integral to Tolkien's philosophy of myth was the belief that creativity was a mark of God's divine image in man. God, as Creator, poured forth the gift of creativity to men, the creatures created in His own image. Only God could create in the primary sense, that is, by bringing something into being out of nothing. Man, however, could subcreate by molding the material of Creation into works of beauty. Music, art and literature were all acts of subcreation expressive of the divine essence in man. In this way, men shared in the creative power of God. This sublime vision found (sub)creative expression in the opening pages of *The Silmarillion*, the enigmatic and unfinished work that forms the theological and philosophical foundation upon which, and the mythological framework within which, *The Lord of the Rings* is structured.

The Silmarillion delved deep into the past of Middle Earth, Tolkien's subcreated world, and the landscape of legends recounted in its pages formed the vast womb of myth from which *The Lord of the Rings* was born. Indeed, Tolkien's magnum opus would not have been born at all if he had not first created, in *The Silmarillion*, the world, the womb, in which it was conceived.

The most important part of *The Silmarillion* is its account of the Creation of Middle Earth by the One. This Creation myth is perhaps the most significant, and the most beautiful, of all Tolkien's work. It goes to the very roots of his creative vision and says much about Tolkien himself. Somewhere within the early pages of *The Silmarillion* is to be found both the man behind the myth and the myth behind the man.

The "myth" behind Tolkien was, of course, Catholic Christianity, the "true myth", and it is scarcely surprising that Tolkien's own version of the Creation in *The Silmarillion* bears a remarkable similarity to the Creation story in the book of Genesis. In the beginning was Eru, the One, who "made first the Ainur, the Holy Ones, that were the offspring of his thought, and they were with him before aught else was made". This, therefore, is the theological foundation upon which the whole edifice of Middle Earth is erected. Disharmony is brought into the cosmos when Melkor, one of the Holy Ones, or archangels, decides to defy the will of the Creator, mirroring the fall of Satan. This disharmony is the beginning of evil. Again, Tolkien's myth follows the "true myth" of Christianity with allegorical precision.

Shortly after describing the rebellion of Melkor, Tolkien introduces Sauron, the Dark Lord in *The Lord of the Rings*. Sauron is described as a "spirit" and as the "greatest" of Melkor's, alias Morgoth's, servants: "But in after years he rose like a shadow of Morgoth and a ghost of his malice, and walked behind him on the same ruinous path down into the Void."

Thus, the evil powers in *The Lord of the Rings* are specified as direct descendents of Tolkien's Satan, rendering impossible, or at any rate implausible, anything but a Christian interpretation of the book. In the impenetrable blackness of the Dark Lord and his abysmal servants, the ring-wraiths, we feel the objective reality of evil. Sauron and his servants confront and affront us with the nauseous presence of the Real Absence of goodness. In his depiction of the potency of evil, Tolkien presents the reader with a metaphysical black hole far more unsettling than Milton's proud vision of Satan as "darkness visible".

Tolkien is, however, equally powerful in his depiction of goodness. In the unassuming humility of the hobbits, we see the exaltation of the humble. In their reluctant heroism, we see a courage ennobled by modesty. In the immortality of the elves, and the sadness and melancholic wisdom it evokes in them, we receive an inkling that man's mortality is a gift of God, a gift that ends his exile in mortal life's "vale of tears" and enables him, in death, to achieve a mystical union with the divine beyond the reach of time.

In Gandalf we see the archetypal prefiguration of a powerful prophet or patriarch, a seer who beholds a vision of the Kingdom beyond the understanding of men. At times he is almost Christlike. He lays down his life for his friends, and his mysterious "resurrection" results in his transfiguration. Before his self-sacrificial "death", he is Gandalf the Grey; after his "resurrection" he reappears as Gandalf the White, armed with greater powers and deeper wisdom.

In the true, though exiled, kingship of Aragorn we see glimmers of the hope for a restoration of truly ordained, that is, Catholic, authority. The person of Aragorn represents the embodiment of the Arthurian and Jacobite yearning—the visionary desire for the "return of the king" after aeons of exile. The "sword that is broken", the symbol of Aragorn's kingship, is reforged at the anointed time—a potent reminder of Excalibur's union with the Christendom it is ordained to serve. And, of course, in the desire for the return of the king, we have the desire of all Christians for the Second Coming of Christ, the true King and Lord of all.

Significantly, the role of men in *The Lord of the Rings* reflects their divine, though fallen, nature. They are to be found among the Enemy's servants, though usually beguiled by deception into the ways of evil and always capable of repentance and, in consequence, redemption. Boromir, who represents man in the Fellowship of the Ring, succumbs to the temptation to use the Ring, that is, the forces of evil, in the naïve belief that it could be wielded as a powerful weapon against Sauron. He finally recognizes the error of seeking to use evil against evil. He dies heroically, laying down his life for his friends in a spirit of repentance.

Ultimately, *The Lord of the Rings* is a sublimely mystical Passion play. The carrying of the Ring—the emblem of sin—is the carrying of the Cross. The mythological Quest is a veritable via dolorosa. Catholic theology, explicitly present in *The Silmarillion* and implicitly present in *The Lord of the Rings*, is omnipresent in both, breathing life into the tales as invisibly, but as surely, as oxygen. Unfortunately, those who are blind to theology will continue to be blind to that which is most beautiful in *The Lord of the Rings*.

This volume will enable the blind to see, and will help the partially sighted to see more clearly, the full beauty of Middle Earth. As a guide for those who would like to know more about the sanctifying power of Middle Earth, this volume will prove invaluable. The sheer magnificence of Tolkien's mythological vision, and the Christian mysticism and theology that give it life, is elucidated with clarity by Professor Birzer in chapters on "Myth and Subcreation", "The Created Order", "Heroism", "The Nature of Evil" and "The Nature of Grace Proclaimed". There is also an excellent and enthralling chapter on the relationship between Middle Earth and modernity, in which Professor Birzer combines his scholarship as a historian, and his grounding in philosophy and theology, to place Tolkien's subcreation into its sociopolitical and cultural context.

With Professor Birzer as an eminently able guide, the reader will be taken deep into Tolkien's world, entering a realm of exciting truths that he might not previously have perceived. As he is led, with the Fellowship of the Ring, into the depths of Mordor and Beyond, he might even come to see that the exciting truths point to the most exciting Truth of all. At its deepest he might finally understand that the Quest is, in fact, a pilgrimage.

TRUE NORTH

I N 1920 C. S. LEWIS WROTE to his friend Arthur Greeves, deploring the "anti-Catholic propaganda" and "rampant Protestantism" in the novels of George Borrow, seeking an explanation for the prejudice in the work of an author that he otherwise admired. Lewis blamed it on Borrow's "northernness": "It lies in the extreme Northernness or Saxonism of his nature. He thrilled, as we once did, to everything Norse ... Hence, of course, a thoroughly Southern, Latin & Mediterranean thing like the Church was antipathetic".

Lewis' words serve as an indication of a common misconception about the nature of Catholicism on the part of those brought up in the Protestant "North". The implicit assumption that Catholicism is something essentially "southern", or Mediterranean, is a product of the supercilious self-righteousness of the Reformation. Since the people of southern Europe had the audacity to remain loyal to the Church during the upheavals of the Reformation, it was assumed that their failure to become "good Protestants" was the result of ignorance or superstition. Unlike the "enlightened" people of the North, the "peasants" of the South were perceived as obstinately "backward" in their faith and culture. Thus was the legacy of Athens and Rome, and Florence and Venice, dismissed with levity by the latter-day barbarians of the "North".

Ironically, this prejudiced presumption of superiority is as unjust to the "true North" as it is to the "true South".

Since, geographically, it is difficult to place the Catholicism of Ireland, France and Poland, or the Orthodoxy of Russia, into the neat division of Europe into a Protestant North and a Catholic South, one is forced to question the criteria by which the advocates of "north-

ernness" define what they actually mean by the "North". Having done
so, we will see that their vision is that of a "false North", quite distinct from the "true North" celebrated in the works of Tolkien and,
to a lesser degree, Lewis. The "false North" is derived from an idolization of the mythical Norse, as seen through the pseudopagan prism
of modern materialist philosophy. "Northernness", thus defined, is the
idolizing and idealizing of the cultural union of all that is perceived to
be Germanic and Scandinavian. Within this cultural *Weltanshauung*,
the Catholics of Bavaria and Austria constitute an embarrassing anom-
aly who are either excluded from the pan-Germanic elite because of
their religion or are admitted as "honorary Germans" in spite of it.
(In fact, since the majority of German speakers have retained their
unity with Rome, there is a logical, and theological, flaw at the very
heart of the whole idolatry of the "false North".)

The ideals of the "false North", propagated by Nietzche and Wagner in the nineteenth century, came to grotesque and caricatured fruition with the advent of the Third Reich. The absurd and perverse
"northernness" of Hitler, which expressed itself in a rampant Prussi-
anism aping, ironically, the "southern" glories of ancient Rome, served
to discredit the ideas and idols of pan-Germanism, or—more correctly, considering its Bismarkian roots—pan-Prussianism. To put the
matter more alliteratively, Prussian pride precedeth the fall of the false
North. This perverse "northernness" was condemned in forthright
terms by J. R. R. Tolkien in a letter to his son Michael in 1941: "I
have in this War a burning private grudge ... against that ruddy little
ignoramus Adolf Hitler [for] ruining, perverting, misapplying and making for ever accursed, that noble Northern Spirit, a supreme contribution to Europe, which I have ever loved, and tried to present in its
true light."

The true North, loved so fondly by Tolkien and Lewis, is that creative seedbed of myth and culture, Christian and pre-Christian, which
springs from the fertile soil of Scandinavia, Germany, England, Ireland, Scotland and Wales and which inspires the spirit and points toward
the truth. Among the fruits of the true North are the *Kalevala*, the
Elder Edda, the *Orkneyinga Saga*, *King Harald's Saga*, *The Dream of the
Rood*, *Beowulf* and *The Seafarer*. Among its heroes are King Arthur and
King Alfred the Great, Merlin and Cuchulain. And, of course, many

of its heroes are also saints: Brendan, Patrick, Aidan, Edmund, Magnus and so on.

And the true North continues to inspire. In the past century, new generations have sought inklings of the truth in the mysteries of the North. George Mackay Brown, ardent Orcadian and Catholic convert, wove the magic of the Orkneys into the mysteries of life. In the islands of his birth, he discovered oases of sanity in an increasingly deranged modernity. His friend, Sir Peter Maxwell Davis, has set Mackay Brown's literary vision to music, bringing his rough-hewn wisdom to symphonic life. Similarly, Sibelius has breathed tonic life into the *kalevala*, and the Estonian composer Arvo Pärt has synthesized the culture of the Baltic North with the universal majesty of Gregorian splendor.

Above all, the true North has inspired the greatest work of literature of the twentieth century—*The Lord of the Rings*. As with the work of George Mackay Brown, Tolkien's work represents a triumphant fusion of northern mythology and Catholic truth.

Tolkien knew something that George Borrow was never able to understand and something that even C. S. Lewis never fully understood. He knew that, at the deepest level, there is no division between North and South. True North and true South were in communion. They are in communion with each other *because* they are in communion with Rome.

37

THE ONCE AND FUTURE KING

K ING ARTHUR. CAMELOT. The knights of the Round Table.
Lancelot. Galahad. Gawain. Merlin. Excalibur. The Lady of
the Lake. The Holy Grail. The very mention of the Arthurian con-
jures up a plethora of images, sacred and profane. One cannot take
a solitary step into the Arthurian past without finding oneself in
a world of wonder. It is a demimonde where the haziness of history merges with the legacy of legend and the mystery of myth. Its
wyrd-woven web of chivalry and chicanery, miracle and magic,
queerness and quest, retains its perennial potency as the centuries
unravel. Amid the ephemeral periphery of human folly it remains as
a monument of the Permanent Things. It continues to fascinate and
inspire.

From the sublime to the ridiculous, new generations have drawn
inspiration from the imaginative wellspring, the living waters, the quick
freshes, that the living legacy of Arthur represents. From the iconoclastic absurdity of Pythonesque irreverence to the dulcified banality
of Disneyed irrelevance, the Arthurian has suffered at the hands of its
abusers. Yet, in the paintings of the Pre-Raphaelites, the poetry of
Charles Williams or the novels of C. S. Lewis, it has breathed the breath
of life into new art and new literature. The paintings of Rossetti, Burne-
Jones and Morris, the Arthurian poems of Williams, and *That Hideous
Strength* by Lewis testify to the power of the Pendragon, the power of
the ancient to beautify the modern.

Ultimately, however, the Arthurian has a power and value that super-
sedes and transcends the merely literary or artistic. It confronts the
presumptions of modernity with the provocative majesty of monarchy.

The Arthurian represents the return of the king, the rekindling of kingship amid the dying embers of dead philosophies. Monarchy or kingship, in the Arthurian sense, has precious little to do with the tawdry trappings of "royalty" that linger, like the fall of the shadow of past glories, over the fading face of modern Europe. Monarchy has everything to do with *authentic* authority—the true authority that resides in the head of the family.

Kingship and kinship are mystically united in the integrity of the *paterfamilias*. Families are not democracies; they are, or at least they should be, self-sacrificial hierarchies rooted in grace. In these self-sacrificial hierarchies, the role of the *paterfamilias* is not to dominere but to serve. In kinship, the one who will reign must rein in his powers. All fathers of families, tribes or kingdoms are called to emulate the calling of the Holy Father, the Pope, whose duty is to be the Servant of the servants of God. To rule is to serve. This is at the heart of the Church's social teaching; it is at the heart of all true authority; it is at the heart of kingship.

King Arthur, the Once and Future King, stands forever as the wielder of Excalibur, the symbol of authority, the sword that serves. Beowulf, destroyer of demons and dragons, stands forever as the wielder of the "fairest of weapons, God-revealed". Aragorn, the king in exile, stands forever as the wielder of the Sword of Elendil, the sword that was broken but is reforged in glory. The Jacobite Pretender, another king in exile, stands forever as the wielder of the hopes of Catholic England and Scotland, hopes that were broken but are reforged in faith. In a truly mystical sense, the Once and Future King and the King over the Water are One. The Arthurian and the Jacobite are united in the authenticity of the authority they represent. They are bound by the Faith and in the Faith. They are the timeless defenders of Christendom against the infidel. They are beyond the transient rebellion of time. They have fought the Long Defeat without ever losing sight of the far-off glimmers of final victory. They are unconquerable. They will return.

"The Sword of Elendil would be a help beyond our hope—if such a thing could indeed return out of the shadows of the past." Boromir's words are those of all who fight for the Faith in the exile of this valley of tears. Only after our exile will we see the Blessed Fruit of her

womb, Jesus, the King of Kings from whom, and in whom, all other
kings must bend the knee in homage, love and service.

> From the ashes a fire shall be woken,
> A light from the shadows shall spring;
> Renewed shall be blade that was broken:
> The crownless again shall be king.

38

TOLKIEN AND THE CATHOLIC LITERARY REVIVAL

I F ONE WERE ASKED to list the key Catholic literary figures of the twentieth century, it is likely that the names of Chesterton, Belloc, Waugh and Greene would spring to mind. It is equally likely that the name of Tolkien would be overlooked. The author of *The Lord of the Rings* is not generally perceived to be one of the key protagonists of the Catholic literary revival, a fact that reflects the extent to which his work is misunderstood. Tolkien's Christian faith is often ignored by critics or else, when alluded to, is dismissed as an aberration that had little or no effect on his subcreation. There is, in fact, an amusing irony in the parallel between Tolkien's position and that of Graham Greene. During the course of his last interview, Greene had reiterated his oft-repeated disclaimer that he was "not a Catholic writer" but "a writer who happens to be a Catholic". Yet, in spite of his protestations to the contrary, Greene's novels are still considered intrinsically to be those of a Catholic writer. On the other hand, if Tolkien had ever made the claim that he was not a Catholic writer, few would have questioned its validity. *The Lord of the Rings* and *The Silmarillion* are not in any sense "Christian", it is claimed, but merely the work of someone "who happens to be a Catholic".

The problem arises when one realizes that Tolkien's own view of the relationship of his faith to his art was almost diametrically opposed to that espoused by Greene. For Tolkien, his faith was of paramount importance and absolutely essential to his subcreation. George Sayer, a friend of Tolkien and Lewis and a biographer of the latter, has remarked that "*The Lord of the Rings* would have been very different, and the writing of it very difficult, if Tolkien hadn't been a Christian. He thought it a profoundly Christian book." Tolkien was also pleased

when Father Robert Murray had written to say that the book had left
him with a strong sense of "a positive compatibility with the order of
Grace" and that the image of Galadriel was reminiscent of the Virgin
Mary. "I have been cheered specially by what you have said," Tolkien
replied, "because you are more perceptive, especially in some directions, than anyone else, and have even revealed to me more clearly
some things about my work. I think I know exactly what you mean
by the order of Grace; and of course by your references to Our Lady,
upon which all my own small perception of beauty both in majesty
and simplicity is founded."

Following his assertion that *The Lord of the Rings* was "fundamentally religious and Catholic", Tolkien had added that he was "grateful
for having been brought up (since I was eight) in a Faith that has
nourished me and taught me all the little that I know; and that I owe
to my mother, who clung to her conversion and died young, largely
through the hardships of poverty resulting from it".

On another occasion, Tolkien sought to emphasize the importance
of his faith in less emotive language, placing it at the pinnacle of a
hierarchy of influences that he called the "scale of significance":

> I object to the contemporary trend in criticism, with its excessive inter-
> est in the details of the lives of authors and artists. They only distract
> attention from an author's work ... and end, as one now often sees, in
> becoming the main interest. But only one's guardian Angel, or indeed
> God Himself, could unravel the real relationship between personal facts
> and an author's works. Not the author himself (though he knows more
> than any investigator), and certainly not so-called "psychologists".
>
> But, of course, there is a scale of significance in "facts" of this sort.

Tolkien then divided the "facts" of his own life into three distinct
categories, namely, the "insignificant", the "more significant" and the
"really significant":

> There are insignificant facts (those particularly dear to analysts and writ-
> ers about writers); such as drunkenness, wife-beating, and suchlike dis-
> orders. I do not happen to be guilty of these particular sins. But if I
> were, I should not suppose that artistic work proceeded from the weak-
> nesses that produced them, but from other and still uncorrupted regions

of my being. Modern "researchers" inform me that Beethoven cheated
his publishers, and abominably ill-treated his nephew; but I do not
believe that has anything to do with his music.

Apart from these "insignificant facts", Tolkien believed that there
were "more significant facts, which *have* some relation to an author's
works". In this category, he placed his academic vocation as a philologist. This had affected his "taste in languages", which was "obviously
a large ingredient in *The Lord of the Rings*". Yet even this was subser-
vient to more important factors:

> And there are a few basic facts, which however drily expressed, are
> really significant. For instance I was born in 1892 and lived for my
> early years in "the Shire" in a pre-mechanical age. Or more important,
> I am a Christian (which can be deduced from my stories), and in fact
> a Roman Catholic.

Considering Tolkien's insistence on the primary importance to his
work of his Christian faith, it is pertinent to place him among the
illustrissimi of the Catholic literary revival and to look more closely at
his place in its historical development.

The revival itself was instigated by John Henry Newman, and its
beginnings can be said to coincide with Newman's reception into the
Church in 1845. The critic George Levine described Newman as "perhaps the most artful and brilliant prose writer of the nineteenth century", and there is no doubt that Newman's literary achievement was
both prodigious and prolific. His works of fiction, *Loss and Gain* and
Callista, are among the greatest novels of the Victorian era, and his
autobiographical *Apologia* is probably the finest exposition of a religious conversion ever written in the English language. His verse, the
most accomplished and most beautiful of which is *The Dream of Gerontius*, places him in the first rank of Victorian poets, and to cap it all,
he is considered a popular theologian of rare distinction who warrants
a place among the foremost doctors of the Church. Almost single-
handedly, Newman's genius had revitalized English Catholicism, and
the quality of his literary output had set the standard that future generations of Catholic writers would seek to emulate.

The enormity of Newman's spirit was to prove a potent influence
on Tolkien's early development. From 1902, when Tolkien was ten

years old, a considerable part of his life revolved around the Birmingham Oratory, a large church served by a community of priests that had been established by Newman in 1849 following the model established in Italy by Saint Philip Neri. Newman spent the last four decades of his life within the oratory walls, dying there in 1890. In 1902 the community still included many priests who remembered Newman as a friend and who had served under him, one of whom was Father Francis Xavier Morgan, destined to become Tolkien's guardian following the death of Tolkien's mother two years later.

If Newman's indirect influence on Tolkien's early life is beyond question, the extent of his influence on Tolkien's work is not so easy to verify. Certainly, the substantial body of Newman's literary output would seem to have little in common with the fantasy genre in which Tolkien excelled. This, however, should not obscure the underlying affinity that exists between the two writers. In spite of the widely different means employed by each, the end result was essentially the same. The difference was not in what they were trying to say but only in the way they were trying to say it. Perhaps the similarity of intention can be seen most clearly in the purgatorial peripatetics employed by both writers. Tolkien's theme in his short story *"Leaf by Niggle"* and his poem "Mythopoeia" is not that dissimilar from Newman's vision of the afterlife in *The Dream of Gerontius*. Yet these surface similarities are merely a reflection of a deeper unity that springs from the Catholicism that animates their work. For Tolkien and Newman alike, the substantial body of their work is "Catholic" insofar as it represents an orthodox Christian response to the cynicism and materialism of the age. The logic of such a response is expressed with characteristic eloquence by Newman:

> Turn away from the Catholic Church, and to whom will you go? it is your only chance of peace and assurance in this turbulent, changing world. There is nothing between it and scepticism, when men exert their reason freely. Private creeds, fancy religions, may be showy and imposing to the many in their day; national religions may lie huge and lifeless, and cumber the ground for centuries, and distract the attention or confuse the judgment of the learned; but on the long run it will be found that either the Catholic Religion is verily and indeed the coming in of the unseen world into this, or that there is nothing positive,

nothing dogmatic, nothing real in any one of our notions as to whence we come and whither we are going. Unlearn Catholicism, and you become Protestant, Unitarian, Deist, Pantheist, Sceptic, in a dreadful, but infallible succession.

There is much in this short extract from one of Newman's sermons that throws light on Tolkien's subcreation of Middle Earth. Newman's description of the Catholic religion as "verily and indeed the coming in of the unseen world into this", offers a key to understanding the hidden forces that give so much depth to *The Lord of the Rings* and *The Silmarillion*. It is the constant awareness of the powers of the unseen world, hidden but real, that fires the imagination and gives these books the creative tension that permeates each page. The other key is Newman's insistence on the stark dichotomy between the Church and the Alternative. There is no murky common ground between the two; it is a fight between the forces of darkness and the forces of light, between orthodoxy and scepticism. One is reminded of Chesterton's words on his deathbed: "The issue is now quite clear. It is between light and darkness and everyone must choose his side."

Nor were the views of Newman, Chesterton or Tolkien the result of an unreasoned religious bigotry. On the contrary, they were anchored in the philosophy of Aristotle and Aquinas and were motivated by a rejection of modern philosophy. The *reductio ad absurdum* that followed on from the Enlightenment's rejection of scholastic philosophy and its espousal of the Cartesian axiom, *cogito, ergo sum*, was all too obvious. Beginning with "I think, therefore I am", the modern world had regressed to the ultimate scepticism about the objectivity of existence itself: "I am but I can't be sure that anything else is." This regression of modern philosophy from the perennial wisdom of the ancients to the primeval soup of sceptical reductionism was at the heart of Newman's claim that to unlearn Catholicism was to "become Protestant, Unitarian, Deist, Pantheist, Sceptic, in a dreadful, but infallible succession".

This philosophical battleground lies at the very core of Tolkien's work and is the ultimate key to its depth and potency. It also explains both its enduring appeal and the continuing hostility it provokes. Those who subscribe, however unwittingly, to the perennial philosophy adopted by the Church will find reassurance in Tolkien's epic tales of the eternal nature of the struggle between good and evil and the moral imperatives and choices this entails. To the philosophically sceptical, who can't be sure of anything, Tolkien's certainties are merely absurdities. His depths are shallows; his truths are falsehoods; his myths are lies. To tamper with a memorable aphorism of Kipling's, it would seem that light is light and dark is dark and never the twain will meet.

The practical implications of Tolkien's philosophical approach are most evident in his enshrining of the objectivity of truth. Far from his "fantasy" world representing a flight from reality, it is, in the metaphysical sense, a flight into reality. The events in Middle Earth are not merely real, they are hyper-real, too real for comfort, so that the reader is genuinely concerned about the characters and the turn of events, the threat of dyscatastrophe and the joy of eucatastrophe. The Ring that Frodo carries is so real that it can't be tossed away and forgotten about. The consequences of doing so would be so disastrous that it would be an unthinkable act. Yet the dangers of not doing so are real also, intensely so, and there is a sublime heroism in the dutiful resolve to bear the burden in spite of the fear and suffering it entails. The Ring is not a fantasy, a figment of the mind, an urge, a desire, or an opinion that can be changed; it is a fact that must be faced, borne and finally overcome. This is true realism, built upon the solid rock of objectivism. It has precious little to do with the false realism of the sceptics, who base their understanding of reality on the shifting sands of subjectivism where nothing is good, nothing evil, nothing true in itself. Perhaps it is not surprising that the sceptics, self-centered in their dogmatic assertion of *cogito, ergo sum*, have sought clues to reality in the most fickle recesses of themselves, in the sexual fantasies and dream analysis of Freudian and Jungian psychology. In this way, most modern "realism" is really little more than surrealism in disguise—an impostor masquerading as the real thing.

Tolkien's preoccupation with the nature and objectivity of truth leads inevitably back to Newman. In Newman's *Apologia*, his semiautobiographical novel *Loss and Gain* and his historical novel *Callista*, he explored the intricate nature of the individual's quest for truth. In *Callista*, a novel set in the third century, Agellius, a Christian, endeavors in vain to convince his sceptical uncle of the claims of the Church:

"O Jucundus," cried Agellius, irritated at his own inability to express himself or hold an argument, "if you did but know what it was to have the Truth! The Christian has found the Truth, the eternal Truth, in a world of error. That is his bargain, that is his hire; can there be a greater? Can I give up the Truth?"

His uncle's reply echoed the words of Pilate two centuries previously and those of sceptics many centuries later:

"The Truth!" he cried, "*this* is what I understand you to say,—the truth. The *truth* is your bargain; I think I'm right, the truth; Hm; what is truth? What in heaven and earth do you mean by truth? where did you get that cant? What oriental tomfoolery is bamboozling you? The truth!" he cried, staring at him, half of triumph, half of impatience, "the truth! Jove help the boy!—the truth! can truth pour me out a cup of melilotus? can truth crown me with flowers? can it sing to me? can it bring Glyceris to me? drop gold in my girdle? or cool my brows when fever visits me? Can truth give me a handsome suburban with some five hundred slaves, or raise me to the duumvirate? Let it do this, and I will worship it; it shall be my god; it shall be more to me than Fortune, Fate, Rome, or any other goddess on the list. But *I* like to see, and touch, and feel, and handle, and weigh, and measure what is promised me. I wish to have a sample and an instalment. I am too old for chaff. Eat, drink, and be merry, that's my philosophy, that's my religion; and I know no better. Today is ours, tomorrow is our children's."

In setting this dialogue more than a millennium and a half ago, Newman was emphasizing the perennial nature of the question. Scepticism, hedonism and materialism were not modern inventions but age-old negations, man's continual denial of the truth that eludes him. Nor were they "progressive". Throughout history, the accentuation of the negative has led to the decay of civilization and the ultimate return of barbarism. It is symbolized in Christian Scripture by Pilate's asking the same question as does Jucundus, coming to the same conclusions and washing his hands of the whole affair. Pilate, the personification of the eternal sceptic, dismisses truth as unknowable and therefore irrelevant.

In *The Lord of the Rings* and *The Silmarillion*, Tolkien uses an invented world for the same reasons that Newman had used the relative distance of antiquity. By placing his epic in Middle Earth, he can deal with eternal verities without the distractions of fads, fashions and the flood of ephemera that clutters modern life. If he had set his story in England during the 1940s, he would no doubt have been commended for his "realism" by contemporary critics, but his "modern" work would appear dated today and possibly less relevant and real to subsequent generations. Tolkien's subcreated world is timeless, enabling him to ignore the peripheral in favor of the perennial problems of existence. For this reason, *The Lord of the Rings* is no more dated today than it was when it was first published. For the same reason, it is safe to predict its continued popularity. If future generations stop reading Tolkien's classic, it will not be because it has become irrelevant or dated. Rather, if they stop reading Tolkien, it will be because they have stopped reading. If technology makes the written word redundant, Tolkien's work may flounder. His books, which have proved too real to be reproduced by any of the new forms of virtual reality, may then be forgotten. If so, it may mark the triumph of technology but certainly not the triumph of "progress". In such circumstances, one is reminded of the wisdom of Coventry Patmore's poem "Magna est Veritas":

> Here, in this little Bay,
> Full of tumultuous life and great repose,
> Where, twice a day,
> The purposeless, glad ocean comes and goes,
> Under high cliffs, and far from the huge town,
> I sit me down.
> For want of me the world's course will not fail;
> When all its work is done, the lie shall rot;
> The truth is great, and shall prevail,
> When none cares whether it prevail or not.

This short verse, written by one of the most celebrated Catholic poets of the Victorian era, displays all the hallmarks of the literary revival heralded by Newman. It shows the same preoccupations that characterize the work of both Newman and Tolkien. There is the insistence upon the transcendent and objective nature of truth and upon its perennial prevalence regardless of the fashionable whims of a largely heedless humanity. More specifically, as far as direct comparisons with Tolkien are concerned, there is the same almost mystical reverence for the timeless endurance of the ocean. At the end of *The Lord of the Rings*, there is more than a glimmer of the poetic poignancy that Patmore felt in the majestic presence of the sea:

> But to Sam the evening deepened to darkness as he stood at the Haven; and as he looked at the grey sea he saw only a shadow on the waters that was soon lost in the West. There still he stood far into the night, hearing only the sigh and murmur of the waves on the shores of Middle-earth, and the sound of them sank deep into his heart.

This reverence for the sea is given theological expression in *The Silmarillion*:

> And they observed the winds and the air, and the matters of which Arda was made, of iron and stone and silver and gold and many sub-stances: but of all these water they most greatly praised. And it is said by the Eldar that in water there lives yet the echo of the Music of the Ainur more than in any substance else that is in this Earth; and many of the Children of Iluvatar hearken still unsated to the voices of the Sea, and yet know not for what they listen.

In prose such as this, Tolkien succeeds in encapsulating theological principles in terms that are evocative of the metaphysical poets. The Ainur are the angelic powers given responsibility for the Creation of Middle Earth by Iluvatar, the One omnipotent God. Their collective act of Creation, overseen by the One, is described as the Music, the symphonic subcreation of the universe. In thus describing water as something in which there still lives the echo of this angelic Music, Tolkien reaches sublime heights of imagery worthy of the great poets.

There is also a striking similarity between the words Tolkien puts into the mouth of Ulmo, the angel most responsible for the Waters, and the words of the Victorian Catholic poet Francis Thompson in his poem "To a Snowflake". First, Tolkien:

> Then Ulmo answered: "Truly, Water is become now fairer than my heart imagined, neither had my secret thought conceived the snow-flake, nor in all my music was contained the falling of the rain."

Compare this with Thompson's verse:

What heart could have thought you?—
Past our devisal
(O filigree petal!)
Fashioned so purely,
Fragilely, surely,
From what Paradisal
Imagineless metal,
Too costly for cost?

Unfortunately, modern ignorance of both philosophy and theology has resulted in this deep love of nature being mistaken for a form of pantheistic paganism. The extent to which Tolkien sought to dispel such misunderstanding is evident in the early pages of *The Silmarillion*, in which he goes to great pains to ensure that his own version of the Creation myth conforms with orthodox Christianity.

Comparison with another Victorian Catholic poet will illustrate the intrinsic unity that exists between Tolkien's "greenness" and the Christian philosophy that underpins his work. Gerard Manley Hopkins had been as devastated by the felling of ten or twelve poplar trees in 1879 as had been the young Tolkien by the felling of a favorite tree during his childhood. In both cases, the wanton destruction inspired literary creativity. For Hopkins, it resulted in the writing of "Binsey Poplars", one of his finest poems:

O if we but knew what we do
    When we delve or hew—
Hack and rack the growing green!
    Since country is so tender
To touch, her being só slender,
That, like this sleek and seeing ball
But a prick will make no eye at all,
Where we, even where we mean
    To mend her we end her,
    When we hew or delve:
After-comers cannot guess the beauty been.
Ten or twelve, only ten or twelve
    Strokes of havoc únselve
    The sweet especial scene,

> Rural scene, a rural scene,
> Sweet especial rural scene.

For Tolkien, this love of nature, and especially of trees, bore fruit in his creation of the arboreal ents and in the charming characterization of Treebeard and Quickbeam. As with Hopkins, the roots from which the fruit sprang were philosophical. The creative vision of both men was shaped to a profound extent by the scholastic philosophy of the Church. For Hopkins, the rigors of his training to become a Jesuit left him thoroughly conversant with the philosophy of both Duns Scotus and Saint Thomas Aquinas. The influence of the former is most evident in the way that *inscape* in Hopkins correlates with the concept of *haecceity* in the metaphysics of Duns Scotus. The concept of *inscape* also explains the omnipresence of nature-reverence and its mystical significance in Tolkien's work, and this in turn represents a further example of the fact that one must plumb the philosophical depths if one is to understand the colorful surface of Middle Earth.

If comparisons with Newman, Patmore, Thompson and Hopkins illustrate the affinity that exists between Tolkien's work and that of the early protagonists of the Catholic literary revival, comparisons with the works of G. K. Chesterton serve as further evidence that Tolkien's achievement should be seen within the context of an orthodox Christian response to secular society. Like Chesterton, Tolkien subscribed to a vision of Merrie England that was an idealized view of what England had been before the Reformation and what she could be again. It was an England free from post-Reformation puritanism and postindustrial proletarianism, an England where individuals owned the land on which they lived and worked. It was Blake's green and pleasant land liberated from the dominion of dark, satanic mills. Chesterton had eulogized this mythical England in his verse, his essays and his novels, and Tolkien had subcreated his own version of it with his descriptions of the Shire. "In many ways," writes Charles A. Coulombe elsewhere in this volume, "the Shire expresses perfectly the economic and political ideals of the Church, as expressed by Leo XIII in *Rerum Novarum*, and Pius XI in *Quadragesimo anno* ... It is the sort of society envisioned by Distributists Belloc and Chesterton".

The linking of the Shire with the distributism of Chesterton and Belloc moves the discussion of Tolkien's place within the Catholic literary revival from the philosophical to the socioeconomic. On this level, there are many striking similarities between Chesterton and Tolkien, most notably in their shared distaste for urban industrialism, which places them in a long plaintive tradition stretching back to Blake and Cobbett almost two centuries earlier. Chesterton had written a study of Blake and a full-length biography of "great Cobbett" describing him as "the horseman of the shires" and the champion of England's dispossessed rural population, the last rustic radical: "After him Radicalism is urban—and Toryism suburban." "In Mr. Chesterton's view," wrote a reviewer, "Cobbett stood for England: England unindustrialised, self-sufficient, relying on a basis of agriculture and sound commerce for her prosperity, with no desire for inflation." Chesterton's view of Cobbett's England conforms with Tolkien's view of the Shire, which he told his publisher was "based on rural England and not on any other country in the world". Comparing Cobbett to Shelley, Chesterton wrote: "Going through green Warwickshire, Cobbett might have thought of the crops and Shelley of the clouds. But Shelley would have called Birmingham what Cobbett called it—a hell-hole." This was certainly a view with which Tolkien would have concurred wholeheartedly, especially as he had seen the village in which he had spent his childhood swallowed up during his own lifetime by the "hell-hole" of the West Midlands conurbation. It is also interesting that Chesterton's description of Cobbett is equally applicable to Tolkien:

> What he saw was not an Eden that cannot exist, but rather an Inferno that can exist, and even that does exist. What he saw was the perishing of the whole English power of self-support, the growth of cities that drain and dry up the countryside ... the toppling triumphs of machines over men ... the wealth that may mean famine and the culture that may mean despair; the bread of Midas and the sword of Damocles.

The evident convergence of opinions raises the question of Chesterton's influence on Tolkien. Chesterton's fame was at its height when Tolkien was still at school and arguably at his most impressionable, and it is clear that Tolkien knew, and largely sympathized with, Chesterton's work. Nonetheless, the danger of overstating the case was apparent in Christopher Clausen's essay "*The Lord of the Rings* and *The Ballad of the White Horse*". Clausen claimed that *The Lord of the Rings* is "heavily indebted" to Chesterton's ballad, particularly in the similarity of Galadriel's role to that of the Virgin Mary in *The Ballad of the White Horse*. Clausen also saw Tolkien's dwarves, elves and men, somewhat incongruously, as parallels of Chesterton's Saxons, Celts and Romans. The basic structure of the two works is similar, in Clausen's view, because both tell the story of a war between good and evil forces in which an alliance of the forces of good, despite all the odds, gains the victory against the vastly more powerful forces of evil. In both works, the culmination of events is the return of the king to his rightful state. Clausen also alludes to the symbolism implicit in the fact that Gandalf's horse, Shadowfax, is the archetypal white horse of English legend.

One suspects that Clausen has read too much into the similarities between the two books, some of which are surely no more than coincidental or superficial. Although Tolkien was well acquainted with Chesterton's *Ballad*, admiring it greatly as a young man before becoming more critical of its undoubted flaws in later years, the extent of his scholarship suggests that his direct indebtedness to Chesterton must be limited. Yet, regardless of the alleged nature of Chesterton's *direct* influence upon Tolkien, there is considerable evidence of his *indirect* influence, and there are clearly discernible links of affinity between the two men.

One of the most notable of these is the sense of wonder that is an essential part of both men's work, and indeed of both men's outlook and philosophy. In *The Lord of the Rings*, the enigmatic figure of Tom Bombadil seems to embody this Chestertonian sense of wonder, in which wisdom and innocence are unified, to a sublime degree: "Tom sang most of the time, but it was chiefly nonsense, or else perhaps a strange language unknown to the hobbits, an ancient language whose words were mainly those of wonder and delight."

Tom Bombadil also appears to be Chestertonian paradox personified. Older than the world, he is perennially young. He has the wisdom to wonder, the wisdom *of* wonder, which sees through worldly cynicism. He has childlike innocence without childish näiveté. These qualities are also present in the character of Quickbeam, an ent who is introduced to the hobbits by Treebeard:

All that day they walked about in the woods with him, singing, and laughing, for Quickbeam often laughed. He laughed if the sun came out from behind a cloud, he laughed if they came upon a stream or spring: then he stooped and splashed his feet and head with water; he laughed sometimes at some sound or whisper in the trees. Whenever he saw a rowan-tree he halted a while with his arms stretched out, and sang, and swayed as he sang.

T. A. Shippey, author of *The Road to Middle Earth*, referred to the infectious nature of this sense of wonder in Tolkien's work when he said that Tolkien had "turned me into an observer. Tolkien turns people into birdwatchers, tree spotters, hedgerow-grubbers." This was certainly one of Tolkien's intentions, springing from his belief that one of the highest functions of fairy stories was the recovery of a clear view of reality:

> We need recovery. We should look at green again, and be startled anew (but not blinded) by blue and yellow and red ... This recovery fairy-stories help us to make ...
>
> Recovery (which includes return and renewal of health) is a re-gaining—regaining of a clear view. I do not say "seeing things as they are" and involve myself with the philosophers, though I might venture to say "seeing things as we are (or were) meant to see them"—as things apart from ourselves. We need, in any case, to clean our windows; so that the things seen clearly may be freed from the drab blur of triteness or familiarity ...
>
> Of course, fairy-stories are not the only means of recovery, or prophylactic against loss. Humility is enough. And there is (especially for the humble) *Mooreeffoc*, or Chestertonian Fantasy. *Mooreeffoc* is a fantastic word, but it could be seen written in every town in this land. It is Coffee-room, viewed from the inside through a glass door, as it was seen by Dickens on a dark London day, and it was used by Chesterton to denote the queerness of things that have become trite, when they are seen suddenly from a new angle.

Perhaps the bonds of affinity between Tolkien and Chesterton are displayed most explicitly in their shared respect for tradition. In 1909 Chesterton had defended traditionalism by labeling it the philosophy of the tree:

I mean that a tree goes on growing, and therefore goes on changing; but always in the fringes surrounding something unchangeable. The innermost rings of the tree are still the same as when it was a sapling; they have ceased to be seen, but they have not ceased to be central. When the tree grows a branch at the top, it does not break away from the roots at the bottom; on the contrary, it needs to hold more strongly by its roots the higher it rises with its branches. That is the true image of the vigorous and healthy progress of a man, a city, or a whole species.

A keen sense of tradition was as important to Tolkien as it was to Chesterton, and the whole of *The Lord of the Rings* resonates with its presence. Yet it is interesting, and perhaps not completely coincidental, that the mythological figure that Tolkien uses to embody this principle of tradition is Treebeard, a treelike creature who was the oldest living being in the whole of Middle Earth. Treebeard appears to be Tolkien's personification of Chesterton's philosophy of the tree.

When Pippin and Merry had first seen Treebeard, they felt that the wisdom of the ages could be glimpsed in the depths of his eyes:

Those deep eyes were now surveying them, slow and solemn, but very penetrating. They were brown, shot with a green light. Often afterwards Pippin tried to describe his first impressions of them.

"One felt as if there was an enormous well behind them, filled up with ages of memory and long, slow, steady thinking; but their surface was sparkling with the present: like sun shimmering on the outer leaves of a vast tree, or on the ripples of a very deep lake. I don't know, but it felt as if something that grew in the ground—asleep, you might say, or just feeling itself as something between root-tip and leaf-tip, between deep earth and sky had suddenly waked up, and was considering you with the same slow care that it had given to its own inside affairs for endless years."

Of course, this traditionalist imagery is rooted in the Catholicism that Chesterton and Tolkien shared, serving as a timely reminder that the bonds of affinity between them subsist within a greater wellspring of inspiration from which both men drank thirstily. Like a host of other Christian writers before and since, Tolkien was concerned principally with what the critic Lin Carter described in her study of *The Lord of the Rings* as "the eternal verities of human nature". What was important to all the writers of the Catholic literary revival was not the accidental trappings of everyday life, the "stuff" of soap operas, but the essential nature of everlasting life, not what human society was becoming but what humanity was being, not the peripheral but the perennial. This was the animus at the very core of the revival heralded by Newman, a revival that enshrined the belief that the highest function of art was the expression of the highest common factors of human life and not the lowest common denominators—life's loves and not its lusts. It is by these standards that Tolkien's work should be judged, and it is by these standards that he shines forth as one of the *illustrissimi* of the revival of which he was part.

39

TRUE MYTH

The Catholicism of The Lord of the Rings

S OME CHRISTIANS REMAIN SUSPICIOUS of *The Lord of the Rings*. They
see within its mythological setting hints of neopaganism, possibly
even Satanism. Can anything containing wizards and elves, and sor-
cery and magic, be trusted? Certainly, in the wake of the worldwide
success of the *Harry Potter* books, many Christians fear the effect that
"fantasy" literature might be having on their children. Are these fears
justified? Should Christian parents prohibit their children from reading these books? Emphatically, in the case of *The Lord of the Rings* at
least, the answer to these questions is no. Far from being prohibited,
Tolkien's epic should be required reading in every Christian family. It
should take its place beside the Narnian Chronicles of C. S. Lewis
(Tolkien's great friend) and the fairy stories of George Macdonald as
an indispensable part of a Christian childhood.

It is intriguing that the same Christians who express their suspicion
of Tolkien are quite happy for their children to be exposed to the
witches and the magic in C. S. Lewis' stories. Clearly, these naturally
concerned parents are oblivious of the profound Christianity that threads
its way through Tolkien's myth. In truth, and "truth" is the operative
word, the power of Christ speaks more potently and subtly in Tolkien's Middle Earth than in Lewis' Narnia.

Many devotees of J. R. R. Tolkien's *The Lord of the Rings* have read
it, often on numerous occasions, without gaining an inkling of its
deeper meaning. Its spirituality, if any is detected, is seen as pagan,
little more than a cocktail of new-age pantheism. It is clear, therefore,
that Tolkien is widely misinterpreted and often misunderstood, a charge

that can seldom be leveled at C. S. Lewis. Is this a weakness in Tolkien's work? The question can be answered only by comparing Tolkien's and Lewis' respective approaches.

The most important difference in Tolkien's and Lewis' approaches lies in their attitude to allegory. Lewis' work abounds with allegorical connections, whereas Tolkien disliked the unsubtle straitjacket that the use of allegory placed upon the weaving of a story. In his foreword to *The Lord of the Rings*, he said about allegory:

> I much prefer history, true or feigned, with its varied applicability to the thought and experience of readers. I think that many confuse "applicability" with "allegory"; but the one resides in the freedom of the reader, and the other in the purposed domination of the author.

Tolkien was well aware that the forsaking of allegory in the telling of his tale gave his readers a freedom that many would not merely use but abuse. Applicability implied the likelihood of its misapplication. It was a price he was prepared to pay. Above all, however, story and allegory had one thing in common. They both subsisted within higher reality with a higher purpose.

> Allegory and story converge, meeting somewhere in Truth. So that the only perfectly consistent allegory is a real life; and the only fully intelligible story is an allegory. And one finds, even in imperfect human "literature", that the better and more consistent an allegory is the more easily it can be read "just as a story"; and the better and more closely woven a story is the more easily can those so minded find allegory in it. But the two start from opposite ends.

Regardless of whether they started from opposite ends, the works of Tolkien and Lewis converged, meeting somewhere in Truth. Both men believed that fairy stories and myths were not, as the "moderns" maintained, lies or falsehoods representing a reprehensible escape from reality. On the contrary, they were the best way of conveying truths that were otherwise inexpressible. They were also the best way of highlighting the difference between facts and truth. Facts were physical, but truth was metaphysical. Facts were scientific, but truth was an art. Specifically, and properly understood, Truth was the Art that governed the cosmos, and the purpose of art, that is, subcreation, was to mirror Art, that is, the primary Creation of the Creator. Thus, in a sublime paradox, myth becomes the highest realism. This was encapsulated by Tolkien in his essay on fairy stories:

> The peculiar quality of the "joy" in successful Fantasy can thus be explained as a sudden glimpse of the underlying reality or truth. It is not only a "consolation" for the sorrow of this world, but a satisfaction, and an answer to that question, "Is it true?" ... in the "eucatastrophe" we see a brief vision... a far-off gleam of *evangelium* in the real world.

In conclusion, Tolkien stressed that Christianity, the true myth, had reconciled all lesser myths to itself. The lesser myths, in the form of fairy story or romance, were "derived from Reality, or are flowing into it." However inadequate in themselves, they still offered a glimpse of the greater truth from which they spring or into which they flow.

Where then is this brief vision of the greater truth, this "far-off gleam of *evangelium*", to be found in Tolkien's work? In his greatest works, those centered on the secondary world of Middle Earth, the careful avoidance of allegory makes the search for the sudden glimpse of reality a wonderful game of hide-and-seek. As Tolkien himself intended, and as millions of his readers continue to demonstrate, it is not necessary to play the game in order to enjoy the story. It is, however, necessary to play the game if one wishes to understand the story more fully and enjoy it at its deepest. One can scratch the surface or plumb the depths. On the surface, one is entertained and swept away in a beautifully dramatic narrative; beneath the surface, one is introduced to the profound Reality that makes the drama beautiful. The true adventure is not in the mastery of prose but in the mystery of praise.

The profoundly Christian nature and supernature of Tolkien's work can be demonstrated by adopting a trifocal approach. First, by looking at Tolkien the man, we shall discover the soul of a Christian mystic; second, by studying Tolkien's philosophy of myth, we shall come to understand the theological basis of his own mythological world; and third, by looking at the myth itself, as revealed in *The Silmarillion* and *The Lord of the Rings*, we shall see that Tolkien's epic goes beyond mere "fantasy" to the deepest realms of metaphysics. Far from being only an escapist fantasy, *The Lord of the Rings* will be revealed as a theological thriller.

In order to get to grips with Tolkien the man—or with Tolkien as the man behind the myth of *The Lord of the Rings*—it is useful to start with how the man saw himself. Specifically, it is useful to see how he saw himself in relation to his work. According to Tolkien's own "scale of significance", his Catholic faith was the most important, or most "significant", influence on the writing of *The Lord of the Rings*. It is, therefore, not merely erroneous but patently perverse to see Tolkien's epic as anything other than a specifically Christian myth. This being so, and considering how the very concept of "myth" is often misunderstood, we should proceed to a discussion of Tolkien's philosophy of myth.

Tolkien understood the nature and meaning of myth in a manner that has not been grasped by his critics. It is this misapprehension on the part of his critics that lies at the very root of their failure to appreciate his work. For most modern critics, "myth" is merely another word for a lie or a falsehood, something which is intrinsically *not* true. For Tolkien, myth had virtually the opposite meaning. It was the only way that certain transcendent truths could be expressed in intelligible form.

Tolkien believed that the story of Christ was simply a true myth, a myth that works in the same way as the others, but a myth that really happened. Whereas pagan myths revealed fragments of eternal truth through the words of poets, the true myth of Christianity revealed the whole truth through the Word Himself. The poets of pagan antiquity told their story with words, but God, the omnipotent Poet, told the true story with facts—weaving His tale with the actions of real men in actual history.

This sublime vision found (sub)creative expression in the opening pages of *The Silmarillion*, in which the "true myth" is reflected through the medium of Tolkien's wonderful imagination. In these pages Tolkien's own version of the Creation bears a remarkable similarity to the Creation story in the book of Genesis. In the beginning was Eru, the One, who "made first the Ainur, the Holy Ones, that were the offspring of his thought, and they were with him before aught else was made". God, the One, "spoke to them, propounding to them themes of music". He then allows the Holy Ones, or archangels, to share his creative gifts, declaring to them their role in Creation: "Of the theme that I have declared to you, I will now that ye make in harmony together a Great Music. And since I have kindled you with the Flame Imperishable, ye shall show forth your powers in adorning this theme, each with his own thoughts and devices, if he will." In this way, the archangels brought forth the Creation of God as a Symphony of Praise in His honor: "And a sound arose of endless interchanging melodies woven in harmony that passed beyond hearing into the depth and into the heights . . . and the music and the echo of the music went out into the Void, and it was not void."

Disharmony is brought into the cosmic symphony of Creation when one of the archangels decides to play his own tune in defiance of the will of the Composer. Instead of being an instrument in the Great Music, the rebel archangel composes his own theme, bringing discord. This disharmony is the beginning of evil. Again, Tolkien's myth follows the "true myth" of Christianity with allegorical precision. The rebel archangel is named Melkor, later known as Morgoth, and is obviously Middle Earth's equivalent of Lucifer, also known as Satan. Melkor is described by Tolkien as "the greatest of the Ainur" as Lucifer was the greatest of the archangels. Like Lucifer, Melkor is the ultimate source of the sin of pride, intent on corrupting mankind for his own spiteful purposes. Melkor desired "to subdue to his will both Elves and Men", envious of the gifts that God had promised them, "and he wished himself to have subjects and servants, and to be called Lord, and to be master over other wills".

The allegory becomes even less mistakable when Tolkien describes the war between Melkor and Manwe, who is clearly cast in the role of the archangel Michael. "And there was strife between Melkor and the other Valar; and for that time Melkor withdrew and departed to other regions and did there what he would."

The parallels between Melkor and Lucifer are made even more apparent when Tolkien explains that the name Melkor means "he who arises in might"—"But that name he has forfeited; and the Noldor, who among the Elves suffered most from his malice, will not utter it, and they name him Morgoth, the Dark Enemy of the World." Similarly, Lucifer, brightest of all the angels, means "light bringer", whereas Satan, like Morgoth, means "enemy". Tolkien's intention, both as a Christian and as a philologist, in identifying Melkor with Lucifer is plain enough.

Taking his inspiration, no doubt, from the book of Isaiah (*Thy pomp is brought down to the grave, and the noise of thy viols: the worm is spread under thee, and the worms cover thee. How art thou fallen from heaven, O Lucifer, son of the morning.* [Is 14:11–12]), Tolkien says of Melkor:

> From Splendour he fell through arrogance to contempt for all things save himself, a spirit wasteful and pitiless. Understanding he turned to subtlety in perverting to his own will all that he would use, until he became a liar without shame. He began with the desire of Light, but when he could not possess it for himself alone, he descended through fire and wrath into a great burning, down into Darkness. And darkness he used most in his evil works upon Arda, and filled it with fear for all living things.

Apart from the scriptural influence, the other overriding influence is Augustinian theology. Evil, as symbolized by darkness, has no value of its own but is only a negation of that which is good, as symbolized by light.

Shortly after this description of Melkor, Tolkien introduces Sauron, the Dark Enemy in *The Lord of the Rings*. Sauron is described as a "spirit" and as the "greatest" of Melkor's, alias Morgoth's, servants: "But in after years he rose like a shadow of Morgoth and a ghost of his malice, and walked behind him on the same ruinous path down into the Void."

Thus, the evil powers in *The Lord of the Rings* are specified as direct descendents of Tolkien's Satan, rendering impossible, or at any rate implausible, anything but a Christian interpretation of the book. Catholic theology, explicitly present in *The Silmarillion* and implicitly present in *The Lord of the Rings*, is omnipresent in both, breathing life into the tales as invisibly but as surely as oxygen.

The sheer magnificence of Tolkien's mythological vision precludes any adequate appraisal, in an essay of this length, of the Christian mysticism and theology that gives it life. In the impenetrable blackness of the Dark Lord and his abysmal servants, the ring-wraiths, we feel the objective reality of Evil. Sauron and his servants confront and affront us with the nauseous presence of the Real Absence of goodness.

Tolkien is, however, equally powerful in his depiction of goodness. His belief that truth, and therefore reality, is ultimately metaphysical leads logically to the subsistent belief that the physical universe is merely a reflection of some greater metaphysical purpose. Thus the physical actions of the hobbits and the other heroes—and villains—in *The Lord of the Rings* are part of some unseen but all-powerful and ever-present metaphysical drama. Those who behave virtuously are doing the will of the One, whereas those who succumb to evil are subjecting themselves to the will of the Enemy.

Seen in this light, the whole drama of *The Lord of the Rings* takes on deeper mystical significance. In the normally shy and retiring hobbits, called unwillingly to acts of unsuspecting heroism, there is the exaltation of the humble. In their reluctant heroism, we see a courage ennobled by modesty. In the Quest, with its trials, tribulations, suffering and sacrifice, there is the Way of the Cross. In the Fellowship of the Ring, collectively facing evil with a defiant adherence to virtuous truth, there is an image of the Church Militant in a hostile world. In the immortality of the elves, and the sadness and melancholic wisdom it evokes in them, we receive an inkling that man's mortality is a gift of God, a gift that ends his exile in mortal life and enables him, in death, to achieve a mystical union with the divine beyond the reach of time. Throughout the whole book, there is a real sense of exile, a feeling that all the struggles in the shadowlands of this physical life are but figments of a fuller life that can be lived only in the metaphysical reality beyond "the circles of the world". This is not realism; it is hyperrealism. Tolkien's fantasy is applicable to the very marrow of our beings in this "real life". We, like the hobbits and men in Middle Earth, are exiles from our true home. We, like they, are poor banished children of Eve, sending up our sighs, mourning and weeping in this vale of tears.

Significantly, the role of men in *The Lord of the Rings* reflects their divine, though fallen, nature. They are to be found among the Enemy's servants, though usually beguiled by deception into the ways of evil and always capable of repentance and, in consequence, redemption. Boromir, who represents man in the Fellowship of the Ring, suc-

cumbs to the temptation to use the Ring, that is, the forces of evil, in
the naïve belief that it could be wielded as a powerful weapon against
Sauron. He finally recognizes the error of seeking to use evil against
evil. He dies heroically, laying down his life for his friends in a spirit
of repentance.

Ultimately, *The Lord of the Rings* is a sublimely mystical Passion play.
The carrying of the Ring—the emblem of sin—is the carrying of the
Cross. The mythological Quest is a veritable via dolorosa. It is true
that Tolkien's detractors, and many of his admirers, have failed to grasp
this ultimate truth at the heart of his myth. Unfortunately, those that
are blind to theology will continue to be blind to that which is most
beautiful in *The Lord of the Rings*. One is reminded of the words of
C. S. Lewis that a diligent atheist, or, for that matter, a delicate neo-
pagan or agnostic, cannot be too careful of what he reads. In straying
too deeply into Tolkien's world, he will be straying into the world of
truths that he had not previously perceived. If he continues to follow
the Fellowship of the Ring into the depths of Mordor and Beyond,
he might even come to see that the exciting truths point to the most
exciting Truth of all. At its deepest, he might finally understand that
the Quest is, in fact, a pilgrimage.

Tolkien's work remains a tour de force in a world of mediocrity. Its
weakness, if weakness it is, lies not with its author but with its readers.
Those who fail to see the far-off gleam of *evangelium* in Tolkien's work
are those who are not looking for it.

> There are none so blind
> (blinded by the night),
> as they who will not see,
> they neither seek nor find,
> (though reminded by the light),
> they are but will not be.

40

LETTING THE CATHOLIC OUT OF THE BAGGINS

IN THE UNITED KINGDOM, back in 1997, Tolkien's *The Lord of the Rings* was voted "the greatest book of the twentieth century" in several major polls, emerging as a runaway winner ahead of its nearest rival, Orwell's *Nineteen Eighty-Four*. Readers of the *Daily Telegraph* voted Tolkien the twentieth century's greatest author, ahead of George Orwell and Evelyn Waugh in second and third place, respectively. Two months later, a poll of the fifty thousand members of the Folio Society produced an even more staggering vindication of the literary position of *The Lord of the Rings*. The Folio Society asked its members to name their favorite books of any age, not simply those published in the twentieth century, and Tolkien's myth triumphed once again. It received 3,270 votes. Jane Austen's *Pride and Prejudice* was second with 3,212 votes and *David Copperfield* by Charles Dickens was third with 3,070 votes.

Tolkien's triumph was greeted with anger and contempt by many literary "experts". The writer Howard Jacobson reacted with splenetic scorn, dismissing Tolkien as being "for children ... or the adult slow". The poll merely demonstrated "the folly of teaching people to read ... It's another black day for British culture." Susan Jeffreys, writing in the *Sunday Times*, described *The Lord of the Rings* as "a horrible artifact" and added that it was "depressing ... that the votes for the world's best 20th-century book should have come from those burrowing an escape into a nonexistent world". Similarly, Griff Rhys Jones on the BBC's *Bookworm* program appeared to believe that Tolkien's epic went no deeper than the "comforts and rituals of childhood". The *Times Literary Supplement* described the results of the poll as "horrifying", while a writer in the *Guardian* complained that *The Lord of the Rings* "must be by any reckoning one of the worst books ever written".

Probably the most bitter response to Tolkien's triumph came from the feminist writer, Germaine Greer, who, a quarter of a century earlier, had attained notoriety for her authorship of the best-selling handbook of women's "liberation", *The Female Eunuch*. Greer complained that the enduring success of *The Lord of the Rings* was a nightmare come true.

> As a fifty-seven-year-old lifelong teacher of English, I might be expected to regard this particular list of books of the century with dismay. I do. Ever since I arrived at Cambridge as a student in 1964 and encountered a tribe of full-grown women wearing puffed sleeves, clutching teddies and babbling excitedly about the doings of hobbits, it has been my nightmare that Tolkien would turn out to be the most influential writer of the twentieth century. The bad dream has materialized. At the head of the list, in pride of place as the book of the century, stands *The Lord of the Rings*.

Rarely has a book caused such controversy; rarely has the vitriol of the critics highlighted to such an extent the cultural schism between the literary illuminati and the views of the reading public.

It is perhaps noteworthy that most of the self-styled "experts" among the literati who queued up to sneer so contemptuously at *The Lord of the Rings* are outspoken champions of cultural deconstruction and moral relativism. It is also noteworthy, however, that their anodyne and anoetic criticism of Tolkien's work betrayed an utter ignorance of the profound debt to, and depth of, Christian theology, which is the work's chief hallmark. No doubt, had they not been so ignorant, they would have sneered with an added degree of derision at the discovery that the work was deeply Christian in inspiration. Either way, the level of critical engagement, or lack thereof, illustrated a collective blindness as regards the Christian dimension in *The Lord of the Rings*. This blindness, or rather, my exasperation at it, was the spark of motivation behind my writing of *Tolkien: Man and Myth* (Ignatius Press, 1998). My intention was to highlight the centrality of the Catholic Church in Tolkien's life and to illustrate the significance of the author's Catholicism to his work. Previously, the major critical works on

Tolkien—those by Tom Shippey and Verlyn Flieger—had concentrated on the linguistic dimension while largely overlooking the religious aspects. Although these scholarly studies were excellent and worthy of the highest praise, the fact remained that the most important ingredient in Middle Earth was not being discussed.

In Tolkien's own "scale of significance" as to the relationship between him and his work, Tolkien had insisted that the fact that he was "a Christian (and in fact a Roman Catholic)" was the most important of the "really significant" elements in his work, stating specifically and explicitly that it was more important than the linguistic influence. This being so, it seemed odd, to say the least, that there had been no major study of the *real significance* of the Catholicism of *The Lord of the Rings*. My own work was, therefore, an effort to rectify a sin of omission.

Now, however, five years after the publication of my book, there seems to be a veritable flood of new religious studies of Tolkien. It is not, perhaps, a plethora, since that suggests that the new phenomenon is in some respects unwelcome or unhealthy; rather, it is an embarrassment of riches. I, for one, am utterly delighted that there is now such a flow of Christocentric studies of "the greatest book of the twentieth century" and would like to offer a brief guide to some of these new titles.

J. R. R. Tolkien's Sanctifying Myth by Bradley J. Birzer (ISI Books, 2002) is arguably the pick of the crop. In chapters such as "Myth and Subcreation", "The Created Order", "Heroism", "The Nature of Evil" and "The Nature of Grace Proclaimed", Professor Birzer elucidates the sheer magnificence of Tolkien's mythological vision and the Christian mysticism and theology that give it life. Perhaps the highlight of the book, at least in this reviewer's judgment, is an excellent and enthralling chapter on the relationship between Middle Earth and modernity, in which Professor Birzer combines his scholarship as a historian steeped in the tradition of Christopher Dawson and Russell Kirk with his grounding in philosophy and theology to place Tolkien's subcreation into its proper sociopolitical and cultural context.

If Birzer's book has a rival to the claim of being pick of the crop, it is Richard Purtill's *J. R. R. Tolkien: Myth, Morality and Religion* (Ignatius Press, 2003). This is not merely my opinion but that of Professor Birzer himself also. "Purtill's book deserves a place alongside the best of Tolkien criticism", Birzer writes.

At once deeply personal, wise, and Christian, Purtill's intellectual and highly readable work offers an overflowing stream of brilliant insights into Tolkien the man, the author, and the Roman Catholic. Especially stunning are Purtill's explorations of myth and the deeper meanings behind serious science fiction and fantasy. One comes away from this book not only with a better understanding of Tolkien, but more importantly, with a greater grasp of truth, beauty, and Grace.

My own thoughts exactly; and since I could hardly express myself more eloquently than Professor Birzer, I shall not attempt to do so.

Time and space do not permit anything other than a cursory glance at some of the other Tolkien books that have been published recently. The appropriately named Inkling Books of Seattle have published *Celebrating Middle-earth: The Lord of the Rings as a Defence of Western Civilization*, a collection of essays edited by John G. West Jr., and *Untangling Tolkien* by Michael W. Perry. The former includes contributions by West himself, by Peter Kreeft and by the present reviewer; the latter describes itself as "a chronology and commentary for *The Lord of the Rings*" and serves as a very useful reference work for those wishing a clearer picture of the time frame within which the action takes place.

There are also several new studies by Protestants, representing a welcome crossing of the denominational frontier. These include *Tolkien in Perspective* by Greg Wright (VMI Publishers, 2003), *The Gospel according to Tolkien* by Ralph C. Wood (Westminster John Knox Press, 2003), *Finding God in The Lord of the Rings* by Kurt D. Bruner and Jim Ware (Tyndale House Publishers, 2001), and *Tolkien's Ordinary Virtues: Exploring the Spiritual Themes of The Lord of the Rings* by Mark Eddy Smith (Intervarsity Press, 2002).

For my final selection from the legion of new works on Tolkien from a Christian scholarly perspective, we shall turn our gaze to the East, not, as Leonie Caldecott would suggest, because it is Dawn, nor (heaven forbid!) because it is Mordor; we shall turn our gaze eastward to Poland, from whence an excellent work of scholarship, *Recovery and Transcendence for the Contemporary Mythmaker: The Spiritual Dimension in the Works of J. R. R. Tolkien* by Christopher Garbowski (Maria Curie-Sklodowska University Press, 2000) is published. In spite of its clodhoppingly clumsy title, its scholarly approach and unifying thesis make it well worth the difficulty of acquiring.

The quantity and quality of Tolkien scholarship has certainly come a long way in the five years since the present reviewer, fraught with frustration at the absence of good Christian scholarship on Tolkien's "fundamentally Catholic" work, felt impelled to gatecrash the ominous silence on the subject. Since then, in the wake of the film adaptation of *The Lord of the Rings*, we have seen how the Peter Jackson entourage has sought to downplay the importance of Tolkien's Catholic faith in its effort to market its product in a global secular environment. No matter. It is too late to subdue the rising tide of Christian Tolkien scholarship. The proverbial cat is out of the bag; or, rather, the Catholic is out of the Baggins.

41

A HIDDEN PRESENCE

The Catholic Imagination of J. R. R. Tolkien

IT IS AN EXCITING TIME to be an admirer of J. R. R. Tolkien. Whereas the reputation of many of Tolkien's literary contemporaries appears to be on the wane, his own formidable reputation continues to wax spectacularly.

The Tolkienian renaissance began in 1997 with the emergence of *The Lord of the Rings* as "the greatest book of the century" in several opinion polls. Then, in 2001, the release of the first of Peter Jackson's three film adaptations of Tolkien's masterpiece introduced the wonders of Middle Earth to millions of new admirers around the world. Now, half a century after the book's initial publication, it is selling in greater numbers than ever. Such is Tolkien's towering presence amid the pygmies of modernity that even the phrase "literary phenomenon" appears something of an understatement that fails to do him justice.

It is gratifying to know that the growth in Tolkien's popularity has been reflected by a similar growth in the quantity and, for the most part, in the quality of Tolkien scholarship. In the past year or so, Bradley J. Birzer's *J. R. R. Tolkien's Sanctifying Myth* (ISI Books) and Richard L. Purtill's *J. R. R. Tolkien: Myth, Morality and Religion* (Ignatius Press) have added considerably to the breadth and depth of the critical approach to Tolkien studies. And these two volumes are only *la crème de la crème* of the plethora of new titles in the field. Since this is the case, one might be forgiven for asking whether there is any need for more of the same. The answer to such a question might be that there is *always* room for more as long as they are *not* the same. More, yes; but more of the same, no.

Thankfully, JRRT's epic myth is so rich, so superabundantly rich, that there is always more to discover. *A Hidden Presence: The Catholic Imagination of J. R. R. Tolkien*, edited by Father Ian Boyd and Stratford Caldecott (Chesterton Press, 2003), is living proof that scholars have only begun to mine the depths for the seams of pure spiritual gold that lie at the heart of Middle Earth.

Boyd and Caldecott are perhaps best known as scholars of G. K. Chesterton, and the book itself is published by the newly launched publishing division of the Chesterton Institute, of which Boyd and Caldecott are luminaries. This, however, is not to detract from their position as scholars of Tolkien. On the contrary, both are well qualified, and Caldecott in particular is a Tolkien scholar of rare insight. Take, for instance, his succinct definition of "mythopoeia" in his introduction to *A Hidden Presence*:

> Mythopoeia is the faculty of making, of creativity, and it is an essential part of our humanity. Escapism in a sense it may be, but in this case we are talking (as Tolkien puts it in his essay on Fairy Stories) of an escape into reality. It is the world of the everyday—boring, banal, dull, meaningless—that is the prison from which this kind of fantasy seeks to liberate us, not by distracting us from the real but by showing us the deeper patterns and meanings that lie concealed within it. (2–3)

Again, from the same introduction, this is what Caldecott has to say about the paradoxical realism at the typological heart of mythology: "Tolkien's imagined beings and characters are neither caricatures nor stereotypes. If anything, they are archetypes. Their larger-than-life quality is necessary, for 'they have their insides on the outside: they are visible souls.' That is all part of the *realism* of myth" (4).

Apart from writing the introduction, Caldecott is the author of the first of the dozen or more essays that grace this volume. He is also the first of several writers in *A Hidden Presence* to refer to the significance of the date on which the Ring is destroyed: 25 March. The significance of this date will not escape the attention of Catholics, though it is certainly overlooked all too often by Tolkien's non-Christian admirers. Tom Shippey, an Anglo-Saxon scholar and Tolkien expert, states in his book *The Road to Middle Earth* that in "Anglo-Saxon belief, and in European popular tradition both before and after that, 25 March is the date of the Crucifixion". It is also, of course, the Feast of the Annunciation, the celebration of the Absolute Center of all history as the moment when God Himself became incarnate as man. As a Catholic, Tolkien was well aware of the significance of 25 March. It signified the way in which God had "unmade" original sin, the Fall, which, like the Ring, had brought humanity under the sway of the Shadow. If the Ring, which is "unmade" at the culmination of Tolkien's Quest, is the "one ring to rule them all . . . and in the darkness bind them", the Fall was the "one sin to rule them all . . . and in the darkness bind them". On 25 March the one sin, like the One Ring, had been "unmade", destroying the power of the Dark Lord.

Always insightful in his own right, Caldecott is also a disseminator of the wisdom of others. I was particularly grateful for his reference to Flannery O'Connor's discussion of what constitutes a "Catholic" novel. It is not necessarily about a Christianized or Catholicized world, but is simply "one in which the truth as Christians know it has been used as a light to see the world by" (11).

The theme of the Catholic novel is taken up by Owen Dudley Edwards in an essay entitled "Gollum, Frodo and the Catholic Novel". At times, Edwards' efforts to forge critical connections between *The Lord of the Rings* and the novels of other Catholic writers, such as Mauriac, Bernanos, Greene and Waugh, are too carelessly, or at least too briefly, argued. The result is that his conclusions appear a trifle tenuous. Similarly, his discussion of the analogous relationship between *The Lord of the Rings* and Orwell's *Nineteen Eighty-Four* is frustratingly incomplete. He is also at pains to point out the inspiration that Tolkien indubitably gained from the Greek classical tradition without balancing his analysis with an acceptance that Norse and Celtic mythology were at least as important as catalysts to Tolkien's imagination. Thus, for instance, he reminds us, in relation to Bilbo's riddle competition with Gollum in *The Hobbit*, that "the story of Oedipus involves a riddle-contest with the Sphinx" (35), while at the same time he fails to allude to the rich riddle-tradition of the Anglo-Saxons. These are, however, relatively minor quibbles. For the most part, Edwards' essay offers valuable illumination of the literary landscape within which *The*

Lord of the Rings was written. Perplexingly, many of his most poignant points are relegated to the footnotes at the end of his essay—for instance, his berating of Edwin Muir for "snobbishly" abusing Tolkien, adding, quite correctly, that a poet of Muir's caliber and sensibility "should have known better" (40). Most particularly, Edwards' footnoted reference to the similarities between Chesterton's *The Flying Inn* and Tolkien's *The Lord of the Rings* was most welcome.

Verlyn Flieger's essay is the low point of the volume. On occasion, her efforts at sociological reductionism reduce her analysis to the level of the inane. Furthermore, it is clear that she has no sympathy with, and no comprehension or conception of, the theological depths from which Tolkien drew the inspiration for his myth-making. Her claim that Tolkien's history in Middle Earth "begins in imperfection" (62) is quite simply wrong, according to any critical criteria. It begins with God! Similarly, her claim that God in Middle Earth "is a curiously remote and for the most part inactive figure, uninvolved, with the exception of one cataclysmic moment, in the world he has conceived" is not only erroneous but plainly contradicted on numerous occasions by the analyses of the other contributors to the volume. Her essay protrudes like an awkward-looking sore thumb from the rest of the book to such an extent that one has to question the wisdom of its inclusion in the first place.

Unfortunately, there is not room in a review of this length to discuss many of the other essays in this splendid volume. Clive Tolley's essay on Tolkien's sublimely beautiful but sadly underrated poem "Mythopoeia" is thoroughly engrossing but flawed, in this reviewer's judgment, by Tolley's misreading of Pope's *Essay on Man*. Dwight Longenecker's short and ingenious essay paralleling hobbit humility with the humility exhibited by Saint Thérèse of Lisieux is full of the deftly expressed wisdom with which his work always abounds.

Perhaps the finest essay in the whole collection, in terms of the pure quality of the prose, is that by Leonie Caldecott. It is not merely what she says that is so delightful but the wonderful way in which she says it. I wish, in fact, that space permitted citation at length, particularly of the concluding three paragraphs of her essay. Entitled "At Dawn, Look to the East", the prose is as bright and as fresh as the dawn itself.

There is much else besides. There are "Perspectives" by those who knew Tolkien personally, including George Sayer and Robert Murray, S.J., and an essay by the exceptionally gifted wordsmith Peter Kreeft that was originally published in the *Saint Austin Review*, a cultural journal of which the present reviewer is honored to be coeditor. Two essays on fairy tales by Chesterton serve as an appropriate appendix to the volume, reiterating the deep-rooted creative affinity between GKC and JRRT. Taken as a whole, and flaws notwithstanding, *A Hidden Presence* deserves a place of honor in any discerning Tolkien-lover's library.

42

FROM WAR TO MORDOR

J. R. R. Tolkien and World War I

A review of

Tolkien and the Great War: The Threshold of Middle-earth
by John Garth[†]

J OHN GARTH'S STUDY of the impact of the killing fields of World War I on the creative imagination of J. R. R. Tolkien begins with an unexpected twist, the ingenuity of which merits its citation in full.

It is December 16th, nearly the dead of winter. Chill gusts buffet the flanks and faces of the attackers struggling to advance across a bare hundred yards or so of mud. They are a ramshackle group, some of them mere novices. The minute these young men muster a concerted effort, a few veterans press forward with all their energy and skill. But most of the time there is chaos. Again and again their opponents shrug off the assault and land a fearsome counterblow, so that all the guile, fortitude, and experience of the veterans can barely hold back the assault. Their captain, J. R. R. Tolkien, tries to bring his own experience to bear; but those around him are, in the words of an eyewitness, "a beaten pack".

The year is 1913: the Great War is eight months away, and this is just a game. Not yet soldiers, Tolkien and his team-mates are Oxbridge undergraduates back in Birmingham for Christmas, and today, in accordance with annual tradition, they are playing rugby against their old school's First XV.

For a scholarly biography, this gimmicky and teasingly tantalizing opening, bathed in bathos, reads suspiciously like the start of a novel. It is,

[†]Boston: Houghton Mifflin, 2003. ISBN 0-618-33129-8, 400 pp., $26.00.

however, neither inapt nor inept that it does so; on the contrary, its originality is positively refreshing. It declares from the very outset that we are in the company of a gifted wordsmith who will spare us the banality of the type of academic jargon, masking ignorance, which is all too common in the myopic miasma of (post)modernity.

Garth's approach is as welcome as it is unusual. His prose is never boring, and he is never bored by, nor boorish toward, his subject. Neither is his book the sort of hackiography (written by hacks who hack to pieces the reputation of their subjects/victims with the machete of scandal and the cudgel of scorn) that is all too common in our meretricious age. "I do not claim any divine insight into Tolkien's mind," Garth declares in the preface, "and I do not pretend to put him on the psychiatrist's couch. I have not gone hunting for shock and scandal, but have focused at all times on matters that seem to me to have played a part in the growth of his legendarium."

If, however, the author's positive approach to his subject is laudable, the narrowness of his historical perspective is less so. His declared belief that World War I was "the crisis of disenchantment that shaped the modern era" is too sweeping in its generalization and too trite in its general understanding of history. It is simply too simplistic to suggest that the "wasteland" of modernity, as epitomized by Eliot's poem of that name, arose from the no-man's-land of the Great War. The wasteland predated the war and was parodied by G. K. Chesterton in his prewar novels, most notably perhaps in *The Man Who Was Thursday* and *The Ball and the Cross*, both of which are peopled with "hollow men" every iota as vacuous and venal as Eliot's postwar counterparts. And if World War I is alleged to have heralded the hedonism of the "bright young things" satirized in the poetry of Eliot and the prose of Waugh, what is to be said of the hedonism of the decadent 1890s reflected in the work of Wilde or Aubrey Beardsley? Similarly, it is a little too easy to state glibly that "disenchantment" began with the protest poetry of Wilfred Owen and Siegfried Sassoon. What about the "disenchantment" of the aforementioned Decadents? And what of Romantic disenchantment? Byron, Shelley, Keats? What of these? And what of the disenchantment of Coleridge and Wordsworth in the aftermath of the Great Terror of the French Revolution, a terror as terrible as the "animal horror" of World War I, to employ Tolkien's description of the latter conflict? And then, of course, there is the cynicism of the so-called enlightened eighteenth century. Finally, and in fact, firstly, there was the Reformation, the mother of all disenchantments, which fractured and fragmented the comparatively unified civilization of medieval Europe. In truth, it would be more accurate to insist that the Reformation was "the crisis of disenchantment that shaped the modern era", compared with which the impact of the First World War was merely a later manifestation of the disunity caused by this greater debacle four hundred years earlier.

In spite of this fundamental flaw, Garth's book has much to recommend it. He provides little-known yet fascinating insights into the literary tastes of the youthful Tolkien, such as his indifference to Milton and Keats and, by contrast, his "passionate approval" of Francis Thompson, the Catholic mystic and poet who died at a young age in 1907 when Tolkien was in his early teens. According to Garth, Thompson's "metrical and verbal accomplishments, his immense imagery, and the visionary faith underpinning his work" was a significant influence on Tolkien's earliest efforts at poetry. We also learn that Tolkien believed that Thompson had successfully bridged the "divide between rationalism and romanticism", a divide that, as a Catholic Christian, Tolkien would see as not merely unhealthy but ultimately even unnatural. The mystical and philosophical marriage of the romantic and the rational, translated more formally as the relationship between faith and reason, *fides et ratio*, would become the kernel of Tolkien's own philosophy as a writer.

Garth is less insightful in his insinuation that Rupert Brooke's famous poem "The Soldier" was the product of "pessimism". In reality, Brooke's self-sacrificial sentiments were the pouring forth of the optimistic naïveté, nourished on jingoism, which typified the British public's attitude toward the war in its earliest days. One suspects that Garth has confused pessimism with melancholy, the latter of which does indeed permeate Brooke's poetry and is an expression of the influence of his poetic mentor, Hilaire Belloc.

Far from representing pessimism, the "Rupert Brooke period", as it has been called, would become a byword for the period of glib pro-war optimism that would be pricked only by the full horror of the realities of trench warfare. By the time the genuine pessimism of the

poetry of Owen and Sassoon burst like bombs of protest on a shell-
shocked public, Rupert Brooke had already spilled out his life as a
martyr to jingoism in "some corner of a foreign field that is forever
England".

The discussion of Brooke, Owen and Sassoon, and the struggle
between jingoism and protest, raises the whole thorny subject of patriotism. Is it good or evil, right or wrong? The question had been
addressed memorably by Chesterton in his witticism that the patriotic
boast of "my country, right or wrong" is like saying "my mother,
drunk or sober". We might love our mother, but should we condone
or encourage her drunkenness? The English nurse Edith Cavell, murdered by the Germans during World War I, had stated that "patriotism is not enough", a phrase that is often used unthinkingly to suggest
that patriotism is in some way wrong. This is not, of course, what
Cavell was saying. To state that a thing is not sufficient is not to say
that it is wrong. Oxygen is not sufficient for the sustenance of human
life in the sense that other things, such as food and drink, are necessary also. It would, therefore, be true to say that oxygen is not enough,
but not to imply from such a statement that oxygen is harmful! Tolkien's contribution to the thorny question is recounted succinctly by
Garth, who relates his defence of nationalism at a college debate shortly
before the war began.

> Tolkien's version [of nationalism] had nothing to do with vaunting one
> nation above others. To him the nation's greatest goal was cultural self-
> realisation, not power over others; but essential to this were patriotism
> and a community of belief. "I don't defend 'Deutschland über alles'
> but certainly do in Norwegian 'alt for Norge' [All for Norway]", he
> told Wiseman on the eve of the debate. By his own admission, there-
> fore, Tolkien was both an English patriot and a supporter of Home
> Rule for the Irish.

In distinguishing between *Deutschland über alles* and *Alt for Norge*, Tolkien is essentially distinguishing between imperialism and nationalism
and insisting that the former is always a negation of the latter. An
imperialist is a "patriot" who tramples on the patriotism of others; a
nationalist is a patriot who respects other nations as he wishes his own
nation to be respected. The former is pernicious and finds expression

in Tolkien's legendarium in the expansionism of Mordor and Isen-gard, whereas the latter is a blessing and finds expression in Rohan, Minas Tirith and, most memorably of all, the Shire. Hobbits are nation-alists; orcs are imperialists.

And this, of course, brings us back to the purpose of John Garth's book. Since it is his intention to show the connection between Tol-kien's wartime experience and his writing of *The Lord of the Rings* thirty years later, the final judgment on his book should rest on his success or failure in doing so. If this is the criterion, it must be said that his book is of only limited value. Tolkien stated that the most important influence on the writing of his magnum opus was religious. His work was "fundamentally religious and Catholic", and the fact that he was "a Christian ... and in fact a Roman Catholic" was at the top of the "scale of significance" that governed the relationship between himself, as author, and his work. Nowhere in Tolkien's scale of sig-nificance is the war even mentioned.

It would be wrong, however, to dismiss the impact of the war—and, in consequence, the relevance of Garth's book—entirely. Nobody could have lived through the "animal horror" of the Somme without its indelible scar being left somewhere on the psyche. Perhaps in the desolation of Mordor we see the desolation of no-man's-land; perhaps in the very darkness of much of the chronicles of Middle Earth we see the shadow of the war and its horrors. Perhaps. Ultimately, however, the shadow of the war is only a dim shadow of the Shadow itself, a shadow that represents not war but the evil that causes war. The work, at its deepest, is a theological thriller, "fundamentally religious and Catholic". As such, and to reiterate, Garth's work is of limited value, especially when compared to those works on Tolkien that concentrate on the more important influences on his life and work. Nonetheless, and this important caveat aside, the work is well written, entertaining and informative.

Anyone seeking a definitive exposition of the depths of Tolkien's life and work will not find it here. If, however, like the present reviewer, he has an insatiable appetite for all things Tolkien, this book will make a valued addition to his presumably already burgeoning collection. *Tol-kien and the Great War* is not the main course—it is not even an appetizer—but it certainly makes a very palatable side dish.

43

DIVINE MERCY IN *THE LORD OF THE RINGS*

Peter Jackson's blockbuster film adaptation of *The Lord of the Rings* has been watched by millions of moviegoers throughout the world, most of whom will be unaware that they are watching a film version of "a fundamentally religious and Catholic work".

The work's author, J. R. R. Tolkien, was a lifelong devout Catholic who poured his Catholic heart into the writing of the myth that is now captivating a new generation, half a century after its first publication.

Yet, if the Catholicism is indeed as "significant" as its author claimed, where exactly are the Catholic signs that bestow this significance?

This is too large a question to answer in a solitary article. Indeed, there are now several whole books dedicated to the Christian heart of Tolkien's myth. This being so, we will concentrate on one aspect of the Christian dimension. Let us examine the manifestation of divine mercy in *The Lord of the Rings*.

"Above all shadows rides the sun", proclaims Samwise Gamgee amid the perilous gloom on the Stairs of Cirith Ungol in *The Two Towers*, declaring his faith and hope in a power beyond the reach of the Shadow. The hopeful hobbit, like the hope-filled Christian, has no need of despair, even in the midst of the greatest evil. Darkness can never ultimately prevail in the presence of the Sun that never sets.

Sam and Frodo are led into the gloom of Cirith Ungol, and into the lurking presence of the monstrous Shelob, by the treachery of Gollum. And it is, ironically, in the relationship between Sam, Frodo and Gollum that we find the key to understanding the role of divine mercy and the workings of divine providence in the whole work.

Throughout the story, Gollum is seeking to betray Sam and Frodo in order to regain possession of the Ring, his "Precious". Knowing his treacherous intent, Frodo initially wished that Gollum had been killed: "What a pity that Bilbo did not stab that vile creature when he had a chance!"

"Pity?" replied Gandalf. "It was Pity that stayed his hand. Pity, and Mercy." Gandalf then went on to say that he believed that Gollum was mystically bound up with the fate of the Ring. "My heart tells me that he has some part to play yet, for good or ill, before the end; and when that comes, the pity of Bilbo may rule the fate of many— yours not least." These words are recalled later by Frodo when he too has the chance to kill Gollum. Like Bilbo, Frodo also chooses the path of mercy over vengeance, and like Bilbo, his charitable choice comes to "rule the fate of many". At the climactic moment on Mount Doom, Frodo finds that he cannot, at the very last, cast the Ring into the Fire. On the very brink of success, he finds himself on the verge of final, and fatal, failure. It is at this crucial moment that Frodo, the Quest and Middle Earth itself are saved by Gollum, who rushes forward and bites the Ring from Frodo's finger before losing his balance and falling into the abyss, destroying himself and the Ring in the process. The scene is not only a triumph of divine providence over fate, it is the triumph of divine mercy, in which free will, supported by grace, is fully vindicated. According to Tolkien himself, Frodo was saved "because he had accepted the burden voluntarily, and had then done all that was within his utmost physical and mental strength to do. He (and the Cause) were saved—by Mercy: by the supreme value and efficacy of Pity and forgiveness and injury." [1] And as for Gollum, he fell into the Fire, clutching his Precious. He made his choice and he has his reward.

The greatest manifestation of divine mercy is, of course, the Incarnation and the Crucifixion, and at its deepest, Tolkien's myth serves as a reflection of this archetypal mercy. The journey of Frodo and Sam into the very heart of Mordor in order to destroy, or unmake, the Ring in the fires of Mount Doom is emblematic of the Christian's imitation of Christ in carrying the Cross. At its most profound level, *The Lord of the Rings* is a sublimely mystical Passion play. The carrying of the Ring—the emblem of sin—is the carrying of the Cross. This is

[1] From Tolkien's *Letters.*

the ultimate applicability of *The Lord of the Rings*—that we have to lose our life in order to gain it; that unless we die we cannot live; that we must all take up our cross and follow him.

All of this would be deducible implicitly from the story itself, but Tolkien makes the parallel even more explicitly. "I should say", he wrote, explaining the final climactic moments on Mount Doom when the Ring is finally unmade, "that within the mode of the story [it] *exemplifies* (an aspect of) the familiar words: 'Forgive us our trespasses as we forgive them that trespass against us. Lead us not into temptation but deliver us from evil'." Tolkien makes the Christian dimension even more unmistakable, and unavoidable, in the fact that the climactic destruction of the Ring, and in consequence the destruction of the Dark Lord who had forged it, occurred on "the twenty-fifth of March". The significance of this date will not escape the attention of Catholics.

Tom Shippey, an Anglo-Saxon scholar and Tolkien expert, states in his book *The Road to Middle Earth* that in "Anglo-Saxon belief, and in European popular tradition both before and after that, 25 March is the date of the Crucifixion". It is also, of course, the Feast of the Annunciation, the celebration of the Absolute Center of all history as the moment when God Himself became incarnate as man. As a Catholic, Tolkien was well aware of the significance of 25 March. It signified the way in which God had "unmade" original sin, the Fall, which, like the Ring, had brought humanity under the sway of the Shadow. If the Ring, which is "unmade" at the culmination of Tolkien's Quest, is the "one ring to rule them all ... and in the darkness bind them", the Fall was the "one sin to rule them all ... and in the darkness bind them". On 25 March the one sin, like the One Ring, had been "unmade", destroying the power of the Dark Lord.

There are, of course, many other examples of divine mercy shining forth from the pages of Tolkien's masterpiece—too many to mention in a solitary article. It is, however, very comforting in the midst of these dark days that the most popular book of the twentieth century, and the most popular movie of the new century, draw their power and their glory from the light of the Gospel. *Deo gratias.*

44

RESURRECTING MYTH

A Response to Dr. Murphy's "Response"

THERE IS SOMETHING A LITTLE FISHY about Dr. Murphy's "response" to my article "True Myth: The Catholicism of *The Lord of the Rings*"—fishy in the sense that it is a large red herring. It seems to me, having read his "response", that the whole argument he constructs is nothing more than a nebulous nonsense that will waft away at the first faint breeze of logical, not to say theological, reality. Ultimately, as we shall see, his less-than-edifying edifice is built upon non sequiturs constructed on fallacious foundations. On the assumption that there is a good deal of truth to be derived from mythology, it can be said, quite truthfully, that Dr. Murphy's position is far less substantial than the castles of the fairies.

Dr. Murphy endeavors to downplay Tolkien's assertion that *The Lord of the Rings* is "of course a fundamentally religious and Catholic work" by quoting another of Tolkien's letters in which he describes the work as "fundamentally linguistic in inspiration". He implies thereafter that the linguistic foundations are as important as the religious. It is, however, interesting that he fails to quote another letter by Tolkien in which the author of *The Lord of the Rings* states unequivocally that the religious element is more important than the linguistic. I say that it is interesting because this particular letter forms the basis of my whole approach to understanding *The Lord of the Rings* in my book *Tolkien: Man and Myth*. Clearly Dr. Murphy has read my book, because he quotes from it selectively throughout his article. Why, therefore, did he fail to quote the very letter that both refutes his own suggestion that religious and linguistic elements are of equal importance and also forms the foundation of my own argument that he is presumably endeavoring to refute?

It is curious that Dr. Murphy asserts that "Tolkien would not want us to take his own suggestions about the meaning of his work as the last word". Possibly not. Yet, as Tolkien states specifically, he knows "more than any investigator". Consequently, assuming that Tolkien is correct in this assertion (and I believe that he is), his words are more reliable than any other words on the subject. I would go further. I would assert that we ignore Tolkien's words at our peril. The author is the anchor that keeps us bedded in the underlying realities that constitute a work. Once we begin to ignore the author, we inevitably drift away from the true meaning of the work. Tolkien's "guardian Angel, or indeed God Himself" might know more about *The Lord of the Rings* than does the author himself, but since we are not at liberty to ask them personally (except perhaps in prayer), we should treat Tolkien as the most reliable arbiter of his own work. To reiterate, therefore, we can assume quite safely that *The Lord of the Rings* is indeed a "fundamentally religious and Catholic work" and that the Catholic dimension is the most important of the really significant factors that animate the book.

Tolkien's secularist admirers never fail to remind us that Tolkien denied that *The Lord of the Rings* could or should be seen as an allegory. Thus, for instance, Dr. Murphy complains that "Pearce omits from his article any discussion of the difference between myth and allegory, a distinction that was important to Tolkien". He then quotes from Tolkien's famous essay "Beowulf: The Monsters and the Critics", in which Tolkien complained that the "defender" of a myth, "unless he is careful, and speaks in parables . . . will kill what he is studying by vivisection, and . . . will be left with a formal and mechanical allegory". Ironically, Dr. Murphy has unwittingly destroyed his own case by the very words of Tolkien that he has sought to employ in his prosecution of it. In this passage, Tolkien is speaking of the dangers of reducing the myth to "a *formal* and *mechanical* allegory" while advocating that the critic employ the more careful and subtle allegorical approach implied by the use of parables.

It is a truth invariably missed by those allergic to allegory that Tolkien's attacks on allegory always and invariably refer *specifically* to this "formal and mechanical" kind. Tolkien considered this form of allegory, exemplified most notably perhaps by Bunyan's *Pilgrim's Progress* and C. S. Lewis' *Pilgrim's Regress*, as being too crude in its mode of conveying the truth. Tolkien preferred the subtler allegorical approach of mythology whereby the *facts* of the story become *applicable* to the *truth* that is present in our own lives. This *applicability* of the literal meaning of a story to the world beyond its pages is no less "allegorical" than other forms of allegory; it is a difference in degree, not essence. It is less formal, less mechanical, more subtle, but no less allegorical. Thus, for example, Tolkien stressed that "any attempt to explain the purport of myth or fairytale must use allegorical language. (And, of course, the more 'life' a story has the more readily will it be susceptible of allegorical interpretations.)"

"The truth is", wrote C. S. Lewis, that allegory is "one of those words which need defining in each context where one uses it." In his early work, *The Allegory of Love*, Lewis defined allegory in its formal, mechanical or crude form, as follows:

> On the one hand you can start with an immaterial fact, such as the passions which you actually experience, and can then invent *visibilia* (visible things) to express them. If you are hesitating between an angry retort and a soft answer, you can express your state of mind by inventing a person called *Ira* (Anger) with a torch and letting her contend with another invented person called *Patientia* (Patience).

Lewis, like Tolkien, often denied that his work was allegorical in this strict sense of the word. In December 1958 he wrote to a correspondent denying that Aslan was an "allegory".

> By an allegory I mean a composition (whether pictorial or literary) in which immaterial realities are represented by feigned physical objects, e.g. a pictured Cupid allegorically represents erotic love (which in reality is an experience, not an object occupying a given area of space) or, in Bunyan a giant represents Despair.

Although Lewis denied that Aslan was "formally and mechanically allegorical" in this crude sense, he would clearly have conceded that Aslan is meant to *remind* the reader of Christ, without specifically representing him per se. Similarly, Gandalf in his death and resurrection is meant to remind us of Christ without any suggestion that we are ever meant to think that he is meant to be Christ Himself. He "dies" as Gandalf the Grey and is washed white in the blood of his sacrifice, returning resplendently transfigured as Gandalf the White. Frodo is depicted as Christlike in his carrying of the Ring, which, like the Cross, is an emblem of evil or sin; yet he is clearly not intended to be seen literally as Christ.

Tolkien's depiction of the Christlike in *The Lord of the Rings* parallels the Christo-subtle images evoked by the great and anonymous Anglo-Saxon *scop* who first recounted the story of Beowulf. Indeed, we should not be the least surprised to discover that Tolkien's approach to the Christocentric applicability of his myth parallels the applicability of the actions of the hero of the Anglo-Saxon epic. Beowulf reminds us of Christ at several points throughout the narrative, but we are never meant to see Beowulf *as* Christ Himself. Clearly Tolkien had drawn deep draughts of inspiration from the subcreative well of this profoundly Christian poem.

There is, in fact, such an abundance of applicable Christian images throughout *The Lord of the Rings* that one scarcely knows where to start or when to stop. Aragorn is the symbol of kingship, that is, authentic authority, and his kingship reminds us not only of Christ himself but of the desire of Englishmen for the return of the true, that is, Catholic, king—the king in exile—whether the resonance surrounding him be Arthurian or Jacobite or both. The "sword that is broken", the symbol of Aragorn's kingship, is reforged at the anointed time—a potent reminder of Excalibur's union with the Christendom it is ordained to serve. One wonders, in fact, whether the very name of Aragorn could be linked to Catherine of Aragon, the saintly queen who, with the support of the Pope, refused heroically to grant a divorce to Henry VIII, staying true to her Catholic faith while her adulterous husband declared himself head of the Church of England. Obviously we are not intended to believe that Aragorn is Catherine of Aragon! It is not a formal allegory, but a story that is applicable allegorically.

Might we not see in the two characters linked ingeniously by Tolkien through the employment of a phonetic anagram, Theoden and Denethor, the victory of Christian hope (hence *Theo*den) over pagan despair (hence Dene*thor*)? Clearly Theoden is not God; neither is

Denethor, Thor. Yet the applicability of their actions to the reality of paganism and Christendom enriches the myth beyond measure. It is not a question of this allegorical applicability impoverishing or "murdering" the myth, as Dr. Murphy implies, but of its breathing the life of God, or "Eru, the One", into it. Again, Tolkien declared in one of his published letters that, as a Catholic who believed in the Fall, he perceived human history as the Long Defeat with only occasional glimmers of final victory; paralleling these words, Galadriel states specifically in *The Lord of the Rings* that she and the Lord of the Galadhrim have, "together through ages of the world . . . fought the long defeat." The elves, like mankind, are exiled in time and, to employ the language of the *Salve Regina*, are like the "poor banished children of Eve" sending up their sighs, "mourning and weeping in this vale of tears". Unlike men, however, the elves are marooned in immortality and are trapped in the Long Defeat of the vale of tears for centuries unnumbered. No wonder the elves call death "the gift of Iluvatar" (that is, God) to man. The elves are painfully aware of the poignant difference between immortality and eternal life. Thus the *Salve Regina* culminates in the faithful Christian's acknowledgement of this gift of death in the plea that, "after this our exile", we may be shown "the Blessed Fruit of thy womb, Jesus".

One is tempted to continue. The Christian applicability, like Tolkien's proverbial "road", goes ever on and on. I shall, however, desist from this seemingly endless tangent and, for the sake of brevity, return to the specific accusations leveled at me by Dr. Murphy. One particular statement of mine was, in Dr. Murphy's estimation, "absurd even by Pearce's standards". My "absurd" statement reads as follows:

> Ultimately, *The Lord of the Rings* is a sublimely mystical Passion Play. The carrying of the Ring—the emblem of Sin—is the Carrying of the Cross . . . the Quest is, in fact, a Pilgrimage.

"A pilgrimage", counters Dr. Murphy, "is a journey to a sacred place; the quest leads to Mordor, hardly a shrine of holiness . . . I fail to see how the quest can possibly be a carrying of the cross *and* a pilgrimage." Although I shall (almost!) resist the temptation to suggest that this statement is "absurd even by Murphy's standards", I cannot help but be perplexed at how Dr. Murphy, who claims to be a Catholic, can fail to see how the carrying of the cross is *not* a pilgrimage. Doesn't every Catholic believe that life itself is a pilgrimage during which we have to carry our crosses in imitation of Christ? Isn't every Christian's life a carrying of the cross *and* a pilgrimage? Is this not, in fact, the ultimate applicability of *The Lord of the Rings*—that we have to lose our life in order to gain it; that unless we die we cannot live; that we must all take up our cross and follow Him? And as for the assertion that "a pilgrimage is a journey to a sacred place", whereas "the quest leads to Mordor, hardly a shrine of holiness", I might remind Dr. Murphy that all pilgrimages are designed to lead us to heaven, to our resurrection after death. The road to the Resurrection passes via the via dolorosa to Calvary. There is no other route. Thus the path to the Mystic West (Tolkien's mystical vision of heaven inspired by the vision-ary voyages of Saint Brendan) passes via Mordor to Mount Doom. The parallels are obvious because they are intentional. Tolkien knew the way to heaven, and Frodo and Sam discovered it. The Way of Life *is* the Way of the Cross.

Ultimately, Dr. Murphy's assertion that "Tolkien was ... creating a pre-Christian mythology" is nothing less, or more, than post-Christian revisionist nonsense.

"Tolkien is more concerned with re-creating the darkness of a pre-Christian world than allowing his readers, Christian or otherwise, to feel safe", opines Dr. Murphy. On the contrary, Tolkien is intent on showing the darkness of the *real* world—past, present and future—the darkness spread by the Shadow of Evil. Whether we call it the work of Satan or Sauron, the evil is the same. Sin, by any other name, would smell as foul. Neither is there anything "safe" about being a Christian. To lay down one's life for one's friends, to love one's enemies, to choose poverty over worldly possessions—this is not the path that a coward would choose. The Way of the Cross is not an easy way, nor does it allow one to feel safe. The Christian, however, has no need of despair. His is the way of Theoden, not Denethor. In the final analy-sis, *The Lord of the Rings* is not about "the darkness of a pre-Christian world" but about the Christian Sun that never sets.

"It is entirely understandable", writes Dr. Murphy, "why neo-Pagans would find Tolkien's work attractive and inspirational." Yes indeed, but only because they have seen half the picture that Tolkien has painted and find that they like it. When they see the whole picture, they will like it even more!

Tolkien wrote a story, continues Dr. Murphy, "in which hobbits live in holes, elves live in the woods, dragons live in caves, and the Creator lives beyond the boundaries of physical space." Really? Is Dr. Murphy saying that God is outside of Creation? Is he implying that He has locked himself out of His own building, or that He has wandered off with indifference into the void? Perhaps He went for a walk and got lost. At any rate, Dr. Murphy's singular view of the absence of the One in Middle Earth does not square with the all-too-obvious presence of providence in the unfolding of events. Neither, ironically, does it square with Dr. Murphy's own words earlier in his article. Discussing Tolkien's discussion of the climactic scene on Mount Doom, in which Tolkien had said that the key to understanding it was the words of the Lord's Prayer (*"Forgive us our trespasses as we forgive those who trespass against us; and lead us not into temptation, but deliver us from evil"*), Dr. Murphy comments thus:

> To anyone acquainted with the book, the reason for this statement will be obvious. Frodo, acting on Gandalf's advice, spared Gollum's life when he could have killed him. Frodo thus forgives Gollum's sins. At the end of his quest, Frodo is led into "temptation", that is, he is placed in a situation where it is impossible for him to complete his quest by his own power. Gollum then, inadvertently, brings the quest to a successful resolution, destroying himself in the process. This escape from the moment of temptation was not planned by Frodo, it was a moment of grace, of divine intervention by the Creator, and defeat is suddenly turned to victory.

Hallelujah! Dr. Murphy has seen how the words of the Lord's Prayer are not only applicable but crucial to an understanding of the final moments of the Quest. Without Frodo's act of mercy in sparing Gollum—if Frodo had sinned instead of acting virtuously—the Quest would have failed. Having done the will of the Creator, he is rewarded at the crucial moment with "a moment of grace, of divine intervention by the Creator, and defeat is suddenly turned into victory". Hallelujah! But where does this leave Dr. Murphy's assertion that the Creator is not to be found within His Creation but that, on the contrary, He "lives beyond the boundaries of physical space"?

In patent contradiction of this assertion that defeat was turned into victory only by the intervention of God, Dr. Murphy still seems to insist that nontheistic readings of the book are valid: "I can accept that there are dragons and elves in the story, but not in the world, and still find useful applications. I do not see any reason why a non-theistic reader could not take the same attitude to Eru, the Creator." This, from Tolkien's Catholic perspective, would be to see the shadows but to deny the sun. It is to state, in perverse parody of Tolkien's vision, that above all shadows there is no sun.

"It seems to me", continues Dr. Murphy, "that the way to find truth in myth is to find ways of applying that myth to reality." I concur wholeheartedly, especially as this is possible only by making the allegorical connections, or applications, that Dr. Murphy had earlier sought to deny. I would, however, remind him that Tolkien believed, as presumably does he, that God is Reality. Without God, there is no reality. He is the Real Presence that makes all else possible. To seek reality without seeking Him is to seek nothing.

Dr. Murphy concludes his "response" to my article by stating that "readers who want a deeper understanding of how Tolkien weaves his subtle magic would do better to turn to Shippey (1982) and Curry (1997) than Pearce (1998)." Speaking personally, I am a great admirer of both these studies of Tolkien offered as "alternatives" to mine. Shippey is a philologist who understands the linguistic dimension in Tolkien's work better than any other living writer; Curry has much of interest to say about Tolkien's challenge to the inanities of modernity. I would join Dr. Murphy in encouraging people to read both these studies. They are, however, not alternatives to mine. Neither writer is Christian, and neither pays enough attention to that aspect of *The Lord of the Rings* that its author thought the "most significant", namely, its Catholic Christianity. I wrote my book precisely because there was no book paying due attention to that spiritual dimension that is of paramount importance in Middle Earth. Thankfully, however, my book has been followed by a veritable host of new Christian studies of *The Lord of the Rings*. I am aware of four new books published within the past year [2003], and I know of at least three more that are due to be published imminently. Readers really wishing to unravel the Christian mysteries in *The Lord of the Rings* have no need to read my book. There are plenty of others to choose from.

I must conclude by returning to Dr. Murphy. He laments at the end of his own article that although "Tolkien is a subtle writer, one might wish that Pearce shared some of this subtlety". For once I find myself agreeing with Dr. Murphy. To have a mere modicum of Tolkien's marvelous gifts would be a blessing indeed. Dr. Murphy then goes on to criticize my "obtuse" comparison of Chesterton with Tolkien. I might lack the subtlety of Tolkien but to be accused by Dr. Murphy of being as unsubtle as Chesterton is singularly gratifying. I thank him for his compliment. Indeed, I kiss the back of the hand that gave it to me.

45

THE GOOD, THE BAD AND THE UGLY

The Successes and Failures of Tolkien on Film

ADMIRERS OF TOLKIEN'S MYTHICAL EPIC, *The Lord of the Rings*, must have approached Peter Jackson's film production with an uneasy trepidation, an anxiety born of a queasy combination of hope and fear. Would their hopes be realized and their fears be unfounded? Or, on the contrary, would their fears become reality and their hopes simply dissolve into disappointment and disillusionment? Would Jackson's vision of Middle Earth by vindicated or vilified?

The ultimate difficulty that Jackson had to overcome arises from the creative conflict between the media of literature and film. The former, at its best, probes psyche-deep in vivid detail and with an eloquent expressiveness that it is simply not possible to convey on film; the latter, at best, shimmers on the psychological surface, offering a vague impression of the truth and a suggestive sense of the spirit conveyed in its literary source of inspiration. Handicapped by the limitations of his chosen medium, there was never any prospect that Jackson's film version of *The Fellowship of the Ring*, the first part of the trilogy, could capture the richness and depth of Tolkien's book. If this is so, it is clearly unfair to expect Jackson to achieve the impossible. Since we are dealing with an impressionistic medium, we should expect the film to convey only an impression of the truth and the spirit of Tolkien's myth.

Does the film achieve this? For the most part, and emphatically, it does. Jackson has resisted the temptation to take too many artistic liberties and has generally adhered closely to Tolkien's text. He is not foolhardy enough to stray too far from a proven winning formula, though he does employ a degree of license that sometimes works and sometimes doesn't. When it works, it is good, sometimes very good, occasionally masterful; when it fails to work, it is bad, sometimes very bad, and occasionally downright ugly!

To begin with the good, Ian McKellen is an inspired Gandalf, exuding mystery and mysticism but also, and of equal importance, merging mirth with mysticism in equal proportion. Similarly, the characterization of the hobbits blends a keen sense of humility with an equally keen sense of humor. This blend of humor and humility becomes a paradoxically potent cocktail, the secret ingredient that makes the hobbits so lovable, both in Tolkien's tale and in Jackson's film. Viggo Mortensen is a convincingly mysterious Strider who metamorphoses into a suitably noble Aragorn. Sean Bean shines faultlessly as the faltering and all-too-fallible Boromir. A lesser-known Sean (Astin) shines— and perhaps even outshines Bean—as the lovable and huggable hobbit Samwise Gamgee.

So much for the good. What of the bad?

Unfortunately, the film fails miserably in its efforts to depict the elven characters. The elves, arguably the most sublime and most beautifully evocative of all Tolkien's creations, are shown either as outrageously effeminate or as provocatively feminine. The male elves are as transexually impotent as their female counterparts are sexually charged. Elven "males", as seen in Lothlorien, are so neutered that it is impossible to determine their sex. Are they supermodels or transvestites? Either way, they are unconvincing as elves.

The choice of Cate Blanchett and Liv Tyler to play, respectively, Galadriel and Arwen, could have worked well if the demands of cryptofeminist and sexist/sexual stereotyping had not dictated that their roles be beefed up. Galadriel, whom Tolkien likened to the Blessed Virgin, becomes a slightly disturbing (and disturbed) white witch, while Arwen teeters on the brink of becoming a reincarnation of Xena, the warrior princess. Seldom has the abyss between modern romance and its medieval namesake appeared so wide and unbridgeable. Whereas the medieval heroine remained chaste, her modern counterpart is merely chased. Tolkien, the medievalist and Anglo-Saxon scholar, would have been horrified at this deflowering of his maidens. And thus the mighty have fallen. The elves, in whose immortal eyes could be perceived glimpses of eternity, are reduced to a hybrid of Marilyn Monroe and Marilyn Manson.

If the good is really good, and the bad is really bad, the ugly is *really* ugly. The orcs are veritable masterpieces of ugliness. These relentlessly hateful servants of the Dark Lord, the products of infernally inspired genetic "modification", are the visible, and visually violent, incarnation of evil. Genetically engineered in Tolkien's imagination, via the perverse will of Sauron and Saruman, the orcs are brought sensationally and horrifically to life by computer-generated images and the ingenuity of makeup artists. The successful re-creation of the orcs in Jackson's film represents the perfect marriage of ancient inspiration and modern technology.

Ultimately, however, Tolkien's book is not merely the product of ancient inspiration but of ancient wisdom. It is not the evil that can be seen in the eyes of an orc that is most hateful to the forces of good, but the invisible evil that lurks in the heart of each of us. The visualization of this invisible evil, and the equally potent visualization of good, was Jackson's greatest challenge. On occasion, he succeeds triumphantly. The scene at the end of the film, when Frodo, weary and frightened, wishes that the Ring, his cross, could pass him by, is a moment of true brilliance. None but the most blind or most hard of heart could fail to perceive parallels with the Gospel. The scene, quite clearly, is the hobbit's "Agony in the Garden". There are other moments also. Aragorn's reverence. Arwen's "prayer" for grace. Gandalf's wisdom and his hints that the hidden hand of providence is invisibly but omnipotently guiding events. Amid the good, the bad and the ugly, it is these magic, or miraculous, moments that represent the film's saving grace.

46

WOULD TOLKIEN HAVE GIVEN PETER JACKSON'S MOVIE THE THUMBS-UP?

AFTER THE RELEASE of the first of Peter Jackson's film adaptations of Tolkien's three-part epic, *The Lord of the Rings*, I acted as defending attorney in the "mock trial of Peter Jackson for the Desecration of *The Lord of the Rings*". Great fun was had by all as we argued the relative merits of Jackson's endeavors to bring Tolkien's myth to the silver screen. On that occasion the jury found Jackson "not guilty", indicating that the first of the movies had received a thumbs-up from the twelve good men and true.

Much water has passed under the Brandywine Bridge since then. With the release of the third of the movies, we can finally judge Jackson's efforts in their entirety. Does he still merit the thumbs-up?

For my part, I am still happy to act as defending attorney. I believe, on balance, that Jackson has done an admirable job. It is, however, not my judgment that is being sought. What would Tolkien himself have thought of the Jackson production of his myth? This is a much more interesting question and one that, in spite of the cautionary admonitions in my ear from the voice of my better judgment, I am foolhardy enough to try to answer.

The first thing we need to understand is that Tolkien was a perfectionist. He worked on the great landscape of myth, upon which *The Lord of the Rings* is little more than a mere blip in the foreground, for more than half a century. At his death, the epic was still uncompleted. Such was his meticulous precision, such was his perfectionism, that a single lifetime was not enough to bring his creative vision to fruition. Something of the frustration that he felt at his inability to complete his magnum opus surfaced in his purgatorial allegory, "Leaf by Niggle". The story's chief protagonist, Niggle, had spent his life trying to paint a landscape but, at the time of death, had not finished even a solitary tree to his satisfaction. The only thing brought to perfection was a lone leaf. Perhaps, in Tolkien's judgment, *The Lord of the Rings* was the lone leaf. To illustrate the same point by switching metaphors, *The Lord of the Rings* was a sublime movement, of which the composer was justly proud, but the Great Music to which he aspired was elusive. The movement confirms the maestro's immortality, but the symphony remained unfinished.

All of this serves as a preamble to illustrate that Tolkien is not merely a hard act to follow but is also a hard judge to please. As such, Jackson was always going to be treading on perilous ground when he chose to follow in the master's footprints. Whether his decision was the result of fearlessness or folly, or both, his bold ambition stumbles, inevitably, on the footfalls of the very footprints he follows. Quite simply, Tolkien would probably have judged Jackson in accordance with his own insurmountable perfectionism and, this being so, would have found the New Zealander wanting.

A few examples will serve to conjure up Tolkien's ghost, enabling him to point a phantom finger of scorn at Jackson's presumption.

Galadriel was modeled, says Tolkien, on his Catholic devotional reverence for the Blessed Virgin; Jackson transforms her into a disturbed and disturbing witch, or an electrifying and electrocuted wench. Faramir serves as an antidote to Boromir's folly, a veritable saint and model of heroic virtue; Jackson turns him into an ignorant rogue and kidnapper. Treebeard embodies the power and wisdom of living tradition, both etymologically and ecclesiologically; Jackson makes him a buffoon who is hoodwinked by the hobbits. Tolkien despised the emerging omnipotence of technology; Jackson allows his besotted attachment to special effects to take over, leaving the technological tail wagging the dog-eared remnants of the tale. Tolkien stated emphatically that *The Lord of the Rings* was "of course, a fundamentally religious and Catholic work"; Jackson barely scratches the surface of the deeper spiritual dimension of the book.

I could go on but will desist. I will also insist, again, that this is how Tolkien the perfectionist would probably judge the imperfections of Jackson's work. It is not how I judge it, though I acknowledge all the above as flaws. I am more inclined to accentuate the positive and turn a beneficent blind eye to the negative. After all, a Hollywood adaptation of *The Lord of the Rings* could have been much, much worse. *Dungeons and Dragons* meets *Conan the Barbarian*! Perish the thought!

In asking the question that serves as the title to this article, I knew that I would have to play devil's advocate. Perhaps I have played it badly. Perhaps Tolkien's shade will point its accusing finger at me, muttering in reproach at my own presumption: *Get thee behind me, Sauron*. Perhaps. I am, however, sticking to my guns. Would Tolkien have given Peter Jackson's movies the thumbs-up? No, I believe that he wouldn't. Should he? Yes, I believe that he should. But then, who am I to question the great man?

47

THE FORGOTTEN INKLING

A Personal Memoir of Owen Barfield

I CANNOT CLAIM to have called Owen Barfield a friend. To claim such intimacy would be preposterous. I met him only once. It was in Forest Row, a small town in Sussex on the edge of the Ashdown Forest, on New Year's Eve 1996. He was the last surviving member of the inner sanctum of the Inklings and, as such, I was anxious to interview him as part of the research for my book *Literary Converts*. He kindly consented to the interview, in spite of his failing health and in spite of the fact that, having recently celebrated his ninety-eighth birthday, he had reached an age at which he could be forgiven for wishing to be left in peace.

He looked his age, a stooped figure of fatigue, frail and fragile, shuffling uneasily around the room. Having settled in an armchair, he regarded me curiously. I'm not sure what he made of me, but for my part, I regarded the skeletal frame and the time-weary face, its skin clinging scantily to the skull beneath, as *a memento mori*. The vision of death was contradicted by the alertness of the eyes, deep with years but shimmering with humor on the mischievous surface. The candor of those eyes exposed the cadaverous lie. I realized as those eyes met mine that the decaying body was merely an inadequate shell for the immortal soul, the husk of time hiding the kernel of eternal truth.

In the next hour or so, the eyes glistened fondly as he shared his many memories of a literary world that had long since passed away, excepting of course its lasting legacy. With words punctuated by interjectory chuckles, he recalled attending a debate between Chesterton and Shaw at a theater in London. "They rather ragged it," he laughed, "because each of them was trying to pretend that the other was hogging the limelight." The antiquated quaintness of Barfield's vocabulary heightened my own sense of nostalgia for a Chestershavian age that had passed into legend even before I was born. Since Chesterton had been dead for sixty years at the time of our interview, I found myself awestruck at the chasm of time that Barfield's experience had straddled. The debate between Chesterton and Shaw belonged to the thirties, possibly even to the twenties, and I imagined Barfield as a vibrantly vigorous young man, hanging onto every word as the tightly packed audience guffawed and applauded.

He spoke of the poets of the twenties, refighting the critical wars of a bygone era when, as a young man with oh-so-modern pretensions, he had held his elders in precocious contempt. "Alfred Noyes was considered very old fashioned. *We* were the Georgian poets. *He* was very Victorian." He spoke of several meetings with T. S. Eliot, including having tea with Eliot and Walter de la Mare at the latter's "rather nice flat" in Putney.

Most memorable of all were the stories about his friendship with Lewis, Tolkien and their fellow Inklings. He spoke of discussing Chesterton with Lewis. "Lewis was very much influenced by Chesterton, especially by *The Everlasting Man*, but he didn't mention anybody else really. We didn't always talk about philosophy. We used to read together ... we never argued from a doctrinal point of view." Specifically, he recalled reading the whole of the *Iliad*, the whole of the *Odyssey* and the whole of the *Divine Comedy* with Lewis.

Although Barfield was too modest to allude to the fact in our conversation, he is generally considered to have exerted an important and benign influence on Lewis throughout the 1920s. Lewis would later describe him as the wisest and best of his unofficial teachers. Barfield's *Poetic Diction: A Study in Meaning*, published in 1928, exerted a profound influence on both Lewis and Tolkien. It was, in fact, a discussion between Barfield, Lewis and Alan Griffiths, one of Lewis' pupils, which was to prove instrumental in edging Lewis closer to Christianity. Barfield and Griffiths were lunching in Lewis' room when Lewis happened to refer to philosophy as "a subject". "It wasn't a *subject* to Plato," Barfield retorted, "it was a way." "The quiet but fervent agreement of Griffiths, and the quick glance of understanding between these two, revealed to me my own frivolity", Lewis wrote in *Surprised by Joy*. "Enough had been thought, and said, and felt, and imagined. It was about time that something should be done."

Even though they had unwittingly played such a crucial role in the coup de grace of Lewis' conversion, neither Barfield nor Griffiths was a Christian at the time of this providential conversation. By a strange coincidence, however, both Lewis and Griffiths converted to Christianity and received their respective First Communions within a day of each other at Christmas 1931, Griffiths as a Catholic on Christmas Eve and Lewis as an Anglican on Christmas Day. A few months after his reception into the Church, Griffiths decided to try his vocation as a religious at Prinknash, the Benedictine priory at Winchcombe in Gloucestershire. On 20 December 1932 he was clothed as a novice and changed his name to Bede, after which he was known as Dom Bede Griffiths and became an influential, and occasionally controversial, writer of popular theology.

In his conversation with me, Barfield recalled his friendship with Lewis and Griffiths in the days before he experienced his own somewhat idiosyncratic conversion to Anglican Christianity in 1949.

> Lewis, Griffiths and I went for long walks together. We talked a good deal about theology ... I was with Griffiths and I told him I was an agnostic and we got talking about being damned and some remark he made elicited the reply from me that "in that case I suppose that I am damned". And I'll never forget the calm, collected way he turned round and said "but of course you are". This amused Lewis very much of course when I told him afterwards.

During my all-too-brief encounter with Owen Barfield, he still displayed, in spite of his magisterial age, tantalizing glimpses of the genius that had so impressed his more famous friends, Tolkien and Lewis, almost seventy years earlier. As I bid him farewell, I sensed that he was not long for this world. The husk was wearing thin and its grip on the kernel within was weakening. It was on the eve of his hundredth New Year, which was to be his last, that I was blessed to have met him, and I shall remain eternally grateful for the blessing.

"I'm not an old man, I'm a very old man", Barfield had told our mutual friend Walter Hooper when Mr. Hooper had visited him on his ninety-eighth birthday, scarcely seven weeks before my own visit. Shortly afterward, he told Mr. Hooper, with characteristic wit, that "I'm not getting on, I'm getting off." A few months later, he did indeed "get off", leaving those who had the good fortune to have met him with many fond memories of a world that seemed to have passed away with him. *Requiescat in pace.*

PART FIVE

MORE THINGS CONSIDERED

48

THE DECADENT PATH TO CHRIST

I T IS PERHAPS A PARADOX of Wildean, Baudelairean or even Chestertonian proportions that the road to hell can sometimes lead to heaven. Had not Baudelaire proclaimed with provocative precision that only Catholics knew the devil? Baudelaire knew, more painfully and grotesquely than most, that we must know our sins in order to know ourselves. One who does not know that he is a sinner does not know himself, nor does he know the God who made him. We must know the hell within ourselves, and the Hell to which it owes allegiance, before we can know the heaven that is promised us. This "discovery" was hardly an original innovation of the French or English Decadents. Six centuries earlier, Dante had discovered the same perennial truth, conveying it with unsurpassed genius in his descent into the inferno en route to Purgatory and paradise.

If it is true that the road to hell is paved with good intentions, it is also true that the road to heaven is sometimes paved with bad ones. Our very sins, if we repent, can be our teachers and guides. In recollecting our sins, and in recoiling from their consequences, we can be kept on the narrow path that leads purgatorially upward toward paradise. Thus the scribes, Pharisees and hypocrites, imagining themselves on the path to heaven, might be heading for an unpleasant surprise, whereas the publicans and sinners, learning from their mistakes and amending their ways, might reach the Kingdom to which Christ has called them.

It is, therefore, a paradoxical pleasure to be able to celebrate the Decadent path to Christ, not as a celebration of Decadence per se (heaven forbid!) but as a celebration of the path to Christ that it represents. God is always bringing good out of evil, and the Catholic literary revival has reaped a wonderful harvest from the seeds planted in Decadence during the nineteenth century. One needs only to examine the key figures of the French and English Decadence to see that the literature of death and decay can prophesy the poetry of resurrection.

Charles Baudelaire, the father of the French Decadent movement, had, according to his fellow Decadent J. K. Huysmans, "gone further" than any other writer in exploring the darker recesses of the soul:

> He had descended to the bottom of the inexhaustible mine, had picked his way along abandoned or unexplored galleries, and had finally reached those districts of the soul where the monstrous vegetations of the sick mind flourish . . . He had laid bare the morbid psychology of the mind.

In spite of Huysmans' assertion, Baudelaire was by no means the first to descend into the depths of "the inexhaustible mine" of the mind's eye. Dante had descended further, and so had Saint John of the Cross, both of whom could see deeper into the depths of the darkness because they carried the torch of holiness with them. If one is to explore the dark places properly, it helps to have a torch. Baudelaire's originality was not in his being the first poet to visit these places; it was in the way he chose to report his experience of them. His *fleurs du mal* were arranged in an enticingly lurid fashion, offering their scent to a new generation of writers who quickly fell under their influence. Most prominent among Baudelaire's French disciples were Paul Verlaine and J. K. Huysmans. Verlaine imitated Baudelaire in delicately poignant verse, whereas Huysmans picked Baudelaire's sick-scented flowers and scattered them liberally throughout his novel *A Rebours*. All three men, Baudelaire, Verlaine and Huysmans, having shocked a generation with what was perceived as their perversity, became Catholics before their death. Having dipped a foot in the Phlegethon and glimpsed the Wood of Suicides beyond, they recoiled from descending further into the inexhaustible mines of the inferno, seeking sanctuary at the foot of the Cross. Baudelaire converted *in extremis*; Verlaine converted in prison and lived long enough to publish poems of penitential beauty; Huysmans, having depicted his path to conversion in his novel *En Route*, spent the final years of his life in a monastery.

These three pillars of the French Decadence exerted a towering influence on the English Decadent movement, whose chief champion was the seductively seditious and self-destructive Oscar Wilde. Gathered around Wilde were a group of young acolytes, his Decadent disciples. These included the poets Ernest Dowson, Lionel Johnson and John Gray, and the artist Aubrey Beardsley. Dowson, Johnson and Beardsley were all doomed to die young; but not, however, before each of them had embraced the Catholic faith. John Gray, having allegedly been the model for Wilde's "Dorian Gray", became a Catholic priest, serving his parish in Edinburgh until his death in 1933. As for Wilde himself, he was received into the saving embrace of Holy Mother Church on his deathbed. Thus the father of the French Decadence and the father of its English equivalent shared a reconciliation with the Bride of Christ *in extremis*. One imagines that Dante, their great precursor, would have smiled with knowing benignity at the divine symmetry of the happy ending. The final words do not belong to Dante, however, nor do they belong to Baudelaire or Wilde; they belong to their fellow Decadent Ernest Dowson, who wrote with beauty and eloquence about the saving power of the Last Rites of the Church in his poem "Extreme Unction":

> The feet, that lately ran so fast
> To meet desire, are soothly sealed;
> The eyes, that were so often cast
> On vanity, are touched and healed.

49

THE QUEST FOR THE REAL OSCAR

*A Century after His Death, Is the Real Oscar Wilde
Finally Emerging from the Shadows?*

A CYNIC, WROTE OSCAR WILDE, is someone who knows the price of everything and the value of nothing. Today, more than a hundred years after Wilde's death on 30 November 1900, the cynics are having a field day. An article in the business section of the *Daily Telegraph* announced solemnly that paying huge sums for Wilde memorabilia was a "sensible investment". It cited the recent sale of a catalog of Wilde's household possessions, printed in the wake of the bankruptcy proceedings following his imprisonment in 1895, which had been sold at this year's London Book Fair for £15,000. The same item, auctioned at Christie's in 1981, had fetched only £2,500. Any letter of Wilde's, however trivial the contents, will sell for at least £1,000, and many change hands for between £10,000 and £20,000. A printed copy of Wilde's early play *Vera*, with extensive handwritten notes penned by Wilde as he watched an early rehearsal, sold for a staggering £50,000 at the London Book Fair. And the list continues. A questionnaire filled in by Wilde when he was at Oxford sold for £23,000; an inscribed cigarette case allegedly given to Wilde by Lord Alfred Douglas sold for £14,000 despite its doubtful authenticity; and two letters from Wilde to Philip Griffiths, described as one of his lovers, reached £16,000 at Christie's. The letters to Griffiths were themselves innocuous, and there is no evidence that Wilde ever had a sexual relationship with him, but the letters sold nonetheless. Wilde's grandson, Merlin Holland, is exasperated by the growing cult surrounding his grandfather, but he adds philosophically that he could "appreciate the humor of questionable pieces of memorabilia from Saint Oscar the Sinner being offered to a credulous public at absurd prices and be proud of my ancestor's ability to take his revenge a century later."

A spokesman for the booksellers who sold the catalog for £15,000 believed that purchasers of Wilde memorabilia were motivated by "Wilde's magic" and believed that the "more they spend, the closer they get" to its source.

One wonders what Wilde himself, the subject of all this idolatry, would have made of it all. It is likely, if his own words are to be believed, that he would have been horrified by the way in which the value of his art had been debased by the sordid cult that has risen from the ashes of the scandal surrounding his private life. "You knew what my Art was to me," Wilde wrote from Reading jail to Lord Alfred Douglas, "the great primal note by which I had revealed, first myself to myself, and then myself to the world; the real passion of my life; the love to which all other loves were as marsh-water to red wine". Clearly, Wilde believed that his true self, his true value, was to be found in his art. By contrast, many of his modern admirers, Judaslike, have betrayed their master with a kiss and have sold his art for the thirty pieces of silver with which they are purchasing the endless ephemera. According to Wilde's own criteria, those who believe that they are closer to his "magic" when they clutch a cigarette case of dubious origin instead of opening the pages of one of his books have succeeded only in changing the finest of red wine into the foulest of marsh water. With "friends" like these, the ghost of Wilde could be tempted to mutter plaintively, who needs enemies?

A century after his death, Wilde is still caught between the prurient and the puritan. To the prurient he is a war cry; to the puritan he is a warning. One betrays him with a kiss, the other with a curse. Now, as ever, Wilde is faced with an unwelcome choice between Judas and the Pharisee. George Bernard Shaw, in his preface to the 1938 edition of Frank Harris' biography of Wilde, admitted that he had "somewhat Pharisaically" summed up Wilde's last days in Paris as those of "an unprofitable drunkard and swindler". Yet, he argued, those of Wilde's admirers who had objected to this description of their hero had forgotten "that Wilde's permanent celebrity belongs to literature, and only his transient notoriety to the police news."

Sadly, the cult surrounding Wilde's "transient notoriety" has a lingering persistence. Happily, however, there are a growing band of Wilde's admirers who are seeking him where he wishes to be sought—in his art.

John Burrows, artistic director of the Bare and Ragged Theatre, based at Stratford-upon-Avon, organized a Festival of Wilde at the Edinburgh Fringe. Apart from the stage dramatization of *The Picture of Dorian Gray*, which the Bare and Ragged Theatre had staged for the past six years, always to sellout crowds, a specially devised play, entitled *Out of the Depths*, was also performed. This was an "impressionistic celebration of Wilde's art", concentrating on Wilde's literary genius while downplaying the "transient notoriety" of the court case, which is only "vaguely mentioned".

The best-selling author Adrian Plass, writing in the *Christian Herald*, compared Wilde to G. K. Chesterton. "I think my own fascination with these writers ... is something to do with sensing that there is a deep desire to be good and lovable beneath the public displays of personal style and crackling paradox." Although Plass admits that "this is much more clearly evident in the case of Chesterton", he emphasizes "the conventional morality at the heart of Wilde's art, even in such pieces as *Salome* and *The Picture of Dorian Gray*, both vilified as obscene and decadent in his lifetime." Plass continues in words that closely parallel those of Shaw:

> The soul of Oscar Wilde, continually reaching for and retreating from the Catholic church, is to be found in its purest form in his prose, his poetry and his plays, rather than in those things which ambushed the pursuit of his deepest instincts.

Wilde's deepest instincts, those that invariably triumphed in his art even when "ambushed" in his life, were profoundly spiritual, not carnal. This spiritual dimension was emphasized by another writer, Mary Kenny. Commenting on Wilde's reception into the Catholic Church on his deathbed, Kenny drew parallels with other leading Decadent writers in England and France who "took refuge in Catholicism". It seems that for Wilde, as for so many of his circle, the way of Decadence became the Way of the Cross.

A further twist to the Catholic dimension in Wilde's art emerged from deep within the very heart of Rome. A report in the *Irish Independent* stated that the Vatican had "rehabilitated Oscar Wilde on the eve of the centenary of his death, praising the turn to spiritual values and 'understanding of God's love' that followed Wilde's imprisonment in Reading gaol." Writing in *La Civilta Cattolica*, a Vatican-backed Jesuit quarterly, Father Antonio Spadaro said that Wilde had seen into the depths of his own soul after a lifetime of "degradation, vanity and frivolity". In his last works, such as *De Profundis* and *The Ballad of Reading Gaol*, he had made "an implicit journey of faith", wrote Father Spadaro.

Father Spadaro could have added that the same implicit affirmation of faith is present in many of Wilde's earlier works, such as his fairy stories, his controversial novel *The Picture of Dorian Gray* and many of his plays, particularly in the challenging symbolism of *Salome*.

Perhaps the last word should belong to Wilde himself. "We are all in the gutter," says Lord Darlington in *Lady Windermere's Fan*, "but some of us are looking at the stars." To look for Wilde in the gutter, whether to wallow with him in the "marsh-water" or to point the finger of self-righteous scorn, is to miss the point. Those wishing a deeper understanding of this most enigmatic of men should not look *at* him in the gutter but *with* him at the stars.

50

MAKING OSCAR WILD

*Unmasking Oscar Wilde's Opposition
to "Pathological" Gay Marriage*

IT's FUNNY HOW URBAN MYTHS can mask reality. Take, for instance, the peculiar case of Oscar Wilde. Ask the average modern intellectual what he knows about Wilde, and he will probably tell you that he was a brilliant artist who was persecuted for his homosexuality and deserves to be remembered as a martyr for the cause of sexual liberation who was sacrificed on the altar of puritanical Victorian values. Ask a homosexual intellectual, and he might even go so far as to describe Wilde as a "gay icon", a poster child for the homosexual movement who has inspired many young men to "come out of the closet". Such is the myth. The reality is very different.

If we take the trouble to unmask the myths surrounding Wilde, we discover a man who is very different from the one imagined by our self-deluded moderns. We find, in fact, a brilliant artist (the moderns get that part of the story right, at least) who was never at peace with his homosexuality, who never managed to "come out of the closet" and who, when at last faced with the reality of his situation, described his homosexual predilections as his "pathology".

Let's play the daring game of removing the masks of self-deception. Let's dare to look reality in the eye, however unpleasant, ugly—or beautiful—it might be. Let's declare ourselves liberated from outmoded forms of repressed truthfulness. Let's whisper the truth that dare not speak its name. In short, let's face facts.

The first thing we must know about Wilde is that he was at war with himself. Wilde the would-be saint and Wilde the woeful sinner

were in deadly conflict, one with the other. In this he was no different from the rest of us. Throughout his life, even at those times when
he was at his most "decadent", he retained a deep love for the Person
of Christ and a lasting reverence for the Catholic Church. In this,
indeed, he differs from many, if not most, of us. Certainly he differs in
this from most of those active homosexuals who seek to claim Wilde
as one of their own.

Wilde almost converted to Catholicism as an undergraduate at Trinity College in Dublin; he almost converted as an undergraduate at
Oxford. There were no doctrinal differences preventing him from being
received into the Church. He believed everything the Church believed
and even spoke eloquently and wittily in defense of Catholic dogmas
such as the Immaculate Conception. The only reason he failed to
follow the logic of his Catholic convictions was a fear of being dis-
inherited by his father if he did so. Years later, after his fall from favor
following the scandal surrounding his homosexual affair with Lord Alfred
Douglas, he spoke wistfully of his reluctant decision to turn his back
on the Church. "Much of my moral obliquity is due to the fact that
my father would not allow me to become a Catholic", he confided to
a journalist. "The artistic side of the Church would have cured my
degeneracies. I intend to be received before long." Wilde would be
received into the Catholic Church on his deathbed, an event that not
only meant that his particular "fairy story" would end happily ever
after but that, through the healing power of the Last Rites, would
finally cure him of his "degeneracies".

In truth, however, Wilde never completely turned his back on the
Church. Throughout his life, and particularly through the medium of
his art, he continued to reveal his love for Christ and the Catholic
Church. His poetry exhibits either a selfless love for Christ or, at its
darkest, a deep self-loathing in the face of the ugliness of his own
sinfulness. His short stories are almost always animated by a deep Christian morality, with "The Selfish Giant" deserving a timeless accolade
as one of the finest Christian fairy stories ever written. His plays are
more than merely comedies or tragedies; they are morality plays in
which virtue is vindicated and vice vanquished. His only novel, *The
Picture of Dorian Gray*, is a masterpiece of Victorian fiction, the overriding moral of which is that to kill the conscience is to kill the soul.

"You knew what my Art was to me," Wilde wrote plaintively to Lord Alfred Douglas, "the great primal note by which I had revealed, first myself to myself, and then myself to the world; the real passion of my life; the love to which all other loves were as mere marsh-water to red wine". These words, written from prison to the man who was largely responsible for the scandal that caused his downfall, show the extent to which Wilde knew that the Christianity expressed through his art was far more important than the sinful passions of the flesh to which he had succumbed. In the same letter to Douglas, he also referred to the homosexuality that had been the bane of his life during the 1890s as his "pathology", his sickness.

Is this the voice of a "sexual liberator"? Hardly. It is the voice of one who had finally freed himself from the slavery of sin. Far from being a sexual liberator, Wilde's life climaxed with a liberation from his sexuality or, at least, a liberation from the slavish addiction to the lustful manifestation of his sexuality.

Would Wilde have supported "gay marriage"? Hardly. He would not have considered it either "gay" or a "marriage". He would have called it what it is: a "pathology".

51

TRUTH IS STRANGER THAN SCIENCE FICTION

A S WITH MOST THINGS that claim to be modern, science fiction is not really modern at all. It is as old as mythology. Take, for example, the myth of Icarus and Daedalus. It has all the ingredients of science fiction. Two men, a father and son, develop new technology that enables them to fly. The older and wiser man, Daedalus, cautions his young and impetuous son against taking the technology too far. Icarus ignores the warning. Putting too much faith in technology, he falls to his death.

Similarly, science fiction is not so much postmodern as postmedieval. One need look no further than Saint Thomas More's *Utopia* for a vision of a strange world, unknown to man, where alien people do things very differently from the way things are done in our world. Two hundred years later, in *Gulliver's Travels*, Jonathan Swift wrote about an intrepid aquanaut who journeys to strange microscopic and macroscopic worlds, who encounters weird horselike creatures enamored of platonic philosophy and who visits strange islands that float above the world. A hundred years after Swift, Mary Shelley gave us *Frankenstein*, a tale in which modern science meets ancient necromancy in a chilling embrace. Again, however, Shelley's tale owes an unpayable debt to the past. Dr. Frankenstein could, after all, have been called Dr. Faustenstein.

What, then, do all these grandparents of science fiction have in common? Apart from their predilection for strange places and "new technology", they are united in the *morality* of their message. In each case, the strangeness and novelty are only means to the moral end, the "science" in the fiction being merely a servant of the morality that the author wishes to convey. Of course, the morality may vary from author to author. In some cases, the fiction will be a servant of good morals; in other cases, it will become a slave of bad morals. Since, however, morals, whether good or bad, are always present, the fiction is to be judged accordingly—that is, according to specifically moral criteria. And, of course, it is the morality that roots the fiction in the facts of everyday life. Morality is the very ingredient, the spice of life, that makes a story relevant to the real world. Its application *within* a story makes it applicable to the world *beyond* the story. This being so, it is chilling to see how truth is often more real, and more terrifying, than science fiction.

Take, for instance, C. S. Lewis' *That Hideous Strength*, the final book in his Space Trilogy. One might think that its plot is fantastic beyond the realms of all possibility. Surely no government organization could be as cruel and as sinister as the National Institute of Coordinated Experiments (N.I.C.E.). Yet today, in the United Kingdom, the National Institute for Clinical Excellence (N.I.C.E.) has called for in vitro fertilization to be made freely available to any childless couple that wants it. Such a policy, if adopted, will mean the slaughter of countless innocent babies, discarded in the test tube as inferior specimens.

Returning to *That Hideous Strength*, surely nothing in the real world could be as bizarre as the N.I.C.E.'s decision to use the scientifically "revived" head of the executed murderer Alcasan as the "head" of their organization. Yet today, in the United States, the head of a former baseball star, Ted Williams, is being preserved, floating in a stainless steel can kept in a freezer vault, by a company called Alcor(*zan?*). Meanwhile, his decapitated corpse is suspended in a nine-foot-high tank of liquid nitrogen.

In life, Williams was a dashing athlete who served in the Second World War and fought as a fighter pilot in the Korean War. As a star player with the Boston Red Sox, he achieved the highest batting average of the modern baseball era. In death, his corpse casts morbid light on the practice of cryonics, the "science" of freezing bodies in the hope that one day scientists may be able to revive them. For a reported fee of $136,000, his body has been stored along with sixty others at an industrial park in Scottsdale, Arizona. The facility is run by the Alcor Life Extension Foundation, which has more than six hundred subscribers paying a monthly fee so that they can also be deep-frozen when they die.

It is indeed a weird and frightening world in which we live, a world that would stretch the fertile imagination of Thomas More, Mary Shelley and C. S. Lewis to the very limits. In pursuit of a scientific *utopia*, Frankenstein Inc., trading as Alcorzan, prepares to revive corpses from the dead while the N.I.C.E. calls for widespread experiments on unborn babies. Truth is indeed stranger than science fiction.

52

HOLLYWOOD AND THE "HOLY WAR"

"**E**VERYONE KNOWS WHAT DAMAGE is done to the soul by bad motion pictures. They are occasions of sin; they seduce young people along the ways of evil by glorifying the passions; they show life under a false light; they cloud ideals; they destroy pure love, respect for marriage, affection for the family." These words, written by Pope Pius XI in 1936, have lost none of their potency. On the contrary, with every passing year they seem to cry out more plaintively than ever to a seemingly heedless humanity.

There is no denying that motion pictures represent an important weapon in the culture war that is gripping the world in the first years of the new Christian millennium. In the battle of ideas and the struggle of contending faiths and philosophies, the medium of film remains a powerful and formidable weapon. Islam, resurgent and resilient, has challenged the fundamental tenets of the West's dominant and decadent materialism. The terrorist attack by Islamic militants on the United States might not be sanctioned by the vast majority of the world's one billion Muslims, but it does highlight the gulf that separates and alienates Islam from the liberal secularism of Britain and America. The two *Weltanschauungen* are ultimately, and profoundly, incompatible.

Where, however, does Christianity place itself in this struggle between contending faiths and philosophies? Do we, as Christians, have a moral duty to side with one side or the other?

The sapient and salient words of Pope Pius XI would suggest that Christians must spurn the overtly agnostic, and often covertly atheistic, assumptions of the prevailing secularism and scepticism of the postmodernist West. Indeed, such is the cultural or anticultural power of Hollywood that the very concept of "the West" sometimes seems synonymous with little more than the west coast of California. Does that mean, however, that we should sympathize with the view of many Muslims that the United States is the "Great Satan"? The desolate decadence, posing as culture and regurgitated from Hollywood, is worthy of the contempt of all Christians—and, indeed, is treated with contempt by millions of good Americans. The United States might not be the "Great Satan", as Muslim fundamentalists would have us believe, but there seems little doubt that the prince of lies has found a very powerful mouthpiece, and foothold, in much (though not all) that emerges from Hollywood. If, however, the prince of lies has gained a foothold in Hollywood, the "Holy Wars" of militant Islam have precious little claim to any communion with the Prince of Peace.

Perhaps the position of Christianity in relation to the war between Islam and secular humanism is best summed up in the words of the Bishop of Como in an interview with the *Saint Austin Review (StAR)*. "There are, it seems to me, clear signs of decay ... exposing Catholicism to the threat of being swamped by violent religious forces, such as Islam; or by the sort of mushy relativism that often goes hand in hand with the widespread availability of a comfortable lifestyle." Certainly these are somber and sobering thoughts.

Are Christians therefore caught between the devil and the deep blue sea? Or, considering the Bishop's evocative description of relativism as "mushy", are we caught between the fierce and formidable deserts of Islam and the stinking and stagnant swamps of postmodernity?

Furthermore—and here is the crux of the matter—if we are caught between these formidable enemies, should we be forced to take sides? The deep blue sea might be more desirable than the devil, but is the desert more desirable than the swamp? Do we have no choice except dehydration of the spirit or drowning in the dregs of decay?

In truth—and "truth" is the operative word—Christians find themselves in the middle because Christianity is the Center. Christians have, as their infallible Guide, Him who is the Way, the Truth and the Life. Through Him, and through the infallible guidance of the Church, His Mystical Body on earth, we can and shall prevail.

In the war between emergent Islam and declining decadence, we must arm ourselves with the weapons of the cultural and spiritual struggle. Apart from prayer, always the most potent of weapons, our army includes the holiest of saints, the mightiest of philosophers and, last but not least, the giants of art and literature. Our army includes Saint Michael, Saint Dominic and Saint Francis; Socrates, Aristotle and Plato; Giotto, Michelangelo and Da Vinci; Palestrina, Mozart and Mahler; and Dante, Shakespeare and Cervantes. Thus is the army of God assembled, rank after rank beneath the radiant splendor of our Lord's and Lady's banner. Called to arms, the Church Militant prepares for what could prove the mother of all battles.

53

THREE CHEERS FOR HOLLYWOOD

THREE CHEERS FOR HOLLYWOOD? Surely not. There must have been some mistake ... How can any conscientious Christian initiate a chorus of praise for such a den of iniquity and vice? Has he lost his senses? Or, worse, has he passed from the purgatory of life to the inferno of the living death that currently squats on the edge of the City of Angels, spreading its filth to a worldwide audience? Has he traded in his true inheritance in the City of God for a few sordid scenes in Tinsel Town?

Fear not. He is merely giving credit where credit is due. He raises his voice in praise for that which is praiseworthy, even though his three rousing cheers might be barely audible amid the deafening hiss that is the usual serpentine chorus emanating from the hell of Hollywood.

The recent release of the first installment of Peter Jackson's bold endeavor to bring the wonder of Tolkien's *The Lord of the Rings* to the silver screen serves as a reminder that the medium of film need not be counterproductive to the life of the soul. On the contrary, it illustrates the film medium's enormous potential, its power to edify audiences. The fact that the potential is all too often squandered, and the fact that the power all too often pollutes the soul instead of assisting in its desire for purity, is not the point at issue. Film, unlike the One Ring in Tolkien's epic, is not intrinsically evil. It has the power for good as well as evil, the power to raise souls heavenward as well as the awful potential to assist in the downward spiral of the hellbound. It should, in fact, be a sobering thought for all producers, directors and screen-writers that Justice will make them accountable for their influence upon audiences. The realization that they are contributing to the raising or the razing of souls should cause them to pause and ponder. The failure to do so is itself a sin of omission screaming for justice.

Over the years, there have been producers, directors and screen-writers who have taken their moral responsibility seriously. Their films have exalted the noble, denigrated the ignoble and uplifted the spirit. Perhaps indeed they represent an exalted nobility of film, outnum-bered perhaps by the ignoble but shining forth in purity like candles in a darkened room. It is these few, these happy few, that warrant the "three cheers for Hollywood".

Thankfully, the Few are not so few that they can be discussed in a solitary article. As such, the following will be a short guided tour of a few of the Few.

A good place to begin any tour of the best of Hollywood is in the presence of Gary Cooper, a fine actor whose understated style belies his natural abilities. *Sergeant York*, *High Noon* and *Friendly Per-suasion* represent a healthy trinity of films starring Cooper, each of which deserves three cheers of its own. The first, a romanticized retelling of the life story of a "real-life" hero of the First World War, dramatizes the subject's prodigal youth, his repentance and conver-sion to Christianity, his efforts to become a conscientious objector on the grounds of a pacifist reading of Scripture, and his final emer-gence as a war hero who saves the lives of many of his comrades through selfless acts of bravery. *High Noon* is probably so well known that its plot, revolving around the hero's self-sacrificial sense of duty regardless of its personal cost in terms of the loss of happi-ness, scarcely needs elucidating. Suffice to say that its masterfully paced ascent to a consummating climax is perambulatory in its persistent patience yet tension-tightening with every successive scene. A cin-ematic masterpiece!

The final piece in our Cooperian trinity is *Friendly Persuasion*, a film about a family of Quakers questioning their principles in the midst of America's civil war. Should they fight for the cause that they believe to be right, or should they refrain from fighting in accordance with their pacifist principles? Interwoven with this dramatic tension between principled pacifism and the concepts of a just war is the tension between two warring concepts of Christianity, namely, the puritanical and the Catholic. Although the Church, as such, does not so much as warrant a mention, the efforts of Cooper's character to overcome the puritan-ical strictures of his wife epitomize the battle between the icono-graphic and the iconoclastic vision of the Faith. Slowly, resolutely and always lovingly, the character played by Cooper introduces beauty and gaity into the life of the family, symbolized by his acquisition of an organ, in defiance of the wishes of his wife, which brings the icon of art, in the form of music, into the life of the family. This theme is played out in various guises, not least in the characterization of the puritanical elder of the Quaker community, whose joyless adherence to his faith finds expression in a pharisaical approach to the letter of the law, particularly in his harshly phrased refusal to question the Quaker position on the war. The hardness of heart is highlighted still further by his sudden *volte-face* following the destruction of his own posses-sions by the enemy. In a moment of poignant symmetry—one of many in this wonderfully scripted tale—we see the erstwhile pacifist's harshly worded defense of the need to fight and are reminded instantly and insistently of his earlier harsh words *against* the war. In his defiant insistence on pacifism and in his later rejection of it, there is, in both cases, an evident absence of love, the Real Absence that renders both viewpoints null and void.

In 1955, the year before the release of *Friendly Persuasion*, another western, of sorts, was released that, subsequently and sadly, has slipped into relative obscurity. *Seven Cities of Gold*, starring Anthony Quinn, Richard Egan and Michael Rennie, recounts the pioneering days of the Spanish settlement of California. Specifically, it shows the struggle of a determined Franciscan priest to establish missions among the Indi-ans in the face of the lust for gold and women of the soldiers among whom he is ministering. The fearless faith of the friar acts as the moral motive force of the film. Paradoxically, however, the movie's ultimate power does not reside with the man of faith and the converts he gains, but with the solitary conversion of a faithless man, whose sin and cynicism have served as a foil to the friar's piety throughout. The cli-mactic conversion of this solitary sinner represents a truly glorious moment in the history of cinematic art.

The final film in the handful selected to justify the "three cheers for Hollywood" is altogether different. *Network*, starring William Holden, Peter Finch and Faye Dunaway, was released more than twenty years after the other movies that have warranted our praise. Released in 1976, *Network* is separated from the other films by that abyss that was the 1960s. In many respects it signifies and symbolizes the hangover with which the world awoke after its flirtation with the narcotic delusions of the hallucinogenic debauch. The film can even be seen as a reply and a riposte to the libertine liberties taken, alongside the drugs, by that decadent decade.

The three central characters in the film, indeed *all* the characters in the film, are hopelessly "mixed up" and "messed up". Confused. Disoriented. Egocentric. Lost. They are filled to the brim with the negativism born of the negations of the previous decade. They are locked up in their libertine worlds, the servants of relativism and the slaves of the virtual reality that has replaced the real thing in their lives. The character played by Peter Finch, a television newscaster, suffers a breakdown and vents his spleen on the air. He is "mad as hell" and wants the world to know. The world, or at least the viewers, clearly want to know. They are also "mad as hell" and tune in by the millions to watch his rantings. The television executives, prompted by the sexually aggressive but emotionally impotent character played by Dunaway, are delighted at the increased audience tuning into the deranged demagogue. The more Finch raves and rants, the more the television moguls rave about the ratings.

Predictably, unpredictability comes at a price. The "bull" being spoken by the proverbial bull in a china shop eventually causes the credulous executives to have more than proverbial egg on their faces. When Finch's rants become xenophobic and anti-Semitic, in the anti-Arab as opposed to the anti-Jewish sense of the word, something has to be done. The deranged dupe is summoned to a private meeting with the mysterious Mr. Big, who heads the network. This disturbing character, an ironic blend of Chesterton's elusively surreal "Sunday" in *The Man Who Was Thursday* and Orwell's menacingly real O'Brien in *Nineteen Eighty-Four*, spouts off an Ayn-Randian antigospel in which he proclaims the new gods of globalization. These demigods obey the ultimate god of Mammon, who has laid down, in letters set in stone, the irrepressible law of omnipresent and almighty market forces. These laws overwrite the right to democracy, to individuality, to freedom. The market is the law before which every knee must bow. The deranged dupe is duped by this new antigospel of hopelessness and proclaims it to his increasingly bewildered viewers.

Mercifully, *Network* is not all doom and despondency. It is lightened by a grimly pervasive irony, darkened delightfully by a countercynical sardonic humor, and, best of all, contains a penetrating morality. This morality, which represents, quite literally, the film's saving grace, is founded on the disturbing vacuum presented by its absence. This paradox is, however, powerful only because of the inkling of something with which the vacuum could and should be filled. The inkling is provided in a memorable scene toward the end of the film, in which the disillusioned character played by Holden confronts the character played by Dunaway with her own superficiality. In the modern terminology, itself the product of the artificiality of modern life, he tells her to "get real". She is living a virtual, virtueless life in an unreal world—an artificial life, defined by television and therefore devoid of any meaningful definitions, through which she is seeking to escape the ultimate realities of life. These ultimate realities, Holden insists, are rooted in love and cannot be divorced from pain and suffering. The glory of life resides in the indissoluble marriage of joy and sorrow. The acceptance of suffering is the beginning of wisdom. Oh, what joy to see such wisdom emanating from Hollywood!

Watching a film like *Network* might encourage people to follow the advice of Malcolm Muggeridge, who, in old age and after having spent many years as a television personality, announced gleefully that he was having "his aerials removed". Having had this particular operation myself, I can confirm that it is relatively painless and allows more freedom and time to live in the real world. Liberated from the televice-like grip of the television networks and their televicious secularism, it is pleasant to spend time enjoying the best of Hollywood on video. Take my advice—have your aerials removed but keep the VCR!

54

PURITY AND PASSION

Examining the Sacred Heart of Mel Gibson's
The Passion of the Christ

I T SAYS SOMETHING about the meretricious spirit of our age that the only "passion" considered controversial is the Passion of Christ. Movies, magazines, newspapers and television programs are full of other, less controversial, passions. They are, in fact, so full of depictions of graphic violence and pornographic sex that these particular passions are no longer considered controversial in the least. On the contrary, voyeurism is not merely acceptable, it is positively de rigueur; it is almost compulsory if one wishes to avoid the heinous charge of prudishness. Prurience is fine; prudishness is not. Vice is fine; so-called Victorian attitudes are not. Vice is victorious, and Victorianism is vanquished. Or so it would seem.

Even the word "sin" has become an expletive, not to be uttered in polite company. Sin has had its day, or so they say. It has been eclipsed by cynicism. And cynics have no time for sin. Or so they say ... In fact, of course, they have no time for anything else. Unable or unwilling to banish sin from their lives, they seek instead to ban it from the language.

It is in the very midst of this stale and putrid scene that the figure of Mel Gibson's Christ staggers onto the stage. He stumbles, bruised and bleeding, into the midst of the party, intent, so it seems, on spoiling the fun. The party-goers, comfortably drunk and heedless of the hangover that awaits them, do not welcome this unwanted and uninvited gate-crasher. Who is He, anyway? And what right does He have to tell them what to do? They are angry. They mutter among themselves that His presence in the midst of the debauch is a scandal. It is intolerable. It will not be tolerated. Who invited Him, anyway? Increasingly angry at His silent reproach, they become violent. They start to bustle Him around. Soon they rain blows upon his battered and defenseless body. He falls to the ground. Unwittingly they have become stars of Gibson's film. It is they who are demanding that Christ be put to death. Crucify Him! Crucify Him!

If this analogy appears a trifle too dramatic—melodramatic, even—we should remember that it is the precise analogy at the very heart of Gibson's movie. It is Gibson's precise point that those calling for Christ to be crucified are not merely historic personages in an obscure corner of the Roman Empire a couple of thousand years ago. They are us. It is we who scourged Him, we who placed the crown of thorns on His head, we who nailed Him to the Cross. It is our sinful hearts that pierced His Sacred Heart. And it is from His Sacred Heart that His mercy pours forth to us—in spite of our sins. This film, and the deep theology it portrays, is nothing less than Gibson's Christian faith poured out as an oblation and as a penance for his sins. In this context it is supremely significant that Gibson's only part in the film itself is to hold the nail as it is hammered into Christ's sinless flesh. As he stressed during a recent interview, the choice of his left hand for the part signifies his sin, figuratively speaking, and the sinister, literally speaking (*sinister* in Latin means *left*). Far from his being, as some suggest, an "anti-Semite" who blames the Jews for crucifying Christ, Gibson is quite clearly blaming himself. He is responsible for the worst crime in human history. And, sobering thought though it be, so are we. This is Gibson's point.

It matters not whether the cynics who find the film so controversial fail to share Gibson's faith. Its truth or falsity has nothing to do with their belief in it. What matters is that Gibson has made a profoundly moving movie depicting the last bloody hours of the life of Christ. He has courageously brought the truth of the Gospel to movie theaters around the world. The fact that many people find the Good News bad news is neither here nor there. It is to be expected. Indeed, the fact that many people find the Good News bad news is not news at all. It has always been thus. The Gospel has always been controversial. It was so controversial that the scribes, Pharisees and hypocrites

put its Founder to death. Nothing has changed. We continue to crucify Him. Yet He continues to live. This is the Sacred Heart of Gibson's film. It is a bleeding Heart, but a beating Heart also. It bled for
us. It beats for us. And this, for Gibson and millions of other Christians around the world, is not merely controversial, it is incontrovertible.

There is no hope that Mel Gibson will ever win an Oscar for *The
Passion of the Christ*. No matter. He has his heart set on an infinitely
greater reward.

55

PAUL McCARTNEY

A Grief Observed

A review of *Blackbird Singing: Poems and Lyrics 1965–1999*[†]

L OVERS OF POETRY could be forgiven for steering clear of any volume of verse by a well-known pop star, even one as generally and genuinely respected as former Beatle Paul McCartney. At the very least, they could be forgiven for approaching such a volume with trepidation. To a degree, their fears and prejudices would be justified. McCartney has written a number of surprisingly good poems, but they are embedded like precious stones in the basest of rock (if the pun be permitted). Indeed, all too often the rock weighs heavily on the blackbird's wings, a millstone around the poet's neck.

There is, in fact, little doubt that McCartney's reputation as a poet would have been enhanced considerably if his reputation as a pop star had not gate-crashed its way onto the pages of *Blackbird Singing*. If the poems had been allowed to stand alone, they would have stood secure. As it is, they have been forced to shuffle uneasily beside a large selection of McCartney's song lyrics. These, stripped of their musical accompaniment, make embarrassingly bad verse, even where they remain eminently memorable as lyrics. It is certainly comical, yet sadly tragic, that legendary and truly lyrical lyrics, such as those in *Penny Lane*, *The Long and Winding Road*, *The Fool on the Hill* and many others, fall flat and lifeless on the dead page, as though, when stripped of their music, they have been stripped of their life. *Hey Jude*, *Back in the USSR*, *Band on the Run* . . . one by one, the lyrical icons of one's youth crumble to dust on the impotent silence of the page. Like an uninvited voyeur, the reader looks on with embarrassed awkwardness at the pathetic sight of the sublime becoming ridiculous.

[†] London: Faber and Faber, 2001.

There are exceptions. *Paperback Writer, She's Leaving Home, Lady Madonna* and *Eleanor Rigby* all salvage some respect as verse even after the musical Muse has been exiled. In each case, however, they were stronger when happily married to their respective musical spouses than when forced to live as aesthetically impoverished divorcees. Only the unforgettable *Yesterday* survives as a poem of true merit, as pristinely pure and sublimely simple in verse as it is on vinyl.

Nonetheless, and leaving these reservations aside, Paul McCartney *is* a genuine poet. He is a poet *in spite* of his reputation as a songwriter, not because of it. It is in the final section of the book, entitled "Nova", that McCartney finally excels. Containing nothing but new verse and mercifully free of old song lyrics, *Blackbird Singing* reaches a late but refreshingly impressive climax. With the rock belatedly removed from around the poet's neck, he begins at last to fly and sing like the bird that gives the volume its title.

Comprising a mere fifteen short verses, the final section is candidly autobiographical, intensely personal, and charts McCartney's enduring love affair with his wife, Linda, following her death from cancer. It is, in fact, the diary of a soul's grappling with bereavement—its feelings, its thoughts, its suffering, its questioning. It is strongly reminiscent of C. S. Lewis' *A Grief Observed*, though it speaks to and from the heart, whereas Lewis spoke to and from the head. It also charts, and chants, a soul's confusion and its eventual conversion, albeit a conversion colored by confusion. The final poem in the volume is a hymn of praise to a long-sought and longed-for God. In the company of other and greater poets, such as Dante, Bunyan, Coleridge and Sassoon, McCartney is a poet on pilgrimage, seeking that he might find. Perhaps, however, his particular pilgrimage is not yet over. Having discovered God, he has still to rediscover His Mother. Across the years, one hears the insistently haunting refrain of one of McCartney's finest songs:

> When I find myself
> In times of trouble
> Mother Mary comes to me
> Speaking words of wisdom,
> Let it be.

56

ABOVE ALL SHADOWS RIDES THE SUN

The Poetry of Praise

A review of

Lion Sun: Poems by Pavel Chichikov[†]

O N FIRST LAYING MY HANDS on a copy of Pavel Chichikov's poems, I was reminded, somewhat incongruously, of C. S. Lewis. The association of the one with the other had nothing to do with any perceived similarity in their poetry. On the contrary, although Chichikov dedicates one of the poems in *Lion Sun* to "C.S.L.", they are as different as the proverbial, or poetical, chalk and cheese. The association arose from the delightful cover art depicting the "Lion Sun" of the book's title as an Aslanesque personification of the Sun or Son, leaping toward the reader from its heat-haze halo. The blending of Lewis' Aslan with Chichikov's "Lion Sun" is itself emblematic of the evocative evolution of ideas that proliferate in Chichikov's work. His imagery leads one from the nature-prophetic to the supernature-profound in a progressive stream of associated ideas pointing to something deeper. Such Franciscan mysticism fused into verse is very reminiscent of Roy Campbell's sonnet sequence "Mithraic Emblems", and, most particularly, his sonnet "To the Sun".

The most powerful and penetrating impression that one derives from Chichikov's verse is a sense that he is a true mystic. His poems resonate with distant yet distinct echoes of others who were similarly blessed with the mystic muse. Apart from Campbell, one senses the presence

†Grey Owl Press, P.O. Box 5334, Takoma Park, MD 20913, USA, ISBN 096719010x.

of Hopkins, Blake and R. S. Thomas. Thus, in "Prayer", the "dapple-shadowed" presence of Hopkins is unmistakable.

> All messengers are angels, and the lesser ones are
> Thermal-riding hawks, foreboding crows and ravens
> Agile swifts, athletic gulls and plunging pelicans
> Cranes that lumber and the geese like cannon-shot
> From silent catapults, ducks on analeptic wings
> And furtive, dapple-shadowed wrens and finches ...

Lines such as these are typical of Chichikov's preoccupation with the beauties of the natural world and its wildlife. He praises the wren as a feathered bell, "A bell that's made of feathers and of fire", and the goldfinch is lauded for its "silver flute" and its "sweet and liquid" song. He is very much a nature poet, though a nature poet who never loses sight of the connection between creature and Creator. For Chichikov, Creation, in its beauty and through its beauty, always points to its Source. As a true romantic, he is deeply distressed by the ugliness that destroys beauty. In particular, he laments with luddite eloquence the encroachments of scientism, the "hideous strength" that destroys creation and desecrates its Source. Occasionally, as in "Dynamite", Chichikov's plaintive voice explodes in the pyrotechnic brilliance of inspired juxtaposed imagery:

> Conquistador technology,
> Exploration of the islands of the cortex of the brain ...

Suffering, and the mystical necessity of its acceptance, is a recurring theme, almost a *leitmotif*. In "Golgotha's Mary", Chichikov relinquishes the modern mode of expression for the medieval, finding inspiration from the Litany of the Blessed Virgin.

> Not alone to shepherds or in caves
> No burning cherub or Creator's slave
> But one of us, Mater Creatoris
>
> Not alone to victims or to innocents
> You also come to help impenitents
> And prisoners, Mater Salvatoris

Elsewhere, as in "Pouring the Moon" or "Empty Church", the medieval meets modernity in a mystic kiss, the metrical jollity clashing in creative bliss with the Baudelairean sin-psychology. Similarly, "Seven Song", possibly my favorite of all the poems in this volume, is a Dantean romp on the subject of the seven deadly sins that skips along with rambunctious and outrageous abandon, the meter as breathless as that employed to immortal effect by Belloc in "The End of the Road".

> Stoop-shouldered Pride
> Slavering Greed
> Eros the stupid
> Envy the weed
> Anger the swollen
> Glutton the base
> Lazy the witless
> Falls on his face
> All of them offspring
> Of Adam the rover
> Who gave up a kingdom
> To scuff the world over.

It is difficult to praise *Lion Sun* highly enough. At his best, Chichikov is himself a feathered bell, chiming with "sweet and liquid" beauty. Several of the poems in this wonder-filled volume have earned Pavel Chichikov a place among my all-time favorite poets: Robert Southwell, Richard Crashaw, George Herbert, Gerard Manley Hopkins, Francis Thompson, Hilaire Belloc, Roy Campbell, T. S. Eliot, R. S. Thomas and Pavel Chichikov. Having read and enjoyed the best of the poems in *Lion Sun*, I believe that Pavel Chichikov does not seem out of place in such illustrious company.

57

THE MAGIC OF TECHNOLOGY

I T MIGHT SEEM A LITTLE ODD to suggest a connection between technology and the occult. It is, however, only a little odd because we live in an age that is more than a little odd. The oddness of the age, and the all-pervasive perversity of its spirit, was summed up recently in the words of a plaintive correspondent to a nameless newspaper. "Why could religion not be as broad-minded as science?" the correspondent inquired indignantly. "Why is religion always looking to the past? Why is it always bogged down with tradition? Why can't it learn from science which always looks to the future?" The words of the correspondent could have been published in the pages of almost any newspaper in almost any country in the world. Such is its universal appeal to the secularist spirit of the age. Indeed, such is its attunement to the *Zeitgeist* that it almost serves as its mantra or its dogma.

In answering these questions, which represent the charges of the secularist Inquisition, we shall discover that they are not merely superficial in their reasoning and supercilious in their *raison d'être*, but that they are ultimately superstitious in their reaction to ultimate reality. Furthermore, we shall discover the synonymous nature of magic and technology; or, to succumb to the temptation to employ more controversial language, we shall expose the unholy marriage of applied science and the occult.

Perhaps it would be simplest to commence by answering the last, and most transparently facile, of the charges, posing as questions, put by our secularist Inquisitor. Science does not, of course, always look to the future. If it did, it would, at that very moment, cease to be science. In fact, it would, at that very moment, cease to be anything at all. Science, as someone quipped with a rare combination of wit

364

and wisdom, is nothing more than the pygmies of the present sitting on the shoulders of the giants of the past. No discipline in the field of human knowledge is more bound to the breakthroughs of the past than the science of the present. No discipline is more dependent on its own rules and regulations, laid down by great figures of the past, than is science. Even its innovations are not really innovations; they are never truly "new" in the sense of being "original". They are merely developments of doctrine, or, at most and only rarely, they might represent new ways of seeing or understanding older truths. And, of course, science never creates any new reality; it merely discovers what was always there. It makes no more sense to pretend that science invents new truths than to pretend that America didn't exist before Columbus discovered it. America was there long before Columbus; and the truth is there long before science discovers it.

Truth is. That is, it is always in the present tense because it is always-present in the omnipresent sense. Truth not only *is*, in the sense of the temporally present, it *was, and is, and is to come.* It is ever-present, not merely within time—past, present or future—but beyond time and space. And this, of course, brings us to religion and the first three of our Inquisitor's questions.

Religion does not always "look to the past", in the sense that it never looks anywhere else, but it always looks to the past in the sense that it is the only way to know where we are in the present and, therefore, where we are going in the future. The past is a map that enables us to know where we are. If we forget the map, we get lost! Those who contemptuously dismiss the past are similar to hikers who contemptuously refuse to carry a map. As such, the past, and the traditions it presents to the present, are a valuable guide to the world in which we live. We discard it at our own peril. The more treacherous the landscape, the more perilous the absence of a map. We live in treacherous times. Facing them without a map is nothing short of foolhardy.

Incidentally, and staying with our topographical analogy, the Church can be likened to a compass in the same way that the past can be likened to a map. She points unerringly to "true north", that is, God.

Where does our refutation of the charges of the secularist Inquisition leave us in relation to our early suggestion that there is an unholy marriage between magic and technology? Quite simply, magic and technology have this much in common—they both seek to manipulate reality for their own, normally selfish, ends. Magic, in the medieval world, was often associated with the art, or science, of alchemy. Alchemists, the precursors of modern scientists, sought to find a way of turning base metals into gold. Now, apparently, modern alchemists, using the latest scientific techniques that involve bombarding the nucleus of an atom with electrons have succeeded where their medieval forebears failed. Modern technology has succeeded in making medieval magic. Base metals can be turned to gold. At present the process is not economically viable, but where there's a proverbial will . . .

At this juncture it is tempting to posit a moral argument about the dangers of the "Midas touch". The temptation will, however, be resisted. One does not wish to offer the secularist Inquisition further cause to point the accusing finger. One can almost hear the same plaintive voice muttering questions. Why does "religion" insist on dredging up the past? Why does it always seek to introduce a moral dimension to the application of technology? Why does it pretend that there is any valuable truth to be found in old myths? Why indeed . . . ?

58

RUSSIAN REVELATIONS

F OR THOSE OF US WHO GREW UP in the icy shadow of the cold war, the very name of Russia can still send a shuddering chill up the spine. It is the chill of the Cheka or the KGB, the Soviet secret police. There remains, for our generation, the lingering suspicion that something in the soul of Russia is dark and cruel. The Russian Bear, though temporarily sedated with the narcotic drug of capitalist consumerism, is only sleeping. When it awakes, it will emerge as menacing as ever.

Such are our fears. Are they justified?

Certainly there is something brutal about Russia's recent history. Estimates of the numbers who perished under the Soviet Terror range from thirty to sixty million. Only Chairman Mao's China can boast more victims than Stalin's Soviet Union. Nor can the Russians escape the censure on the grounds that Josef Stalin was not a Russian but a Georgian. One might as well excuse the Germans for the barbarities of the Third Reich on the basis that Hitler was not German but Austrian.

Yet who are we to judge? England's record is scarcely without blemish. We had our own "revolution" almost four centuries earlier, in which it became an act of treason to profess the Catholic faith. Many Catholic priests were butchered in the most barbaric way, by being hanged, drawn and quartered. Even members of the laity were in peril. Margaret Clitherow, an expectant mother, was tortured to death in horrific fashion in the city of York because she would not renounce her Catholic faith and because she refused to betray the priests she had harbored. Perhaps, as Englishmen, we should examine the plank in our own eye before we are too hasty in pointing out the mote in the eye of the Russian people.

In fact, and indeed, the English and the Russians have a great deal in common. Having abandoned their rightful but spurned inheritance, the orthodox Christianity of their fathers, the English and the Russians find themselves in a post-Reformation or post-Revolution no-man's-land of doubt and desolation. Between us and our past is an abyss of betrayal—the betrayal of God and His Church on the altar of failed utopias that have decayed into the sin, cynicism and insincerity of postmodern pseudorationalism. In place of the priceless treasure of God Himself, offered on Catholic and Orthodox altars, we have accepted the devil's bargain. We have abandoned Life Itself for the living death of self-consumerism, an empty religion that has nothing to offer but "consumer products". These trinkets and gadgets are the idolized gadgets of self-worship. Oh, how we have sold our very souls for so very, very little!

To quote the words of Hardy, not Thomas but Oliver, what a fine mess we have gotten ourselves into! The question is, how do we get ourselves out?

It is all a matter of Time . . .

It is often said that time is a great healer, and, as with so many truisms, this particular truism happens to be true. Ultimately, the cure for the modern malaise affecting England, Russia and, for that matter, the rest of the world, is to be found in the healing hands of Time. It is, in fact, a question not only of Time but of Timelessness. Paradoxically, the present is always passing away. It is, in fact, never really here or, at least, is never within our grasp. By the time we think about the present moment, it is already in the past. The temporal point, like the mathematical point, doesn't really exist except as a metaphysical concept. It exists in the realm of truth, but not in fact. Consequently, we are always living in the past and thinking about the future!

What exactly does such abstruse metaphysics have to say about our present problems? Quite simply, it is to show that our future depends on our past. The antidote to modern despair is ancient wisdom. The cure for decadence is renewal. The cure for postmodern deconstruction is Christian Reconstruction. The cure for post-Reformation England and post-Revolution Russia lies in their respective, and shared, cultural heritage: Shakespeare and Pushkin; Dickens and Dostoyevsky; Chesterton and Chekhov; Belloc and Blok; Tolkien and Tolstoy.

Perhaps we should conclude with some "Russian revelations" that might constitute a prophecy, or possibly merely wishful thinking. They are, at any rate, a prayer. They are fed by faith, rooted in hope and lived in love. The prophecy or prayer is this: that when the Russian bear awakens, it will roar in union with the British Lion. And both will lie down before the Lamb.

59

DANTE

Assent's Ascent

S OME TIME AGO, at a Catholic Writers' Festival on the campus of Franciscan University in Steubenville, I was privileged to be part of a forum discussion on the subject of poetry. At the end of a very lively and fruitful debate as to what constituted Christian poetry, the panel members were asked by a member of the audience to name the greatest Christian poem of all time. The two other panel members answered, without the slightest hesitation, that Dante's *Divine Comedy* warranted this singular accolade. I was, of course, in total agreement with my colleagues. Yes indeed, I replied, Dante's masterpiece deserves to be crowned with the supreme laurel.

The concord between me and my colleagues was hardly surprising. The *Divine Comedy* is such a magnificent achievement that it has no equal within the sphere of poetry. It is a literary edifice that towers over its rivals. As such, the question from the audience was almost superfluous. After all, what's the point of asking a question to which only one answer is possible? I was reminded, in fact, of T. S. Eliot's judgment on Dante: "I feel that anything I can say about such a subject is trivial. I feel so completely inferior in his presence—there seems really nothing to do but to point to him and be silent." [1] If the greatest poet of the twentieth century was rendered speechless in the presence of the medieval master, what hope was there for three mere "experts"? Like Eliot, we had little option but to point to Dante and

---

[1] Valerie Eliot, ed., *The Letters of T. S. Eliot* (London, 1988), 1:374–75.

be silent. Such was the apt if somewhat anticlimactic end to our discussion of Christian poetry.

In spite of his own cautionary words on the subject, Eliot did not always remain silent. In *The Sacred Wood*, he wrote that "Dante's is the most comprehensive, and the most *ordered* presentation of emotions that has ever been made."[2] He also insisted that Dante was superior to Milton, dismissing the latter's claim as a worthy contender or pretender to the Italian's crown. "Dante seems to me so immeasurably greater in every way, even in control of language, that I am often irritated by Milton's admirers."[3]

As usual, I find myself in essential agreement with Eliot. The difference between these two great poets, Dante and Milton, is truly abysmal, in the sense that an abyss separates them. It is an abyss that is analogous to the chasm that separates heaven from hell. One does not need to agree wholeheartedly with William Blake's assertion that Milton was "of the Devil's party without knowing it" to agree nonetheless with his judgment that "Milton wrote in fetters when he wrote of Angels & God, and at liberty when of Devils & Hell". Whether or not Milton truly had sympathy for the devil, he certainly gave him many of the best lines.

The difference between Milton and Dante can be summarized succinctly. Milton's approach is devious, deviant, even devilish; Dante's is divine. Milton's focus is principally infernal, concentrating on infernal principalities and powers; Dante's is always on paradise, even when he is in hell. Milton's heaven is a military dictatorship with Satan as the leader of an army of rebel freedom fighters; Dante's heaven is a communion of saints living in harmony within a hierarchy of virtue, moved by Love. Milton points to hell, even from heaven; Dante points to heaven, even from hell. Milton descends from the positive to the negative; Dante ascends from the negative to the positive. Milton's is the tragedy of a Paradise Lost; Dante's the comedy of a Paradise Attained.

If modernity does not perceive the profound difference between these two masterful poets, it is not particularly surprising. Modernity

[2] T. S. Eliot, *The Sacred Wood* (London, 1960), 168.
[3] Valerie Eliot, *The Letters of T. S. Eliot*, 1:426.

does not perceive *anything* very profoundly, least of all those things that are truly profound. The cry of the *De profundis* cannot be heard by the moderns because in order to cry *de profundis*, one must first have some perception of the depth from which one is crying. Paradoxically, modernity cannot cry from out of the depths because it is out of its depth. It simply does not understand the deeper things.

This lack of insight on the part of the modern world, particularly within the context of a discussion of the importance of Dante, was expressed by Chesterton with his customary eloquence.

> If we compare . . . the morality of the *Divine Comedy* with the morality of Ibsen's *Ghosts*, we shall see all that modern ethics have really done. No one, I imagine, will accuse the author of the *Inferno* of an Early Victorian prudishness or a Podsnapian optimism. But Dante describes three moral instruments—Heaven, Purgatory, and Hell, the vision of perfection, the vision of improvement, and the vision of failure. Ibsen has only one—Hell.[4]

The irony, of course, is that modernity is left with hell because it has rejected Purgatory and heaven. And this takes us from Ibsen back to Milton. As a fanatical Puritan, Milton had rejected the medieval vision of heaven and Purgatory. Perhaps indeed he "wrote in fetters when he wrote of Angels & God, and at liberty when of Devils & Hell" precisely because he despised Dante's vision of the Church Triumphant and the Church Suffering. The Puritans condemned the Catholic veneration of the saints and rejected the very existence of Purgatory. Quite simply, heaven and Purgatory, as Dante envisioned them, were "off limits" to Milton. He could not write of saints, nor of repentant souls being cleansed of their sins. He was left with hell. Having rejected the vision of success (heaven) and the vision of improvement on the path to success (Purgatory), he is left only with the vision of failure (hell). What, ultimately, is *Paradise Lost* but a vision of failure?

Like Milton and Ibsen, the modern world is more at home in hell than in heaven. It is where it wants to be. It comes as no surprise,

<hr />

[4] G. K. Chesterton, *Heretics* (London, 1905), 29–30.

therefore, that Dante's *Inferno* is far more widely read than the *Purgatorio* or the *Paradiso*. For most moderns, even those who profess to teach literature at our centers of higher learning (so-called), Dante is often seen as "the poet of the *Inferno*". Not only is this the only part of the *Divine Comedy* that is studied, it is generally considered to be far superior as literature to the other two books. The absurdity of such a position, literarily speaking, beggars belief. It beggars belief not so much because the *Purgatorio* and the *Paradiso* are better as literature (though it can certainly be argued convincingly that they are at least the *Inferno's* equal) but because they are all part of the same book. Imagine the absurdity of suggesting that Tolkien's *The Fellowship of the Ring* was superior to *The Two Towers* or *The Return of the King*, so much so that it was considered unnecessary to read the whole of *The Lord of the Rings*. Imagine the absurdity of suggesting that the first book of Waugh's *Brideshead Revisited* was superior to the second and third books and that, therefore, it was necessary to study only the first third of the novel. Imagine the suggestion that it is necessary to read only the first third of any book in order to understand it! Yet, astounding though it may seem, this is exactly the way in which the *Divine Comedy* is often studied.

The full extent of the absurdity is made apparent once we perceive the work as a whole and not as three distinct books. Taken as a whole, the *Divine Comedy* depicts the ascent of the spirit of assent, the soul's slow but sure acceptance of the will of God. It begins, however, with the descent of the spirit of dissent, the soul's obstinate rejection of the divine will. The deeper the dissent, the deeper the descent until, at last, we find ourselves with the traitors in the diabolic presence of Satan himself. The vision thus far is all negative, rooted in rejection of the will of God. It is, however, only the preamble, only the prelude or the prologue to the ascent and assent that follows. From now on, the soul ascends Mount Purgatory and from thence is lifted into the spheres of heaven itself and, finally, into the very presence of the beatific vision. Seen in this context, the descent into Hell is the *diminuendo* that accentuates the increasing power of the *crescendo* that follows it. Remove the *crescendo*, and the *diminuendo* is devoid of ultimate purpose.

Perhaps it takes a Catholic sensibility to understand fully the *Divine Comedy*, and this perhaps is the reason for modernity's failure to

comprehend this greatest of all poems. At any rate, it takes a great
Catholic like Chesterton to elucidate fully the lucidity of Dante's vision.
Take, for instance, Chesterton's comparison of Dante to Shakespeare.

> Do we not know in our hearts that Shakespeare could have dealt with
> Dante's Hell but hardly with Dante's Heaven? In so far as it is possible
> to be greater than anything that is really great, the man who wrote of
> Romeo and Juliet might have made something even more poignant out
> of Paolo and Francesca. The man who uttered that pulverizing "He
> has no children", over the butchery in the house of Macduff, might
> have picked out yet more awful and telling words for the father's cry
> out of the Tower of Hunger. And when Dante is really dealing with
> the dance of the liberated virtues in the vasty heights of heaven, he is
> spacious. He is spacious when he talks of Liberty; he is spacious when
> he talks of Love. It is so in the famous words at the end about Love
> driving the sun and stars; it is the same in the far less famous and far
> finer passage, in which he hails the huge magnanimity of God in giv-
> ing to the human spirit the one gift worth having; which is Liberty.
> Nobody but a fool will say that Shakespeare was a pessimist; but we
> may, in this limited sense, say that he was a pagan; in so far that he is
> at his greatest in describing great spirits in chains. In that sense, his
> most serious plays are an inferno. Anyhow, they are certainly not a
> *Paradiso*.[5]

Although I can't concur with Chesterton's conclusion that some of
Shakespeare's plays were an inferno, believing instead that they were
in fact a *purgatorio*, his insistence on Dante's superiority as a visionary
of paradise is utterly valid. Nor can one argue with Chesterton's ultimate appraisal of Dante's munificent and magnificent accentuation of
the positive: "Dante is drawn as a dark and bitter spirit; but in fact he
wrote the only one of the great epics that really has a happy ending."[6]
    The final word on Dante's masterpiece belongs not to Eliot, nor to
Chesterton, but to Chesterton's great friend, Maurice Baring. A greatly
underrated novelist and poet in his own right, Baring has captured

    [5] G. K. Chesterton, *Chaucer* (London, 1949), 226–27.
    [6] G. K. Chesterton, "On Dante and Beatrice", in *All Is Grist* (Freeport, NY.:
1967), 126.

better than anyone the love of liberty and the liberty of love at the heart-leaping core of the *Divine Comedy*, the assent's ascent.

> Scaling the circles of the *Paradiso*, we are conscious the whole time of an ascent not only in the quality of the substance but in that of the form. It is a long perpetual crescendo, increasing in beauty until the final consummation in the very last line. Somebody once defined an artist ... as a man who knew how to finish things. If this definition is true—and I think it is—then Dante was the greatest artist who ever lived. His final canto is the best, and it depends on and completes the beginning.[7]

[7] Maurice Baring, *Have You Anything to Declare?* (London, 1936), 106.

60

SHAKESPEARE

Good Will for All Men

A s an Englishman, I must confess an element of pride (in the nontheological sense!) at the very mention of the name of William Shakespeare. The knowledge that my country has spawned, nurtured and nourished such a genius is certainly a cause for joy. It is, however, a little presumptuous to feel proud about something for which one deserves no credit. One might as well feel proud or superior because one is the offspring of rich parents. The baby, fresh from the womb of a wealthy mother, has clearly not merited the silver spoon that he has inherited any more than the newborn babe of penurious parents deserves censure for the plastic spoon with which it is fed. Clearly, therefore, we Englishmen have not *merited* the honor of calling William Shakespeare our fellow countryman. Nonetheless, he *is* our fellow countryman, and we have the right—nay, the duty—to feel grateful for this fortuitous gift. It is, indeed, the sort of fortuitousness that breeds fortitude. After all, if we can call Shakespeare our countryman, shouldn't it inspire us to emulate his example, however imperfectly?

Shakespeare is, however, not merely or only an Englishman. He is no more *merely* English than Dante is *merely* Italian, Cervantes *merely* Spanish or Dostoyevsky *merely* Russian. He was, and they were, spawned, nurtured and nourished by something greater than their respective nationalities. They were all children of Christendom, inheritors of the seed of Christ. They were cultivated by the grace of God Himself and grew to creative fruition in the profound culture of the Church. As such, they are catholic and Catholic. Their appeal is universal. They speak nothing less than the language of Truth. They speak to Everyman in a powerful language that Everyman understands. Thus Shakespeare the Englishman is also Shakespeare for Everyman, regardless of Everyman's nationality. Shakespeare is for sharing!

There is, however, a problem that comes with this liberality. There is the danger—nay, the inevitability—that the Shakespearean pearls will be cast before swine. So be it. The swine will not be harmed by it. It might even do them some good! Even relativists may come through relatively unharmed! They might even find themselves relatively cured of their relativism. Perhaps, however, this is merely wishful thinking. There are none so blind, as the saying goes ... I suspect, in fact, that the only people more blind than those who will not see are those who see only what they want to see!

I am reminded—if I might be permitted a brief peripatetic aside—of the exchange between Chesterton, the prophet of absolute or gospel truth, and Holbrook Jackson, a preacher of relative or secularist opinion:

> Jackson: *A lie is that which you do not believe.*
> Chesterton: This is a lie: so perhaps you don't believe it.
> Jackson: *As soon as an idea is accepted it is time to reject it.*
> Chesterton: No: It is time to build another idea on it. You are always rejecting: and you build nothing.
> Jackson: *Truth and falsehood in the abstract do not exist.*
> Chesterton: Then nothing else does.
> Jackson: *Truth is one's own conception of things.*
> Chesterton: The Big Blunder. All thought is an attempt to discover if one's own conception is true or not.
> Jackson: *Negations without affirmations are worthless.*
> Chesterton: And impossible.
> Jackson: *No opinion matters finally: except your own.*
> Chesterton: Said the man who thought he was a rabbit.

Chesterton, the absolutist, is absolutely right; Jackson, the relativist, is more than relatively wrong.

What, however, has this to do with Shakespeare? I will answer, if I may, with a further peripatetic aside, this time in the form of a cautionary tale.

I was born with the proverbial plastic spoon in my mouth and endured the worst of educations in an east London comprehensive school (which shall remain nameless). This citadel of secularism was full of the sort of relativist and "multicultural" nonsense that, with reference and deference to the dialogue quoted above, could be called almost "Jacksonian" in its inanity. Now, this school had, as its motto, emblazoned above the assembly hall, the Shakespearean epithet "This above all: To thine own self be true." As a youth, steeped in an unconscious agnosticism and entirely ignorant of Christian orthodoxy, I took this motto very seriously. It became, in fact, and in the absence of a creed, my own personal motto. I even claimed, somewhat whimsically and a trifle unjustly, that it was the only useful thing I ever learned at school.

Why, one wonders, did such a school choose such a motto? The answer, of course, is that it is safe. It cannot offend anyone, regardless of his faith or lack thereof. It smacks of relativism. It reminds us of Jackson's trite trifles, posing as philosophy. *Truth is one's own conception of things ... No opinion matters finally: except your own ...* It is a short step from these self-centered notions of truth to the Shakespearean version of the same: *This above all: To thine own self be true.* Can this not be paraphrased or interpreted as "Be true to thine own selfishness"; or "Be true to thyself, to hell with the rest"; or, more blasphemously, "I am the way and the truth (not anyone else, including God)"?

What does all this mean? Does it mean, horror of horrors, that Shakespeare was a protosecularist or a protorelativist? Certainly many secularist critics would have us believe so. They are, however, wrong. Shakespeare was possibly, perhaps probably, a Catholic. He was certainly a believing and profoundly orthodox Christian whose plays were full of profoundly Christocentric perceptions of life.

Yet, if this is so, where does it leave our cautionary tale? How do we explain the apparent secularism of the Shakespearean epithet quoted above? The answer, of course, is that the words are not Shakespeare's at all; or rather, they are words that Shakespeare placed into the mouth of someone else. They were uttered by a character in one of his plays and, as such, represent the beliefs of the character, not necessarily the beliefs of the poet who enabled him to speak. The character in question is Polonius, the well-meaning, bungling and ultimately shallow adviser to King Claudius in *Hamlet.* The words are spoken as part of Polonius' famous advice to his son, Laertes, a monologue that can be seen as a secularist discourse, more sublime in expression than Jackson's platitudes but ultimately almost as banal. Shakespeare paints Polonius as a meddling and blundering buffoon, as facile and impotent in life as he is fatuous in philosophy. In short, Polonius looks as silly in the hands of Shakespeare as does Jackson in the hands of Chesterton. In both cases, the folly of falsehood is exposed by a master of truth.

In the words of the Bard himself, life in the fallen world might continue to be a comedy of errors, but all's well that ends well!

61

MODERN ART

Friend or Foe?

I S MODERN ART MERELY A LOAD of old rubbish—or, rather, a load of old new rubbish? Certainly much that passes as "art" in our muddled modern world is not worthy of the name. Take, for instance, the garbage posing as art during an exhibition of the shortlisted "artists" for the 2004 Beck's Futures Prize at London's Institute of Contemporary Art. Among the finalists for the £20,000 prize was a British "artist" who had produced a video of two Cilla Black impersonators singing the star's first big hit, *Anyone Who Had a Heart*. Another finalist, who described himself as an avid train spotter, had produced a twenty-seven-minute video of a freight train. The winner, however, was a Brazilian "artist" who specialized in making sculptures of animals by scraping fluff from new carpets.

Meanwhile, in Cardiff, the Artes Mundi prize, worth £40,000, was won by a Chinese "artist" who had gathered dust from the ruins of the World Trade Center and had scattered it on the floor before tracing a short verse about dust in the dust. Works of "art" honored with major prizes in previous years include piles of bricks, soiled nappies (or soiled diapers for our American readers), an unmade bed decorated with debris such as condoms, dead animals, "sculptures" made by urinating in snow, and the work of an "artist" who specialized in sewing things to the soles of his feet. *Et cetera ad nauseam.*

The exhibition at the Institute of Contemporary Art (ICA) opened a few hours before the millionaire collector and patron of modern "art", Charles Saatchi, threw a celebrity-thronged party at his private gallery to launch a new exhibition, titled *New Blood*, which also professed to champion the avant-garde. The exhibition was greeted with howls of derision by Saatchi's rivals at the ICA. "We're showing the new blood. Saatchi's got old blood", sneered a spokesman for the ICA. Philip Dodd, the ICA's director, added that "the nicest thing to say about Charles is that several artists in his show were in our Beck's exhibition a year ago." In dismissing his rival, Dodd had also unwittingly dismissed himself, and the so-called "art" he promotes, to the dustbin of history. As his comments make abundantly clear, this sort of self-styled modern "art" is not about quality but novelty. It's not about how good it is but how new it is. This year's artists are better than last year's artists purely because they are this year's artists. Last year's artists are already *passé*. It is, therefore, easy to dismiss this sort of "art" as nothing but dust and fluff that will be blown away by the winds of fashion. After all, as C. S. Lewis quipped, fashions are always coming and going ... but mostly going.

So much for fashion and the false "art" it promotes. What about real modern art? What about art that is truly modern and truly art? Is such art a friend or foe of the Faith? Should Christians be suspicious of such art? Should we trust it?

Such questions cannot be answered—and should not even be asked— until we have asked and answered the more fundamental and radical question *What is modern art?* And, as is so often the case, it is best to begin by asking what a thing is not before we proceed to a discussion of what it is.

The first thing to be understood is that modern art is not particularly "modern". In the same way that modern history begins several centuries ago, modern art is already many centuries old. It is, in fact, impossible to point definitively to a particular moment when art became modern. The departure from iconography was "modern"; the science of perspective was "modern". Giotto was "modern" in the fourteenth century; Leonardo da Vinci and Raphael were "modern" in the fifteenth and sixteenth centuries. If "modern" means up-to-date or innovative within the context of one's own time, these artists qualify in every respect as "modern". Paradoxically, they are permanently modern, in the sense that the freshness of their vision is perennial. Their art is fresh because it is incorruptible. One can hardly say the same of soiled nappies, condom-strewn beds or carpet fluff. In this sense, Giotto, Leonardo and Raphael have far more claim to being modern than have the nameless and soon-to-be-forgotten "artists" of today. And, of course, they have a far better claim to being artists.

If we move our discussion of modern art to the nineteenth century, we can see the paradoxes and the tensions at the heart of any discussion of art and modernity. Impressionism, for instance, was perceived as very avant-garde, even dangerously so. According to G. K. Chesterton, a critic who should never be taken lightly, impressionism was the product of philosophical relativism, the absence of definition in the former being the result of the absence of definitive objectivity in the latter. One can see Chesterton's point, and even agree with it, but are we to conclude that there was no good impressionist art? Surely not. *Pace* Chesterton, we cannot see Monet's masterful vision of Rouen Cathedral in full sunlight as anything but sublime. Similarly, the protoimpressionism of J. M. W. Turner was truly "modern" in the sense of being avant-garde or ahead of its time. Although one critic dismissed a particularly monochromatic Turner seascape as nothing but "soap-suds", it is the artist and not the critic who has stood the test of time or, more correctly, the test of timelessness. It is indeed a paradox worthy of note that Turner's greatest champion among his contemporaries was John Ruskin, who, as both artist and critic, is better known as a neomedievalist who championed Gothic "tradition" than as an advocate of modern concepts of "impressionism". It is, in fact, an even greater paradox that Ruskin's championing of another artistic movement, the Pre-Raphaelite brotherhood, exhibited the surprising fact that even tradition can be modern.

The Pre-Raphaelites, as their name suggests, sought a return to the purity of a medieval vision of art. In contradistinction to the pastel haze of the impressionists, the Pre-Raphaelites painted in the bold daylight of primary splendor. Their subjects were often taken from literature and myth and were imbued with neomedievalist romanticism. It is a medieval victory *over* Victorianism, and yet it is also medievalism modified and modernized *by* Victorianism. And herein lies the dynamism of the paradox. Neomedievalism is both *new* and *medieval*. It is the light of tradition seen through the telescope of modernity.

And so to the twentieth century.

Arguably, of all centuries, the last was the worst—at least in terms of the divorce of modernity from tradition. And if this is true of culture in general, it is certainly true of art in particular.

Perhaps Pablo Picasso is more culpable than most for the divorce. He was certainly guilty of adultery, in the sense of the adulteration of the gifts he was given. Unlike many of the modern "artists" who followed his example, Picasso could paint beautifully. The problem is that he ceased to do so. Having established a solid reputation, he sullied himself with inferior "primitive" experiments utterly unworthy of his talent. This, in itself, might not have mattered too much except for the fact that a legion of disciples who, unlike their master, could not paint, crept wormlike through the crevices of credulity that the weight of Picasso's fallen talent had caused. The result was an artistic revolution as nihilistic and destructive as were the political revolutions of the century. The cubist castration of art heralded the omnipotence of impotence made manifest in the dust and fluff of today's artless moderns.

It is not all bad news, however. Much art of real stature has emerged in the twentieth century. The art of Otto Dix is as gruesome as Grünewald in its graphic depiction of the ugliness of sin, and the surrealist symbolism of Salvador Dali has more in common with the artistic vision of Hieronymus Bosch than with the heinous bosh of "postmodern" pretentiousness. Unlike many of their contemporaries, Dali and Dix have retained the critical connection with tradition that is essential to all true art. Their art is the product of the marriage of tradition and modernity and, in consequence, will survive alongside the modern art of previous centuries. The rest of the ephemera masquerading as "art" will decay in the putridness of its own corruption. Will anyone remember the nameless Brazilian artist who creates "art" from fluff in a century or so, or next year for that matter? Of course not. Ashes to ashes, dust to dust ... Will genuine art, modern or otherwise, survive the test of timelessness? Of course it will. *Vincit omnia veritas*.

62

SALVADOR DALI

From Freud to Faith

Around Dali everything is real except myself.

—Salvador Dali

S ALVADOR DALI IS AN ENIGMA. He is such an enigma that it is almost trite to describe him as such. He is as elusive as a butterfly— infuriatingly so, self-contradictorily so. He is so elusive, flittering from one flippant frivolity to another, that the pursuivant's sadistic curiosity desires to pin him down and, like a lepidopterist, examine the color-ful concoction of beauty and ugliness with which he revealed himself to, and concealed himself from, the world.

It is never possible satisfactorily to explain a man, least of all a man of Dali's contradictions, through a process of biographical vivisection whereby the investigator seeks to dissect his subject's secrets with the scalpel of subjectivism and the forceps of Freudian self-deception. It is, however, possible to arrive at sensible conclusions through a pro-cess of good solid detective work. In the case of one as self-consciously elusive and artfully deceptive as Dali, it becomes more necessary than ever to stick resolutely to the facts and not to fly off in pursuit of Dali's flights of fancy. Such flights will simply lead to the pursuit of the elusive butterfly with no hope of pinning him down. Instead, the Dali detective must keep his feet on the ground and his eyes on the facts, remembering in true surrealist fashion that red herrings can fly.

Salvador Dali was born in 1904 in Figueres on the plains of Anda-lusia in northern Spain. From 1921 until his expulsion in 1926, he studied at the San Fernando School of Fine Arts in Madrid. During his period as a student, he became attracted, albeit briefly, to revolutionary politics and was jailed for thirty-five days for anarchistic tendencies. His early paintings were somewhat eclectic, vacillating between the traditional and the avant-garde and betraying the influence of artists as diverse as Jan Vermeer, Francisco de Zurbarán and Pablo Picasso. His artistic identity attained coherence, or at any rate cohesion, following his joining of the surrealist movement in the summer of 1929. Thereafter, the bizarre dreamscapes awash with the remnants of Freudian psychoanalysis became the hallmark with which he attained global prominence.

In the same year in which Dali formalized his relationship with the surrealists, he was introduced to the captivating Helena, who would soon become Gala, his beloved wife. According to Dali expert Antonia Spanos, Gala became a "Beatrice figure" who would serve as his muse for the next fifty years. Her influence on Dali is certainly as striking as was that of Beatrice on Dante, and she emerges and reemerges in his art in guises as disparate as Leda and the Blessed Virgin.

In 1932 Dali's painting *The Persistence of Memory* caused a sensation at an exhibition of his paintings at the Julien Levy Gallery in New York. Its evocation of the psychoanalysis of Freud mixed with the scientific relativism of Einstein tapped into the *Zeitgeist* of the interwar years. If, however, his art had succumbed to the allure of the *Zeitgeist*, neither Dali nor his art would be a slave to its wiles. In 1934 he was summoned to appear before the *illustrissimi* of surrealism at the home of its leader, André Breton, to answer charges that he had become "a counterrevolutionary". According to Dali's own account, the "Order of the Day", which had apparently been circulated prior to the meeting, berated him for failing to kowtow before the avowed communism of the rest of the surrealist movement: "Dali having been found guilty on several occasions of counter-revolutionary actions involving the glorification of Hitlerian fascism, the undersigned propose— despite his statement of 25 January 1934—that he be excluded from Surrealism as a fascist element and combated by all available means." In true Stalinist fashion, Dali had become the victim of a show trial and had been found guilty *in absentia* on the charge of "political incorrectness". He was, of course, no more guilty of "Hitlerian fascism"

than were the numberless victims of Stalin's show trials. He was, however, guilty, if guilty be the word, of treating Lenin with evident contempt in his painting *The Enigma of William Tell*, which had been
exhibited, to the anger of his "comrades" in the surrealist movement,
only a few months before the travesty of a "trial".

In the following years, he would make himself, and his work, even
more anathema to his former comrades as a result of his opposition to
the communists in the Spanish civil war and his scarcely concealed
support for Franco's Nationalists. In 1936, the year in which the war
began, he painted the bizarrely titled *Soft Construction with Boiled Beans:
Premonition of Civil War*. Dawn Ades, in her study of Dali, wrote per-
ceptively that "Goya was clearly in Dali's mind as he planned this painting, and the monstrous figure broods over the landscape like Goya's
Colossus presiding over a ruined land." Dali described the painting
himself in terms that were more graphic, if less allusive: "In this picture I showed a vast human body breaking out into monstrous excres-
cences of arms and legs tearing at one another in a delirium of auto-
strangulation." The painting is certainly ugly, horrifying even, but not
more so than the war of which it was an uncanny premonition. If this
is surrealism, it is also realism at its most symbolically resonant.

In a similar vein, *Autumn Cannibalism*, painted at the end of 1936,
after the war had started, depicts two dehumanized human forms locked
in a morbid embrace while eating each other. Commenting on this
painting, Dali distanced himself from the communist sympathies of
Pablo Picasso: "These Iberian beings, eating each other in autumn,
express the pathos of the Civil War considered (by me) as a phenomenon of natural history as opposed to Picasso who considered it as a
political phenomenon." These words have been misunderstood, by
Dawn Ades among others, as an indication that Dali was an historical
determinist who sees "the events of contemporary history . . . as being
as inevitable as evolution, a phenomenon equivalent to a biological or
geological cataclysm." The truth is, however, that they indicate something far subtler than a purely deterministic approach to history. Dali
does not deny the role of free will in shaping history but is stressing
that human will works within the parameters of an inherent dynamic
within history defined by the perennial tension between the power of
tradition and the power of the reaction against it. Ades is closer to

Dali's true position when she discusses his attitude to "change" and to "tradition": "Change is irresistible, and though Dali has an acute horror of it, he believes that it is none the less paradoxically necessary in order to reveal the true strength of tradition." The war in Spain was, therefore, a manifestation of this inherent conflict between change and tradition, with Dali siding very firmly with tradition. This much is evident from his own words about the war and its significance:

> It was going to be necessary for the jackal claws of the revolution to scratch down to the atavistic layers of tradition in order that, as they became savagely ground and mutilated against the granitic hardness of the bones of this tradition they were profaning, one might in the end be dazzled anew by that hard light of the treasures of "ardent death" and of putrefying and resurrected splendours that this earth of Spain held hidden in the depths of its entrails.

Writing in 1942, Dali was even more explicit in his support for the forces of tradition under General Franco. Describing how "the cadaverous body of Spain" had been "half devoured by the vermin and the worms of exotic and materialist ideologies", he contrasted the morbid nihilism of the anarchists with the life-affirming faith of the Nationalists: "The Spanish Anarchists took to the streets of total subversion with black banners, on which were described the words VIVA LA MUERTE! (Long Live Death!) The others, with the flag of tradition, red and gold, of immemorial Spain bearing that other inscription which needs only two letters, FE (Faith)." Dali's triumphalism at Franco's victory is almost salacious, to such an extent that his description of the triumph of faith over death continues with the use of phallic imagery to metamorphose the war from a destructive debauch to a fertility rite. The Faith is phallic. It represents the triumph of life over death.

Appropriately enough, Dali's most powerful reaction to the war in Spain is to be found not in his words but in his work, particularly in the paradoxical serenity of *Spain, 1938*. Unlike the two earlier angst-ridden paintings, *Premonition of War* and *Autumn Cannibalism*, both of which were painted two years earlier when most people expected the communists to emerge as the victors, the statuesque serenity of the later work signifies the artist's relief that the forces of tradition were emerging triumphant. *Spain, 1938* depicts Spain personified as a beautiful woman. Her upper body is delineated by fighting figures who are struggling through her, with her and within her, presumably for the right to possess her. She, however, is seemingly indifferent to the struggle and reclines in the tranquility of her own transcendence. She seems to know, even if the combatants do not, that her victory is assured. She has faith; her enemies have only death—not her death but their own.

The similarity of Dali's *Spain, 1938* to Roy Campbell's poem "Posada" cannot pass without comment:

> Outside, it froze. On rocky arms
> Sleeping face-upwards to the sun
> Lay Spain. Her golden hair was spun
> From sky to sky. Her mighty charms
> Breathed soft beneath her robe of farms
> And gardens: while her snowy breasts,
> Sierras white, with crimson crests,
> Were stained with sunset.

As with Dali, the Spanish civil war was to prove a decisive event in Campbell's life. Having experienced the anarchist uprising in Barcelona in 1934, shortly after his arrival in Spain, Campbell perceived immediately that the stage was set for a bloody war between the opposing forces of tradition and revolution. "From the very beginning my wife and I understood the real issues in Spain. There could be no compromise ... between the East and the West, between Credulity and Faith, between irresponsible innovation ... and tradition, between the emotions (disguised as Reason) and the intelligence." For Dali, her native-born son, and for Campbell, her acolyte by adoption, Spain was the embodiment of faith and tradition. For both men, the artist and the poet, she found personified perfection in the perfect beauty of femininity enshrined. For the artist and the poet alike, conversion to Catholicism was a natural progression from their traditionalist stance. Campbell was received into the Church in Spain in 1935; Dali would be reconciled to the Church following his arrival in the United States in 1940.

In the years following the Second World War, many of Dali's greatest works would be inspired by his religious faith. From his first major painting on a religious theme, *The Temptation of Saint Anthony* (1946), until his celebrated illustrations of the Bible in 1965, Dali blended the sacred and the surreal with innovative, if sometimes controversial, zeal. *The Disintegration of the Persistence of Memory*, painted in the mid-1950s, signaled his apparent rejection of the dominant Freudian influences of his earlier work. In truth, however, he never managed to cleanse the "damn'd spot" of Freudianism from his life or work. Its ubiquity in his youth had psychoanalytically scarred his psyche, preventing any thorough purgation of its stain. Its presence was at least curtailed, and, for the most part, the Freudian was replaced by the ascendant if eccentric nature of his Catholic faith. The other major influence to emerge in the postwar period was an almost obsessive interest in the apparent overlap between physics and metaphysics in the wake of the dawn of the nuclear age.

The mystical relationship between Catholic theology and nuclear physics is the dominant inspiration in several of Dali's postwar works, including *Nuclear Cross* (1952), *Crucifixion* (*Corpus Hypercubus*) (1954), *Angelic Crucifixion* (1954) and *Anti-Protonic Assumption* (1956). In *Crucifixion* (*Corpus Hypercubus*), Christ and His Mother are depicted as being outside time and space, symbolizing the eternal significance of Christ's Passion. In *Angelic Crucifixion*, the crucified Christ is placed within cubes, signifying the reality of His suffering within time and space, but the Crucifix and the cubes that encompass it are set upon a sphere, presumably signifying the world, and the sphere itself is set upon an island from which protrude several needles, presumably signifying heaven and the angels. The use of needles is, of course, a comic touch, alluding to the oft-quoted reference to scholastic philosophers arguing about how many angels could dance upon the point of a needle. Dali's point is, however, not so much comic as cosmic; indeed, not so much cosmic as hypercosmic. The whole of the cosmos, as represented by the cubic representation of time and space, is quite literally dancing on the point of a needle. One angel, in the sense that he is eternal, is greater than the cosmos; and, of course, by extension, every man is also greater than the cosmos, in the sense that he too is eternal. Christ's Presence on the Cross within time and space signifies human destiny beyond time and space. Paradoxically, the Blood from the Cross drips onto the island, signifying heaven, but is not spilled on the sphere, signifying the world. Since orthodoxy dictates that Christ's Blood was poured forth for all humanity, one is tempted to detect an element of heterodoxy in Dali's symbolic representation of the Crucifixion. The suggestion that Christ's suffering is not fully universal, that is, for the salvation of *all* men, appears to show Dali as being guilty of error in his understanding and portrayal of the Faith. The problem might possibly be overcome, however, by the realization that the world, as signified, is representative of those who preferred darkness to the Light. In this sense it does not signify Creation but the denial of Creation, and, by extension, the denial of the Creator. Put simply, the sphere at the base of the Cross represents the rejection of God and the eternal consequence of such a rejection: hell. Seen in this light, the eternal contradiction between the Cross and the sphere in Dali's sculpture is akin to the contradiction that forms the heart and the inspiration of G. K. Chesterton's novel *The Ball and the Cross*.

In *Nuclear Cross*, the Cross itself is made of cubes, signifying its material nature and the historical setting of the Passion of Christ in a particular time and place. Underneath the Cross of cubes, and therefore outside and beyond the confines of time and space, is an altar, signifying the eternal significance of the Mass. In the middle of the Cross, framed by it but beyond it, is a piece of bread, signifying the Real Presence of Christ Himself in the Blessed Sacrament.

Finally, of course, the employment of cubes as the medium for his metaphysical musings enabled Dali to counter the cubist movement in general, and Picasso in particular, whose atheism and communism were anathema to him. Although Dali's metaphysical symbolism had nothing in common with cubism, he could nonetheless express his disapproval indirectly, and with comic adroitness, through the use of symbol association. As for his attitude to Picasso, he had shown his contempt for his great artistic rival in 1947 with much less subtlety, though perhaps with the same degree of comic adroitness. His *Portrait of Picasso* lampooned his rival with caricatured grotesqueness in the manner of the great sixteenth-century protosurrealist Giuseppe Arcimboldo. Picasso is disheveled, decrepit, eyeless and toothless; his tongue lolls out flaccidly in canine abjection, and his skull is crowned with the horns of a goat. The combined effect is one of blindness, bestiality and, above all, impotence, all of which is crowned with a suggestion of the satanic. Seldom had Dali's surrealist wit been so acerbically obvious.

Apart from his mystical journeys to the trysting place of physics and metaphysics, Dali's other religious works include *The Sacrament of the Last Supper* (1955), *The Discovery of America by Christopher Columbus* (1958–59) and *The Ecumenical Council* (1960). *The Discovery of America by Christopher Columbus* is a robust defense of the Christian significance of Columbus' arrival in the New World. It is filled to the brim with an unabashed love for the Church Militant and the Christendom she forged, and the whole work is executed with unapologetic conquistador zeal. It is Dali at his most "politically incorrect". *The Ecumenical Council*, painted a year or so later, is filled with the idealistic hope with which many Catholics approached the opening of the Second Vatican Council.

Dali's best known, if not necessarily his best, religious painting is, without doubt, *Christ of Saint John of the Cross* (1951). This work, inspired by a drawing of Christ attributed to Saint John of the Cross in Avila, Spain, is now one of the most popular religious pictures in the world. Printed reproductions are sold by the millions to Protestants and Catholics alike, and the work has become an object of, or at least a channel for, pietistic devotion on an enormous scale. It is indeed ironic that Dali is best known to the world at large as the painter responsible for *Christ of Saint John of the Cross*, in much the same way that Jean-François Millet is best known as the painter of *The Angelus*. The irony springs from the fact that Dali was obsessed throughout his life with Millet's painting, beguiled no doubt by its iconographic status, and variations on *The Angelus* recur as a potent motif in many of his works. One wonders what the shade of Dali would think of one of his own works being judged by posterity as pietistically synonymous with Millet's masterpiece.

Another intriguing coincidence, or providential correlative, connected with Dali's painting of *Christ of Saint John of the Cross* relates to the fact that Roy Campbell published his award-winning translations of the poems of Saint John of the Cross in 1951, the same year in which Dali was working on his painting. In both cases, and in both cases somewhat unjustly, the artist and the poet have become best known as translators of the work of their saintly predecessor.

It was also in 1951 that Dali was commissioned by the Italian government to produce two hundred watercolor illustrations for an edition of Dante's *Divine Comedy*. It was a labor of love in which Dali clearly identified himself with Dante. He also illustrated *Don Quixote* and, in 1965, the Bible, for which he produced one hundred watercolors. In working so conscientiously and diligently on *Don Quixote*, the *Divine Comedy* and the Bible, Dali was genuflecting before the giant works of Christendom and was pouring out his thoroughly modern genius as a libation before the altar of traditional Christianity.

In 1958 Dali finally solemnized his marriage to Gala, setting his moral life in order, and in the following year he had an audience with Pope John XXIII in Rome. After years of wandering in the wilderness of Freudian self-delusion, Salvador Dali was finally coming Home. In 1982 Gala, Dali's beloved wife, his Beatrice, died. "She is not dead", Dali insisted. "She will never die." Following her death, he abandoned public life and lived a largely reclusive existence until his own death at the age of 85 on 23 January 1989.

Having played the detective and having examined the facts, we are closer to understanding the real Salvador Dali. Nonetheless, he remains an enigma, a conundrum of contradictions, who defies simple categorization. He was a genuine Catholic and a genuine genius, but he was clearly not a saint or a naturally pious believer, at least not in the sense that sanctity and piety are normally measured. His eclecticism and eccentricity are, at one and the same time, both beguilingly charming and incongruently irritating. He remained adolescently fixated with the phallic and other forms of eroticism, a weakness that continued to mar his work long after he had sought to shed the Freudian dream-fixations of his youth. He was also, on occasion at least, surprisingly candid about his philosophy of life, most notably in his exposition of a personal credo in the form of a list of pros and cons. He was, he wrote, for diversity and against uniformity; for hierarchy and against equality; for the individual and against the collective; for metaphysics and against politics; for eternity and against progress; for dreams and against mechanics; for the concrete and against the abstract; for maturity and against youth; for theater and against cinema; for tradition and against revolution; for religion and against philosophy; and for folly and against scepticism. There is enough material in this list alone to facilitate another full-length article in the quest for Salvador Dali, and the list, as quoted, is not even exhaustive.

Although the quest for Dali will doubtless continue, we can certainly get closer to the real Dali than many of his critics imagine. Take, for example, the critic John Russell Taylor, who wrote an opinionated article in *The Times* entitled "Will the Real Dali Ever Stand Up?" The crux of his argument was the fact that the real Dali had never stood up because he lacked both sincerity and the ability to be sensible:

> Obviously the word "sensible" could never be applied to Dali, being as irrelevant to his art as "sincere". He was a showman, a show-off, an illusionist: he deliberately challenged his public to find him out, to discover where the divine madness ended and the commercial calculation began.

There is clearly a non sequitur in this line of reasoning. Dali was indubitably a showman, a show-off and an illusionist, and he obviously challenged his public to find him out, but it does not follow that a showman or a show-off or an illusionist lacks sincerity or is devoid of the ability to be sensible, nor does it follow that one who lays down a challenge lacks sincerity or good sense in so doing, nor that he expects or desires that those challenged should not rise to the challenge offered. The fact that one wears masks does not mean that one lacks a face underneath. The challenge is in revealing the face behind the mask, the truth behind the myth. And the truth is, as we have seen, that Dali had a good deal of sincerity in spite of his showmanship and that he was perfectly capable of being sensible in spite of the absurdity of some of his eccentricities.

To return to John Russell Taylor's question, did the real Dali ever stand up? Yes, he did; and not only did he stand up, but in the important things in life, he stood up to be counted. He might not have been a saint or an angel, but for the most part, he was on the side of the angels and the saints.

63

MR. DAVEY VERSUS THE DEVIL

A True Story

P ICTURE THE SCENE. A black night in the autumn of 1968. The moon is banished. Invisible clouds, hidden by the impenetrable darkness of which they are themselves the cause, cover the earth in an ominous cloak, threatening rain. There's a chill in the air. A solitary walker, out for a midnight stroll in the solitude of the Norfolk countryside, trudges up Houghton Hill. The silence is stifling. The occasional scream of a screech owl and the soft rustling whisper of dying leaves break the unspoken conspiracy of silence that seems to permeate the breeze. At the top of the hill, the walker stumbles across the crumbling remains of two cottages, the remnants of a long-deserted village. Silhouetted against the murkiness, black on gray, their petrified carcasses act as ghostly guards of the dead village's long-forgotten memories. It is then that the walker is surprised by the most startling discovery of all. There, in the midst of the deserted village, far from the nearest hearth or home, he finds himself in the presence of half a dozen parked cars. In the middle of nowhere, in the middle of the night, on an unpaved track leading nowhere ... In these surroundings, the cars strike him as rather alarming incongruities. How did they get here? Why did they come? Who brought them? And where were the owners now?

Furtively, the walker looks around but finds no sign of life. Peering into the darkness, he believes he can see a leafy tower looming skyward, about twenty yards from the path. Straining his ears, he thinks he can hear human voices. Are they singing? Curiosity overcoming fear, he creeps through the overgrowth toward the dark tower. As he edges closer, the voices grow louder. They are joined in some sort of incantation. In Latin. Reaching the tower, he discovers that it is the derelict and ivy-covered ruin of the village church, long neglected, long forgotten and long ignored—except, apparently, by those whose voices he can now hear clearly.

Peering discreetly inside, he stops dead in his tracks, aghast at the sight in front of him. Around an altar in the middle of the nave, flickering in candlelight, are clustered a group of hooded figures, one of whom is holding aloft a skull from which drips blood, or is it wine? Bringing the upturned skull to his lips, he drinks from one of its crevices, the dark liquid spilling wantonly from other orifices of his cadaverous chalice as he swallows lasciviously.

Stifling a gurgling exclamation of disgust, the walker stumbles back into the sanity of the darkness . . .

SCENE TWO: DAVEY TAKES ON THE DEVIL

Picture the scene. Twenty and more years later. June 1992. Another walker stumbles across the ruined church of Houghton-on-the-Hill, this time in broad daylight on a bright summer's day. The walker is Bob Davey, a gray-bearded elderly man, who moved to the nearby village of North Pickenham a few years earlier from Pulborough in Sussex. Clambering through the overgrown churchyard, he enters the church and is confronted by the sickening evidence of satanic practices. The church has been vandalized; the chancel steps have been smashed up; in the center of the nave is a satanic altar. Worst of all is the desecrated grave of a former pastor from which the skull and crossbones have been removed, no doubt for use in the satanists' perverse rite.

There and then the intrepid Mr. Davey resolves to put the devil to flight and to restore the once-proud church of Saint Mary to its former glory. Almost single-handedly, he sets about clearing the undergrowth and overgrowth. He plants flowers and tidies the graves. Finally he begins on the restoration of the church itself, repairing the roof and making many other renovations. He is threatened by death. An anonymous phone call tells him that a satanic curse has been placed on him and that he will "wither and die". As a practicing Christian who trusts in the power of the One who never withers or dies, the intrepid Mr. Davey carries on regardless. The satanists still show signs of returning. Calling on the service of the Norwich unit of the Territorial Army, Mr. Davey lies in wait. When the devil worshipers arrive for one of their midnight debauches, they are greeted by a standing army that springs in ambush from the bushes. Shrieking in fear, the coven scatters, stumbling in fear back into the insanity of their darkness.

SCENE THREE: IT ROSE FROM THE DEAD

Picture the scene. Ten years later. Your intrepid reporter meets the intrepid Mr. Davey. The glorious English sunshine kisses the glorious churchyard of Saint Mary's in a nuptial embrace. The day is as delightful as the Davey!

Mr. Davey's rambunctiously gentle appearance and rustic Sussex accent reminds the reporter of Grizzlebeard in Belloc's *The Four Men*. As the reporter has always desired, in his heart of hearts, to meet Grizzlebeard, he is more than happy to have met his spitting image in Mr. Davey.

Mr. Davey is clearly at home in this charming church, which is hardly surprising since it has literally served as a home from home over the past decade. He is also more than happy to offer any visitor a guided tour of the church's restored splendor. With surprising speed and agility for one so resplendent in years, he ascends the narrow steps and ladder that lead to the roof of the tower. He then proceeds to point, north, south, east and west, indicating with pointed finger and eagle eye the notable landmarks in all directions. The tower of the church, standing as it does on the apex of a hill that, according to Mr. Davey, is the second highest summit in the whole of Norfolk, certainly offers spectacular views for miles around.

The most spectacular views are, however, to be found inside, and not outside, the church. On the east wall of the nave, uncovered during the renovation, are wall paintings depicting the "seat of mercy Trinity", a very rare image of the Holy Trinity. God the Father is seated in the center, with a smaller image below His right hand depicting Christ on the Cross, and above this, a dove representing the Holy Spirit. Archaeologically, this represents a major discovery. According to Mr. Davey, the painting dates back from "at least three hundred years earlier than any "seat of mercy Trinity" wall paintings in England" and, even more intriguing, "at least two hundred years earlier than any 'seat of mercy Trinity' in France". Since it had been thought previously that this particular depiction of the Trinity originated in France, it has left the experts baffled. A major rethink is required. Either there must be older "seat of mercy Trinity" depictions as yet undiscovered in France, or else the "seat of mercy Trinity" might actually have originated in England before being exported to France.

Mr. Davey's enthusiasm for his subject is contagious. He points out with evident relish that this is not the only mystery uncovered during the renovation that has baffled the experts. "No expert agrees on the dating of the other wall paintings. Some say between 1000 and 1020, others insist they are prior to 950, and others suggest that they might be as late as 1090." The wall paintings also represent "some of the earliest examples of the three-dimensional perspective".

The many charms of Saint Mary's are not consigned to the prestigious nature of the wall paintings. The keyhole arch was probably an original feature of the seventh-century Celtic church. Meanwhile, Mr. Davey recounts how he had recovered the original Saxon stoop from a garden in a nearby village, where it was being used as a birdbath. The original Saxon font was being used by a local rector for growing spring bulbs! It is now, thankfully and thanks to Mr. Davey, back in its rightful place in the church.

The parish chest, dating from 1724, is a veritable treasure chest of antiquities. These include a Bible, dating from 1708, and a *Book of Common Prayer*, dating from the following year. Listed in the latter tome are all of the "holy days of obligation" imposed by the "established church" on the people of England, for which they would be fined one shilling for failure to attend. These included 5 November, at which people were compelled to celebrate the foiling of the "traitorous and bloody" Gunpowder Plot and the subsequent execution of Guy Fawkes; the execution of Charles I by "cruel and unreasonable men"; and the restoration of Charles II, which was described as an "unspeakable mercy". Clearly, the restored Saint Mary's is itself the result of "unspeakable mercy" and astounding grace.

Throughout the years, the church has witnessed "unspeakable" events, both ancient and modern. Sacrifice. Celebration. Renewal. Reformation. Defamation. Destruction. Desolation. Desecration. Devil worship. A litany of use and abuse. In the past century, it has witnessed the destruction of the village it had served for centuries. The last villagers left in 1936; four years later, the cottages were demolished. The last regular service was held in Saint Mary's in 1938; and the final service, held in 1944, was celebrated for the benefit of the U.S. airmen stationed nearby. By that time, its roof was gone. There was talk of pulling the church down. Its contents were burned. Then came the satanists, whose practices were witnessed by a local man as early as 1968. He was "thoroughly frightened" by the experience and left the area. For more than twenty years, the devil worshipers attempted to turn the doomed village into the village of the damned. Thanks to one man, they have failed. In recent years, for the first time since the Reformation, the holy sacrifice of the Mass has been celebrated within its once-more-hallowed walls.

The village has died. Its church, suffering an even worse fate, descended into hell. Yet, as with the Master for Whom it was built, it rose from the dead and is once more, in liturgy and praise, ascending to heaven.

64

TOTUS TUUS

A Tribute to a Truly Holy Father

When a Turkish assassin seriously wounded Pope John Paul II, he almost brought to an end one of the most remarkable episcopates in the history of Christianity. Cardinal Wojtyla of Cracow was elected Pope in October 1978. He inherited a divided, demoralized church. But he was exceptionally well-qualified to take over a world religion in crisis. Vigorous and assured, a born mixer and gifted linguist, with long experience of pastoral work, church-state relations and Catholicism's own internal machinery, he also possesses a robust philosophy of Christian humanism, which gives him inner serenity and natural authority.

T HE ABOVE WORDS WERE PUBLISHED on the jacket of *Pope John Paul II and the Catholic Restoration*, an excellent study of the Holy Father by Paul Johnson. The blurb concludes thus: "Paul Johnson describes, step by step, how the new Pope set about imposing order, restoring morale and giving back to 700 million Catholics the security and self-confidence they were beginning to lose." The most remarkable thing about these words is not what they actually say. Few would argue that the present Holy Father has indeed imposed order, raised morale and restored a sense of security and self-confidence to the world's Catholics. Even the sweeping grandeur of the claim that his has been "one of the most remarkable episcopates in the history of Christianity" does not seem an overstatement. No, the remarkable thing about these words is not what they say but when they were said. They were written in 1982, less than four years after that remarkable episcopate had begun. The fact that such words could be written after such a short time is itself an astounding testimony and tribute to the immediate impact that this most indefatigable of men made upon the world.

Pope John Paul II began as he meant to go on. Since then, thanks be to God, he has gone on and on and on. Now, after more than twenty-five years as the Servant of the servants of God, it would be somewhat presumptuous, not to say impossible, to summarize the achievement of the present Holy Father within the confines of a solitary short essay. Prudence precludes such presumption, and the attempt shall not be made.

On a purely personal level, Pope John Paul II has touched my own life in ways too powerful to encapsulate in words. Like so many millions of others around the world, I have been fortunate enough to see him in the flesh on several occasions, most memorably with my wife on our honeymoon, when the Holy Father blessed our marriage. Ten years earlier, I had seen him on his own native soil in Poland at a truly memorable World Youth Day. Our tiny English contingent was lost in a sea of young people from all over the world. The noisy presence of thousands upon thousands of boisterously joyous young people from Spain, Italy and many other countries waving their nation's flags in a sea of fervor that seemed to bear witness to Belloc's "Europe of the Faith" stays with me as a memory of particular resonance and poignancy. The multitude of foreign visitors was reinforced by the million or so Poles, many of whom had walked hundreds of miles on a pilgrimage of thanksgiving for the deliverance of Poland from nearly half a century of communist oppression. Even more impressive were the many pilgrims from Russia and Ukraine who had walked even further to pay homage to the man who, perhaps more than any other, had helped to bring down the communist empire.

I shall conclude my own short and entirely inadequate tribute to His Holiness by returning to the place whence I began. Paul Johnson, in his book on the Holy Father, recorded that in August 1978, just before the conclave opened that would elect him Pope, Cardinal Wojtyla, as he then was, included among his devotional exercises in Rome a visit to the tomb of Josemaría Escrivá de Balaguer y Albas, the founder of Opus Dei. Shortly after becoming Pope, he wrote a letter to Opus Dei, dated 15 November 1978, on the occasion of its fiftieth anniversary, congratulating it on its work. Thereafter, Opus Dei found in the person of the Holy Father a powerful champion of its work. As early as 1982, Paul Johnson saw the significance of this partnership in faith and works:

> Opus Dei appears to be the kind of instrument John Paul needs to assist him in carrying through his restoration on a permanent basis: orthodox, loyal, dedicated, superbly organized and disciplined, ubiquitous and youthful.
>
> The Fact that Opus Dei has many enemies, has been the object of a liberal campaign in the media, and is widely presented as obscurantist and reactionary will not deter John Paul ... One virtue he does not lack is moral courage, including the courage to stand out against the conventional wisdom. He is rightly suspicious of fashion, especially in religious matters. He detects in Opus Dei some highly unfashionable merits. That is in itself high commendation to him. (184–85)

Once again, the words written more than twenty years ago are at least as applicable today. When Pope John Paul II began his twenty-fifth year as Pontiff, he celebrated the occasion with an even greater one. He presided over the canonization of Blessed Josemaría, the founder of the "unfashionable" Opus Dei, proving once again that, though fashions come and go, the Faith remains. Thus we see the undying and imperishable unity between the Church Triumphant and the Church Militant; a saint being made by a saint in the making.

65

FAITH AND THE FEMININE

A S Catholics, we should celebrate the feminine. We should
celebrate its beauty—which is certainly breathtaking—and also
its centrality. We should celebrate the fact that the feminine is fundamental. It is at the very core of life itself, the very heart of humanity.
Indeed, mystically and paradoxically, it is at the very Heart of God
Himself. Thus the Church is both the Mystical Body of Christ and
the Bride of Christ at one and the same time. In the mystical marriage of Christ and His Church, we see how the Bride of Christ has
become one flesh with the Bridegroom. The Church is the perfect
archetypal unity of masculine and feminine. She *is* the sacramental
union of marriage; she is the marriage to which every other marriage
owes its significance.

It goes without saying, of course, that none of these thoughts is
original, in the sense of being originally mine. "Mine" is always a
minefield of self-delusion. As Saint Augustine observed, the only thing
that is truly mine is a lie. Everything else, everything *other*, is a gift.
Thus, in this self-centered sense, the only truly original thing is sin!
Such an understanding of the nature of reality animated Chesterton's
self-effacing assertion that he had spent his life diligently discovering
things that other people had already discovered before him. In the
case of the ecclesiology outlined above, the mystical union of masculine and feminine was expounded with timeless beauty in the wisdom
of Solomon and was interpreted with almost matching beauty by Saint
Bernard in his sermons on Solomon's Song of Songs. Then, of course,
there is the Gospel itself, in which Christ teaches the essential truths
in terms of the Bridegroom and His Bride.

Finally, one cannot discuss the place of the feminine at the heart of reality without paying homage to the Mother of God, she who is the feminine personified and the feminine perfected. Mary's faith and humility at the Annunciation was the final triumph of the eternal feminine over her ancient adversary. It was the triumph of her eternal fertility over her enemy's infernal sterility. Her *fiat* was the annunciation of her victory carrying with it the logical and theological assumption of her coronation as Queen of Heaven.

If, however, the feminine is at the very heart of the joyful and glorious mysteries of reality, it is also the broken heart in the depths of humanity's mysterious sorrows. The feminine is not only the core but the crux; it is the *cri de coeur* at the foot of the Cross. The sword that pierced the Son of Man also pierced the Immaculate Heart of His Mother. Mary, impassioned and impaled, shares her Son's suffering. His Passion is hers also. Thus the feminine is the crux as well as the core of reality. It is crucial because it too was crucified.

Throughout the twentieth century, the feminine was crucified by feminism. Acting like a female Faust selling her soul for an illusory dream of "liberty" and "equality", feminism stripped women of their womanhood, scourged them with the Promethean promise of promiscuity, crowned them with the thorns of contraception and laid upon them the cross of futile and infertile sexual relationships, rooted in lust masquerading as love. Finally, the feminine is nailed to the cross of male lasciviousness, where she is held up as an object to be leered at, abused and ultimately scorned. Such is the legacy of woman's "liberation".

The feminine, hanging upon the cross of feminist crassness, thirsts. She thirsts as her Master thirsted upon His own archetypical Cross. She hungers. The feminine, famished and starved of the fertile fruits of her own natural motherhood, seeks in vain for fertility amid the sterility of the just deserts of the deserts of modernity. Eventually, she dies. Thus has feminism brought about the death of the feminine on the altar of *male*volent desire.

The feminine is not vanquished, however. Following her death comes her resurrection. Following in her Master's footsteps, she rises from the dead. Her womb, no longer a tomb of false philosophies and empty promises, brings forth new life. As faithless feminism fades, we witness with gratitude the enduring faith of the feminine.

66

OUR LIFE, OUR SWEETNESS AND OUR HOPE

*B*EATI QUORUM TECTA SUNT PECCATA. Blessed are they whose sins are forgiven. Blessed indeed! For, and to turn from the ancient majesty of the penitential psalms to the modern medium of an Elvis Presley gospel song, "I remember my days of darkness, without sunshine or light to lead the way." I still remember, and every time I remember, I recall once more my blessings. Thus the Trinitarian life of the soul, centered on the life-giving trinity of confession, contrition and satisfaction, leads us from the darkness of ignorance and sin to the sunshine of grace and the light of His Presence.

It was not always so.

In the years before the light of Christ entered my dismal life, I groped in the gloom of my own grievances, griping at others in the miasmal myopia caused by the plank lodged obstinately in my eye. One of my biggest grievances was against the Catholic Church. She, it seemed, was to blame for so much. The ignorance of the Dark Ages, the ignominiousness of the Middle Ages and, of course, the infamy of the Inquisition. I considered myself so much smarter than those ignorant papists who still clung superstitiously to their antiquated Creed. I was so "clever" that I became embroiled in the bigoted barbarism of the politics of Northern Ireland. Thus, as a "brother" of the Orange Order, I learned that the Church of Rome was the Scarlet Woman, the Whore of Babylon and the Servant of Satan. Similarly, the Pope of Rome was not merely a foolish or evil man, he was the anti-Christ who sought to lead Christians away from Christ. I was not so much green with envy against the Church of Rome, but orange with pride. God help me! *Beati quorum tecta sunt peccata.*

404

No Pope! No Rome Rule! No Surrender! *"No nuns and no priests, no rosary beads; every day is the Twelfth of July!"* No! No! No! The affirmation *ad nauseam* of the negative. I was under the influence of the anathema anesthetic, the deranged drug that dupes and dopes the bigot and blinds and binds him to his blunder. *Beati quorum tecta sunt peccata.*

One result of the blindness of my bigotry was an implicit distrust of our Lady. Not that I would have dreamed of calling her "our Lady"; she was simply "Mary". Since she was "worshiped" by the Catholics, who even used superstitious beads to pray to her, she had to be guilty by association. She was a goddess of idolatry and therefore not to be trusted. Father, forgive me, for I knew not what I did.

Beati quorum . . .

Times change and so do people. Sins are committed and yet are forgiven. It is, therefore, with all due humility that I confess my devotion to the Blessed Mother of God. In doing so, I am tempted to echo the words, and the warning, of G. K. Chesterton that anything I say on the subject of the Mother of God could be tainted by enthusiasm. In fact, and instead, I am reduced to echoing the words of T. S. Eliot: "I feel that anything I can say about such a subject is trivial. I feel so completely inferior in [her] presence—there seems really nothing to do but to point to [her] and be silent." (Actually, Eliot said these words in honor of Dante, but they seem so apposite to my own feelings of inadequacy in the presence of the Blessed Virgin that I have tampered with the gender of the original quotation to suit my need. I am confident that neither Eliot nor Dante will take offense at such tampering.)

Since "anything I can say about such a subject is trivial", I shall remain silent and point to others who have said what I would like to say so much better than I could ever hope to do. I shall commence, in the company of Eliot, by pointing to Dante and remaining silent. It was he, in the *Paradiso*, who put the following sublime words onto the lips of the heavenly vision of Saint Bernard:

> Thou Virgin Mother, daughter of thy Son,
> Humble and high beyond all other creature,
> The limit fixed of the eternal counsel,

Thou art the one who such nobility
To human nature gave, that its Creator
Did not disdain to make himself its creature.

Similar praise and honor to her who is "our life, our sweetness and
our hope" was the inspiration for the anonymous author of the fifteenth-
century "Carol" that ends with this charmingly simple, yet utterly
profound, verse:

Mother and maiden
Was never none but she;
Well may such a lady
God's mother be.

Finally, my dumb devotion finds voice in "A Hymn to the Virgin". It
dates (how appropriate an example of divine symmetry!) from the
very Middle Ages that I had once spurned but which now I honor as
the bearer of the light that penetrated my darkness:

Of one that is so fair and bright
Velut maris stella,
Brighter than the day is light,
Parens et puella:
I cry to thee, thou see to me,
Lady, pray thy Son for me,
Tam pia,
That I might come to thee
Maria.

67

THE PRESENCE THAT CHRISTMAS PRESENTS

W HAT IS CHRISTMAS? Presumably the asking of such a question is hardly necessary in the pages of this volume, whose readers have no doubt already found their way to Bethlehem and have discovered its priceless treasure for themselves. The question is, however, not as superfluous as it seems. The billion people living under the cloak of Islam have probably never asked the question. Certainly they have never answered it correctly. Similarly, those caught in the Confucian confusion of China or those hindered by Hinduism in India have failed to ask or answer the question. It is a question to which the Buddhists remain blind, and its answer the Sikhs have not found.

These many millions who have never asked or answered the question are barely culpable. They simply cannot see because their faiths have made them blind. But what of the many millions who have asked the question but have answered it incorrectly? What of the millions of agnostic consumers who "celebrate" Christmas but have apparently rejected its meaning? Truly they are a greater cause of sorrow during this season of joy than any number of heedless Muslims, Hindus or Sikhs. They are not the blind who *cannot* see but the blind who *will not* see.

Perhaps the quest for the real Christmas could be presented to these doubting millions by asking a different question. Rather than asking what Christmas is, perhaps we should ask what it isn't. It isn't an annual shopping spree; it isn't advertisement *ad nauseam*; it isn't the annual office party, nor is it the hangover that follows it. It isn't any of these perennial seasonal rituals—all of which, in any case, take place in the season of Advent before Christmas has even begun.

407

Does such a "negative" attitude place one in the role of an Eben-ezer Scrooge, grumbling self-righteously at the desire of others to cel-ebrate? Do sober-minded Christians wish to celebrate Christmas by spoiling the party? Certainly not. And heaven forbid! The spirit of Christmas might not be found in the ringing of a cash register, nor on television, nor in the bottom of the twelfth glass of whiskey; but it is to be found in the ringing of church bells, the singing of carols and the sharing of a bottle of the finest Scottish malt with friends. It is to be found in the giving of gifts, the faces of children, red-nosed rein-deer, red-nosed Santas, red-nosed carol singers, red-breasted robins and glowing fires. It is to be found in snowmen, snowballs and snowflakes; and in the holly and the ivy, the mistletoe and the wine. Yule logs, Christmas trees, colored lights, candles, plum pudding, fruit cake and a partridge in a pear tree. It is to be found in all these things . . . but all these things are not it.

"It" is something infinitely greater, infinitely larger, infinitely smaller; it is infinitely more beautiful, more bountiful, more blissful, more bash-ful and more bold. It is the Kiss of God on the unworthy lips of man. It is man warming himself in the physical Presence of God. It is God warming Himself in the physical womb of a woman. It is humility exalted. It is Life. It is Love. It is the love of life and the life of love. It is He. His is the Presence that Christmas presents.

Life . . . Love . . . Man . . . God . . . Man-God.

The Kiss of Life.

What is Christmas? Christmas is He—and He is worth celebrating!

May He who breathes life into Christmas bring its message of love, its warmth and its light to Everyman. May God bless us every one.

INDEX

A Rebours (Huysmans), 34–36, 38, 336
"Absolution" (Sassoon), 164
Acton, Lord, 250
Adam, Karl, 14
Ades, Dawn, 386–87
Allegory of Love, The (Lewis), 316
Alton, Lord David, 85
Angelic Crucifixion (Dali), 389–90
Angelus, The (Millet), 203, 391
Anglican Difficulties (1850 Newman
   lectures), 29
Animal Farm (Orwell), 53, 101–2
Anti-Protonic Assumption (Dali), 389
Apes of God, The (Wyndham Lewis), 184
apologetics, cultural, 14–18
Apologetics and Catholic Doctrine
   (Sheehan), 14
Apologia (Newman), 14, 26, 46, 142,
   274, 277
"Arbor Vitae" (Sassoon), 166
Arthurian legacy, 267, 269–71
"Ash Wednesday" (Eliot), 165, 176
Asquith, Katherine, 115
"At Dawn, Look to the East"
   (Caldecott), 304
Athenaeum, 123
Auden, W. H., 196
Augustine, Saint, 15, 116, 402
Autobiography (Chesterton), 33, 69
"Autumn" (Campbell), 201
Autumn Cannibalism (Dali), 386, 387
Avowals and Denials (Chesterton), 95

Bad Child's Book of Beasts, The (Belloc),
   110
Balfour, Charlotte, 133

Balfour, Reggie, 130–31
Ball and the Cross, The (Chesterton), 44,
   69, 106–7, 307, 390
Ballad of Reading Gaol, The (Wilde), 36,
   37, 341
Ballad of the White Horse, The
   (Chesterton), 42, 67, 284
"Ballad of Walsingham, The"
   (anonymous), 28
"Ballade of Illegal Ornaments" (Belloc),
   45
Barbey d'Aurevilly, Jules, 36
Barfield, Owen, 329–32
Baring, Maurice, 39–41, 128–37, 214
   and Belloc, 39, 40–41, 130, 133, 135
   and Chesterton, 39, 40–41, 131–32,
      135
   conversion of, 39, 132–34
   on Dante's *Divine Comedy*, 374–75
   early life and education of, 129–31
   and Waugh's *Brideshead Revisited*, 54
Barker, Pat, 160
"Base Details" (Sassoon), 163
Basil Howe: A Story of Young Love
   (Chesterton), 80–84
Battle of Agincourt (Drayton), 157–58, 161
Baudelaire, Charles, 34, 36, 77, 335, 336
Beardsley, Aubrey, 34, 77, 337
Beerbohm, Max, 128
"Beethoven" (Baring), 134
Belinda (Belloc), 45, 71–72, 111, 112
Belloc, Elodie Hogan, 109–10
Belloc, Hilaire
   apologia of, 73–74, 110
   and Baring, 39, 40–41, 130, 133, 135
   and Benson, 46, 140

Belloc, Hilaire (*continued*)
 and Brooke, 308
 and Copper, 125–27
 and distributism, 50–51, 73, 110,
  247–49, 260
 on faith of Old Europe, 167
 liberals' misunderstandings of, 91
 life of, 109–11
 novels of, 45, 71–72, 111
 personality of, 111
 poetry of, 45, 68–69, 111
 Reformation studies by, 46, 110, 140
 and the theology of place, 114–16
 and Waugh, 54, 216
 and Wells, 107, 111
 and World War I, 51, 172
 See also Chesterbelloc; *Path to Rome,*
  The (Belloc)
Benson, A. C., 139
Benson, E. F., 139
Benson, E. W., 45, 138
Benson, Robert Hugh, 45–47, 138–45
 and Belloc, 46, 140
 and Chesterton, 47, 142
 conversion of, 45–46, 138
 death of, 46, 143
 family of, 45, 138–39
 and Knox, 47, 48, 142
 and Maisie Ward, 150
 and Newman, 45–46
 novels of, 46, 139–41
 other writing, 46, 141–42
 "triumphalism" of, 143–45
 and the truth of the Church, 144–45
 and Waugh, 216
 and Wilde, 47, 142–43
"Beowulf: The Monsters and the
 Critics" (Tolkien), 315
Bergonzi, Bernard, 160–61
Bernanos, Georges, 223–24
Bernard, Saint, 402, 405
"Binsley Poplars" (Hopkins), 281–82
biographies of Christian writers, 214–15
Birzer, Bradley J., 261–65, 298–99, 301

Blackbird Singing: Poems and Lyrics
 1965–1999 (McCartney), 359–60
Blake, William, 283, 371
Blessings in Disguise (Guinness), 57
Bloomsbury group, 135, 186, 192–93,
 231, 232
Bloy, Leon, 35
Bookworm (BBC program), 296
Borrow, George, 266, 268
Boyd, Father Ian, 302
Bratt Tolkien, Edith, 242
Brave New World (Huxley), 46, 141
Braybrooke, Patrick, 79
Breton, Andre, 385
Brideshead Revisited (Waugh), 53–54,
 108, 177, 212–13
Bridges, Robert, 30, 32
Brighton Rock (Greene), 52, 218
Bring Me My Bow (Seymour), 153
Broken Record (Campbell), 203, 206
Brooke, Rupert, 158, 170, 172, 308–9
Brown, George Mackay, 268
Browne, Sir Thomas, 219
Bruner, Kurt D., 299
Burke, Edmund, 250
Burrows, John, 340
Bystander, 211

C (Baring), 39, 134–35
Caesar, Adrian, 161
Caldecott, Leonie, 299, 304
Caldecott, Stratford, 302, 303
Callista (Newman), 25, 274, 277–78
Campbell, Mary, 187, 197, 201, 205,
 206, 209, 236
Campbell, Roy, 184–209
 and Africa, 184–85, 190, 191, 200–201
 conversion of, 187, 194–95, 194–96,
  206, 388
 early influences, 184–86, 190–91,
  200–201
 early poems, 190–91, 194, 201
 and Eliot, 184, 185
 and Fascism, 197–98, 238

and *The Flaming Terrapin*, 184, 185,
  186, 191–92, 198
and *The Georgiad*, 52, 186–87,
  192–93, 206
and the Inklings, 235–39
and John of the Cross, 204–5, 391
and Lewis, 235–39
life of, 184–87, 190
and *Mithraic Emblems*, 187, 188,
  194–95, 204–5, 206, 361
in Provence, 193–94, 204
religion and politics of, 189–99
and Sitwell, 182, 184
in Spain, 187, 194, 200–209
and the Spanish civil war, 187–88,
  196–97, 209, 216, 236, 238, 388
and subsidiarity, 198
and Tolkien, 235–36, 237
Campbell Lyle, Anna, 201, 202–3, 208
Campion, Edmund, Saint, 17
"Candlemas" (Baring), 134
Caraman, Philip, 216
"Carol" (anonymous), 406
Carpenter, Humphrey, 243
Carter, Lin, 286
Catechism of the Catholic Church, 73, 92,
  260
*Catholic Intellectuals and the Challenge of
  Democracy* (Corrin), 89–92
Catholicism and the true North, 266–68
Cat's Cradle (Baring), 135
Cautionary Tales for Children (Belloc),
  69, 110
Cavell, Edith, 309
Celebrating Middle-earth (West, ed.), 299
Centesimus annus (John Paul II), 73, 92
Cervantes, Miguel, 169
Chambers Biographical Dictionary, 227
Characters of the Reformation (Belloc), 110
Cherwell, The, 236
Chesterbelloc, 65–75
  as defenders of the Faith, 73–74
  and distributism, 50–51, 73, 247–49,
    252, 260

mutual admiration of Chesterton and
    Belloc, 66–67
  Orwell on, 128
  and respective bodies of work, 45,
    67–72
  and Seymour, 153–54
  Shaw's affectionate attack on, 45,
    65–66
  as socioeconomic and political
    commentators, 50–51, 73
  Wells on, 74
  See also Belloc, Hilaire; Chesterton,
    G.K.
"Chesterbelloc, The: A Lampoon"
  (Shaw), 65
Chesterton, Frances, 44, 47, 78, 132
Chesterton, G.K., 41–45
  apologia of, 73–74
  artistic reaction to wasteland of
    modernity, 51, 167–69, 172, 372
  and Baring, 39, 40–41, 131–32,
    135
  and Benson, 47, 142
  and the Christian literary revival,
    33–34, 41–45, 59, 105–6, 108,
    128, 282–86
  conversion of, 78, 211, 212
  as critic of modern trends in poetry,
    180, 181
  on Dante, 372, 374
  debate with Darrow, 212
  and Decadence, early interest in,
    33–34, 59, 76–77, 81–83
  and Decadence, reaction against, 77,
    123, 169
  and distributism, 50–51, 73, 103,
    247–49, 260, 262
  and early novel *Basil Howe*, 80–84
  and Eliot, 50, 105–6
  on evolution/revolution, 22
  exchange with Jackson on
    absolute/relative truth, 377
  and Fascism, 93–104, 216
  on Hardy, 221

Chesterton, G. K. (*continued*)
  idealized view of pre-Reformation
    England, 282
  and Jews/anti-Semitism, 97–98
  and Knox, 47, 49, 142
  on Mary, 405
  on modern art, 382
  novels of, 42–45, 69–71, 80–84
  and orthodoxy, 105–8
  poetry of, 42, 45, 67–69
  popularity with contemporary
    politicians, 85–88
  and Saint Francis, 42, 76–79
  and Shaw, 44, 59, 107, 329–30
  socioeconomic and political
    commentary, 50–51, 73, 86–88,
    94–98, 102–3
  and Thompson, 33
  and Tolkien, 247–48, 282–86
  on tradition, 41–42, 57, 105–8,
    285–86
  on Vatican II, 91
  on the Victorians, 22
  and Wilde, 76, 82, 340
  and World War I, 51, 172, 307
  youth of, 76–77, 81–82
  See also Chesterbelloc
Chichikov, Pavel, 361–63
"Choosing a Mast" (Campbell), 201
Christ of Saint John of the Cross (Dali),
    391
Christian Herald, 340
Christian literary revival, 25–30, 33–34,
    39–55, 58–61
  Baring and, 39–41, 128
  Belloc and, 128
  Benson and, 45–47, 48, 138–45
  Chesterton and, 33–34, 41–45, 59,
    105–6, 108, 128, 282–86
  and deaths of Nietzsche and Wilde,
    58–59
  Eliot and, 50–51, 60, 105–6
  Greene and, 52–53
  Knox and, 47–49

  Lewis and, 55, 60–61
  Maisie Ward and, 151
  Newman and, 25–30, 29, 34, 41, 59,
    274–78, 287
  and the quest for truth, 277–80
  and the rejection of modern
    philosophy, 276
  Tolkien and, 55, 60–61, 231, 272–87
  Waugh and, 51–52, 54, 55–56, 60,
    216–17
  World War I and, 50–51
  World War II and postwar pessimism,
    53–55
  See also modern English literature,
    tradition and conversion in;
    modernity, cultural reaction to
    wasteland of
Christmas, 407–8
Chronicles of Narnia (Lewis), 288
Churchill, Winston, 100, 227
Civilta Cattolica, La (Jesuit quarterly),
    341
Clark, Ken, 85
Clausen, Christopher, 284
Coat without Seam, The (Baring), 135,
    136
Cobbett, William, 283
Coleridge, Samuel Taylor, 22–23, 37–38
Collected Poems (Baring), 39
Collins, Dorothy, 80
Collins, Michael, 87
Come Rack! Come Rope! (Benson), 46,
    48, 131, 140–41
Comedians, The (Greene), 218
Complete Guide to Self-Sufficiency, The
    (Seymour), 153
Complete Memoirs of George Sherston, The
    (Sassoon), 165
"Concert-Interpretation" (Sassoon), 164
Confessions of a Convert (Benson), 46,
    138, 142, 143–44, 150
Conlon, Denis J., 80–81
Conversation Piece, The (Gunn painting),
    39, 128

"Converted to Rome: Why It Has
  Happened to Me" (Waugh), 52,
  210–11
Cooper, Gary, 352–53
Copleston, Father F. C., 14
Copper, Bob, 125–27
Corrin, Jay P., 89–92
Coulombe, Charles A., 245, 282
Crucifixion (Corpus Hypercubus) (Dali),
  389
Cruise of the "Nona", The (Belloc), 111,
  114
cubism, 383, 390
Curry, Patrick, 321

da Vinci, Leonardo, 134, 381
Daily Chronicle, 37, 123
Daily Express, 52, 210–13
Daily Herald, 164
Daily Mirror, 179
Daily Telegraph, 296, 338
Dali, Salvador, 383, 384–93
  conversion of, 388
  early life and work of, 384–85
  and Fascism, 385–86
  and the Spanish civil war, 386–88
  and surrealism, 385–86
Dante Alighieri, 370–75
  and Baring, 136
  and Decadence, 38, 336, 337
  and Eliot, 51, 173–74, 176, 178,
    370–71
  on Mary, 405–6
  and modernity, 371–74
  and Newman's The Dream of
    Gerontius, 27
Danton (Belloc), 110
Daphne Adeane (Baring), 40, 135
Darby and Joan (Baring), 40, 133
D'Arcy, Martin, 216
Darrow, Clarence, 212
Darwin, Charles, 191
Davis, Sir Peter Maxwell, 268
Dawson, Christopher, 100, 150, 216

Day-Lewis, Cecil, 196
Dayrell-Browning, Vivien, 220
de la Mare, Walter, 330
De Profundis (Wilde), 36, 47, 142, 341
Dead Letters (Baring), 134
"Dead Samurai to Death, The"
  (Baring), 134
Decadent movement
  Chesterton's counter-Decadence, 77,
    123, 169
  Chesterton's youthful interest in,
    33–34, 59, 76–77, 81–83
  and conversions of Decadents, 77,
    335–37
  and Dante, 38, 336, 337
  and Eliot, 60
  English, 34, 336–37
  French, 33–35, 336–37
  and Huysmans, 34–36, 336
  sin and despair for, 34–35, 38
  and Wilde, 34, 35, 37–38, 77, 82, 337
Decline and Fall (Waugh), 60
deconstructionism, 231–32, 234
"democracy" and Catholic intellectuals,
  89–92
Diminutive Dramas (Baring), 134
Discovery of America by Christopher
  Columbus, The (Dali), 391
Disintegration of the Persistence of Memory,
  The (Dali), 389
distributism
  Belloc and, 50–51, 73, 110, 247–49,
    260
  Chesterton and, 50–51, 73, 103,
    247–49, 260, 262
  Seymour and, 153–54
  and social teaching of Pope Leo XIII,
    73, 92, 103, 248–49, 260
  and subsidiarity, 73, 92, 252, 260
  and Tolkien's The Lord of the Rings,
    247–49, 252
Divine Comedy (Dante), 51, 178,
  370–75, 392
Dix, Otto, 159, 170, 383

Dodd, Philip, 381
Don Quixote (Cervantes), 169, 392
"Donkey, The" (Chesterton), 67
Douglas, Lord Alfred, 58, 338, 339,
    343, 344
Dowson, Ernest, 77, 337
Drayton, Michael, 157–58, 161
Dream of Gerontius, The (Newman), 27,
    274, 275
"Driving Cattle to Casas Buenas"
    (Campbell), 209
"Drowned Suns" (Sitwell), 179
Dublin Review, 149
"Dulce et Decorum Est" (Owen), 51,
    159, 171–72
Duns Scotus, 31, 282
Durrell, Lawrence, 196
"Dying Reservist, The" (Baring), 134
"Dynamite" (Chichikov), 362

Ecumenical Council, The (Dali), 391
ecumenism, Benson and, 143, 145
Edwards, Owen Dudley, 303–4
"Elegy in a Country Churchyard"
    (Chesterton), 51, 172
Eliot, T. S.
    and the Anglo-Catholic tradition,
        29
    artistic reaction to wasteland of
        modernity, 50, 51, 60, 172–76,
        177, 178
    and Barfield, 330
    and Campbell, 184, 185
    and Chesterton, 50, 105–6
    and the Christian literary revival,
        50–51, 60, 105–6
    conversion of, 51, 175, 195
    and Dante, 51, 173–74, 176, 178,
        370–71
    and Decadence, 60
    on Hopkins, 30–31
    on Mary, 405
    and modern trends in poetry,
        179–81

and The Waste Land, 50, 51, 60,
    172–74, 179–80, 191–92
    and Waugh, 60, 216
"Empty Church" (Chichikov), 363
En Route (Huysmans), 39, 336
"End of the Road, The" (Belloc), 45,
    68, 111, 122–23
England, post-Reformation, 367–69
"Englishman, The" (Chesterton), 68
Enigma of William Tell, The (Dali),
    386
Escrivá de Balaguer, Josemaría, 400–401
Essay on the Restoration of Property, An
    (Belloc), 73, 110, 153
"Europe of the Faith" (Belloc), 14
Everlasting Man, The (Chesterton), 14,
    107–8, 110, 330
"Exposure" (Owen), 159
"Extreme Unction" (Dowson), 337

Fabian Society, 231
Fabiola: A Tale of the Catacombs
    (Wiseman), 25–26
Façade (Sitwell), 179–80
Fascism
    Campbell and, 197–98, 238
    Chesterton and, 93–104, 216
    Dali and, 385–86
    defining, 93, 95, 100–102
    of Franco, 95, 98–99, 101
    of Hitler, 95–98, 99
    of Mussolini, 93–95
    Orwell and, 101–2
    and the Spanish civil war, 91–92,
        99–101, 197–98
    and state power/state control, 102–3
    Waugh on, 100–101
"Father Brown" stories (Chesterton),
    45, 212
Fellowship of the Ring, The (film), 323
feminine, 402–3
"Fight, The" (Campbell), 206–7
"Fight to a Finish" (Sassoon), 51, 159,
    163, 170–71

Finding God in The Lord of the Rings
   (Bruner and Ware), 299
"Finis Coronat Opus" (Thompson), 38
"Fish, The" (Chesterton), 67
Fisher, David, 97–98
Flaming Terrapin, The (Campbell), 184,
   185, 186, 191–92, 198
Fleurs du mal, Les (Baudelaire), 36
Flieger, Verlyn, 298, 304
Flowering Rifle (Campbell), 236, 239
Flying Inn, The (Chesterton), 45, 68,
   69, 304
Food of the Gods, The (Wells), 88
"For the Dead" (Newman), 27
Forster, E. M., 39, 135
Four Men, The (Belloc), 111, 114
   and Chesterton's *The Flying Inn*, 45
   Grizzlebeard of, 116, 126, 396
   literary excellence of, 72
   and metaphor, 116
   songs/verse of, 68, 69
   and the theology of place, 115
Four Quartets (Eliot), 176, 178
Francis of Assisi, Saint, 42, 76–79
Franco, Francisco, 92, 95, 98–99, 100,
   238, 387. *See also* Spanish civil war
Frankenstein (Shelley), 345
Friday's Business (Baring), 129
Friendly Persuasion (film), 352–53

Galsworthy, John, 42
Garbowski, Christopher, 299
Garth, John, 306–10
"General, The" (Sassoon), 159, 163
George, Lloyd, 87
Georgiad, The (Campbell), 52, 186–87,
   192–93, 206
Gibson, Mel, 15, 356–58
Gill, Eric, 151
G. K.'s Weekly, 96
"Glory of Women" (Sassoon), 163
God and the Atom (Knox), 53
Gold Coast Customs (Sitwell), 182
"Golden Prison, The" (Newman), 27

"Golgotha" (Sassoon), 159, 164
"Golgotha's Mary" (Chichikov), 362–63
"Gollum, Frodo and the Catholic
   Novel" (Edwards), 303–4
Gospel according to Tolkien, The (Wood),
   299
Gosse, Edmund, 180–81
Gothic revival, 24–25
Goya, Francisco, 386
Grant, Duncan, 231
Graves, Robert, 162–63
Gray, John, 337
Gray, Thomas, 172
Great Divorce, The (Lewis), 61
"Great Inspirations" (Radio Four
   broadcast), 85
Greene, Dana, 147–52
Greene, Graham, 52–53, 161, 218–22
   as "Catholic writer", 52–53, 272
   and Chesterton, 42, 108
   conversion of, 108, 219–21, 222
   early life of, 219
   novels of, 52, 218–19, 222, 224, 272
   vertical vision of, 223–24
Greer, Germaine, 297
Greeves, Arthur, 266
Grief Observed, A (Lewis), 360
Griffiths, Alan, 330–31
Griffiths, Philip, 338
Guardian, 296–97
Guinness, Alec, 57, 183
Gulliver's Travels (Swift), 345
Gunn, Sir James, 39, 128

Hague, William, 85
"Ha'nacker Mill" (Belloc), 45, 68, 111,
   115, 125
Handful of Dust, A (Waugh), 60, 176
Hardy, Thomas, 221
Harry Potter books (Rowling), 288
"Harvest in Russia" (Baring), 134
Have You Anything to Declare? (Baring),
   135–36
Helbeck of Bannisdale (Ward), 136, 214

"Heresy of Race, The" (Chesterton), 96
Heretics (Chesterton), 47, 59, 88, 107, 131, 142
Hidden Presence, A: The Catholic Imagination of J. R. R. Tolkien (Boyd and Caldecott, eds.), 302–5
High Noon (film), 352
Hilaire Belloc Society, 125
History of England (Belloc), 110
Hitler, Adolf, 95–98, 99, 244, 267
Hobbit, The (Tolkien), 258, 303
Holland, Merlin, 338
Hollis, Christopher, 100
"Hollow Men, The" (Eliot), 60, 174–75, 176
Hollywood
   moral responsibility in, 351–55
   and the Western worldview, 348–50
   See also *Lord of the Rings, The* (film); *Passion of the Christ, The* (film)
Hooper, Walter, 332
Hopkins, Gerard Manley, 30–32, 33, 34, 161, 281–82, 362
"Hound of Heaven, The" (Thompson), 37, 39
Hours, The (film), 175–76
How the Reformation Happened (Belloc), 46, 110, 140
Howe, Lord, 85–88
Humanae vitae (Paul VI), 90
Huxley, Aldous, 46, 141, 161
Huysmans, J. K.
   and Baring, 39
   on Baudelaire's exploration of the soul, 336
   conversion of, 36, 77, 336
   and Decadence, 34–36, 336
"Hymn" (Chesterton), 67
"Hymn to the Virgin, A" (anonymous), 406

Ibsen, Henrik, 372–73
Illustrated London News, 95
impressionism, 382

Inferno (Dante), 51, 373
Ingrams, Richard, 225–26
Inklings, 231–34, 244
   Barfield and, 329–32
   Campbell and, 235–39
   Lewis and, 231–33, 235–39, 244
   Tolkien and, 231, 235–36, 237, 239, 244
Institute of Contemporary Art (ICA), 380–81
Insurrection versus Resurrection (Ward), 152
Irish Independent, 341
Irish Statesman, 185
Islam, militant, 348–50

Jackson, Holbrook, 377
Jackson, Peter, 15–16, 300, 311, 323–25, 326–28, 351. See also *Lord of the Rings, The* (film)
Jacobson, Howard, 296
Jebb, Dom Philip, 123–24
Jeffreys, Susan, 296
Jews and anti-Semitism, 97–98
John of the Cross, Saint, 204–5, 336, 391
John Paul II, Pope, 73, 92, 151, 399–401
John XXIII, Pope, 392
Johnson, Lionel, 77, 337
Johnson, Paul, 399–401
Jones, David, 150, 151, 161
Jones, Griff Rhys, 296
J. R. R. Tolkien: Myth, Morality and Religion (Purtill), 298–99, 301
J. R. R. Tolkien's Sanctifying Myth (Birzer), 261–65, 298, 301

Kafka, Franz, 43
Kaye-Smith, Sheila, 211
Keating, Karl, 14
Keep the Aspidistra Flying (Orwell), 128
Kenny, Mary, 340
Kerr, Douglas, 161
King Henry V (Shakespeare), 158

Knox, Ronald
  and Benson, 47, 48, 142
  and Chesterton, 47, 49, 142
  on Chesterton's *The Everlasting Man*,
    107–8
  and the Christian literary revival,
    47–49
  conversion of, 47, 48, 49, 59, 142,
    211, 212
  and the Spanish civil war, 100
  and *A Spiritual Aeneid*, 48–49, 142
  and Waugh, 48–49, 212, 213, 216
Kreeft, Peter, 299, 305
Kristallnacht: The Nazi Night of Terror
  (Read and Fisher), 97–98

Lady Windemere's Fan (Wilde), 341
Las Vergnas, Raymond, 133
"Leaf by Niggle" (Tolkien), 249, 275,
  326–27
"Lenten Illuminations" (Sassoon), 165
Leo XIII, Pope, 73, 92, 103, 110, 151,
  248–49, 260, 282
"Lepanto" (Chesterton), 42, 45, 67–68,
  167–69
Levine, George, 26–27, 274
Lewis, C. S.
  on allegory, 316
  on anti-Catholic Protestantism, 266
  artistic reaction to wasteland of
    modernity, 177
  and Barfield, 330–31
  and Campbell, 235–39
  Chesterton's influence on, 42, 59,
    105, 108, 330
  on Chesterton's *The Everlasting Man*,
    108
  on Chesterton's *The Man Who Was
    Thursday*, 43
  and the Christian literary revival, 55,
    60–61
  conversion of, 59, 108, 243, 331
  and the Inklings, 231–33, 235–39, 244
  and modern trends in poetry, 180

  on myth, 243
  and *That Hideous Strength*, 55, 177,
    346
  Tolkien's influence on, 243, 262
Life of Waugh (Patey), 214–17
Light Invisible, The (Benson), 48, 139
"Lines to a Don" (Belloc), 45, 68, 111
Lion Sun: Poems by Pavel Chichikov,
  361–63
"Litany of the Lost" (Sassoon), 53, 165,
  177–78
Literary Converts (Pearce), 329
Literary World, 123
Living of Maisie Ward, The (Greene),
  147–52
Lodge, David, 161
"Logical Vegetarian, The" (Chesterton),
  68
Longenecker, Dwight, 304
"*Lord of the Rings, The*: A Catholic
  View" (Coulombe), 245–46
Lord of the Rings, The (film), 15–16, 55,
  300, 301, 311, 351
  successes and failures of, 323–25
  what Tolkien would have thought of,
    326–28
Lord of the Rings, The (Tolkien)
  and allegory, 289–90, 292, 315–17
  and the Arthurian legacy, 264,
    270–71
  Catholicism of, 16, 245–46, 247,
    257–58, 261–65, 272, 288–95,
    314–22
  and Chesterton, 247–48, 283–86
  and Chesterton's *Ballad of the White
    Horse*, 284
  and the Christian literary revival, 61
  Christlike images of, 312–13, 317–18
  and contemporary Tolkien
    scholarship, 298–300, 301–5
  and Creation, 252–54, 262–63,
    291–92
  and date of the ring's destruction,
    259, 302–3, 313

Lord of the Rings, The (continued)
  and depiction of evil, 244, 258,
    263–64, 292–94
  and distributism, 247–49, 252
  Divine Mercy in, 311–13
  as fundamentally religious/Catholic
    work, 247, 257–58, 272–73, 298,
    310, 311, 314, 327
  and idealized view of
    pre-Reformation England, 282–83
  the individual and
    community/communitas in, 247–56
  and Lewis' fiction, 55, 289
  as mystical Passion play/pilgrimage,
    265, 295, 312–13, 318–19
  political significance of, 259–60
  popularity of, 247, 257, 296–97, 301
  and pre-Christian mythology, 319
  and principle of self-limitation, 249–52
  religion and politics in, 257–60
  religious applicability of, 258–59,
    317–18
  sociopolitical/sociocultural
    applicability of, 247–56
  and Tolkien's philosophy of myth,
    243, 249–51, 262–64, 277, 291–92
  as Tolkien's reaction to modernity,
    55, 177, 244–45
  and the "true North", 268
  Truth/realism in, 262, 277, 278–79,
    289–90
  and World War I, 242, 310
  writing of, 244, 326–27
  See also Lord of the Rings, The (film);
    Tolkien, J. R. R.
"Lord of the Rings and The Ballad of the
  White Horse, The" (Clausen), 284
Lord of the World (Benson), 46, 141
Loss and Gain (Newman), 14, 25, 274,
  277
Lost Diaries (Baring), 134
"Love and the Child" (Thompson), 33
Lunn, Arnold, 100
Lyrical Ballads (Wordsworth and
  Coleridge, eds.), 22–23

Macdonald, George, 288
Mackenzie, Compton, 54, 211
MacNeice, Louis, 196
Magic (Chesterton), 143
"Magna est Veritas" (Patmore), 279
Malcolm Muggeridge: A Biography
  (Wolfe), 225–28
Man Who Was Thursday, The
  (Chesterton), 43–44, 79, 307, 354
  as Chesterton's response to
    Decadence, 59, 77
  excellence of, 43–44, 70–71, 72
Man Within, The (Greene), 219
Manalive (Chesterton), 44–45
Manchester Guardian, 123, 179–80
Manning, Cardinal (Henry Edward),
  233, 248
Marconi Scandal (1913), 97
Maritain, Jacques, 215
Martindale, C. C., 47, 133, 142
Mary, Mother of God, 403, 405–6
"Mass at Dawn" (Campbell), 194, 201
Masters, Brian, 139
Mauriac, François, 40, 136
Maurois, André, 39, 135
McCartney, Paul, 359–60
McNabb, Father Vincent, 151
"Me Heart" (Chesterton), 68
Memoirs of a Fox-Hunting Man
  (Sassoon), 165
Memoirs of an Infantry Officer (Sassoon),
  165
Meynell, Alice, 32–33
Meynell, Wilfrid, 32–33
Millet, Jean-François, 203, 391
Milton, John, 371, 372
Mithraic Emblems (Campbell), 187, 188,
  194–95, 204–5, 206, 361
Mithraism, 204–5
modern art, 380–83, 385, 390. See also
  Dali, Salvador; Picasso, Pablo
modern English literature, tradition and
  conversion in, 21–57
  and the Christian literary revival,
    25–30, 33–34, 39–55

and the Decadent movement, 34–39
and the Gothic revival, 24–25
Hopkins and, 30–32, 33, 34
and the Oxford movement, 23–24, 25
Patmore and, 32
and post-Enlightenment traditions, 22–23, 37–38
and the Pre-Raphaelites, 24–25
and the romantic movement, 22–23
Ruskin and, 24–25
Thompson and, 32–33, 38–39
and Victorian era, 22, 24, 30
and World War I, 50–51
and World War II era, 53–55
See also Christian literary revival
modernity, cultural reaction to
wasteland of, 167–78
Campbell and, 191–93
Chesterton and, 51, 167–69, 172, 372
Eliot and, 50, 51, 60, 172–76, 177, 178
Lewis and, 177
Maisie Ward and, 148–51
and modern poetry, 179–83
Newman and, 150, 275–76
Tolkien and, 55, 177, 244–45
and Vatican II, 56–57, 90–91
Waugh and, 52, 55–56, 151, 176, 177
World War I era, 50–51, 170–75, 307–9
World War II era, 53–54, 165, 176–78, 182, 244
More, Thomas, 345
More Beasts (for Worse Children) (Belloc), 110
Morgan, Father Francis Xavier, 241–42, 275
"Mozart" (Baring), 134
Mrs. Dalloway (Woolf), 176
Muggeridge, Malcolm, 221, 225–28, 355
Muggeridge: The Biography (Ingrams), 225
Muir, Edwin, 304
Murder in the Cathedral (Eliot), 50, 176
Murray, Robert, S.J., 273, 305
Mussolini, Benito, 93–94

"Mythopoeia" (Tolkien), 243, 249, 275, 304

Napoleon of Notting Hill, The (Chesterton)
Baring and, 131
Chesterton's appraisal of, 69
distributism of, 73, 248
Knox and, 47
politicians' misunderstanding of, 85–88
themes of, 43, 44, 86–87, 88, 103
National Institute for Clinical Excellence (N.I.C.E.), 346–47
Neale, John Mason, 23–24
Necromancers, The (Benson), 141
Network (film), 353–55
Nevinson, C. R. W., 170
New Statesman, 100–101
New York Times, The, 123
Newman, John Henry, 25–30
and Benson, 45–46
and Catholic response to modernity, 150, 275–76
and the Christian literary revival, 25–30, 29, 34, 41, 59, 274–78, 287
conversion of, 25
and English Catholicism, 25–30, 34
and the individual quest for truth, 277–78
on issue of conversion, 25–26
poems of, 27–28
and Tolkien, 274–76
Nicolson, Harold, 52
Nietzsche, Friedrich, 58–59, 191, 267
Nineteen Eighty-Four (Orwell), 46, 53, 354
and Benson's The Necromancers, 141
and Chesterton's Napoleon of Notting Hill, 103
and Fascism, 101–2
and Tolkien's Lord of the Rings, 296, 303
Norse sagas, 157, 267–68
North, true and false, 266–68

Notes towards the Definition of Culture
  (Eliot), 105–6
Noyes, Alfred, 330
  conversion of, 59, 183, 211
  and modern trends in poetry, 180–82,
    183
  and the Spanish civil war, 100
Nuclear Cross (Dali), 389, 390

"O God of earth and altar"
  (Chesterton), 67
Observer, 42
O'Connor, Flannery, 303
Old Century, The (Sassoon), 165
"On Fairy Stories" (Tolkien), 248, 249,
  253, 290
"On Irony" (Belloc), 72
"On the Nature of the Gothic"
  (Ruskin), 24
One Poor Scruple (Ward), 161
Open Letter on the Decay of Faith, An
  (Belloc), 133–34
Opus Dei, 400–401
Orkneyinga Saga, 157, 267
Orthodoxy (Chesterton), 14, 43, 81,
  105–7, 110, 132
Orwell, George
  Animal Farm, 53, 101–2
  on Chesterbelloc, 128
  on Fascism, 101–2
  Nineteen Eighty-Four, 46, 53, 101–2,
    103, 141, 296, 303, 354
  on the Spanish civil war, 99
Outline of History (Wells), 107
Outline of Sanity, The (Chesterton), 73,
  153
Owen, Wilfred
  and poetry of war, 159, 162, 170,
    171–72
  and Sassoon, 162, 164
Oxford movement, 23–24, 25

Pall Mall Gazette, 107
Papers of a Pariah (Benson), 47, 142
Paradise Lost (Milton), 27, 372

Paradiso (Dante), 27, 136, 373, 405–6
Paradoxes of Catholicism, The (Benson),
  141–42
Part, Arvo, 268
Passing By (Baring), 39, 134
Passion of the Christ, The (film), 15,
  356–58
Patey, Douglas Lane, 214–17
Path to Peace, The (Sassoon), 166
Path to Rome, The (Belloc), 72, 111,
  112–24, 248
  basic narrative/structure of, 113, 114
  concluding verse of, 122–23
  critical praise for, 123–24
  and love for mankind, 117–18
  major themes of, 114–23
  metaphors of, 115–19, 120–21
  and modernity, 120
  and nature mysticism, 120–21
  and the theology of place, 114–16,
    120
Patmore, Coventry, 30, 32, 33, 279–80
Perry, Michael W., 299
Persistence of Memory, The (Dali), 385
Picasso, Pablo, 383, 386, 390–91
Picture of Dorian Gray, The (Wilde), 36,
  38
  and Chesterton, 82
  morality of, 77, 340, 341, 343
"Pilgrim Queen, The" (Newman),
  27–29
Pilgrim's Progress (Bunyan), 316
Pilgrim's Regress (Lewis), 61, 316
Pius X, Pope, Saint, 149
Pius XI, Pope, 73, 94, 151, 282, 348
Plass, Adrian, 340
Poe, Edgar Allan, 181
Poems (Benson), 46, 141, 150
Poetic Diction: A Study in Meaning
  (Barfield), 330
poetry, modern trends in
  Eliot and, 179–81
  Sitwell and, 164, 177, 179–83
  See also modernity, cultural reaction
    to wasteland of

poetry of war, 157–61
  Baring and, 134
  Owen and, 159, 162, 170, 171–72
  Sassoon and, 53, 159, 162–65,
    170–71, 177–78
  World War I, 51, 158–59, 162–64,
    170–72
  World War II, 53, 165, 176–78, 182
*Pope John Paul II and the Catholic
  Restoration* (Johnson), 399–401
Portrait of Picasso (Dali), 390–91
"Posada" (Campbell), 200, 201, 388
Potting Shed, The (Greene), 218
"Pouring the Moon" (Chichikov), 363
Power and the Glory, The (Greene), 52,
  218
Pratchett, Terry, 43–44, 85
"Prayer" (Chichikov), 362
"Prayer at Pentecost, A" (Sassoon), 166
"Prayer in Old Age, A" (Sassoon), 166
Pre-Raphaelites, 24–25, 382
Premonition of War (Dali), 387
"Prussian Nights" (Solzhenitsyn), 159
Pugin, Augustus, 24
Puppet Show of Memory, The (Baring),
  129
Purgatorio (Dante), 27, 373
Purtill, Richard L., 298–99, 301

Quadragesimo anno (Pius XI), 73, 282

"Race Memory (by a dazed
  Darwinian)" (Chesterton), 190
Read, Anthony, 97–98
Read, Sir Herbert, 32
"Reconciliation" (Sassoon), 164
*Recovery and Transcendence for the
  Contemporary Mythmaker*
  (Garbowski), 299
"Redeemer, The" (Sassoon), 164
"Reflections on a Rotten Apple"
  (Chesterton), 73
Reformation
  Baring's view of, 131
  Belloc's studies of, 46, 110, 140

and Benson's novels, 139–40
and Catholicism of southern Europe,
  266
Chesterton's idealized view of
  pre-Reformation England, 282
as "crisis of disenchantment", 308
Tolkien's idealized view of
  pre-Reformation England, 282–83
Regeneration Trilogy (Barker), 160
Rerum novarum (Leo XIII), 73, 92, 110,
  248, 260, 282
Resurrection of Rome, The (Chesterton),
  93–94, 216
Retrieved from the Future (Seymour), 154
Reunion All Round (Knox), 212
Reynolds, Barbara, 49, 108
Richard Raynal, Solitary (Benson),
  139–40
Richards, I. A., 51
Rilke, Rainer Maria, 208
"Rime of the Ancient Mariner, The"
  (Coleridge), 23
Road to Middle Earth, The (Shippey),
  285, 303, 313
Robert Peckham (Baring), 131, 135
Rock, The (Eliot), 176
"Rolling English Road, The"
  (Chesterton), 67, 68
"Rose" (Belloc), 45
Rossetti, Christina, 29
Rossetti, Dante Gabriel, 24–25
Rowling, J. K., 85
Ruskin, John, 24–25, 382
Russell, Bertrand, 129, 193
Russell, George, 185
Russia, 367–69
Ryland, Tim, 14

Saatchi, Charles, 380–81
Sackville-West, Edward, 210
Sackville-West, Vita, 52, 186, 193, 231
Sacrament of the Last Supper, The (Dali),
  391
Sacre du printemps, Le (Stravinsky), 164
Sacred Wood, The (Eliot), 371

"Sailor's Carol" (Belloc), 69
Saint Austin Review (StAR), 16, 305, 349
Saint Francis of Assisi (Chesterton),
　78–79
"Saint Peter of the Three Canals"
　(Campbell), 194
Saint Thomas Aquinas (Copleston), 14
Salome (Wilde), 340, 341
"Saracen's Head, The" (Chesterton), 68
Sargent, John Singer, 170
Sassoon, Siegfried, 162–66
　autobiographical prose, 165
　conversion of, 165, 178
　and Knox, 49
　military career of, 162–63
　and Owen, 162, 164
　and poetry of war, 53, 159, 162–65,
　　170–71, 177–78
　and World War II, 53, 165, 177
Sayer, George, 272, 305
Sayers, Dorothy L., 29, 59, 105, 108
Schopenhauer, Arthur, 58
Schumacher, E. F., 103, 119, 153, 250,
　252
science fiction, 345–47
"Secret People, The" (Chesterton), 42,
　67
secularists, 231–34
"Selfish Giant, The" (Wilde), 343
"Serf, The" (Campbell), 191, 201
Sergeant York (film), 352
Sermons Addressed to Mixed Congregations
　(Newman), 26
Servile State, The (Belloc), 73, 110, 153,
　248
Seven Cities of Gold (film), 353
"Seven Song" (Chichikov), 363
Seymour, John, 153–54
Shadow of Cain, The (Sitwell), 53, 177,
　182
Shakespeare, William, 17, 158, 185,
　374, 376–79
Shaw, George Bernard
　and Chesterbelloc, 45, 65–66
　and Chesterton, 44, 59, 107, 329–30

and Muggeridge, 226
　and secular "progress"/the
　　perfectibility of man, 226, 231,
　　233
　and Stalin, 95
　on Wilde's celebrity, 339
Sheed, Frank, 32, 151
Sheehan, Archbishop Michael, 14
"Sheldonian Soliloquy" (Sassoon),
　164–65
Shelley, Mary, 345
Shelley, Percy Bysshe, 283
Sherry, Norman, 52–53
Sherston's Progress (Sassoon), 165
Shippey, T. A., 285, 298, 302–3, 313, 321
Sibbett, C. J., 202
Sibelius, Jean, 268
Siegfried's Journey (Sassoon), 165
"Sign of the Cross, The" (Newman), 27
Silmarillion, The (Tolkien), 61, 265, 272,
　276, 278–79, 291–93
　and Creation myth, 262–63
　and reverence for the sea, 280–81
　Sauron in, 258, 293
　and Tolkien's philosophy of myth,
　　243, 262–63, 291–92
Sinister Street (Mackenzie), 54
"Sisters, The" (Campbell), 201
Sitwell, Edith, 179–83
　and Campbell, 182, 184
　conversion of, 182–83
　and modern trends in poetry, 53,
　　164, 177, 179–83
"Skeleton, The" (Chesterton), 67
Slade School of Art (London), 33, 59,
　81, 82
"Sloth" (Waugh), 215–16
Small Is Beautiful (Schumacher), 119,
　153
Smith, Mark Eddy, 299
Smyth, Ethel, 132–33
*Soft Construction with Boiled Beans:
　Premonition of Civil War* (Dali), 386
"Soldier, The" (Brooke), 158, 170, 308
"Soldier's Declaration" (Sassoon), 163

Solzhenitsyn, Alexander, 159, 171, 250
"Song of Quoodle, The" (Chesterton),
    68
"Song of the Pelagian Heresy ... "
    (Belloc), 69
"Song of the Strange Ascetic, The"
    (Chesterton), 68
Sonnets and Short Poems (Baring), 134
Sort of Life, A (Greene), 219–20
"South Country, The" (Belloc), 115
Southwell, Robert, Saint, 17–18
Spadaro, Father Antonio, 341
Spain, 1938 (Dali), 387–88
Spanish civil war, 99–101
    Campbell and, 187–88, 196–97, 209,
        216, 236, 238, 388
    Chesterton and, 99
    Dali and, 386–88
    and Fascism, 91–92, 99–101, 197
    liberals' misunderstandings of, 91–92
    understanding Catholic involvement
        in, 91–92, 99–101, 198
    Waugh and, 100, 216
Spanos, Antonia, 385
Speaight, Robert
    and Baring, 40, 136
    on Belloc, 71–72, 124
    and reforms of Vatican II, 56–57
Speaker, The, 77
Spender, Stephen, 196
Spirit of Catholicism, The (Adam), 14
Spiritual Aeneid, A (Knox), 48–49, 142
Spiritual Letters (Benson), 46, 141, 150
"Spring Offensive" (Owen), 159
Stalin, Josef, 95, 100, 244
"Stand-To: Good Friday Morning"
    (Sassoon), 164
Stannard, Martin, 215
"Still Falls the Rain" (Sitwell), 177, 182
Stopes, Marie, 193
Strachey, Lytton, 231, 233
Stravinsky, Igor, 164
subsidiarity, 73, 92, 198, 252, 260
Sunday Times, The, 215, 296
Surprised by Joy (Lewis), 331

surrealism, 385–86
Survivals and New Arrivals (Belloc),
    73–74, 110
Swift, Jonathan, 345
Sykes, Christopher, 55–56

Tablet, 54, 213
"Tarantella" (Belloc), 45, 68, 111, 115
Taylor, John Russell, 393
technology and the occult, 364–66
Temptation of Saint Anthony, The (Dali),
    389
Tennyson, Alfred Lord, 158
That Hideous Strength (Lewis), 55, 177,
    346
"Theology of Bongwi, the Baboon,
    The" (Campbell), 190
Thomas, Dylan, 184
Thomas Aquinas, Saint, 15, 31, 42, 116,
    173–74, 282
Thompson, Francis, 32–33, 38–39,
    280–81, 308
Thoughts on Art and Life (da Vinci), 134
Time magazine, 54, 213
Times, The, 40, 56, 143, 173, 393
Times Literary Supplement, 180, 296
"To a Snowflake" (Thompson), 33,
    280–81
"To Roy Campbell" (Lewis), 239
"To the Author of Flowering Rifle"
    (Lewis), 236
"To the Sun" (Campbell), 361
Tolkien: A Celebration (Pearce), 15–16
Tolkien, J.R.R., 240–46
    on allegory, 289, 315–16
    and Barfield, 330
    and Belloc, 247–48
    and Campbell, 235–36, 237
    and Chesterton, 42, 247–48, 282–86
    and the Christian literary revival, 55,
        60–61, 231, 272–87
    and contemporary Tolkien
        scholarship, 298–300, 301–5
    early life and "cradle conversion",
        240–42

Tolkien, J. R. R. (*continued*)
  education and academic vocation,
    242
  and the film adaptation of *The Lord
    of the Rings*, 326–28
  on Hitler, 244, 267
  and idealized view of England,
    282–83
  importance of Catholic faith for, 258,
    261, 272–74, 291
  and the Inklings, 231, 235–36, 237,
    239, 244
  and Lewis, 242–43
  life of, 240–46
  nature-reverence of, 280–82
  and Newman, 274–76
  philosophy of myth of, 243, 249–51,
    252–54, 262–64, 277, 291–92
  and the rejection of modern
    philosophy, 276–77
  and World War I, 242, 306–10
  See also *Lord of the Rings, The*
    (Tolkien); *Silmarillion, The*
    (Tolkien)
Tolkien, Mabel, 240–41
Tolkien: Man and Myth (Pearce), 15–16,
  297, 314
*Tolkien and the Great War: The Threshold
  of Middle-earth* (Garth), 306–10
Tolkien in Perspective (Wright), 299
Tolkien's Ordinary Virtues (Smith), 299
Tolley, Clive, 304
"Toys, The" (Patmore), 33
Tree and Leaf (Tolkien), 243
Trevelyan, Robert, 129
"True Myth: The Catholicism of *The
  Lord of the Rings*" (Pearce), 314–22
Turner, J. M. W., 382
"Twelfth Night" (Belloc), 45, 68
Twelve Types (Chesterton), 78

Undset, Sigrid, 223–24
Unmasking of Oscar Wilde, The (Pearce),
  16–17
Untangling Tolkien (Perry), 299

Usher, Jerry, 14
Utopia (More), 345

Vatican Council, Second
  Chesterton on, 91
  Maisie Ward and, 151
  and modernity, 56–57, 90–91
  and the "vertical man", 223–24
Vera (Wilde), 338
Verlaine, Paul, 77, 336
Verses and Sonnets (Belloc), 110
Vertical Man (Whitehouse), 223–24
Victorian era scepticism, 22
Vile Bodies (Waugh), 52, 210
"Virgin's Cradle Hymn, The"
  (Coleridge), 23
"Vita Nuova" (Baring), 39, 132, 134

Wagner, Richard, 267
"Wagner" (Baring), 134
Walton, William, 179
war poetry. See poetry of war
War Poets and Other Subjects (Bergonzi),
  160–61
Ward, Mrs. Humphrey, 25, 136, 214
Ward, Josephine Hope, 148
Ward, Maisie, 32, 143, 146–52
Ward, Wilfrid, 105, 148, 149–50
Ward, Mrs. Wilfrid, 161
Ward, William George, 149
Ware, Jim, 299
Waste Land, The (Eliot)
  and Campbell's *The Flaming Terrapin*,
    191–92
  and Dante, 51, 173–74
  depiction of modernity in, 50, 51,
    60, 174
  publication and critical reaction to,
    50, 51, 173, 179–80
Watkin, E. I., 150
Waugh, Evelyn
  artistic reaction to wasteland of
    modernity, 52, 55–56, 151, 176,
    177
  and Belloc, 54, 216

and *Brideshead Revisited,* 53–54, 108,
177, 212–13
and Chesterton's influence, 54, 108,
212–13, 216
on Chesterton's *The Everlasting Man,*
107–8
and the Christian literary revival,
51–52, 54, 55–56, 60, 216–17
conversion of, 51–52, 60, 108, 176,
210–13, 215–16
and Eliot, 60, 216
and Fascism, 100–101
and Knox, 48–49, 212, 213, 216
literary influences on, 54, 108,
212–13, 216
Patey's biography of, 214–17
and Sitwell, 182–83
and the Spanish civil war, 100, 216
Weald of Youth, The (Sassoon), 165
Well and the Shallows, The (Chesterton),
14, 73
Wells, H. G.
and Belloc, 107, 111
on Chesterbelloc, 74
Chesterton's attack on, 59, 88
and scientism/secular "progress", 231,
233
and Seymour, 154
and Stalin, 95
West, Anthony, 161
West, John G., Jr., 299
West, Rebecca, 161
Wheels (anthology), 179
Whitehouse, J. C., 221, 223–24
Wilde, Oscar
and Benson, 47, 142–43
Catholic dimension of art of, 340–41,
343–44
celebrity cult of, 338–41
and Chesterton, 76, 82, 340
conversion of, 16, 36–37, 59, 77,
337, 340, 343
death of, 37, 58–59
and the Decadent movement, 34, 35,
37–38, 77, 82, 337

homosexuality and myth of, 16–17,
342–44
influence on secular culture, 58–59
Wilfrid Wards and the Transition, The
(Ward), 149–50, 151–52
"Will the Real Dali Ever Stand Up?"
(Taylor), 393
Williams, Charles, 231, 235
Williams, Ted, 346–47
Wilson, Edmund, 54, 213
"Wine and Water" (Chesterton), 68
Wise, Rabbi Stephen, 97
Wiseman, Nicholas, Cardinal, 25–26
Wolfe, Gregory, 225–28
Wood, Ralph C., 299
Woodhouse, A. S. P., 27
Woolf, Virginia
on Baring's novels, 40, 135–36
and Bloomsbury, 135, 186, 193, 231
and Eliot, 175–76, 195
Wordsworth, William, 22–23, 37–38
World, The, 123
World War I
artistic reactions to modernity and,
50–51, 170–75, 307–9
Belloc and, 51, 172
Chesterton and, 51, 172, 307
early optimism of, 170, 172, 308–9
and patriotism, 309–10
and pessimism, 308–9
and poetry of war, 51, 158–59,
162–64, 170–72
Tolkien and, 242, 306–10
World War II
artistic reactions to, 53–54, 165,
176–78, 182, 244
and postwar pessimism/anxiety,
53–55
Sassoon and, 53, 165, 177
Tolkien's *Lord of the Rings* and, 244
Wright, David, 185
Wright, Greg, 299
Wyndham Lewis, Percy, 184, 202

"Zulu Girl" (Campbell), 191